POLITICAL ISSUES
IN BRITAIN TODAY

Politics today

Series editor: Bill Jones

POLITICAL ISSUES IN BRITAIN TODAY

Third edition

Edited by
Bill Jones

Manchester University Press

Manchester and New York

Distributed exclusively in the USA and Canada by St. Martin's Press

Published by Manchester University Press
Oxford Road, Manchester M13 9PL, UK
and Room 400, 175 Fifth Avenue,
New York, NY 10010, USA

Distributed exclusively in the USA and Canada
by St. Martin's Press, Inc.,
175 Fifth Avenue, New York, NY 10010, USA

British Library cataloguing in publication data
Political issues in Britain today. – 3rd ed – (Politics today).
  1. Great Britain. Social conditions
  I. Jones, Bill, 1946–   II. Series
  941.085′8

Library of Congress cataloging in publication data applied for

ISBN   0 7190 3019 6 *hardback*
       0 7190 3024 2 *paperback*

Phototypeset in Great Britain
by Northern Phototypesetting Co, Bolton

Printed in Great Britain
by Billing and Sons Ltd, Worcester

Contents

Introduction

It was Peter Byrd from Warwick University who first pointed out to me the dearth of books which cover a range of current political issues. The studies which do exist tend to be weighty investigations into single issues which are too long and complex for most students of politics, whether at advanced or undergraduate level. Their need, it seemed to me, is for a shorter treatment which conveys the important facts and arguments and places them in the context of the present political debate. This book is designed to do just that.

Political issues develop and change rapidly, so to help reduce preparation time a number of contributors were invited to write their chapters during the months of August and September 1984. Contributions to the second edition were produced in July 1986, and for this third edition in January 1989. The format used follows that of the MUP's successful 'Today' series: students seem to appreciate a style which is crisp, concise and highlights the major points. As with the other volumes in the series the aim is to provide a complement rather than a substitute for the more comprehensive studies. We hope that the brief, clear introduction provided here will encourage students to follow up and deepen their knowledge via the further reading suggestions which appear at the end of each chapter.

Are the issues dealt with in an unbiased fashion? Total objectivity, of course, is an impossible ideal, especially in the teaching of politics, and I have always felt that too earnest an aspiration towards it robs the subject of much intrinsic interest. Contributors have their own views which will have played a part in the selection and presentation of their material, but the aim has been to offer a balanced approach which explains and discusses all the major arguments and value positions. This is not to say that on occasions certain values or positions – for example the chapter on racism – are not explained, elaborated and defended.

The seventeen issues covered are loosely organised into four sections: institutional questions, economic issues, social policy, and keeping the peace. Inevitably the coverage is not comprehensive but it is as wide as the length of the volume allows and certainly takes in a wide range of political controversy. Interestingly, following the example of certain university departments, a number of examination boards have moved away from the traditional institutional approach to one which also embraces issues. This trend can only be applauded: issues are the stuff of politics and more attention must be paid to them by teachers if they want to interest, challenge and truly involve their students. Elections, after all, are not fought over delegated legislation or the office of the Comptroller and Auditor-General but over the economy, social policy, law and order – those subjects which influence the way we live, think and cast our votes. I said in my introduction to the first edition that I hoped this book would nudge the movement a little further along its way. The fact that second and third editions have followed so swiftly suggests that perhaps it has indeed achieved a degree of success in this area. All the chapters have been updated and in most cases substantially revised. One new chapter, on the political role of television, has been added. The splintering of the Alliance after the 1987 election has created a few problems. The policy positions of the SLD and the SDP are given where known but where pre-1987 matters are dealt with Alliance policies are still cited.

Finally, thanks are due to all the contributors for producing their material so efficiently and delivering it so promptly, and to Manchester University Press for all their help and encouragement.

Bill Jones
Manchester, February 1989

Notes on contributors

Bill Jones is Director of Extra-Mural Studies, University of Manchester. He is editor of Manchester University Press's 'Politics Today' series.

Peter Byrd is Lecturer in Politics at the University of Warwick.

Andrew Gray is Senior Lecturer in Administrative Studies at the University of Kent at Canterbury.

Karen Hunt is Tutor Organiser for Women's Education in the North-West District of the Workers' Education Association.

Geoff Lee formerly lectured in Government and Management at Manchester Polytechnic and currently works in management training in industry.

John McIlroy is Staff Tutor in Industrial Relations, Department of Extra-Mural Studies, University of Manchester.

Lynton Robins is Senior Lecturer in Politics at Leicester Polytechnic and edits *Talking Politics* for the Politics Association.

Paul Wilding is Professor of Social Policy, University of Manchester.

INSTITUTIONAL ISSUES

1 *Bill Jones*

The Thatcher style

Just before the 1983 general election, *The Economist* lead editorial read: 'The Issue is Thatcher'.[1] This provided the theme for my opening chapter in the first edition of this book in August 1984. Nineteen months later, in the middle of the Westland crisis, the same journal judged: 'Her style is no longer her asset. It is her biggest liability.'[2] Three editions and six years on, is Mrs Thatcher's political style still a major issue in British politics? This question will be addressed, after considering the pros and cons of seven critical propositions which encapsulate the chief charges against her way of conducting the country's government.

(1) Mrs Thatcher pursues an excessively ideological line

The case for

Mrs Thatcher claims she is 'in politics because of the conflict between good and evil' and she believes 'that in the end good will triumph'.[3] This morally righteous dogmatic approach is anathema to traditional Conservatives like Pym and Gilmour, who argue that Conservatives never hold fast to any specific set of policies. Whilst seeking to defend and promote principles like freedom, competition, property and patriotism, they employ whatever policies are appropriate given the circumstances: pragmatism has always been their overriding principle.[4] Mrs Thatcher, however, has turned this fundamental tenet of Toryism on its head. She has expounded, passionately, a view of Conservatism which is closer to nineteenth-century liberalism: drastically reduce the role of government in the economy; let market forces liberate the economy from the dead hand of high taxes and bureaucratic state intervention. To this she has added her own Grantham shopkeeper version of Victorian middle-class values: thrift, hard work, getting on, acquiring property, self-reliance and the central importance of family life. She treats the nation's economy like the family budget, preaching, in her own words, 'the homilies of housekeeping' and 'the parables of the parlour'.[5] When asked if Thatcherism was an aberration in the history of the Conservatives, Edward Heath replied simply: 'Yes.'[6]

Yet her biggest mistake, say her critics, was to lay such store by the ideas of Milton Friedman, the economist who enshrined the idea that inflation could only be cured by controlling the money supply: the circulation of cash and credit in the economy. The principal control employed – high interest rates – caused massive and unnecessary industrial failure and helped produce a 250% increase in unemployment.

The case against

As with so many of the criticisms levelled against her, Mrs Thatcher would accept parts of this one proudly. She freely admits she is a 'conviction politican' who wishes to 'change the heart and soul' of the nation.[7] She shared Lord Blake's view, expressed in 1976, that 'Nothing less will suffice than a major reversal of the trends which ever since 1945 Labour has presented and Conservatives have accepted.'[8] She realised she was a 'rebel amidst a government of squares', and that her commitment disturbed and even embarrassed the complacent scepticism of the Conservative establishment. Consequently, she believed her own role to be crucial: 'If I give up we will lose.'[9] It follows that as leader of the counter-revolution against socialism she needs to express her ideas honestly, clearly and passionately at every opportunity. She wants her government to be remembered as one 'which decisively broke with a debilitating consensus of a paternalistic Government and a dependent people; which rejected the notion that the State is all powerful and the citizen is merely its beneficiary'.[10] But 'Thatcherism' is wrongly named in one sense, her defenders would say, for it incorporates the ideas of some of the best Conservative brains like Enoch Powell, Keith Joseph and Rhodes Boyson. And just because she holds strong views this does not mean that she cannot change her policies when necessary or back away when the occasion requires.

She would also claim that on the central issue of the economy her so-called 'ideological' line has proved practical and highly effective. From 1981 seven years of growth increased output by 43%, generated over two million jobs and pushed up Britain's overseas assets to a level exceeded only by Japan. Moreover, Mrs Thatcher can claim, with some justice, that her mission to change our political culture is succeeding. Her instinct that the centre ground of British politics was further to the right than Edward Heath supposed has been vindicated. According to her supporters she has catalysed a drift to the right into a major shift in popular attitudes on issues like the economy, defence and law and order. Even a critical writer like the *Guardian's* Hugo Young allowed that 'a substantial process of national education has taken place in the past few years . . . Thatcherism remains the body of belief which dominates political thinking . . . Up to a point, we are all Thatcherites now.'[11]

(2) Mrs Thatcher protects middle-class interests and is insensitive to the suffering caused by her policies

The case for
The Prime Minister is often reported as referring to the Conservative voting middle class as 'our people'. Critics point out that 'her people' have prospered greatly since 1979. A married man on five times average earnings has seen his total tax burden (income tax, national insurance, VAT, rates, etc.) drop from 48.8% of gross earnings in 1979 to 34.2% in 1989. A married man on average earnings, however, has seen his tax burden actually *increase* from 35.1% of gross earnings to 37.3% in 1989 – despite the claims of Mrs Thatcher to lead a tax-cutting government. For those at the bottom of the pile life has become more miserable. In July 1986 the DHSS revealed that the numbers living in poverty had increased from 11.5 million in 1979 to 16.3 million in 1983.

It is no secret that Mrs Thatcher identifies with the wealth-creators in society, especially self-made entrepreneurs. She has less sympathy for people employed in the public sector, avoids visits to the depressed north, and on one famous occasion castigated those who 'drool and drivel' about caring for those in need.[12]

The public judges accordingly. In a series of polls between 1977 and 1986 Gallup revealed that the numbers thinking Mrs Thatcher 'was not in touch with working/ordinary people' had increased from

54% to 77% and that those thinking she 'was a snob' and 'talks down to people' has increased from 40% to 60%.[13] Ferdinand Mount perhaps expressed the source of this complaint in 1979 when he noted in Mrs Thatcher 'a certain impatience with subtlety of feeling, a lack of sympathy with people unlike her and a definitely limited range of experience'.[14]

The case against

Mrs Thatcher's defenders would argue that tax cuts for high earners were necessary incentives to effort and that much unemployment was caused in any case by the international recession and companies shedding superfluous manpower. Now that companies have become more efficient and started to expand, then, as Mrs Thatcher puts it: 'Even the people at the bottom are coming up.'[15] Her economic strategy, therefore, has not been designed to benefit merely the already privileged but all sections of society.

The editor of the *Sunday Express*, Robin Esser, cannot believe why her opponents claim Mrs Thatcher is uncaring. 'As we talked', he reported in an interview in July 1988, 'it was clear that she cares an awful lot about people from all walks of life. Two weeks have gone by since the Piper Alpha disaster yet she still cannot speak of it without a catch, an emotional tremor in her voice.' Even critical writers like Alan Watkins in the *Observer* allow that Mrs Thatcher can be 'warm and compassionate'.[16]

Her supporters can also point out that her preferences lie not with the privileged aristocratic element in the Conservative party but with those from humble origins like herself. For her own part she stresses the advantages she received through being brought up in a small town: 'We knew everyone, we knew what people felt. I sort of regard myself as a very normal ordinary person with all the right instinctive antennae.'[17] She insists that her policies reflect the basic wishes of the majority of the British people. 'Everything I do is done on the basis that it finds an echo way and beyond just the number of people who vote for me.'[18] The vital supporting evidence in any case, she would claim, is provided by the fact that in 1987 43% of skilled workers voted for her compared with 34% for Labour.

(3) Mrs Thatcher is stubbornly confrontationist

The case for

Some of her critics maintain that Mrs Thatcher came to power spoiling for a fight with the trade unions: 'My God, I'll confront them,' she said on the Jimmy Young Show in 1979. This confrontationist approach, with its concomitant division and bitterness, violates the traditional Conservative approach which, argue the 'wets', has been to strive for harmony and balance in the nation. Even worse, Mrs Thatcher is stubborn, making a fetish of getting her own way. Examples abound. Over the GCHQ issue, Mrs Thatcher was so determined to ban trade union membership in Britain's top-secret communications establishment that she refused a trade union offer giving her virtually all she asked and forced through the ban in the face of outrage in the opposition, trade unions and her own party.

Another example was her opposition to economic sanctions against South Africa in the summer of 1986. In direct contradiction to the views of the Commonwealth, not to mention the front-line states and black leaders within South Africa itself, she insisted on roundly condemning such measures as 'immoral'. Her defence of such divisive action? 'If I were the odd one out and I were right, it wouldn't matter would it?'[19]

Yet another was her conduct over the attempted extradition from Belgium and then Ireland of a suspected IRA terrorist, Patrick Ryan, in the autumn of 1988. In a situation where delicate diplomacy was necessary, Mrs Thatcher upbraided the governments of Belgium and Ireland in the House of Commons and shortly afterwards attempted a near-public carpeting of their respective premiers at a European summit meeting.

In retrospect, say her critics, her promise upon her election to office in 1979 that 'where there was discord' she would 'bring harmony' now seems to be the most grotesque piece of hypocrisy. Since the Falklands war she has tended to see every opponent – at home as well as abroad – as a Galtieri to be defeated and destroyed. Unsurprisingly the Marplan poll revealed that 78% thought Mrs Thatcher 'stubborn'; 33% thought Kinnock so. More worrying for Mrs Thatcher, though, was the 1986 'Gallup Survey of Britain' revelation that 74% of people interviewed believed that she 'divides the country', compared with 31% in October 1977.

Her abrasive style makes matters worse. Ex-Cabinet minister

David Howell recalls that 'the general atmosphere in the government of which I was a member was that everything should start as an argument, continue as an argument and end as an argument'.[20] Anthony King suggests that one of the reasons is that Mrs Thatcher has noticed that most 'well brought up Englishmen . . . have no idea what to do with a strong assertive woman'. In consequence she has 'conceived a considerable contempt for the whole tribe', thinking all men – according to Sir John Nott – to be 'wimps'.[21] The various nicknames bestowed upon her – 'the Boss', 'Leaderene', 'Attila the Hen' – further reflect her fearsome reputation. This is not the way, say her critics, the English way, to conduct government. When projected each week from the despatch box it offends unnecessarily, provoking angry responses at home and abroad.

The case against

Again, Mrs Thatcher would probably accept much of this criticism as praise. She is proud of her ability not to turn, not to compromise, to stick to a task until it is complete. 'I am extremely patient', she says, 'provided I get my own way in the end.' She has always, quite openly, rejected consensus politics as the insidious process which has protected uneconomic industries and hastened our relative national decline. Rather, like her left-wing opponents, she believes conflict to be necessary, for antiquated socialist ideas to be called out into the open and defeated. Only then can Britain begin to build on a new consensus built around her own economic ideas.

   Her critics fail to realise that these qualities are the inevitable complements of those which have singled her out for leadership. As Harold Wilson observed, 'I have no doubt Margaret was elected [leader of the Conservatives] because of her courage.' In the Falklands crisis, where national humiliation and tragic loss of life threatened, it was her willingness to confront the fascist military junta in Argentina, her stubborn refusal to evade the conflict and compromise, which eventually won for us a famous and honourable victory. Her perfect composure under great stress was again demonstrated in the wake of the 1984 Brighton bomb explosion. The 78% of respondents in the *Observer*/Harris poll who saw Mrs Thatcher as 'Britain's toughest Prime Minister since Churchill' were surely paying her a compliment.

   In Cabinet she is concerned to get things done and quite naturally uses her formidable strength of personality as an instrument. She chooses to lead from the front and wins many battles but she also quite often has to accept defeat. And her ministers *do* occasionally answer back in kind. Julian Critchley MP gleefully relates how Nigel Lawson, irritated beyond measure by his leader's continual interruption of Sir Keith Joseph during one Cabinet meeting, suddenly said, 'Will you please shut up?' (In response the Prime Minister is said to have gone pink and remained silent for over fifteen minutes.)

Mrs Thatcher, moreover, is no reckless juggernaut; as King has noted, 'Thatcher not only respects power; she is unusually adept at weighing it.'[22] Thus she gave in to the miners in 1981 but fought them in 1984 when she felt a big majority, plentiful coal reserves and a divided NUM enabled her so to do. Naturally she loses her temper occasionally – few prime ministers maintain their equanimity indefinitely – but the fact that so many of the complaints emanate from ex-Cabinet members perhaps helps explain – say Thatcherites – why they lost their jobs in the first place.

(4) Mrs Thatcher is excessively authoritarian

The case for

Soon after her elevation to power one political correspondent wrote: 'whilst not actually surrounded by sycophants she gives the impression that she would like to be'. Some would say that by 1984 this unspoken wish had come to pass. In 1981 a showdown with the 'wets' in her Cabinet shifted the balance of power finally in her favour. She used the Falklands war and her crushing election victory in 1983 to weed out some of the remaining waverers and after the 1987 election the removal of John Biffen left Peter Walker as the only Cabinet member with views known to differ from Mrs Thatcher. 'To be loyal means one hundred per cent acceptance of Government thinking: any dissent, even admittance of doubt is treachery and treason', wrote Frances Pym.[23] Regular checks are kept on loyalty: twice a year the whips meet to discuss the voting record and opinions of every Tory MP. 'All this is sifted and considered when she makes her appointments; nothing is forgotten and little forgiven.'[24] The public seem to have gained a similar impression; 62% of respondents in the *Observer*/Harris poll agreed 'she acts too much like a dictator'.

For several years she has seemed not to listen. According to Whitehall folklore civil servants have at most four minutes (some say less than a minute) to explain an issue to her, however complicated.

'Beyond that point, unless her interest is awakened, Mrs Thatcher's eyes glaze over. To continue is to jeopardize future promotion.'[25]

Her behaviour can sometimes be 'terrifying', according to Robert Harris of the *Observer*: 'Like the female monster at the heart of a Rider Haggard adventure story: ripping apart some helpless official for an ill thought-out answer or casually disposing of some Minister who has loyally served her for a decade.' Sir John Hoskyns, once head of her Policy Unit, believes she uses the fact she is female 'very powerfully to get her own way'. She can be 'deliberately unreasonable, emotional, excitable, instead of being calm and consensus seeking'.[26] She lectures and bosses about interviewers and foreign heads of government alike. Her public style is a kind of authoritarian populism which is reflected and reinforced by the *Sun's* style of journalism.

Not content with the shift to the right which Rupert Murdoch's entry into Fleet Street has caused, she has used her power to manage the press to a worrying degree. Indeed, some students of the political personality have seen in some of Mrs Thatcher's behaviour signs of the paranoia widely recognised as symptoms of the disease Lord Acton diagnosed so memorably: the corruption of power. An example occurred during July 1984 when Mrs Thatcher's leadership was suffering a mini-crisis. No. 10 put it about that Francis Pym had convened a meeting of MPs to organise opposition to their leader – when Pym proved to be perfectly innocent, No. 10's accusations appeared not only foolish, but sinister.

Finally, say her critics, she is unique amongst post-war Prime Ministers in having no sense of humour. An example was provided at Prime Minister's Question Time (19 January 1989) when she was asked by Ann Clywd whether her 'advice to women consists of following her example and finding a wealthy husband?' The house found this amusing, but instead of a witty or relaxed reply Mrs Thatcher stiffly responded that the question was 'cheap' and 'singularly offensive'.

The case against

Mrs Thatcher's supporters have no difficulty in dismissing these criticisms as the resentment of sacked ministers, passed-over MPs and the predictable bias of left-of-centre journalists. It is absurd to compare Mrs Thatcher to a dictator; as Prime Minister she works purely within the parliamentary system and is dependent upon the support of her party, a formidable array of ability and intellect in which groups of MPs regularly assert their independence by abstaining or voting against the government. But its overwhelming support for Mrs Thatcher has never been doubted and for this support she has worked hard and democratically. Harry Greenway, a Tory MP, puts it like this: 'A Prime Minister gets the authority he or she can command by brilliance at the job and personality and above all by dominance of the House of Commons; in this Margaret Thatcher is quite exceptional.'[27]

According to this view, Mrs Thatcher is no dictator but a tough, determined, very successful Prime Minister who so dominates the democratic process that she appears more authoritarian than she really is. The weakness of the Labour opposition and tribal loyalties of the 'wets' merely enhance this effect.

Ivor Crewe, moreover, uses a wealth of survey evidence to suggest that Mrs Thatcher's strong leadership is a key electoral factor: 'Cohesion, purpose and success take precedence over policy and ideology in voters' eyes; that is the lesson of Mrs Thatcher and Thatcherism's astonishing success.'[28]

Her supporters also deny she is as grim as her critics like to present her. Anthony King observes that 'she has no trouble in winning the affection and loyalty of those in her immediate circle'.[29] And she has shown she can relax and laugh at politics – as she did when she wrote and performed in a televised *Yes Prime Minister* sketch. The popular singer, Cliff Richard, probably spoke for many who have met Mrs Thatcher informally: 'She really is a woman just like my mum.'

(5) The Prime Minister is poorly advised

The case for

For some time now a vacuum of policy advice in No. 10 has been discerned by Whitehall watchers. Whilst previous prime ministers had teams of able political advisers, Mrs Thatcher has few. Indeed, one of her first actions after returning to power in 1983 was to abolish the Cabinet 'think-tank', complaining that all it churned out was 'guffy stuff like Ph.D. theses. We could do that kind of thing ourselves.'[30] According to *The Economist* (7 July 1984): 'No. 10 Downing St., the epicentre of Britain's political life, is a curiously empty place. The Prime Minister flaps round its corridors like a solitary hawk looking for prey.' Her advisors are often part-time or transient 'court favourites' and real influence is given to shadowy figures, like Bernard Ingham (Press Secretary), Charles Powell (Personal Secretary) and Brian Griffiths (head of her Policy Unit): scarcely a heavyweight line-up. After the Westland débâcle *The Economist* pointed out that most of the crucial misjudgements had been made by incompetent 'kitchen courtiers'. 'This is a portrait of high office reminiscent of Watergate hearings', remarked the journal.

The problem seems to lie in the fact that Mrs Thatcher recognises only her own immovable certainties. 'We have,' writes Hugo Young, 'the most politically confident government of modern times.'[31] He points out that Mrs Thatcher has dispensed with Royal Commissions and lengthy enquiries in favour of short investigations, often undertaken by accountants. She is so sure of the answers she does not see the need for advice. The consequences of this illusion, say her critics, were manifest in the series of misjudgements and errors following her reaccession to power in 1983: GCHQ, the top people's pay award in July 1985, Westland, the failure of the important Shops Bill (April 1986), and so on.

The case against

Against this charge, it can be pointed out that Mrs Thatcher's office in January 1983 was in fact 'slightly larger than the staff of 69 which was in place when Mr. Callaghan departed',[32] and since 1983 her Policy Unit has doubled in size.

In addition, a number of very distinguished experts – often drawn from the outside world – have tendered their advice, e.g. Sir Alfred Sherman, director of the right-wing Centre for Policy Studies (why fund a think-tank when the Conservative party has its own?), Professors Douglas Hague and Alan Walters (recalled in 1988) and on diplomatic matters, Sir Anthony Parsons. Robert Harris in the *Observer* asserts that Mrs Thatcher has 'the most extensive retinue of personal advisors of any prime minister in our history'.[33] And why waste public money if their contributions can be effectively made part-time? Remember also that in 1982 Mrs Thatcher proposed that all the advisers and assistants at No. 10 be gathered together into a 'Prime Minister's Department', but this idea was criticised on the grounds that it would make her office too powerful. Notwithstanding, Mrs Thatcher would probably accept one element of the charge against her: she *is* sure of what she wants to do and is determined to go straight for it; overwhelming majorities in three elections are her authority for doing so. As *The Economist* itself recognises: 'The Prime Minister herself is the guardian of the government's strategy. She knows in broad outline what she wants done. What she needs is advice on how to do it.'[34]

(6) Mrs Thatcher has subverted the constitution

The case for

The Duke of Wellington wrote to a friend after his first Cabinet meeting, 'I gave them their orders and they wanted to stay behind and discuss them.' He had not yet realised that in parliamentary government, military-style decision-making is not possible. Since his day the conventions have been strengthened so that it became accepted that all important interest groups are consulted before decisions are taken, all major decisions are taken collectively in Cabinet, and implementation is by a politically neutral civil service. The charge against Mrs Thatcher is that she has ignored these conventions by:

(a) *Downgrading the Cabinet as a decision-making body*   The Iron Lady is cleverer than the Iron Duke: she avoids bringing important matters before the Cabinet in the first place. Take economic policy: 'The single most important fact about Mrs Thatcher's first period in government,' writes Burch, 'is that the main thrust of economic policy was effectively hived-off from the scrutiny of the whole Cabinet. Apart from discussions on expenditure reviews, the Cabinet as a body did not consider the general economic strategy until July 1980: 14 months after entering office.'[35] All this, combined with her abrasive style, her habit of eschewing calm discussion for what David Howell has called 'high pitched argument';[36] her tendency to state her own view at such great length that none dared challenge her, proved too much for her Defence Minister, Michael Heseltine. When a Cabinet committee meeting scheduled to discuss the Westland issue on 13 December 1985 was cancelled, it was the last straw: he walked out of a Cabinet meeting on 9 January (see p. 35). 'I resigned,' he told Fred Emery on *Panorama*, 'on my judgement of a breakdown of constitutional procedures.' There has been an 'affront to the constitution'. Later in the year on the Terry Wogan chat show he was asked his opinion of the *Spitting Image* satirical puppet show. He recalled a sketch in which Mrs Thatcher was supposedly dining out with her Cabinet colleagues. Having ordered her meat course, the waiter asked, 'And what about the vegetables?' 'Oh, they'll have the same as me', replied the Prime Minister with weary contempt. That sketch, Heseltine thought, would come to be seen by historians as symbolic of politics in the eighties.

Even so, according to Jim Prior, the Cabinet worked reasonably well until the crucial ditching of the 'wets' in the September 1981 reshuffle. After that, 'there was more and more control by the Prime Minister . . . I don't think it was as good a Cabinet and certainly the debates on economic policy really ceased to exist.'[37]

In his book, *Cabinet*, Peter Hennessy reveals that Mrs Thatcher has relied less and less on Cabinet meetings, halving their number compared with Attlee and Churchill, and reducing the flow of Cabinet papers to only one-sixth of the annual totals during the fifties and sixties.[38] And whilst she has utilised the devices of Cabinet committees – as Richard Crossman noted, the classic way in which modern prime ministers divide and rule Cabinet – she has not used them as much as some of her predecessors. Her favoured *modus operandi* is the *ad hoc* grouping of ministers and civil servants, specially convened to report on a problem or solve it, and responsible directly to her rather than via the Cabinet network. She had always made it clear that she was going to be in charge. 'As Prime Minister', she said in February 1979, 'I could not waste any time having internal arguments.'[39]

When things go well there are few complaints about this dominant style and, as the Falklands war proved, this is a quick and direct way of making policy. However, when things go badly this prime-ministerial style means that there is no one to blame but Mrs Thatcher herself. When her judgement is sound she is vindicated but when it is not she must accept heavy criticism, and not just from enemies. Paul Johnson, the ex-socialist turned Thatcherite, for example, believed she was wrong not to support Reagan's invasion of Grenada in 1983. Without her hitherto good judgement, he wrote, Mrs Thatcher 'is a very ordinary woman occupying a position where ordinary virtues are not enough'.[40]

(b) *Politicising the civil service* The charge here is that civil servants are being appointed on the basis of their political views, rather than their ability. Largely as a result of retirement, eleven out of the twenty-five top permanent secretary posts became vacant between 1981 and 1983. Mrs Thatcher took a close interest in the new appointments and, it is alleged, did her best to fill them with civil servants who had either worked for her or were thought sympathetic to her views. Thus her ex-Private Secretary, Clive Whitmore, went to Defence, Peter Middleton, who helped design the Medium Term Financial Strategy, to the Treasury and David Hancock, who had worked on EEC matters in the Cabinet Office, to Education. 'The permanent secretaries at most major departments', writes *The Economist*, 'are now known as Mrs. Thatcher's personal appointments, often promoted over the heads of more senior candidates.'[41] Sir Robin Butler in a television interview even went so far as to admit to 'worries' within Whitehall over possible politicisation.[42]

The case is further strengthened by the example of Bernard Ingham who fills the highly political office of Press Secretary: he too is a civil servant. Civil servants have, moreover, been asked to work in a different way. Mrs Thatcher requires results: she wants departments to 'execute policy without constant reference back to the centre and without wasting time and effort on elaborate Cabinet Office coordination'. Civil servants are expected to have one overriding loyalty: to the objectives set by No. 10. This alleged politicisation of the civil service has been offered by some as an explanation for the constant series of leaks from within the govermment machine which has plagued Thatcher administrations from their earliest days.

(c) *Overcentralising government decision-making*   Mrs Thatcher claims that she wants to return responsibility to the individual, to take government out of their lives. In practice, say her critics, she has achieved the opposite: 'central government', says Pym, 'now exer cises direct control over more and more aspects of our lives'.[43] Two important examples illustrate this point. Firstly, local government has been progressively brought under central control: in April 1986 the Labour-controlled GLC and the six other metropolitan counties were formally abolished. Secondly, Mrs Thatcher has ceased to pay the respect traditionally accorded to pressure groups which seek to influence specific policies. The trade unions, of course, she has systematically weakened – some say crushed – by ignoring them and passing restrictive legislation.

A Gallup poll, reported on BBC's *Panorama* (9 January 1989) revealed that 65% of British people thought that government power

had grown more under Mrs Thatcher whilst only 10% thought freedom for the individual had grown more.

The case against

(a) *Downgrading Cabinet* In her defence it can be argued that Mrs
Thatcher has not broken any rules: none of the conventions about
prior Cabinet discussion of important issues and the formulation of a
consensus have any legal status at all. Heseltine's complaint that a
consitutional outrage had occurred over Westland is dismissed by
Hugo Young as 'a total absurdity . . . The rules of Cabinet in my view
are largely determined by the balance of political power between the
different forces which exist.'[44] In other words, if the Prime Minister
enjoys the overall support of a party in Parliament then it matters not
how decisions are reached. Sir Frank Cooper, outspoken former
Permanent Under-Secretary in the Ministry of Defence, in an interview with Peter Hennessy, did not believe that she had put 'severe
dents in the traditional model of collective cabinet government'. 'I
think she's changed a number of things', judged Sir Frank. 'She
believes it's the duty of any prime minister to lead from the front and
I would have a great deal of sympathy with that view quite frankly.'[45]

Both Hennessy and Young deny that Cabinet government has
been dismantled by Mrs Thatcher. 'Cabinet government
undoubtedly still exists despite rumours sometimes heard to the
contrary', says Hugo Young. He discerns 'a collective mood of those
who are in Cabinet which acts, maybe often, as an inexplicit veto on
what Prime Ministers may want to do.'[46] Hennessy cites examples
of issues which Mrs Thatcher did not take to full Cabinet for fear that
they would be defeated, e.g. 'the total abolition of the closed shop,
the radical breaking-up of the National Health Service, student
loans, rates, vouchers for schools . . .'.[47]

Her defeat in the Cabinet (spring 1986) over the sale of parts of BL
to American buyers is surely further evidence that Cabinet
government is alive under Mrs Thatcher, if not particularly well.
After the débâcle of Westland she simply could not get her own way
and had to back down.

Inevitably any prime minister will run things with the help of a
small, possibly informal, group of colleagues. As David Howell
pointed out, 'This country, really since the sixteenth century has
basically been run by five or six people. I don't think its very different
today: five or six is what you need and that's what any prime minister

tends to form around them.'[48]

Burch argues that it would be 'misleading to suggest' that Mrs Thatcher intervened more in the work of individual departments than previous prime ministers. Her style is interventionist; she wants to influence policy in its formative stage and quite naturally seeks to involve and encourage the civil servants concerned. Anthony King argues that Mrs Thatcher is uninterested in the 'nuts and bolts of government. Faced with a problem she instinctively asks not "what organisation shall I create?" but "who can help me?" '[49] Ignoring bureaucratic procedures, she then assembles those people who can produce the desired results quickly and efficiently.

(b) *Politicisation of the civil service*   She is less interested in the political views of civil servants – professionally trained to serve any master – than their energy and ability. Sir Robin Butler is 'quite certain that the Prime Minister's wish . . . is that the Civil Service should remain an apolitical organisation and I believe that is remaining so'.[50] Other mandarins point out that it is only natural that the more dynamic civil servants who thrive on change should win preferment under a radical administration – just as they did during the nationalisation process after the war.

(c) *Overcentralisation*   It is the spendthrift local councils which intervene so unjustifiably into our lives, argue Thatcher loyalists: it is necessary to curb them. The public also benefited from the removal of metropolitan county councils which proved to be an unnecessary, expensive and bureaucratic tier of government. They also argue that pressure groups have a right to tender advice but governments are not obliged to take it. Mrs Thatcher believes that the practice of consulting myriad pressure groups in the hope of creating some kind of consensus tends either to prevent the right decision being made or to produce immobilism.

(7) Mrs Thatcher has become a president rather than a prime minister

The case for
The criticism is really a synthesis of all those discussed earlier. From the original idea of a British prime minister as first among equals within the Cabinet, Mrs Thatcher seems to have travelled a long way.

Her style of government is intensely personal – more so than any prime minister within living memory. As Pym says, 'she would ideally like to run the major Departments herself and tries her best to do so'. It is *her* will which dominates, not the Cabinet's. By degrees she has gathered all the threads of power into her own hands, bypassing Cabinet and its committees in a number of crucial areas; if Cabinet has no collective force it is little different from its American equivalent which is purely the creature of the President.

The corollary of this is that Mrs Thatcher tries to do too much. *The Economist* criticises her hectic schedules, her short attention-span, her tendency to be 'not quite in intellectual control'.[51] Other commentators regularly discern a desperately tired Mrs Thatcher, looking drained and grey: Mr Edward Du Cann MP in March 1984 even had the temerity to suggest that a deputy should be appointed to help carry her excessive workload.

Interestingly, the suite of rooms in the Grand Hotel, Brighton, used by Mrs Thatcher at the time of the 1984 bombing, has been rebuilt and renamed 'The Presidential Suite'! Some would say, however, that left to her Mrs Thatcher would have named it 'The Royal Suite'. According to some she increasingly assumes a royal demeanour when visiting abroad and at home pre-empts royal visits to scenes of disaster. Even Norman Tebbit has likened her to Queen Victoria, but most telling of all is her extraordinary use of the royal 'we': 'We have learned so much and shall never forget the beauteous things we have seen', she wrote in a museum's visitors' book.[52] And then in February 1989 came the definitive example: 'We have become a grandmother.'

The case against

(a) A 'presidential tendency' in the British premiership has been noted ever since Richard Crossman's famous introduction to Bagehot's *English Constitution*. It was inevitable that a strong character like Mrs Thatcher would help this tendency develop.

(b) Unlike the American President, Mrs Thatcher was not elected directly for a fixed term. She is always beholden ultimately to her party in Parliament. As long as they loyally support her, it is arguable that she has more relative power than the US President who always faces opposition from Congress but, if her party deserts her, then, unlike the President, she is lost. The point is that she has to *earn* this support. The fact that she commands the kind of support which enables her to act like a president should not be held against her: it is really a compliment rather than a criticism.

A century ago Sir William Harcourt said that 'In practice the thing very much depends on the character of the man . . . the office of Prime Minister is what its holder chooses and is able to make of it.' In the present day Joe Haines, a former aide to Harold Wilson, dismisses 'presidential' descriptions of Mrs Thatcher as an exaggeration: 'If you have a powerful man like Churchill was, or Macmillan was, or Mrs Thatcher is, then they tend to dominate their colleagues.'[53] Hennessey also holds well back from claiming that Mrs Thatcher has 'privatised' the Cabinet from the Constitution.

(c) Mrs Thatcher is human and of course becomes tired, though her energy is prodigious. She rises at 6.00 a.m. each day and stays up into the small hours dealing with her red boxes and reading the first editions of the national newspapers. Each day is highly organised and involves a gruelling schedule of high-level meetings, interviews, visits and appearances in the House of Commons. Her supporters would claim she has a genius for making decisions – the vast majority of them good ones. These special abilities enable her to do more than the normal prime minister: she overflows the boundaries of the office and consequently appears to be presidential. But again, it is her achievement.

Even one of her opponents, Paddy Ashdown, leader of the SLD, had to admit in 1988 that 'Mrs Thatcher will go down as one of the great Prime Ministers of this country.' Supporters claim it is not her fault if her bearing and manner resemble those of a queen.

(d) Mrs Thatcher herself dismisses any suggestion that she has royal pretensions but she has admitted that she has 'become a bit of an institution – you know, the sort of thing people expect to see around the place'. She has also said that she would like to be seen as 'the mother of the nation', rather like Golda Meir was for Israel.

Conclusion

Is Mrs Thatcher's political style still an issue? I would conclude that it is but less so than it was – especially since Westland. In January 1986 this crisis threatened to prove the truth of most or all of the critical propositions considered above plus a few more besides. The conflict was a dispute over the future of the Westland helicopter company between Michael Heseltine at Defence and Leon Brittan at Trade and Industry in which Mrs Thatcher sided with the DTI. The real issue, however, quickly became the alleged impropriety of Mrs Thatcher's conduct. It emerged that her personal staff had been involved with DTI officials in authorising the leak of a highly confidential letter from Sir Patrick Mayhew, the Solicitor-General, which undermined Heseltine's position.

In the furore which surrounded Heseltine's resignation on 9 January 1986 the most penetrating attention was focused on the way Mrs Thatcher managed her Cabinet and her Private Office. Did she authorise the leak personally as much evidence suggested? Had she lied? Was this the way she usually ran things? The crisis was averted when Leon Brittan eventually accepted the blame and resigned but his subsequent evasions in front of a Select Committee enquiry suggested he was protecting his Prime Minister. Doubts over her position grew within the Conservative party and in the country her ratings plummeted. But after a difficult six months the economy started to improve, she was able to put Westland behind her and march on to electoral victory in June 1987. Brittan remained on the backbenches but was rewarded for his loyalty in 1988 with a knighthood and a job as an EEC Commissioner.

The gathering discontent over Mrs Thatcher's political style reached its apotheosis with Westland: perhaps her opponents concluded that if she could survive this test she could survive anything. Since then – halfway through her third term – her position appears unassailable. The public do not like Mrs Thatcher or – if poll data is any guide – her policies either, but in the absence of any credible opposition they respond to her strength, certainty and competence. Her faults are well known and perhaps accepted as the necessary complements of her strengths. Dennis Healey suggested in 1988 that she is now seen as 'a force, an elemental force of nature'.[54] But political events can change rapidly and so can apparently impregnable political positions. A week is still a long time in politics.

Notes

1 *The Economist*, 14 May 1983.
2 *The Economist*, 18 January 1986.
3 Quoted in *The Observer*, 23 October 1984.
4 See D. Kavanagh, *Thatcherism and British Politics*, OUP, 1987, pp. 26–63.
5 Her words to the Lord Mayor's Banquet, 1982, quoted in Peter Riddel, *The Thatcher Government*, Martin Robertson, 1984, p. 9.
6 *Guardian*, 22 October 1988.
7 Interview with Ronald Butt, *Sunday Times*, 3 May 1981.
8 Quoted in Arthur Aughey, 'Mrs Thatcher's philosophy', *Parliamentary Affairs*, Autumn 1983, p. 393.
9 Interview with Hugo Young, *Sunday Times*, 3 August 1980.
10 Dennis Kavanagh, *Thatcherism*, p. 252.
11 *Guardian*, 10 July 1985.
12 Interview with David Dimbleby, 10 June 1987.
13 Kavanagh, *Thatcherism*, p. 273.
14 Riddel, *Thatcher Government*, p. 2.
15 *Sunday Express*, 27 July 1988.
16 *Observer*, 15 January 1989.
17 *Sunday Times*, 3 August 1980.
18 *Sunday Express*, 27 July 1988.
19 Interview with Hugo Young, *Guardian*, 24 September 1986.
20 Kavanagh, *Thatcherism*, p. 251.
21 Anthony King, 'Margaret Thatcher as a political leader', in Robert Skidelsky (ed.), *Thatcherism*, Chatto & Windus, 1988, p. 58.
22 *Sunday Times*, 15 April 1984.
23 Francis Pym, *The Politics of Consent*, Hamish Hamilton, 1984, p. 14.
24 Simon Hoggart, 'Mrs Thatcher: five years on', *Observer*, 29 April 1984.
25 Peter Hennessy, *Cabinet*, Blackwell, 1986, p. 98.
26 Robert Harris, 'Mrs Thatcher's kitchen cabinet', *Observer*, 27 November 1988.
27 Interview given to Tyne Tees TV, 'Is Democracy Working?', 29 April 1984.
28 Ivor Crewe, 'Has the electorate become Thatcherite?' in Skidelsky, *Thatcherism*, p. 49.
29 *Ibid.*, p. 57.

30 *Observer*, 27 November 1988.
31 *Guardian*, 24 September 1984.
32 Martin Burch, 'Mrs Thatcher's approach to leadership in government 1979–1983', *Parliamentary Affairs*, 36(4), p. 408.
33 *Observer*, 27 November 1988.
34 *The Economist*, 10 March 1984.
35 Burch, 'Mrs Thatcher's approach', p. 411.
36 Hennessy, *Cabinet*, p. 97.
37 *Ibid.*, p. 95.
38 *Ibid.*, p. 99.
39 *Observer*, 25 February 1979.
40 Paul Johnson, *Sunday Times*, 24 November 1983.
41 *The Economist*, 10 March 1984.
42 Channel 4, 20 December 1988.
43 Pym, *Politics of Consent*, p. 17.
44 Tyne Tees, 'Is Democracy Working?', 19 April 1986.
45 Hennessy, *Cabinet*, p. 105.
46 Tyne Tees, 'Is Democracy Working?', 16 April 1986.
47 Hennessy, *Cabinet*, p. 111.
48 *Ibid.*, p. 96.
49 Anthony King, *Sunday Times*, 11 April 1984.
50 Channel 4, 20 December 1988.
51 *The Economist*, 7 July 1984.
52 *Observer*, 5 April 1987.
53 Tyne Tees, 'Is Democracy Working?', 16 April 1986.
54 *Guardian*, 23 July 1988.

Reading

Peter Hennessy, *Cabinet*, Blackwell, 1986.
Dennis Kavanagh, *Thatcherism and British Politics*, OUP, 1987.
A. King, *The British Prime Minister*, Macmillan, 1985, pp. 96–133.
Francis Pym, *The Politics of Consent*, Hamish Hamilton, 1984.
Peter Riddel, *The Thatcher Government*, Martin Robertson, 1984.
R. Skidelsky (ed.), *Thatcherism*, Chatto & Windus, 1988.
Hugo Young, *One of US*, Macmillan, 1989.

2 *Andrew Gray*

Secrecy and openness in government

'Open government is a contradiction in terms. You can be open –
or you can have government.' (Cabinet Secretary in *Yes Minister*
(J. Lynn & A. Jay, BBC, 1981, p. 19))

Even those with a distaste for such Alice-in-Wonderland type quota-
tions at the head of chapters will have to admit to the lure of a quip
such as this. As on so many other occasions, the series *Yes Minister*
captured the essence of the issue. In this chapter, therefore, we shall
examine the forces for secrecy and openness and identify the purposes served by freedom of information and the problems faced by
would-be reformers. But first the issues must be placed in their
historical context.

Historical landmarks

In George Orwell's *Nineteen Eighty-Four* the Ministry of Truth is of
course really the Ministry of Falsehood. Its job is to present an
interpretation of the world which protects the Party. Oceania may be
a fiction but it illustrates issues which have exercised minds not only
in the real 1984 when the Campaign for Freedom of Information was
mounted, but both before and since. Indeed, Des Wilson's Campaign, which has been supported by such establishment figures as Sir
Douglas Wass and Sir Patrick Nairne, both former permanent
secretaries in the Civil Service, and Sir John Hoskyns, former policy
adviser to Mrs Thatcher, is only a part of a notable saga.

The origins of the Official Secrets Acts

(a) *Marvin and* The Globe, *1878*   At least as far as the past century or so is concerned the saga begins with Marvin, a clerk who worked for the diplomatic service. In 1878, in preliminary discussions for the Berlin Peace Conference, the British and Russian governments were hatching a secret deal. Marvin simply took some of the drafts to representatives of *The Globe* newspaper who rewarded him for his services and published what they saw. As Marvin had not actually stolen the documents, the government found they had no case for a prosecution under the existing legislation. This was one of the reasons for the first Official Secrets Act of 1889.

(b) *German spies, 1911*   In the summer of 1911 anxiety grew about German espionage, especially after some of its nationals were found drawing pictures of fortifications at Dover. As a result, the government hurriedly passed the Official Secrets Act of that year. It is this Act which is still in force and of which section II causes so much controversy for the way it proscribes the passing of *any* unauthorised information.

Some recent confusions

(c) *The* Sunday Telegraph *Case, 1971*   This prosecution arose out of an article on a government document about British military equipment being sent to help the federal Nigerian government in its struggle with the secessionist state of Biafra. The document also contained a highly critical analysis of the prospects of the federal government. After a four-week trial, the journalist (Jonathan Aitken), the editor, and the army colonel who leaked the document were acquitted. In one of the more robust judgements of British legal history, the judge said that Section II of the Official Secrets Act, 1911, should be 'pensioned off'. This appeared to make Section II inoperative.

(d) *The Crossman diaries, 1975*   The diaries of the former Labour Cabinet minister, Richard Crossman, were less important for what they contained (which was anyway rather too verbose) than the issue raised by their publication. An attempt was made by the Attorney-General, the law officer of the Labour government of 1974, to prohibit publication by the *Sunday Times* and Jonathan Cape Ltd. This attempt eventually failed in the Court of Appeal, thus confirming the courts' liberal trend of the 1970s.

(e) *Civil servants and the Ministry of Defence, 1984* These steps towards greater openness were reversed by two prosecutions brought in 1984. Both concerned civil servants in the Ministry of Defence. The first was a junior official who was convicted for passing to the *Guardian* documents about the installation of Cruise missiles in the UK. The second was a senior civil servant who was acquitted of leaking to an MP documents about the sinking of the Argentinian battleship *Belgrano* during the Falklands War of 1982. This acquittal implied that an MP might be an authorised person to whom under Section II information could be passed.

(f) *The Westland Affair, 1985–86* The Westland Affair confirmed that ministers may be just as prone to leaking as their officials. Judging from the hearings of the Select Committee on Defence, this long and complex series of incidents involved ministers, their press officers and regular civil servants in a good deal of underhand activity. Even the Prime Minister and head of the civil service themselves appear to have been guilty of at best misjudgement, if not actual collusion, in the manipulation of disclosure and witholding of information. In the end it was Mr Leon Brittan, as Secretary of State for Trade and Industry, who resigned. Ostensibly, this resignation arose from Mr Brittan's disclosure of part of a letter from the Solicitor-General which impugned the validity of arguments used by the Defence Secretary (Mr Heseltine) in the debate on whether the Westland Helicopter Company should be rescued financially by a consortium led by the American competitor Sikorsky. In part, however, the resignation arose from the manner in which Mr Brittan failed to present a credible account to the House of Commons (see Ch. 3). The story suggests a very fine dividing-line between what constitutes official and unofficial disclosure.

(g) *'Spycatcher'* More recently, of course, those interested in freedom of information have been feasted on the events surrounding the memoirs of a former MI5 official, Peter Wright. The author appears to have had a grievance against his employers over his pension entitlements and hoped to publish his memoirs in recompense. The royalties must have surpassed his wildest hopes for, thanks to the British government's single-minded attempts to prevent publication anywhere (which included despatching the Cabinet Secretary to be a witness in the Australian High Court), the publicity fanned interest in the book out of all proportion to its intrinsic worth.

For the government, the issue was ostensibly the very proper one of maintaining the oath of confidentiality of its MI5 employees. For the champions of publication, the issue has been the determination of what constitutes material which should be released into the public domain; the memoirs offered observations on the loyalty of a former head of MI5 and on alleged plots by the agency to destabilise a previous Labour government. Perhaps of most interest, however, has been the government's avoidance of the use of Section II of the Official Secrets Act, 1911 and its recourse to injunctions through the civil law, a device used in subsequent actions against the mass media not only in relation to 'Spycatcher' publications but also over the broadcast of programmes on other security matters.

Conservative government reforms of Section II

Realising that Section II of the 1911 Act had become unworkable, and frightened by the strength of support for an earlier attempt to reform the law by Richard Shepherd (one of its own back-benchers), the government published its own proposals to reform the criminal law in this area (Cm. 408, 1988). Its objective was to clarify the grounds for non-disclosure to include principally defence, security, intelligence matters (including international co-operation), and information useful to or relating to the apprehension of criminals. Liberalisation was proposed in that some important blanket classifications (such as Cabinet minutes and advice to ministers) would cease but might still fall under the restrictions mentioned above. More restrictively, it would not be a defence to argue that a matter needed to be disclosed in the public interest nor that material had already been published abroad. Similarly, disclosures by members of the security services would by definition constitute a criminal offence.

The content of the proposals is complex. Interested readers should consult the White Paper itself and newspapers published on 30 June 1988. In the latter they will also find that the proposals were not universally welcomed, even on the government's own side. The Home Secretary's efforts to clarify and liberalise were supported by senior colleagues, including Mr Leon Brittan, the casualty of the

Westland affair. But Mr Shepherd reiterated his long-held concern with the 'very repressive measures' by which ministers were able to determine the extent of disclosure without redress. Labour party spokesmen also criticised these catch-all provisions while an SDP criticism related specifically to the absence of a public interest defence.

The history of these cases indicates that both the law and administration of government information are based very largely on chance and political discretion. However, before you come to your own judgement on the recent government proposals we should consider the forces which shape this practice and the objectives and potential beneficiaries of greater openness.

Objectives and beneficiaries

Objectives of greater openness

Perhaps one of the reasons for the rather sterile discussion of open government in recent years has been the scant attention paid to the objectives it should promote. The obvious links between power, liberty and openness may be justifications in themselves. The practice, however, has often been a confusion of ends and means. One way to resolve this is to consider the objectives in terms of Birch's characterisation of *Representative and Responsible Government*. By representative, Birch understands three notions: election as the means by which governments are chosen, government by representatives of the people, and government as representative or reflective of the people. By responsible government he understands three further notions: responsive government, considered and unarbitrary government, and accountable government. In this context the objectives of open government relate primarily to government by representatives, the promotion of responsive and accountable government, and the protection against arbitrary government.

Specifically these objectives may be expressed as three propositions:

(1) *The civil rights objective:* secrecy should be relaxed to allow the individual to see files containing his personal records and thereby protect his individual rights.

(2) *The policy-making objective:* governments should be obliged to outline in greater detail the nature of the problems they face and provide for public use the information thought relevant to the search

for solutions.

(3) *The accountability objective:* governments should be obliged to provide more detailed accounts not only of their decisions but also the reasons for them and the conduct of their implementation.

Whether these objectives have equal weight in the current debate is not easy to determine. What is clear, however, is that each might have its own implications for the development of greater openness and that these might even be mutually inconsistent.

Beneficiaries of openness

As secrecy is about the protection of information and openness about its dispersal, we might expect the potential beneficiaries of greater openness to be MPs and other representatives of the public, whether groups or individuals, who presently depend on government disclosure. This generalisation, however, conceals a complex pattern.

(a) *Members of Parliament* This complexity is reflected in the attitudes of front benches in the House of Commons: in opposition each has been broadly in favour of greater disclosure, while in government each has resisted progress. Back-benchers of all parties, however, appear to be prime beneficiaries; at least they make such claims in the support for private members' bills on the subject, based on their requirements for more information in the performance of their various parliamentary functions.

(b) *The mass media* It is clear that the press regards itself as a major beneficiary. This was expressed formally in a *Times* leading article of 1852: the press's ability to 'enhance its dignity and freedom . . . [is] trammelled from the moment it accepts an ancillary position' to government. In some quarters the dependence on the lobby system of unattributable government briefings is clearly regarded as corruptly ancillary. No doubt the press also hopes (perhaps unrealistically) to obtain good copy from less secrecy.

(c) *Interest groups* A further beneficiary is suggested by the experience of the Freedom of Information Acts in the USA where corporate business has gained perhaps more than any other group. Some commentators have described legislation as providing for legalised industrial espionage and the largest corporations have benefited most. But not all interest groups would appear to gain equally; those without established and institutionalised links with government might certainly gain, but those already close to the policy-making process in this way might actually see their positions in jeopardy.

(d) *Individual members of the public*   This category of beneficiaries would appear directly affected only by systematic and effective attempts to promote the civil rights objective outlined earlier, either by allowing individual access to personal files or by enhancing the access of officers such as ombudsmen.

Forces for secrecy and openness

The variability of these complex issues and the practice of secrecy is reinforced by the way many of our political institutions and processes can act as forces both for and against secrecy.

Forces for secrecy

(a) *The unwritten constitution*   The absence of a written document which lays down the rights of governed and government and the very dependence on custom and practice for the operation of so much of our system of government are themselves important sources of secrecy. The fact that it is for a prime minister, for example, to decide how much shall be revealed about the structure of Cabinet committees is reflective of an inbuilt inertia towards secrecy which only conscious and active attention can prevent pervading the whole system.

(b) *Statutes*   Those parts of the Constitution which are written as legislation tend to reinforce this tendency. Two sets of statutes are significant here: those relating to official secrets and the publication of official records. Of the Official Secrets Acts, that of 1911, and especially Section II, is the most important. As we have seen earlier, it is this section which makes it an offence to pass unauthorised information. The all-embracing nature of these provisions are so restrictive in theory as to make government unworkable. The Public Records Act of 1958 (as amended) stipulates that official information may not be published for at least thirty years. We are almost unique in this country in having such a rule and in many countries it is possible to inspect personal files upon application and to see documents relating to a decision or policy once it has been made. This

Act, then, helps to keep a prying public at bay.

(c) *Parliament*   Many of our parliamentary arrangements also constitute a force for secrecy. At the heart of this is the party system itself. The divisions of government and opposition, and the attendant constraints of party discipline and the management of the party game, have tended to provide obstructions to those seeking information. The fact, for example, that no incoming government may see the papers relating to its predecessors is characteristic. Similarly, parliamentary questions, which many textbooks refer to as a cornerstone of Parliament's ability to scrutinise government, are constrained by ministers' ability to refuse an answer. Some of these are very properly refused as they relate to matters of security, the confidentiality of individuals, or areas outside the minister's direct responsibility (e.g. the activities of nationalised industries or local government). It is not difficult, however, to see how such definitions might be stretched so as to prevent unfavourable revelations. Indeed, so secretive was this tendency that it was not until the late 1970s that the Speaker allowed an MP even to ask about the sorts of questions which a minister could refuse to answer!

Another constraint here, of course, is the inadequacy of a political and parliamentary system which neither attracts the most talented and informed members of the community nor provides them once elected with the facilities for gaining information on their own account. This is underwritten by a part-time ethic amongst many MPs and reinforced in much of the regular cycle of parliamentary business. MPs are thus dependent on the government for information.

(d) *The mass media*   In general, relations between the government of the day and the mass media are controlled by the various press officers in the departments and especially that of No. 10 Downing Street. But of special note here is the 'D' (for Defence) Notice Committee. This comprises journalists and civil servants and represents an instrument for the voluntary censorship in the media of defence matters. Each notice suggests whether or not the media may publish matters relating to the issue in question. It is described by those who have researched the area as working tolerably well. If it did not exist legislation would certainly take its place. Nevertheless, in so far as the press accepts the guidelines laid down it represents an unaccountable force against disclosure and in favour of secrecy. In areas other than defence the media is almost toally dependent on the lobby. This is essentially a system of government handouts supported by unattributable briefings by press officers.

(e) *Civil service*   It is also true that the organisational development of the civil service, i.e. its hierarchical tendencies, division of tasks, rules and procedures, helps to induce a bureaucratic organisation and mind which are both structurally and attitudinally unsympathetic to openness.

(f) *Wider cultural forces*   Perhaps this attitude in the civil service reflects more general cultural traits in our society. Even if it is now rather old-fashioned to speak of a deferential political culture in this country, it is still perhaps true that we have a tendency to be trustful of government and that our political institutions and practices are built on an assumption of trust. Nevertheless, this can support a relative invisibility and inaccountability of government, a world of private and secretive operations.

Forces for openness

All the above illustrations have been drawn rather starkly in order to clarify the tendencies at work. That the reality is more ambiguous, however, is indicated by the fact that each of the above features of our constitution and practice can also act as a force for openness.

(a) *The unwritten constitution*   As we saw earlier, a responsible government is a responsive government, i.e. responsive to the demands and interests of the public. It can demonstrate its responsiveness only by informing the people what it is doing and how. Thus it provides data about houses built, people unemployed, money spent, and so on. But this provision of information is also a facet of accountable government in the sense that it is part of the obligation to give an account (see Ch. 3). Similarly, in order to show that they have not been arbitrary, governments are obliged to bring groups into the decision-making processes such as in enquiries and other participatory mechanisms. In short, the government can open itself up as part of the process of displaying its responsibility.

(b) *Statutes*   Even the legislation which we have seen as a force for secrecy can work two ways; law is only effective if it is enforced. In the case of the Official Secrets Act of 1911, we may have seen the passing of Section II into the dignified (rather than effective) parts of the Constitution. In addition, some of the provisions of relevant legislation can be used for openness. The Public Records Act, for example, contains an important discretionary provision (Section V) whereby the Lord Chancellor may extend *or shorten* the thirty-year rule.

(c) *Parliament*   Changes in Parliament have also had their effects. The break-up of the two-party system (and perhaps also the size of recent government majorities) has given rise to an increasingly numerous band of MPs unwilling to accept the old order of things as arranged by the two front benches. The new select committee system has also provided an opportunity for MPs to dig out the information they need as well as to specialise and become more expert in chosen fields of policy. There are signs, too, that a number of MPs have established their own networks of contacts within the civil service and other public organisations which can provide them with useful ammunition on such committees. In short, there is evidence of a new professionalisation of MPs which, whatever its drawbacks, will act as a force for openness.

(d) *The mass media*   These MPs' activities have been much supported by the development of investigatory journalism and the public's interest in it. This is a field made notable by the *Sunday Times* Insight Team but now more widespread. Granada television has also over the years gained a similar reputation from its early series on 'The State of the Nation' and 'Decision' to its use of 'hypotheticals' to simulate government activities in particular contexts. Perhaps this development falls behind that in other countries such as the USA but it is nevertheless contributing to the opening up of government.

(e) *Civil service*   Both the MPs and the journalists now enjoy closer links with the civil service. This has been an area of important developments, from provisions in the Establishment Officer's Guide (the civil service 'Bible' on conduct) and the forgotten Croham Directive of 1977 (which encourages the publication of background papers), to the development of consultative Green Papers on government thinking and the changing experiences and attitudes of more recent generations of civil servants. The latter are now less anonymous both in public and parliamentary contexts and have been brought up administratively in a time of greater experience of the more open ways of the European Economic Community and other supra-national organisations. It has also been observed that the civil service is increasingly less prepared to accept the secrecy of a government which itself so publicly criticises the administrative machine on which it depends.

(f) *Wider cultural forces*   If this last point suggests a rising anti-authoritarianism, it reflects a changing attitude to government in the country as a whole. Some have 'blamed' this on the educational system, others on an increasing affluence and therefore independence generally. Whatever the cause, there does appear to be less willingness to accept what governments say at face value. The sagas of the Belgrano and Westland affairs are perhaps indicative of this.

Problems in the pursuit of openness

It is with these forces for openness that successive campaigns for greater freedom of information have been launched to promote the sort of objectives cited earlier. Yet each campaign has faced four sets of practical problems which it has been obliged to resolve:

(1) *The subject matter of disclosure*   What to exempt from disclosure presents problems not so much in the matter of *real* secrets (matters of genuine national security) as in drawing the line in a feasible way between what is to be disclosed and what protected.

(2) *Decisions about disclosure*   The fuzziness of the dividing-line may mean that we have to depend on some agency or other to decide whether matters should be disclosed on their merits. This is liable to rest finally with ministers. The problem then would lie with the clash between their own and the public interest. As a result some have suggested a kind of ombudsman for secrets to check up on ministerial decisions.

(3) *The form of disclosure*   The simple availability of files, even if this were feasible, would be helpful to few other than those familiar with the workings of the system. Perhaps, therefore, special documents should be prepared. The problem is who by and at what cost. Many doubt the value of such an exercise.

(4) *Effects of disclosure*   Some fear that the consequences of

greater disclosure would be a distortion of the democratic process as, for example, institutions with the resources necessary for capitalising on the opportunities of greater openness came to wield greater influence. These are not inconsiderable problems; often they raise fundamental questions about the nature of our political system.

Conclusion

The issues in government secrecy and openness are many and varied, the objectives and beneficiaries sometimes conflicting and the problems faced by reform difficult to resolve. Des Wilson, the founder of the 1984 Campaign for Freedom of Information, was confident that it would lead to a successful repeal of Section II of the 1911 Official Secrets Act as a committee chaired by Lord Franks recommended as long ago as 1972. But recent events surrounding 'Spycatcher' and the Westland affair have confirmed that governments are still inherently protective of the information they hold and that reform must unravel not only the legal but also the administrative problems. The question remains whether another government would propose more freedom of information in practice.

Reading

Birch, A. H., *Representative and Responsible Government*, Allen & Unwin, 1964.

Hunt, R. A. & Chapman M., *Open Government*, Croom Helm, 1978.

3 *Andrew Gray*

The individual accountability of ministers

When a small group of Argentinian scrap-metal workers landed on the tiny island of South Georgia in March 1982 they set off a chain of events which, following their country's invasion of the Falkland Islands on 2 April, led eventually to the resignation of Lord Carrington, the British Foreign Secretary. Then in January 1986 Mr Leon Brittan, Secretary of State for Industry, resigned over his part in the Westland affair, in particular the unofficial disclosure of a confidential letter from the Solicitor-General to the Secretary of State for Defence, Mr Michael Heseltine. For many, these cases have shown that the principle of ministerial accountability – that for every policy or action of a department its minister is accountable, answerable and if necessary culpable – is still alive and well in the British Constitution. After a gap of nearly thirty years ministers have accepted the ultimate responsibility for the policy and conduct of their departments.

Is such an interpretation justified? This chapter will attempt to answer this not only by reference to the circumstances of these and other cases of the past few decades but also by setting them into an analysis of what accountability is and how it is exercised. This will involve an examination of *stewardship*, which is at the heart of accountability, and the different *codes* which govern its form and content. We will also explore the way *accounts* are presented, noting a distinction between judicial and theatrical settings. All these considerations will be important for our understanding of what has been going on.

The story so far

Carrington and the Falklands
Before their departure on Sunday 28 March 1982 for an EEC meeting in Brussels, the Foreign Secretary (Lord Carrington) and the Prime Minister considered intelligence reports of Argentinian forces who were threatening the security of the British Falkland Islands in the South Atlantic. The next day saw the Prime Minister herself order three nuclear-powered submarines to the region. By Thursday, when Lord Carrington returned from Tel Aviv (whence he had flown after Brussels), all who were privy to these discussions knew they could do nothing to prevent what Carrington later called a 'humiliating affront to this country', the Argentinian invasion of the Falklands.

During the evening of Friday 2 April, Carrington and John Nott (Minister of Defence) gave a press conference and confirmed what most of the world had already gathered; that the invasion had taken place and that the Argentinian forces were secure. The full Cabinet then met and implemented the contingency plans, including the launching of the counter-invasion task force. Richard Luce suggested to Carrington that as junior minister responsible for the negotiations with the Argentine government he should resign. But Carrington played it down. On the following day, in a unique Saturday session of Parliament, Nott took a pounding in the Commons. With Carrington in the Lords, Nott was the obvious target for the vengeance-seekers who promptly made the most of his inept performance. The Minister of Defence had previously offered his own resignation, but the Prime Minister had rejected it on the grounds that it had not been *his* department's responsibility.

Perhaps unwittingly, the Prime Minister had thereby pointed the finger at the Foreign Secretary. This and his absence from the Commons appeared to persuade Carrington that it was he who should go. To his surprise, Carrington found the Prime Minister exerting great pressure on him to stay. But the Press was hostile over the weekend and not even the counsels of former premiers Home and Macmillan could prevail. Carrington thus resigned and with him his deputy, Humphrey Atkins, and his junior minister, Richard Luce.

Brittan and the Westland Affair
On 13 and 14 December 1985 the Board of Directors of the helicopter company, Westland plc, resolved to reject a financial rescue package

from a consortium of European companies and to accept that from the American Sikorsky Company. Despite Defence Secretary Heseltine's recorded protest at the 12 December Cabinet meeting, Mrs Thatcher must have hoped that this was the end of the matter as far as the government was concerned. Yet within a month or so two of her colleagues had resigned and her own position was as much under threat as at any time in her premiership.

That the issue would not lie down was much the result of Mr Heseltine's determined and unusually public lobbying on behalf of the European Consortium. In the end, he walked out of the Cabinet on 9 January, unable to accept a collective responsibility for the decision-making process and its outcome. Thus far, the main issue was therefore that of collective responsibility.

Yet even as Mr Heseltine resigned, Mr Brittan's department (Trade and Industry) was under suspicion for having leaked to the Press Association selected passages from a letter written by the Solicitor-General, a government law officer, to Mr Heseltine. These extracts referred to 'material inaccuracies' in the latter's own communications to Lloyds Bank, the European Consortium's bankers. Mr Brittan's presentations to the House of Commons accounting for this were not only unacceptable to the Opposition parties but also to large numbers of his own back-benchers. Mr Brittan then resigned. Thus, an affair which had begun as important for collective responsibility became significant for individual ministerial accountability.

This, however, was not the end of the affair. It soon became clear that the Prime Minister's Press Officer and private office as well as the Cabinet Secretary had been involved in the decision to disclose the Solicitor-General's letter. The subsequent accounts both to the House of Commons itself and its Select Committee for Defence suggested, first, a certain lack of co-ordination between the Department and the centre over the decision and, second, evidence of collusion in concealing the real state of affairs from the House of Commons and the wider public. The latter included the most deadbat performance from the Cabinet Secretary that one is likely to witness from an official and the non-appearance before the Committee of the Prime Minister's Press Officer and other officials involved in the disclosure decision. Thus a third issue arose, that of Parliament's right to examine civil servants.

The story is full of paradoxes. Mr Brittan resigned probably only because, first, he was found to have improperly disclosed a law officer's letter and, second, he gave such inadequate accounts to the House. If the matter had remained a strictly internal departmental error, history suggests he would have been able to pass responsibility down the hierarchy. Mrs Thatcher's misjudgements do seem to have been protected by deflecting responsibility to members of her private office while, through the Cabinet Secretary, she protected them from the Select Committee.

Hoare and Abyssinia

The above reference to historical precedent suggests the value of an appreciation of the way the principles involved have developed. As we saw earlier, many have found in the Carrington and Brittan resignations the restoration of the principle that for every policy or action of a department the minister is responsible and, if necessary, culpable. The previous occasion when a Foreign Secretary had resigned had been in 1935. On that occasion Sam Hoare had negotiated a deal with the French relating to the fate of Abyssinia. He returned to find that the details had been leaked, with a resulting press outcry. The Cabinet felt the need to disassociate itself from the deal and Hoare resigned.

Dugdale and Crichel Down

Of course, the previous occasion on which *any* minister resigned over the policy or actions of his department was in 1954 in the case of Crichel Down. Then, Sir Thomas Dugdale, Minister of Agriculture, found himself the inheritor of a long-running saga involving a number of departments and some private land which had been compulsorily purchased during the Second World War. The original owner had found difficulty in buying back his land, despite earlier assurances from Whitehall. A subsequent committee of enquiry found negligence on the part of agriculture officials and Dugdale resigned on the grounds that 'I, as Minister, must accept full responsibility to Parliament for any mistakes and inefficiency of officials in my Department.'

Amery and Ferranti

However, apart from a few who have resigned over their personal misconduct (one of the latest of whom was Cecil Parkinson in 1983), ministers have not been exactly leaping over themselves to follow Dugdale's example. In 1964, for example, Julian Amery did not resign as Minister of Aviation over the excess profits which were later discovered to have been made by the Ferranti company from contracts with the Ministry to make the Bloodhound missile. Amery's defence was that the fault lay with cost accountants and not with himself. This was accepted by the hard-pressed government of the day and the large Conservative majority in the House of Commons.

Davies and Vehicle & General
A similar case arose in the 1971 Vehicle and General affair. The V&G was an insurance company which had struggled with liquidity problems for a decade. Under the Insurance Acts the Department of Trade and Industry (the successor in these matters to the Board of Trade) had the discretionary powers to intervene in a company's affairs if it had reason to doubt the company's solvency. When the V&G was suddenly and compulsorily wound up in March 1971 there was a good deal of outcry over the conduct of the department in leaving so many people uninsured, a situation which the Acts were designed specifically to prevent.

The Tribunal of Enquiry which followed named and blamed certain officials, in particular the Under-Secretary, whose division was directly responsible for monitoring the affairs of such companies. The Tribunal reported negligence and incompetence in the handling of the V&G case. Ministers, however, remained unmentioned; indeed, they were not even asked to give evidence. And when the Secretary of State, John Davies, made a statement to the House on the Tribunal's Report he made no comments about his own or his colleagues' positions. Mr Davies had joined the government in 1970, after serving as Director-General of the Confederation of British Industry. He was an inexperienced politician with a huge and complex department to control. Nevertheless, the question of his resignation was barely touched upon in the whole affair.

Callaghan and devaluation
The closest parallel in recent years with the Falklands case, however, was the devaluation crisis of 1967. James Callaghan had been Chancellor of the Exchequer since the Labour victory of 1964. The economy had been in some difficulty throughout this time, eventually leading to a run on sterling from the summer of 1966. (In those days governments regarded the protection of the pound's value as a very high priority.) When the government eventually devalued the pound

in 1967, Callaghan's personal policy was defeated and he immediately offered his resignation to the Prime Minister, Harold Wilson. Wilson, however, felt that at such a time it was important for the government to stick together. Callaghan therefore stayed on to introduce the package of measures designed to help the devaluation achieve its desired effects but later that year, in a minor Cabinet reshuffle, he changed places with Roy Jenkins at the Home Office.

What can be made of these stories? On the one hand there is the principle of ministerial accountability so clearly stated and (admirably?) followed by Dugdale; on the other is the trend of later cases which supports Lord Hunt's evidence to the Expenditure Committee of the House of Commons in 1977 when he was Secretary to the Cabinet: 'The concept that because somebody whom the Minister had never heard of, has made a mistake, means that the Minister should resign, is out of date, and rightly so.' Although much has been written about accountability, including these cases, there have been very few attempts to *understand* what accountability is and how it is exercised. In the remainder of this chapter, we will attempt to do this by setting these incidents into an analysis of accountability.

Ministerial accountability and stewardship

Definitions

(1) *To be accountable* is to be liable to present an account of and answer for the discharge of responsibilities to the person or group entrusting those responsibilities. Thus at the heart of accountability is stewardship.

(2) *Stewardship* is a relationship where one party is entrusted with the property and/or resource of another.

(3) *There are three parties involved* in stewardship and accountability.

(a) *The steward* (or accountor) is the party to whom the responsibilities are entrusted and who is obliged to give an account of their execution.

(b) *The principal* (or accountee) is the party entrusting those responsibilities and to whom the account is presented.

(c) *The code* (or set of codes) is the collection of understandings that govern the content and conduct of these responsibilities as well as the manner in which the account shall be presented.

A minister is thus a steward in the way he is responsible to Parliament (the principal) for the discharge of his duties and for presenting an account of this. In turn civil servants are stewards in the way they are responsible for accounting to ministers for their duties. This idea of ministers and civil servants as stewards is a very old one in British government. In the Middle Ages, for example, sheriffs were the King's stewards responsible for the collection of revenues. They were held accountable when they were summoned to appear before the King's commissioners (the Exchequer). If they satisfied the Exchequer as to their activities on the King's behalf, they were literally 'discharged'. Much more recently, Mrs Thatcher's government has sought to enhance the accountability of the civil service. Since 1982 the Financial Management Initiative (FMI) has been trying to install a system of accountable management whereby civil servants are made responsible for more clearly-defined resources and operations. In the way that the FMI is dealing with the content and conduct of stewardship it represents a new code of accountability.

Codes of accountability

These codes are often overlooked in traditional discussions of accountability mainly because they are not obvious, unlike ministers and civil servants. But they are important, for they define (a) the nature of the relationship between (say) Parliament and minister, or minister and civil servant; (b) the content and manner of the execution of the responsibilities; and (c) the terms in which the account is presented and evaluated. Thus, they give rise to what some refer to as different types of accountability, i.e. political, legal or financial.

There are, however, many different codes at work:

(1) *Specific codes* are those designed to relate to a specific relationship.

(2) *General codes* are those which already exist (e.g. professional codes of conduct) and are applied to a general set of relationships between stewards and principals.

(3) *Outcome codes* refer to the expectations principals have about the results of the stewardship.

(4) *Process codes* refer to the methods by which these outcomes are to be achieved.

(5) *Symbolic codes* are those which stewards and even principals might acknowledge but which have no practical effect on the conduct of the stewardship even if they are alluded to in the account itself.

(6) *Substantive codes*, on the other hand, do have a direct practical

effect in the way they seek, for example, to promote a particular style of reasoning in the decisions taken, for example, economic, social or legal reasoning.

You will notice that these types of code appear here as contrasting pairs. This is deliberate. Of the first pair there is a tendency in ministerial accountability for *general* codes to predominate over specific ones. One of the features of our relatively unwritten constitution is that the responsibilities of ministers are rarely made explicit; rather they are based on the development of practice in often widely differing fields and contexts of government. The ambiguities which arise may allow an individual minister to escape censure because principals may be unclear as to what the steward was actually entrusted with (see the cases of Amery and Davies above).

Of the second pairing there has been an emphasis on *process* codes rather than those relating to outcomes of accountability. Thus concepts such as due process and equity of treatment are stressed in the conduct of government. At one point in the saga of the government and the General Communications Headquarters (GCHQ), the courts found that the government had neglected due process by not adequately consulting the trade unions involved. Similarly, in the evaluation of financial accounts which departments present to Parliament, more attention has been paid to what is called *regularity* (whether what has been spent has been so authorised) than to the effectiveness or efficiency of that expenditure.

Reference to symbolic codes draws attention to the whole doctrine of ministerial responsibility itself. Many have commented that it is a myth: Parliament, ministers and civil servants may all symbolically acknowledge it but it has little practical effect on these stewards and principals either in the execution of responsibilities or in the adjudication of accounts. On the other hand, there clearly are codes which do affect accountability in the way that they encourage decisions and actions embodying certain types of reasoning (such as complying with the law or making greater use of financial resources).

Stages of accountability
For analytical purposes we can see accountability as passing through several stages:

(1) *The establishment of stewardship* arises when one party entrusts the other with resources and/or responsibilities. Almost certainly, the steward takes on this trusteeship in return for some

reward. In this way accountability can impose a reciprocal obligation upon the principal.

(2) *The execution of the trusteeship*, whether this be the guardianship of public assets, the use of such assets for some mutual gain, or the performance of general or specific duties, is followed by:

(3) *The presentation of the account* and its examination in accordance with the codes by which the stewardship was struck.

(4) *The adjudication of the account* confirms, modifies or terminates the stewardship.

These stages thus constitute the *cycle of accountability* and are repeated for each stewardship struck in turn by a steward with sub-stewards (as between ministers and civil servants). They show how the obligation to give an account arises and how the account may be examined with a view to establishing responsibility for desired and undesired outcomes and activities. The trouble with ministerial accountability, of course, is that these stages are not so neatly distinct. As a result, not only may the terms of the minister's responsibilities (the codes) be unclear to both parties (Parliament and minister), but the occasion when they are laid down is most uncertain. The moment when a minister accepts his trusteeship, for example, is formally when he receives his seals of office from the monarch; Parliament is only remotely involved. These ambiguities may be exploited in the presentation of ministers' accounts.

The presentation of the account

This stage of accountability may be regarded in at least two ways:

(1) as a *quasi-judicial process* in which the account is presented and examined as evidence might be in a court of law; and

(2) as a *dramatic performance* in which the account is presented and examined as a script in a theatre.

Originally, the process of accountability in government *was* judicial; sheriffs, for example, were charged and (all being well) discharged in a king's court. In the passage from the court-room to other arenas, however, the possibilities for theatrical performance (which were already present in the court-room) multiplied. Thus ministers presenting their accounts to Parliament may be seen as actors in the way, for example, they rehearse their scripts in order to prevent any embarrassing and revealing incidents. Similarly, Parliament (as the audience) adopts devices to help the minister sustain his performance such as signals of appreciation during and at the close of the performance, warnings when it is less happy with the performance and wants it altered in some way, and the disregarding of errors or obvious acceptance of ministers' explanations. In short, there may be a collusion between minister and Parliament (steward and principal) more appropriate to theatrical than judicial settings.

Such a view of ministerial accountability may help to explain why so many ministers appear to escape censure. One of the reasons for the collusion we have identified is that the style of Parliament is more appropriate to some of its functions (e.g. debating and legislating) than to others (holding the executive to account). It may also be, of course, that Parliament has come to be filled by those who *wish* to collude (at least in this arena). Perhaps this also explains why the various reforms in this area, e.g. ombudsmen, select committees and tribunals, have all been attempts to get backstage to break down the performance.

The changing accountability of ministers

The selected illustrations show that ministerial accountability has been changing. The analysis of how accountability is established and maintained demonstrates that it is not as straightforward as many have supposed. It is now possible to draw some conclusions about our definition of ministerial accountability, its changing form and content, and the different arenas in which it is now discharged.

(1) *Ministerial accountability* In speaking of this we have been referring to the individual responsibility of ministers for the policy and conduct of themselves as ministers and of their departments (and not, therefore, for their actions as private individuals, however much these may affect their suitability for office, nor for their share of the collective responsibility of the government as a whole).

(2) *The form and content of ministerial accountability* The character of ministerial responsibilities has changed over the years as different *codes of accountability* have come to be adopted and discarded. Traditionally, three substantive codes characterised the responsibilities:

(a) *Financial* codes originally stipulated that ministers (or the monarch's servants) were responsible for using financial resources in the way authorised by king and Parliament. More recently, economic constraints have extended these codes to encompass a responsibility for the effectiveness and efficiency of the expenditure as well.

(b) *Legal* codes have for centuries subjected ministers to the rule of law (even if they have sometimes been in a handy position to say what it is) and thereby charged them to act both within their powers and in the way stipulated. An important characteristic of such codes was the anonymity of departmental officials when acting on behalf of the department.

(c) *Political* codes came to be important when Parliament and the electorate replaced the monarch as the source of ministerial patronage. Ministers' policies and actions came to require the general support of colleagues: Parliament and ministers remained in office only so long as this support was maintained. This too implied an anonymity of the ministers' officials.

While these codes (or types) of accountability have continued to be significant, ministerial accountability has more recently been affected by the rise of different codes, both administrative and professional.

(d) *Administrative* codes have bestowed a public responsibility and accountability on *officials* for their activities on behalf of ministers and their departments. Thus civil servants are increasingly obliged to account before all sorts of bodies (as in the cases of Crichel Down, Ferranti, and Vehicle & General above). Thus this administrative accountability has weakened the anonymity of officials. Further, there has been the development of a process for allocating administrative responsibilities (for example, for finance and operations) in a specific way. This process is sometimes referred to as *accountable management* and is at the heart of the Conservative government's Financial Management Initiative. Together, these two aspects of administrative accountability have made officials more publicly accountable for more precise sets of responsibilities.

(e) *Professional* codes have developed in government as its activities have become both more specialised in themselves and required the practice of professions to undertake them. The incorporation of groups of professionals such as doctors, lawyers and more recently accountants imports sets of codes developed originally outside government and without recognition of its requirements (including the judgement of electors as opposed to fellow professionals).

The effect of these two sets of codes has been to lessen the direct responsibility of ministers for detailed work in their departments, though not for its general conduct and oversight.

(3) *The arenas in which accountability is discharged*   Traditionally,
there have been only two arenas in which ministers have been obliged
to give accounts directly: Parliament and the courts. The latter
remain significant. However, as the political (and especially
governing) parties have come to dominate the membership and
conduct of Parliament so the theatrical tendency of this arena has
been intensified. Reformers have therefore sought to subject
ministers and departments to alternative arenas in which the latter
have less control. The development of the select committee system
and the use of the tribunal of enquiry provide evidence of this, as
does the rise of the institution of ombudsman. We may call these
arenas *quasi-judicial* for the way they seek to subject accounts to a
more judicial type of scrutiny. But their enhancement of more
detailed examination paradoxically allows for more detailed specifi-
cation of the responsibility of *officials* rather than of ministers.

Conclusions

Ministerial accountability involves a complex set of relationships.
There have been changes to the form and content of this accountability and to the arenas in which it is discharged. As a result, and
despite the two cases described at the beginning of this chapter, the
principle that for every policy or action of a department a minister
must answer has been replaced by a practice which limits this responsibility to personal involvement.

Reading

You will find sections on ministerial accountability in almost any
textbook on British government. They will contrast with the way the
issues are presented here. The ideas are developed in more detail in
Ch. 6 of A. G. Gray & W. I. Jenkins, *Administrative Politics in
British Government*, Wheatsheaf Books, 1985.

4 *Geoffrey Lee*

Town Hall versus Whitehall

The traditional tension between central and local government reached an unprecedented pitch of intensity under the Thatcher government. This chapter examines the idea of local democracy, the constitutional perspective, local government finance, the abolition of the metropolitan counties, and the community charge, or poll tax.

Background

Local democracy
Democratically elected local representatives have the responsibility of controlling local government. The benefits are:

(i) Participation – by the people in their own governance. As a by-product they become educated about the process.

(ii) Responsiveness to local needs by local representatives who will control the administration and frame policies accordingly.

(iii) A training ground is created for those who wish to enter national politics.

(iv) Political parties are able to test candidates, policies and their own procedures and maintain morale and effectiveness between general elections.

Advocates of local autonomy, such as the council associations, the Alliance parties and other opponents of centralising policies usually refer to the threat to the first two factors.

Critique
This ideal model is cast into doubt by:

(i) The low turn-out in local elections – often below 30%.

(ii) The incursion of party politics and the salience of national issues in local elections. In June 1986 the Widdicombe inquiry said that politics could be a 'malign influence' leading to a distribution of spoils. It recommended a larger role for the ombudsman and Audit Commission, party balance on committees, a register of councillors' interests, national party rules and no officials to be politically affiliated above principal officer.

(iii) The lack of accountability for spending decisions. Only a third of voters pay full domestic rates, which in turn contribute less than a quarter of local income – business rates and government grant make up the rest.

This last factor was used strongly by the business community and the Conservative government as the premise for further control over waste and deliberate irresponsibility.

(iv) The secrecy in decision-making. Following a court case against Hackney Council in 1984 the government supported a Freedom of Information Bill in 1985 (though critics pointed to the retention of secrecy in Whitehall).

Agents of central goverment

(i) *The constitutional relationship* Local authorities require statutory authorisation, through public, private or adoptive Acts of Parliament, provisional orders or statutory instruments, for all that they do. If they exceed their powers, they can be judged *ultra vires*, and sued in the courts. This judicial control was exercised against the GLC fares policy reviewed later.

Government, through Parliament, has the power to remove powers or even abolish a tier of government – as it did in Northern Ireland. In a unitary state it has to be accepted that national policy prevails. Local government has suffered a steady erosion of its influence, as energy provision, water, health and some education functions were transferred to *ad hoc* agencies, public corporations or central government. Indeed in 1982 it was suggested that a separate block grant would remove the control of education to central government completely. This can become a self-fulfilling prophecy – in 1983 the GLC's loss of water, ambulance service, housing planning and transport were cited as reasons for its abolition, its role having diminished so much.

(ii) *Uniformity of services* Public demand for a relatively equal level of services, and concern that one authority should not disadvantage its neighbours all foster central intervention. The 1975 Layfield Committee had prophetically explained the logic – if more government control was exerted, it would have to ensure equity and to do that more detailed intervention would follow.

(iii) *Finance* Government have varied the proportion of specific grants to services and block grants, but the overall position is clear – even after government cut-backs they were still providing 53% of council spending in 1983–84. The Layfield Committee had wanted to align responsibilities for decision-making and fund-raising – that central government should assume control directly or local authorities be allowed to raise a local income tax (LIT). But in addition to the technical problems of change it is politically convenient for both sides that responsibility and blame cannot be clearly apportioned.

Dialogue

The truth lies somewhere in between. Councils are clearly not autonomous, nor can a partnership exist when the power, including dissolution, is on one side. But neither are local authorities mere agents:

(i) There are policy differences and local initiatives are possible.

(ii) It is significant which party is in power – government circulars have been ignored, and policies delayed – on comprehensive schools, council house sales and rate levels.

(iii) Government grants allow different patterns of allocation.

(iv) Since reorganisation in 1972, attempts have been made to loosen controls over the appointment of officers and auditors and over planning authorities and entertainments (300 controls were scrapped in 1979 and legislation passed in 1981).

(v) Though the Department of the Environment is of central importance, there is no single ministry for local government. Different departments, themselves interest groups, deal with councils collectively or individually. The process of consultation and bargaining was institutionalised in 1975 when a Consultative Council was created. And through their Associations the councils can command media attention.

(vi) *Rates* This independent source of revenue brings councils over £5 billion each year. It has been heavily criticised as a regressive tax,

falling heavily on businesses and bearing no relation to services used. But it is a simple system and neither the Conservative Green Paper of 1971 nor that of 1981 could find a viable alternative. Sales tax, poll tax or local income tax were deemed to be open to evasion, resentment or to incur expense and would not improve accountability to electors. The 1974 Conservative pledge to abolish rates was therefore dropped, to the delight of Labour who adopted it as their own in 1981 in favour of LIT. In 1987, however, the Conservatives chose a community charge or poll tax as their alternative.

The balance upset?

It was contended that the Conservative government upset this balanced relationship in favour of ever-tightening control because its priorities, controlling public expenditure and unburdening industry, so dictated. The case of one interest group – the business community – was accepted, i.e. that rates increased costs, destroyed jobs and recovery. They pressed for rate-capping, compulsory consultation on rate levels and abolition of rates on empty buildings – all of which were incorporated into legislation. As privatisation was extended there were claims that councils' inability to modify or mitigate policies was turning them into residual supermarkets, no longer worthy of their name – enthusiastic privatisers such as Bradford were said by Labour to be abolishing themselves. When the government reintroduced its 'gag' powers in November 1987 restricting publication by councils of party material, it met the opposition of all the associations, including the Conservative ADC.

Process

(i) Spending crisis, 1974–76

By 1975 there were fears that local government spending was out of control; it was consuming 16% of Britain's gross domestic product, with an overspend of 5.4%. This was a function of:

(a) Reorganisation: in reducing 1,390 English and Welsh councils to 422, staffing had risen by 4.7% or 100,000 people. Larger populations helped to increase salaries and costs as did the duplication of functions.

(b) Demand: intentions to provide better services, developed in the 1960s, led to increased staffing e.g. 500,000 more in education in a decade.

(*c*) Inflation: salaries grew to be 60% of local spending with many groups being made 'special cases'.

(*d*) Government requirements: e.g. in 1973, 64 new Acts and 2,229 ministerial orders required action (*Sunday Times*, 23 February 1975).

In 1974–75 rates rose 30% on average and as high as 138%, as rate-payers' organisations complained of town-hall overstaffing and incompetence and challenged the rises in court. As Britain approached a financial crisis, Secretary of State Anthony Crosland declared that 'the party' was over.

(ii) *Stabilisation, 1976–79*

By 1976–77 there was a 1.8% underspend, and NALGO and NUPE produced a booklet, 'Breakdown – the crisis in your public services'. The 1978 Public Expenditure White Paper allowed for a modest 2% to 5.5% growth.

(iii) *Retrenchment, 1979–83*

The economic policy of the Conservative government elected in May 1979 was based on the premise that expansion would be facilitated by reducing public expenditure, of which local government claimed a quarter.

(*a*) Cut-back: in the June 1979 Budget, local authorities were told to reduce spending by £360 million in addition to an overbudgeted £450 million – a 7% cut in nine months. The reaction to this first collision was more vociferous than during later, more fundamental confrontations – the Institute of Municipal Engineers asserted that sewage could swill through the streets and NALGO promised strike action against redundancies.

(*b*) Rate Support Grant: the 1979 RSG settlement was supposed to cover 61% of spending, but was said to be a reduction to 58%.

(*c*) Hit list: the first list of 'spending councils' was produced to pressurise them.

(*d*) Legislation: the Local Government Planning and Land Act 1980 altered the whole framework of financial support by replacing the old RSG formula with a block grant calculated on Grant Related Expenditure (GRE).

(*e*) Hold-back: in 1981 local authorities were deprived of £300 million to ensure government monetarist targets were achieved and it threatened to hold back £450 million more unless cuts were made.

The Association of Metropolitan Authorities (AMA) thought compliance would cost 150,000 jobs. The government, however, had already declared the 2% cut in manpower over the previous year to be insufficient.

(f) Rate referenda: encouraged by the example of Coventry City Council's referendum in August 1981, when electors chose cuts rather than rate increases, the government moved to establish such a process nationally. Pressure from Conservative peers, back-benchers and councillors forced its abandonment, but

(g) The Local Government Finance Act 1982 banned supplementary rates and increased the grant withdrawal powers of government.

The atmosphere was one of uncertainty; there were discrepancies between disciplinary and GRE targets, pay awards increased cuts beyond planned percentages, and the Treasury based its 1982 plans on only cash figures – implying 7% cuts and 120,000 lost jobs.

Confrontation

(a) Legal: the right of government to send in agents to sell Norwich City Council's housing went to the High Court where the 'bullying' powers were criticised and both Strathclyde Regional Council and the London Borough of Hackney took ministers to court for withholding grants.

(b) Propaganda: by 1982 the AMA was conducting a £½ million advertising campaign and interest groups were using official reports detailing the damage done to services. The government responded by stretching the powers of the new 1982 Act to compel publication of spending league tables to embarrass the 'profligate'.

(iv) *The second attempt, 1983–87*

The process described above did not satisfy the government whose targets had been exceeded every year, with a total overspend in 1983–84 of £770 million. The overall expenditure figures, they conceded, concealed the massive rise in current spending given a 50% decrease in capital expenditure between 1978–79 and 1982–83. While local authorities managed a 4% reduction in their 2½ million total manpower from June 1979 to March 1983, this trend had reversed. Noting that three-quarters of the overspending was incurred by sixteen authorities, the 1983 Conservative manifesto promised to legislate to control them and introduce a general scheme.

The Scottish example

The Scottish Office, since 1929, has had the power to penalise authorities for levying excessive rates. In 1981 this was changed from a retrospective to an immediate response and in 1982 rate-capping was introduced. The main target became the rebellious Lothian Regional Council which had to reduce its rate from 116p to 100p and then to 86p in the pound. These powers and their successes acted as an example and a spur and countered objections that they were incompatible with local government in Britain. This process was continued with the decision to implement the poll tax first in Scotland in 1988 – amid accusations that Scotland was being used as a laboratory.

Rate limitation

Following its White Paper in August, the government published its Rates Bill in December 1983. It contained two main elements:

(a) A selective power to single out 'extravagant' authorities and control their spending and rate levels.

(b) A reserve general power to control the spending of all councils. The government was at pains to point out that this would only be used with the approval of Parliament.

Excluded from the selective scheme are district councils spending less than £10 million or below the GRE assessment. The government claimed only twelve to twenty councils would be caught.

Opposition

(a) *Conservatives*   Some twenty to thirty MPs, backed by Francis Pym, attacked the rate-capping proposals and particularly the general reserve powers as 'dangerous and unconstitutional' (*Sunday Times*, 18 December 1983). The Conservative-controlled Association of District Councils had declared its opposition in June 1983, and doubts were expressed in the House of Lords. But while this coalition had stymied referenda in 1981 and was to embarrass the government again in 1984, on this occasion the manifesto commitment was fulfilled. Conservative shire councils, such as Buckinghamshire and Essex, made no attempt to disguise their anger in July 1984 when cuts were made in their grants for 'overspending'. In 1985 the government eased the system of penalties to remove the pressure from 'low-spending' shires, but encountered fury in 1986 for moving £224 million to the inner cities. Nicholas Ridley's claims that he had won a

£3.8 billion increase from the Treasury did not pacify Tory back-benchers facing Alliance pressure in counties such as Surrey and Hertfordshire which could lose 59% and 37% of their grants. Advice to privatise or ignore national agreements to cut wages were not well received. In 1987 councils were still overspending by 3% despite more generous grants, and the government move to stop 'recycling' or redistributing grants from high spenders to other councils led to more accusations of 'muddle, misanthropy, incompetence, and illegality and sometimes plain malevolence' (John Fraser, Labour spokesman, House of Commons, 5 February 1987). A £1.1 billion increase was made at the end of 1988 to keep spending steady as the government sought escape from the tangle via the poll tax.

(b) *Labour 'hit list' councils*   Of the eighteen councils singled out for rate-capping in 1983 only Brent and Portsmouth were Conservative. They were chosen for spending 4% above their 1983–84 target and 20% above GRE assessments. Most were told to make a cut the size of inflation.

In July 1984 the sixteen Labour councils agreed on non-compliance, in refusing to cut jobs or services and boycotting the new derogation procedure of renegotiating their spending limits. Labour's local government conference discussed options which included:

(i) Mass resignations.

(ii) Illegally refusing to make a rate, to create a crisis for councils and government, by losing interest payments and having to borrow more to pay workers.

(iii) Deficit budgeting – making a legal rate and illegally failing to reduce expenditure accordingly.

Councillors pointed to their own mandates, and statutory obligations to provide services. This resistance was endorsed by the Labour NEC and TUC Conference. In September 1984 the AMA set up a £175,000 fighting fund.

Labour councils employed *(ii)* and some moved to *(iii)* during 1985, but eventually withdrew their opposition until only Liverpool was left. Despite Mr Jenkin's embarassment in trying to avoid explaining how his figures were calculated, there was never any question of the government conceding. At the same time, no major cuts were made as the limits were set reasonably high initially, and public support was not forthcoming as anticipated, with three out of five electors opposed to rate-capping (Mori poll, *Sunday Times*, 7 May 1985).

By 1986 the Comptroller and Auditor-General had condemned capital spending controls while he and the Audit Commission had damned the Rate Support Grant system and its effects on the rates and spending. Mr Jenkin had by now resigned, unhappy at being a scapegoat for unpopular legislation. In fact, rate-capped authorities accounted for only 8% of the total overspend.

In July 1986 the government added another £1 billion, bringing local authority current account spending to £25.2 billion, while at the same time stopping deferred payment of capital funding, rate-capping another nine authorities and stopping the aid given to compensate for metropolitan county abolition. By setting realistic targets in line with inflation it was seeking the appearance of 'control', no rate rises to damage Conservative electoral prospects, and to show that any blame for overspending was appointed to (mainly Labour) councils. In 1987 seventeen councils were capped, with Ealing having to cut its spending by £20 million and its rates by over 40%. In the following year London councils were to cut 5,500 jobs because of rate-capping.

(c) *Liverpool* Labour took control of Liverpool City Council in 1983. It was left with no rate as 'hard' left councillors tried to pass 'no cuts' budgets and confront the government. As Labour made gains in the 1984 elections, the government prepared to take over the council functions with commissioners and surcharge councillors. Instead a package was agreed in July 1984 which involved a 17% rate rise. Labour leaders there claimed a victory and £8 million new money from central government, an assessment with which *The Times*, in its editorial 'Danegeld in Liverpool', disgustedly agreed (11 July 1984). As a result, when the council refused to set a rate in 1985 and then did so at a level that ensured the money would run out, the government did not intervene. The council had to withdraw redundancy notices and the six-month confrontation ended in November as the 31,000 work-force would not support a closure of all but emergency services. By this time Labour councils were reluctant to help after the Liverpool leaders rejected the Stonefrost Report recommendations and Neil Kinnock condemned the 'Tendency tacticians'. By 1986 forty-seven councillors had been surcharged, Militant leaders expelled from the Labour Party and the city, according to the district auditors, was in financial chaos with large financial commitments, poor budgetary control, high costs and overmanning. In March 1987 the forty-seven lost their final legal battle and their seats and faced bankruptcy with a debt of £590,000.

Capital spending and debt

To further undermine goodwill, the government announced restrictions on capital spending in July 1984, less than two years after criticising councils for underspending. While avoiding the complete moratorium of 1980, cuts of up to £1 billion were involved. Doubts were raised about the legality of preventing reinvestment of 80% of funds from the sale of council houses and the short-term stop-go treatment of a long-term issue.

In 1981–82 and 1982–83 councils underspent by 17% and 14%, but in the following three years they overspent by 15%, 30% and 36% respectively. The Audit Commission severely criticised the DOE's long-winded vetting of capital projects (March 1985).

The Labour leadership were warned in 1986 that councils were using deferred purchase agreements – leasing property to banks – to support revenue expenditure and were heading for a £2 billion crisis. In 1987 the *Sunday Times* revealed that this was nearer to £5 billion and the government took powers to close the loophole the following year. Again, Tory councils forced changes to avoid hundreds of shopping, leisure and industrial schemes being stopped.

In 1988 a new system was announced – making councils use their council-house receipts to redeem their debts, being free to spend the rest and finance capital spending from revenue. Beginning in 1990 the system would seek to control borrowing rather than spending, removing creative accounting.

Statistics in doubt

From the outset a war of figures began as local government leaders in 1979 claimed to have been deliberately misled by the government's omission of specific grants from totals. Grants for pay rises were said to be too low and councils on 'hit lists' claimed they were there on bogus figures, having earlier been called underspenders. Targets for 1981 were chosen on national averages related to spending in 1978–79, so arbitrarily some councils faced 20% cuts.

Local government came to believe that the Treasury in particular could not be trusted: in 1981 they were said to be planning a surreptitious cut of £1,500 million by technical changes, and their July 1982 figures were so unrealistic that the cuts were quickly reduced from 7% to 2% (redundancy payments had been forgotten). The GREA target system, based on its fifty-six items of spending needs, was queried in December 1983 when the DOE was forced to release its figures.

One reason for the discrepancies on cuts and grants is that they were based on councils' reporting of spending, and some had disguised the true level by the 'creative accounting' reviewed above.

Most serious was the report of the government-appointed Audit Commission in August 1984 which complained of the complexities and uncertainties of the grant system which had caused ratepayers to be charged £1.5 billion more than necessary over three years. To the government's embarrassment, it had to introduce legislation in 1986/87 to rectify the admission that the grant system used since 1981 to distribute £70 billion was unlawful. In 1987 amendments had to be made as councils such as Greenwich won court victories against the DOE and as they issued the wrong figures.

The metropolitan dimension

Discrimination
The retrenchment described above was not uniform in its application, but was more severe upon the metropolitan authorities. County councils were granted concessions to win their support and help the 1980 Bill through the House of Lords. The switching of grants worth £1,445 million from district to county councils was said to increase the latters' share from 32% to 53%.

To add insult to what urban Labour councils described as the injury of grant 'gerrymandering', the government proposed to cover only 60% of the costs of the 1981 inner-city riots, leaving them to find another £18 million.

Abolition

Background Prior to May 1981 the Labour Party controlled the metropolitan county councils of Tyne and Wear and South Yorkshire. In the elections that month they won West Yorkshire, Greater Manchester, Merseyside, West Midlands and, by a narrow majority, the Greater London Council. Only the Liberal Party consistently demanded abolition of this tier of government during the campaigns. The Conservatives, as their creators and as incumbents, were more disposed to defend their achievements. The Labour Party showed signs of ambivalence; while they saw and wanted the opportunity to take control, many district councillors resented county level interference. On the other hand, at the time of reorganisation in 1970–72 Labour had favoured stronger metropolitan authorities with responsibility for education and social services, and some still advocated incremental or radical restructuring of local government.

After 1981 these councils, and in particular the GLC, emerged as strident opponents of government policy. Two months after taking office Mr Ken Livingstone called for a campaign of disruption in Parliament and a general strike to stop legislation designed to curb councils' spending. Pronouncements followed on Northern Ireland, nuclear weapons and unemployment – large banners on County Hall reminded Parliament across the river of the number of London unemployed. As Mr Livingstone turned into a major public figure the Conservatives raged against the GLC's grant policy which saw donations to 'Babies Against the Bomb', 'The Southall Black Sisters' and 'The Irish Women's Group' (e.g. *Daily Mail*, 16 February 1983).

The first confrontation over the GLC policy came in November 1981 when the Appeal Court ruled that reducing public transport fares by 25% was illegal. In upholding the appeal of the Conservative-controlled Borough of Bromley, the Court decided that the Transport (London) Act, 1969 required services to 'break even' and that the GLC had acted in an arbitrary and unreasonable manner. A High Court ruling in February 1982 that this did not apply to metropolitan councils, who could subsidise fares from the rates, was to little avail as government grant penalties forced the abandonment of these manifesto promises.

In January 1983 it was revealed that a Cabinet Committee, MISC 79, had recommended the abolition of the GLC and metropolitan county councils. The Conservative manifesto of 1983 described them as 'a wasteful and unnecessary tier of government' and briefly stated that their functions would either be given to districts and boroughs or administered over a wider area by boards of representatives.

The case for The government's case, in a nutshell was that the councils did too little and cost too much. It was set out in detail in the White Paper, 'Streamlining the Cities', of October 1983.

   (a) Lack of responsibilities: their three main functions were fire

services, police and public transport. In the case of public transport day-to-day management was vested with separate executives, and London Transport was scheduled to obtain autonomy in 1983/84. Residual oversight was also the case with police matters in metropolitan counties and in London responsibility was direct to the Home Secretary. Conflicts between the Chief Constables of Greater Manchester and Merseyside and their police committees in the aftermath of the 1981 riots led to conflicting claims of political interference and public accountability. The attempt of the GLC to establish its own police committee similarly fuelled the controversy about the role of the councils.

(b) Overlapping functions: the failure of the counties to find a strategic role or develop a working relationship with districts in areas such as planning is deemed to have led to confusion, duplicating of work and waste.

(c) Overspending: by straying into peripheral or politically mischievous areas, government control of spending has been cast into doubt. The example is cited of the GLC whose current expenditure rose by 185% between 1978–79 to 1983–84 and a 111% rise by the metropolitan counties (against an average of 80%). Between 1981–82 and 1983–84 the GLC's precept rose 118% and the metropolitan counties 29% while the rest managed 20% against 14% inflation *(Politics Today*, p. 30). Not surprisingly, these councils appeared regularly in the DOE's 'hit lists'.

(d) Savings: the government refused to specify the size of expected savings, as this would depend on the management abilities of successor bodies. Eight Conservative-controlled councils in Greater Manchester, Merseyside and the West Midlands reported in May 1984 that Price Waterhouse believed £20 million would be saved by rationalisation alone. By early 1986 the NALGO union was predicting 5,000 redundancies, over 1,000 being in Merseyside.

The case against
(a) Cost: in February 1984 the six metropolitan counties paid £40,000 to another group of consultants, Coopers and Lybrand, who reported that no savings would accrue from abolition, though by 1985 they were estimating that abolition of the GLC would cost £150 million, but save £30 million a year in operating costs (half what the government had hoped).

In response to the White Paper the GLC produced its report, 'The future of the Greater London Council', which began by criticising the absence of testable financial and expenditure analysis, and pointing out the new costs that would result from more managements, and the impact on the Inner London Education Authority and joint services. In addition, 40% of the GLC budget was for debt charges – some £300 million.

The transfer to boroughs and districts of twenty-one responsibilities could result in increased staffing there, and the creation of what Labour believed would be at least fifty new bodies would cause a massive increase in bureaucracy: new premises, staff and expense. Council finance chiefs concurred with this analysis in October 1983. Most embarrassingly for the government, the GLC Conservatives presented proposals in January 1984 for a restructuring costing £200 million less than abolition.

By 1986 the costs argument had been relegated. It was clear, for example, that only 1% of the GLC staff of 23,000 and work-force of 180,000 had not found another post and would be made redundant, and that the successor joint boards would be the largest local authority overspenders (at 15% over, they were five times worse than Labour controlled London boroughs).

(b) Complexity: while the White Paper saw abolition as streamlining, enabling the public to understand the system, critics described the web of 39 joint boards and 48 committees as a confusing mess. The Labour Environment spokesman condemned the conversion of a 2-tier system into a 27-tier system in London and 22-tier system in the provinces. The GLC's functions split 58 ways to 7 quangos, 15 joint boards, one joint committee, one housing trust, one directly elected education authority, 32 borough councils and the City of London.

(c) Weakening accountability: the joint boards and committees were to be made up of indirectly elected members, drawn from district and borough councils. This was condemened as a weakening of local democracy and Mr Jenkin's own criticism of the ILEA in 1977 as a 'constitutional monstrosity' free to be extravagant and irresponsible was recalled. More than 70% of the GLC's responsibilities went to non-elected or indirectly nominated quangos. Many Conservatives who favoured abolition of the metropolitan councils doubted the wisdom of leaving the capital, alone among great cities, without directly elected representatives.

(d) Quality of services: concern was expressed that devolved

services, such as tourism, support for the arts, green belt land, housing, historic buildings, planning and traffic management, etc., would not fare so well in the hands of all districts and boroughs. And it was warned that far from assisting industrial development, authorities would compete and duplicate efforts. The Bishop of Rochester voiced concern for voluntary work and the fate of London's homeless. The West Midlands lost its consumer protection service, said to be the best in Britain. In London, £200 million was transferred from the shires to soften the rates blow, but elsewhere ratepayers suffered rises up to 37.4% (Calderdale) while the bus-users of South Yorkshire saw a cut in services and a 230% increase in fares.

(e) Public opinion: opinion polls consistently showed the public supporting retention of the councils. A Harris Research Centre Poll in April 1985 showed 74% opposed to abolition with 80% wanting an elected body for London. Polls in the metropolitan counties showed similar opposition, and by July 1984 they were showing 66% against and 18% in favour (*Guardian*, 23 July 1984). Reflecting this, two-thirds of MPs and a majority of Conservative MPs thought abolition a vote-loser (MORI poll, *Guardian*, 29 August 1984).

The process of abolition

(a) *Opposition pressure* The campaign against abolition began immediately, with the GLC co-ordinating a formidable publicity campaign which by July 1984 had cost £10.6 million, despite Conservative protests. In addition to its campaign unit, the councils employed a professional lobbying company.

The local government union NALGO instructed members not to co-operate with the government in 1983 and the Labour party pledged restoration of the GLC in September 1984.

(b) *Timetable* A major difficulty for the government were the scheduled elections of May 1985. Councillors nominated from the district and borough councils took over the running of the abolished authorities in 1985. The government, accused of engineering a change of political control without elections, was determined that the local elections, which would turn into a referendum, would not take place, and preferred this substitution to the threat of deferral and the threat of disruption.

The Paving Bill

To facilitate substitution, a Local Government (Interim Provisions) Bill was brought forward in March 1984 to pave the way for abolition (it thus became known as the Paving Bill). It sought to control events by giving powers to stop abortive work and obstruction.

Problems came in the House of Lord, which not only disliked the measure but its arrival before the Abolition Bill itself. The combination of a Bill that seemed unconstitutional, was not covered by the manifesto and tested the *raison d'être* of the Lords was irresistible. The government mustered their in-built Conservative majority on a three-line whip for its second reading but the Lords defeated the Bill by a majority of forty-eight on an amendment, despite Mr Jenkin's offers to accept changes and his leaks of it being a resigning issue. It was hailed as the most serious defeat for the government in five years. In fact, the goverment quickly switched to deferral of elections and added more restrictions.

Conservative back-benchers continued to oppose parts of the abolition Bill on the grounds that too much power was being transferred up to central government.

The House of Lords continued to cause problems, only failing by four votes to substitute an elected authority (May 1985) and imposing four defeats – making the government agree to a representative body for planning. The government tried to counter the counties' successful public relations with glossy pamphlets, but the campaign went on – pointing to the inadequacy of the parliamentary process, when only sixteen of the ninety-eight clauses were debated by MPs.

The GLC had one last populist triumph in banning lorries from the roads at nights and weekends and won its case in the High Court. It was less successful in the courts, however, in its attempt at a death-bed spending spree – a £40 million grant to the ILEA and £77 million to umbrella organisations to pass on to voluntary groups were stopped, but £5.8 million left to forty organisations on its last working day was released after a legal challenge.

Power politics

Beneath the constitutional and administrative debates ran the theme that a political vendetta was being waged. Ken Livingstone was convinced that Mrs Thatcher was attacking the GLC because 'she is appalled that we are an example of a Labour administration which gets elected and continues to fight for its policies' (*Guardian*, 15

January 1983). The *Daily Telegraph* was equally convinced that abolition would see the end of 'many sinecures used as power bases from which to wage political warfare and subversion not only against this Government but against the British polity' (8 October 1983). It is in the heat of this political debate that the models and conventions described at the outset have to be tested. Nor did the process or argument cease: the ILEA was abolished by Cabinet decision in 1988 and while the government claimed savings of £431 million from the GLC and met county abolition, other experts believed the cost of running London to have risen by £180 million, that unfilled vacancies were hidden costs, and that many services and groups had suffered or disappeared where Labour councils had not co-operated in the transition – e.g. in Merseyside.

Opposition

In April 1986 the NEC and MPs had drawn up a policy of re-creating the GLC, leaving abolished the metropolitan counties (always resented by Labour districts) and moving towards a single tier of local governments. This would entail the organic change favoured by Labour in 1977 whereby the nine large city districts such as Bristol, Leicester and Southampton would regain wider powers, many shire districts would disappear, and a directly-elected regional tier would be created. The latter would control services such as water, transport, police and economic planning – a policy long favoured by the Liberal party and the Alliance. Labour would also increase grants to enable councils to play a major part in combating unemployment, and approached the general election of 1987 proposing a new regional tier of government, annual elections and a quality commission.

The government, however, saw a clear area of weakness for Labour – using the Audit Commission's report on mismanagement, party chairman Norman Tebbit circulated a list of excesses by fourteen councils – concern for gay and lesbian organisations, resignation of officials, staff increases and tributes to the Mandelas. Rhodes Boyson spoke of 'bullying . . . socialist Soviets . . . people live in fear of an Orwellian or McCarthyite challenge to their integrity' (*Guardian*, 13 December 1986). While Labour remained committed to assisting with the councils' debts, it stepped back from a major job-creation role and issued reassurances that there would be no blank cheques. That the 'loony' councils label was a problem for Labour was reinforced in September 1988 when the leadership moved to ensure councils adhered to the manifesto and did not advocate illegal action, that trade unionists be banned from strategy meetings and that councillors should declare any self-interest as employees.

Privatisation

The government pressed for increased privatisation of services, citing examples such as Wandsworth. In 1986 they were answering Tory critics on cuts by its advocacy and preparing compulsory competition for all refuse collection, street cleaning, building cleaning, catering and ground and vehicle maintenance – worth £2.5 billion per annum. These followed previous measures on direct labour, buses and services in the NHS. In 1988 tendering was also introduced for sports and leisure facilities, though protests led to pricing and opening hours being left to councils. At the same time direct labour tendering was extended to services with five employees or more.

Metropolitan councils in particular criticised the outcomes – lower wages, poorer hygiene and nutrition. Controversy surrounded the zealous Westminster city council, which by the end of 1988 had ten enquiries running into its sale of graveyards, Tory headquarters (in a secret sale) and the privatisation of leisure centres.

From rates to poll tax

(i)   *Background*   Under attack for its control of local spending the government announced a review of finance in October 1984 and began to discuss the Whitehall collection of the £6.9 billion business rates.

This was accentuated in 1985 when revaluation in Scotland produced rises of up to 50% and an outcry from small businesses. A £40 million aid bill was speedily passed and the government resolved to promise reform in England and Wales. In January 1986 the Green Paper, 'Paying for Local Government', proposed to replace the domestic rates over ten years by a community charge (a 'poll tax' sounded like a penalty for voting). Business rates would be collected centrally and distributed with grants. Councils would keep only a light rate on industry, though the system of a need equalisation grant would transfer £70 million from the shires of the south to London and the North. Nevertheless 75% of a local spending would be disbursed centrally, as opposed to 44%, and the system was likely to produce large fluctuations in rates. This sweeping change, including the new rating valuation for four million businesses, was postponed until after the 1987 general election.

(ii) *Arguments for the poll tax*
  (a) *Lack of accountability* Only eighteen million out of the thirty-five million electors actually pay rates. The poll tax, being levied on every adult in the country would increase significantly the number of people contributing to local services. In Liverpool, where the average rates bill was £500, the intended poll tax would be £301: two adults in the same house would pay nearly twice as much.

  (b) *Political responsibility* The government believed the change would counter extremism. Labour would not be tempted to offer 'ill-concealed bribes' in the form of higher spending and subsidies to the three out of four people who vote in local elections to 'spend other people's money' (Nicholas Ridley, *Independent*, 4 August 1987). Rather, voters would have an incentive both to turn out and to vote for curbs on high-spending councils.

  (c) *Fairness* The tax would remedy some of the inequities of the rating system – the oft-cited example being the old lady paying the same as the family next door with four wage-earners. Exemptions under the poll tax for the very poor, handicapped and those in care would be offered under the poll tax. Under the old system, rate poundages would vary between 98.9p in the pound in Kensington and Chelsea and 330p in Greater Manchester.

  (d) *Help for business* A single business rate was designed to deal with councils that drove away or even bankrupted businesses by high rates. Complaints from disenfranchised businesses in city centres had long been a feature of local elections there.

(iii) *Arguments against the poll tax*
  (a) *Local accountability* It was contended that the real motive for the change was to control local spending and that previous attempts had failed. The introduction was not linked to structural reform and the financial system would remain heavily dependent on central grants – the business rate, standard and needs grants. There would be no extension of local discretion but continuing frustration of responsibility. This was confirmed for opponents in April 1988 when

the government included 'capping' in the community charge legislation.

(b) *Unfairness*   The poll tax does not take into account a person's
ability to pay and is, like the rates, a regressive tax – it bears most
heavily on those least able to pay it. A study in Cleveland in 1987
concluded that the worst hit would be those in properties with low
rateable values and families on low incomes. In that those in an
extended family system such as Asians were further penalised, it was
dubbed racist. Those on low incomes were to be given a rebate of up
to 80% and people on social security would have benefits increased to
pay their 20% – but that was against a national average of the charge
and those in high rate areas would lose. Benefits would be deducted
from defaulters. Uncomfortable calculations were made – the 'Dul-
wich factor', that the Thatchers would be £2,000 better off, and that
the 'backwoodsmen' Lords who voted for the charge would be paying
less than a tenth of their rates.

(c) *Cost*   The cost of compiling and maintaining registers for the
charge soon became apparent. A government-commissioned report
in June 1988 confirmed earlier pessimistic estimates that the charge
would cost twice as much as the rates to collect – £435 million
compared to £200 million (plus a total of £357 million for start-up on
new computers and extra staff).

(d) *Policing*   Unlike the rates – a tax on property – the advent of the
community charge gave rise to fears of evasion by non-registration.
The government was prepared to concede that evasion could run at
10%, rather than the 1% on rates, with particular problems among
young people in large cities. Early debates included the potential
inclusion of vagrants, submariners when serving under water, and
separated couples. This latter gave rise to fears of invasion of privacy
and new powers of enforcement being given to councils without
recourse to court – the system could only work efficiently by asking
personal questions, computerising identification and having the right
to imprison those who refused to pay. The chief finance officer of
Wakefield council described his new role as a 'bounty-hunter'.
Strathclyde began to levy the first £50 fines against 5,000 people in
September 1988.

(e) *Political problems* The Conservatives ran into problems of both ideology and implementation. On ideological grounds they found that the CBI preferred market forces which enabled them to move from high-spending areas or induce grants from local authorities – if change was intended they wanted radical derating, privatisation, and the removal of education from councils. It was pointed out, too, that in encouraging the young to leave home and constituting a 'granny tax' the measure was against family values.

In terms of implementation the Conservative back-benchers were dubious about rendering 8.3 million people worse off in 1990, before the next election. It was also feared that voters would support local Labour opposition as a protest despite high spending. And in Scotland, where the charge was offered as a vote-winner after the protest over revaluation, the Conservatives lost eleven of their twenty-one Scottish seats in the 1987 general election. Far from re-establishing the unionist base there the poll tax was seized upon by a resurgent SNP to attack London rule.

(f) *Public opinion* Confidential Central Office research showed the Conservatives before the 1987 general election that the poll tax worried more people than unemployment. Opinion then hardened steadily against the tax – in February 1986 45% were in favour and 39% against, but by March 1988 60% were against and only 22% in favour (in Scotland, 68% to 18%). And only a narrow majority of Conservatives were in support – 41% to 35% (MORI, *Sunday Times*, 27 March 1988). Ministers were forced to consider a £1 million TV campaign, newspaper advertising and leaflet drops to counter this. The government could respond that much of this was due to ignorance or political misinformation, and despite the campaigns and dire warnings 99% of Scots registered by November 1988.

(iv) *Implementation*
The government guillotined debate to bring in the poll tax in Scotland in May 1987. Two months later they began the process for England with a reported lack of enthusiasm, reminding back-benchers of the manifesto commitment and absence of an alternative. A wary Tory conference pressed for a 'one-go' implementation – a record number of thirty critical resolutions had been submitted – but this was blocked by the Treasury and in cabinet committee as too disruptive.

Tory rebels concentrated their opposition around a proposal for a graduated charge, related to the ability to pay – originally devised by the Chartered Institute of Public Finance and Accountancy and the London School of Economics. In December 1987 seventeen voted against the government and fifteen abstained and in April 1988 they had reduced the government majority to twenty-five. The front bench argued against the rival scheme as impractical, and fostering the poverty trap and unequal charges. But government attempts to defuse opposition by adding £130 million to take another million people into the rebate scheme were thwarted by a leaked document indicating this would be added to everyone else's payments.

The government attempted to block opposition in the House of Lords by defining the measure as a finance bill and outside their constitutional remit. This failed and they had to mobilise sixty to seventy peers who had not previously appeared, in a vote of 500 peers in May 1988 – the second highest this century. Further opposition was softened by concessions on the disabled, student nurses and community service volunteers, and by cushioning the effect on business by phasing in and setting maximum limits.

The most important opposition came from within the Conservative fold. The Labour Party encouraged Tory rebels and adopted a policy of advocating lawful frustration in Scotland by appeals and complaints. But they were wrong-footed by the SNP campaign of refusal to pay and the support of fifty Labour MPs (including Robin Cook) and the Scottish TGWU for a tougher line. The SNP exploited this in winning the Govan by-election and the Conservatives accused Labour of having no policy. In September 1988 Labour moved towards a policy of a property tax based on actual value, supplemented by a local income tax for 10–20% of the total bill and rebates for the poor and for small businesses. The government could ruefully reflect that they had not faced the same kind of opposition as Richard II in the 1377 and 1380 attempts to introduce a poll tax – major non-registration and a peasants' revolt.

Reading

S. Bristow *et al.* (eds.), *The Redundant Counties?*, Hesketh, 1984.

Conservative Research Department, *Politics Today*, 13 February 1984.

J. Dearlove, *The Reorganisation of the British Local Government*, CUP, 1979.

GLC, *The Future of the Greater London Council*, 1984.

5 *Bill Jones*

Reforming the electoral system

The results of recent elections have strengthened calls for reform of the British electoral system. This chapter considers the arguments for and against such reform together with the two most likely alternatives: the single transferable vote system and the additional member system.

Introduction

When Prime Minister, the Duke of Wellington declared that the British Constitution required no further improvement: it was already perfect. Shortly afterwards in 1832 came the Great Reform Act and the subsequent transformation of the voting system from one involving a quarter of a million votes to the present day when forty million men and women aged over eighteen elect 650 Members of Parliament from single member constituencies on the basis of a simple majority vote. In the wake of recent elections not only Mrs Thatcher but her vanquished opponents dismissed the idea of further electoral reform, but will history make their attitudes seem as short-sighted as Wellington's and if so, how long will it be before another Great Reform Act is passed? The fact is that a growing consensus is emerging across the political spectrum in favour of electoral reform. In the nineteenth century, the first-past-the-post (FPTP) system was relatively advanced compared with the sundry authoritarian regimes in Europe, but many of those countries which went on to adopt the British system have since rejected it for proportional representation. Why should this be and what are the arguments against our present system?

The case against first past the post

The core idea behind representative government is that it enables all sections of society to have a say in the formation and conduct of government. This fulfils a basic right which all are held to have and, we have good reason to believe, makes it more likely that government will be carried out in the interests of, and with the general consent of, the governed. Critics maintain that because our present system is insufficiently representative if offends against basic human rights and delivers the wrong kind of government:

(1) *FPTP discriminates against smaller parties*

A party with thin national support might poll a substantial number of votes but win very few seats. Thus in 1983, despite the fact that 26% of votes cast went to the SDP–Liberal Alliance and that their candidates came second in 313 contests, they won only twenty-three contests outright: 3.5% of the seats in the House of Commons. Over a quarter of the voting population, therefore, received minimal representation. Under FPTP such parties struggle to win seats until they pass the threshold of about one-third of the poll after which they begin to win seats in great numbers. Small parties face a virtually insuperable catch-22: they have to become big in order to stop being small!

(2) *FPTP favours the two big parties disproportionately*

This criticism is the corollary of the last. In 1979 Conservatives won 44% of the votes yet 53.4% of the seats: Labour 36.9% of the vote yet 42.4% of the seats. In 1983 the entry of the SDP helped split the non-Tory vote and the Conservatives were able to win 61% of the seats on 42.5% of the vote. Mrs Thatcher therefore gained some 100 seats compared with 1979 from a *reduced* vote.

(3) *FPTP elects on minority votes*

In 1979, 203 candidates were elected on less than 50% of the votes cast in their constituencies; in 1983 the figure rose to 334. Again in 1987 over half of MPs were elected in contests where the majority of voters did not support them. At the national level, as already shown, the same applies. In October 1974 Labour formed a government on

39.3% of votes cast. The *Hansard Commission on Electoral Reform* (1976) commented (p. 22), 'if fewer than 40% of voters (29% of electors) can impose their will on the other 60% or more, distortions are no longer a question of "fairness" but of elementary rights of citizens'.

(4) *FPTP favours parties with concentrated regional support*

It follows under FPTP that even small parties with highly-localised support, e.g. nationalist parties, will do relatively well – as they did in 1974. But Labour has its support concentrated in the north where it duly wins the vast majority of its seats, and the Conservatives in the south where they do likewise. In 1987, excluding London, Labour won no seats south of a line joining the Bristol South, Oxford East and Norwich South constituencies. In Scotland, on the other hand, Labour won fifty seats to the Conservatives' ten. Moreover, can it be good that few Labour MPs represent rural constituencies or towns and cities with expanding new industries, whilst few Conservative MPs have first-hand experience, in their constituency surgeries, of decaying inner cities and the problems of obsolescent traditional industries? All this could change, say the reformers, if the system were changed.

(5) *FPTP creates artificially large majorities*

Over 70% of constituencies are 'safe' Labour or Conservative seats: their majorities are so large that defeat is unlikely. The reason for this is that the majority of Labour supporters are working-class and are concentrated in the traditional industrial areas of south Wales, the north of England and central Scotland. In these areas the election of Labour candidates is virtually automatic. The Conservative party gained over a third of working-class votes in 1987 but its main strength still lies in the middle classes, especially in the south. Elections are decided therefore by about 25% of constituencies, mostly with mixed social composition, which are 'marginal': where majorities are such that the contest will be decided by small shifts in the voting either way. Psephologists calculate that a swing of 1% from one of the large parties to the other will usually result, these days, in about ten marginal seats changing hands. A swing of only a few percentage points in voter preferences therefore can make the difference between defeat and victory, a small or a very large majority. Critics argue that such majorities, created by the vagaries of the voting system and the geography of class, are not true reflections of public opinion and provide a false mandate for the winning party's programme. When combined with a strong showing by a third party the results can be a gross distortion as in 1983 and, to a slightly lesser extent, in 1987.

(6) *FPTP produces 'wasted' votes*

Those votes which do not contribute directly to the election of a candidate are said by some to be 'wasted' because they are not reflected in the House of Commons. Where the seat is safe these might comprise a substantial minority but, as we have seen, they might easily comprise the majority of voters in a constituency. It is also argued that the huge majorities piled up for some candidates are wasted votes which might be better used to reflect different and important shades of opinion. Small wonder, say reformers, that over 20% of the electorate regularly fail to vote. By contrast, voters in marginal seats exercise a disproportionate influence over the outcome of elections: their votes can be infinitely 'more equal' than those in other constituencies.

(7) *FPTP perpetuates the two-party system*

Because only the governing and opposition parties appear to have viable chances of gaining majorities in general elections, voters tend to withhold their support for small parties which more accurately reflect their beliefs, and cast their vote for the party they dislike least. For reformers this produces a number of evils. Firstly, voter choice is limited to two rival philosophies which can be bitterly and irreconcilably antithetical especially when radical voices win party arguments. Secondly, it encourages the maintenance of unwieldly political coalitions like the Labour party, which endeavours for electoral benefit to pretend it is united. Thirdly – and perhaps most importantly – it sustains adversary politics whereby real issues are lost in the unseemly ritual rhetoric of the party debate, and winning parties immediately set about undoing the work of their predecessors. The end result is that millions of voters occupying the centre ground go unrepresented, the political process falls into disrepute and the uncertainty surrounding our political future deters proper economic planning and investment for both the private and public sectors.

(8) *FPTP discriminates against women and ethnic minorities*

Women comprise over 50% of the population but only 6.3% of MPs. Coloured ethnic minorities gained representation for the first time in 1987 for fifty-eight years but nevertheless numbered only four. The simple reason for this is that candidates are chosen by local party selection committees who 'tend to choose a "safe" candidate who will be as near to an identikit model of an MP as it is possible to find. The candidate will be white, middle-aged and male' (Bogdanor, p. 113).

(9) *FPTP leads to undemocratic government*

Exploiting the lack of constraint which Britain's unwritten constitution allows, it is argued that FPTP enables a modern political party, elected on a minority vote, to impose measures for which there is no popular approval. According to Professor Ridley, 'Britain seems to have the most powerful and least representative system of government in Western Europe' (*Guardian*, 11 January 1989).

Reformers believe therefore that FPTP is inadequate when two parties dominate, farcical when a third party challenges strongly and inferior to certain of the proportional representation systems used by other countries. Unsurprisingly, defenders of the present system will have none of this.

The case for the first-past-the-post system

Understandably, proponents of FPTP are found within the ranks of those parties which benefit from it: Labour and Conservative. As they are defending the status quo – always the high ground in British politics – they do not need to elaborate their views with the enthusiasm and detail of their opponents but they do, in any case, have a substantial case to put forward. They maintain:

(1) It is not the chief aim of government to be *representative* but to be *effective*. By creating administrations with healthy majorities, FPTP, with occasional exceptions, has provided strong, stable governments which have been able to fulfil most of their election promises.

(2) The close personal relationship between MP and constituent is a valuable (and much admired) aspect of the present system.

(3) By-elections enable sections of the public to register their views on the progress of a government between elections.

(4) Adversary politics is as much a reflection of a new volatile mood amongst the electorate as it is of the FPTP system.

(5) Parties *do* have a chance to win seats once they pass a certain threshold; if smaller parties were to keep working instead of pursuing a sour-grapes reformist campaign they might be able one day to enjoy the system's benefits.

(6) In 1979 the Liberals asked the European Court of Human Rights in Strasbourg to judge whether FPTP was a violation of their democratic rights – the Court ruled that such rights had not been violated.

(7) FPTP is well known and understood and has been in existence for some time. The disruption which a shift to another system would cause could scarcely be justified in terms of the movement for change, which is not widespread and intense but is confined to those parties with a vested interest in change, sundry pressure groups and individuals. As Angus Maude and John Szemerey point out in *Why Electoral Change?*: 'It is not enough to assert that it (electoral change) *might* be better, or even that it *must* be better than what we have. It is necessary to show pretty conclusively that it *would* be better and could *not* in any circumstances make things worse.'

(8) It is a mistake to think, as is often argued, that economic success is closely related to voting systems. It is the skill, energy and character of its people which make a country prosperous, not the way it elects its legislature.

(9) FPTP may have disadvantages but they are not as grievous as those of its alternatives.

Proposals for electoral reform in Britain

What are the alternatives on offer? The human mind seems particularly fecund in this respect: there are literally hundreds, but only a few have been seriously considered in the British context. Having said this it sometimes comes as a surprise to British people that their government came close to changing our electoral system on two occasions. In 1910 the Royal Commission on Electoral Reform suggested that the alternative vote (AV) be adopted for parliamentary elections, with some experimental use of proportional representation – the single transferable vote (STV) – at the local level. The alternative vote is based upon the numbering by voters of candidates according to preference in single-member constituencies.

Any candidate who receives over 50% of first preferences is elected. If no one manages this, the candidate with the least votes is eliminated and second preferences distributed accordingly to the other candidates. This process is repeated until one candidate receives a majority and is declared the winner. The system is not strictly proportional but gives more voter choice and reduces wasted votes.

In 1917 a Speaker's Conference on Electoral Reform unanimously recommended a combination of both systems for parliamentary elections but the resultant Representation of the People Bill (1917) foundered on the Commons' preference for AV on its own and the Lords' for STV. The bill lapsed but, writes David Butler, 'the survival of the existing system plainly expressed not so much an endorsement of its merits as a failure to agree upon the remedy for its faults' (Butler, p. 39).

The industrious Proportional Representation Society maintained the pressure, winning the support for several leading politicians. Following the hung parliament of 1929, MacDonald's minority government – partly to appease their Liberal allies – set up another Speaker's Conference. This time AV was favoured, but not without fierce opposition from advocates of PR and opponents of all electoral change. The Commons endorsed the reform by fifty votes but the Lords rejected it and the government fell before the upper chamber could be overruled (Butler, pp. 58–83). Since then no serious legislative attempt has been made to reform the basis of the voting system. Indeed, during the period of two-party hegemony after the war the issues became the virtual preserve of small pressure groups and the Liberal party. The 1974 election results, however – which in February gave the Liberals only fourteen seats from six million votes – put new and indignant fire into the reformers' cause. Their case had been already strengthened by the 1972 decision of the British government to introduce PR into non-parliamentary elections in Northern Ireland: if it was thought PR could help heal the divisions over there then why not use it to counteract the increasingly intractable polarities on the mainland? PR now became part of the political atmosphere of the decade, and the most favoured type of alternative system for Britain. It was recommended by many bodies and study groups for a reformed House of Lords, was used increasingly by professional bodies and, in its 'list' form, was the dominant electoral system used by Britain's new EEC partners. In 1979 Britain was conspicuous in refusing to use PR in elections to the European

Assembly; in 1981 electoral reform received the support of a whole new political party of converts in the shape of the SDP. Minority support also grew in the two big parties, but the results of the 1983 election elevated the issue into one of constant underlying importance. Table 1 illustrates the distortions. The right-hand column shows the way seats would have been distributed according to a strictly proportional system. Obviously the political complexion of any resultant government would have been very different to Mrs Thatcher's, not to mention the policies pursued. Supporters of FPTP

Table 1 *1983 election results for England, Scotland and Wales*

	Votes (in 000's)	% of poll	Seats won	% of seats	Theoretical seat allocation in proportion to votes won
Conservatives	13,012	43.5	397	63	277
Labour	8,457	28.3	209	33	180
Lib–SDP	7,794	26.1	23	3.5	166
Nationalist (SNP & Plaid Cymru)	458	1.5	4	0.5	9
Others	189	0.6	0	0	1 (Ecology)

Source: Adapted from Michael Steed, lecture to a conference, 27 April 1984.

accuse the reformers of having centrist, moderate axes to grind and claim that PR's dubious advantages are won at too great a cost. PR supporters maintain that such criticisms are either biased, ill-informed, exaggerated or based on selective use of evidence. The major elements in the debate are explained below.

The case for and against PR

(1) *Representativeness*

Against: opponents of PR, such as Enoch Powell, argue that it is not the purpose of Parliament to offer a perfect reflection of society: the existing system is held to give adequate representation of most important interests, regions and ideas.

For: advocates of PR do not claim it will give a perfect reflection, merely a better one, which will give better representation to women, ethnic minorities and those views at present stifled by the simple majority system.

Professor Ridley pointed out (*Guardian*, 11 January 1989) 'that the 1987 Conservative government was elected on a smaller proportion of the electorate than any other in Europe'.

(2) *Complexity*

Against: the system is too complex for voters to understand.

For: a small number of votes will always be spoiled or filled in unthinkingly but whilst some of the mathematics behind PR systems might be complex, filling in the ballot paper is invariably straightforward. Are we to assume that British voters are less able to cope than Irish, Italian or Belgian voters or the hundreds of thousands who fill in complicated football pools or bingo cards each week?

(3) *The MP–constituent connection*

Against: PR would destroy the traditionally close link which exists between MP and constituent and for the recognisable, single MP would substitute a group of members, none of whom would have the same feeling of responsibility for their vastly enlarged constituencies.

For: the single-member seat is no sacred British institution: multi-member constituencies functioned right into the present century and local government district council wards are usually represented by three members. Moreover, the Irish STV system arguably strengthens the connection (see below) and some PR systems (e.g. West Germany) retain single member seats.

(4) *By-elections*

Against: PR systems do not allow for this traditional means of testing public opinion between elections.

For: this argument is exaggerated in that local elections and regular opinion polls provide barometers of public opinion and, again, under certain forms of PR, by-elections can be fought.

(5) *Extremism and proliferation of parties*

Against: PR lets small extremist parties into the legislature, e.g. the Nazis under the Weimar Republic constitution, and causes the proliferation of small parties, e.g. Denmark and Finland, which have nine each.

For: where – as in Israel – the whole country is one multi-member constituency, this can and does certainly happen, but by stating a specific threshold below which parties will not be awarded seats this problem can be minimised or eliminated: Sweden's 4% limit has limited party numbers to five and only four parties currently operate under West Germany's 5% limit.

(6) *Party power and selection of candidates*

Against: under PR, political parties, not voters, determine the names which appear on the candidate lists, meaning that they are often of low calibre.

For: even under FPTP it is a small minority of the party faithful who choose candidates. Moreover the German and Irish systems allow equal or more voter choice in candidate selection (see below).

(7) *Coalitions*

Against: PR increases the number of parties and hence the chances of an indecisive result, making coalition politics the order of the day. This in turn produces:

(a) Indecisive government and political immobilism.

(b) Long delays whilst coalitions are being constructed, e.g. anything up to six months in Holland.

(c) Regular crises when they break down and frequent changes in government.

(d) Flagrant unfairness in that politicians in smoke-filled rooms decide the colour of governments, not the voter.

For:

(a) Indecisive results do occasionally happen under PR but it must be remembered that eight out of the past twenty-four elections in Britain have been indecisive. Moreover coalitions under PR *have* produced stable governments in a number of countries including Sweden, Germany and Austria, and in Greece and Spain majority single-party governments.

(b) Delays, crises and changes of government are exaggerated: between 1945 and 1975 Britain had more general elections and changed finance and foreign ministers to a greater degree than many PR countries including Belgium, Austria, Ireland, Israel, Sweden, Switzerland and West Germany (Finer, p. 24).

(c) Some PR systems, like those in Ireland and West Germany, give the voter a chance to express an opinion on proposed coalitions (see below).

(d) Coalitions which reflect consensus might reduce the potential role of conviction politicians like Mrs Thatcher or Tony Benn, but it can be powerfully argued that if the majority of voters desire centrist or moderate policies then it is the function of a democracy to deliver them. Moreover governments which people want are more likely to be stable, and unifying and, if West Germany and Austria are anything to go by, encourage economic growth and development.

Criteria of acceptability

Clearly, defenders of PR are justified in complaining that their opponents seek to highlight those, of the many available examples of PR in practice, which display it to least possible advantage as a potential system for Britain. However, this alone does not rebut the charge that PR will be bad for Britain; most reformers recognise that a British PR system should retain – as far as possible – the valued features of the present system:

(1) Simplicity.
(2) Strong and stable, preferably one-party, government.
(3) Good constituency–MP links.
(4) A manageable number of minor parties.

It might already have become apparent that the systems employed in West Germany and Ireland appear to go a long way towards meeting these criteria and indeed, the German additional member system (AMS) together with the Irish single transferable vote (STV) system are the two only serious candidates offered by the reform lobby. Both systems are explained below and their merits debated.

The additional member system

AMS seeks to marry the advantages of FPTP with those of PR. Out of the 497 seats in the West German lower house (Bundestag) 248 are elected according to the British system from one-member constituencies; the other 249 are elected proportionately through a regional list system of nominated party candidates. Voters make two crosses on their ballot papers: one for a constituency candidate and the other on an adjacent list of political parties. It is the *percentage of the vote gained by parties in the latter ballot which determines, usually within a few decimal points, the total number of seats finally allocated.* Seats gained from the constituency ballot are topped-up to the requisite levels from the 248 regional list seats. For example, in 1987, the Social Democrats gained seventy-nine constituency seats and 39.2% list votes. The latter figure meant an entitlement of 186 seats, so 107 list seats were added, taken in rank order from the regional SPD candidate lists. The Christian Democrats (CDU) did better in the constituency section with 169 seats and therefore needed only fifty-four list seats to make up their entitlement earned by 47.7% of this ballot (223 seats in all).

The Free Democrats (FDP) won no consituency seats but 9.1% of the list votes won forty-six seats and similarly the Greens gained forty-two seats on 8.3% of the vote. Seat allocations are nearly but not quite proportional with votes because parties must gain *at least 5% of list votes or three constituency seats* before they are allotted *any* list seats.

Most voters are politically consistent in their choice but some split their votes for a variety of reasons, for example:

(1) Knowing that their constituency candidate has no chance, Green supporters might vote for the candidate they dislike least from the other parties, but cast their regional list votes for their own party.

(2) Knowing that their party plans a coalition with the Free Democrats, SPD voters might cast their regional list vote for the FDP.

Advantages of AMS

(1) From total collapse in 1945, AMS (introduced in 1949) has helped provide stable coalition government in Germany which has itself enabled old wounds to heal and the economy recover. Two parties have dominated the legislature and since 1961 only two small ones have been represented in addition; in 1969 the far right NPD just failed to reach the 5% limit; in 1987 it scored only 0.6% in the list section.

(2) It enables voters to express an opinion on proposed coalitions (traditionally declared by parties before elections).

(3) It retains the constituency link yet delivers a proportional result.

(4) With only two crosses required on the ballot paper it is simple to understand.

Criticisms

(1) Coalition government has produced a very crowded political

centre ground in Germany which discourages radical new initiatives.

(2) It has enabled a small party, the FDP, the play a disproportionately big part in every government except one since 1961.

(3) It creates two 'classes' of MP: those popularly elected and the
list representatives (in practice, though, this does not seem to matter
in Germany).

(4) Constituencies are relatively large by British standards.

(5) Political parties determine candidatures in the regional lists
(though electoral law insists that democratic selection procedures be
adhered to), and it often occurs that candidates who fail to be elected
in constituencies get into the Bundestag through their nomination in
the regional list. Moreover, the whole idea of party lists is attacked
on the grounds that the voter is asked to choose not between individual candidates with personalities of their own but faceless political
parties. This last characteristic in particular seems to go against the
grain of the Anglo-Saxon political tradition.

Some reformers have concluded that to be suitable for British
political conditions, AMS needs to be modified. In 1976 the *Hansard
Society Commission on Electoral Reform* accordingly offered its
well-considered thoughts.

The Hansard Society Commission's (HSC) variation
The last mentioned criticism weighed particularly with the HSC
which felt it was of overriding importance that all candidates should
be elected directly by voters (HSC, paras. 116–17). Their proposals
were as follows:

(1) Of 640 House of Commons seats three-quarters (not half)
should be directly elected by FPTP from constituencies which would
be enlarged but not doubled as under the German system.

(2) 160 seats would be available to make up party strengths to
accord with votes cast but they would not be allocated to party lists.
Instead they would be taken up by parties on a regional basis according to the percentages gained by losing candidates. The 'top-up' seats
therefore would go to the best losers and only one not two votes
would be required.

(3) Parties gaining less than 5% of the votes cast in any region
would not gain any additional seats.

This variation offers several advantages: it requires no change in
existing voting procedure; it would give representation to parties
with substantial but not majority support in certain regions of the

country, e.g. Labour in the south, Conservatives in the north; it would retain the constituency connection; it requires all MPs to submit themselves to the voters.

However the scheme has several disadvantages, as Bogdanor notes (pp. 72–3): 'failed' candidates would be able to sit in the House; it could easily happen that some constituencies could gain an unfair two, or even three, MPs; 'best losers' will frequently be determined by the number of candidates fighting their constituencies; small parties will be encouraged to fight every constituency in order to make the 5% threshold; the lack of a second vote would remove the possibility of indicating a preference for a coalition partner – PR after all would make coalitions much more likely, and disproportionality would often result if only 25% of seats were available to add to constituency seats.

The single transferable vote (STV)

In Ireland voters are divided into multi-member constituencies and at elections register their preferences for candidates as 1, 2, 3, 4 or as far down as they wish or there are candidates. In a four-member constituency a quota is set of *one-fifth* of the votes cast plus one: a simple calculation will reveal that only four candidates can possibly reach this quota figure. The quota can be expressed thus:

$$\text{Quota} = \frac{\text{total valid votes cast}}{\text{total number of seats} + 1} + 1$$

Any candidate who receives the quota number of first preferences is elected. However, in the likely event that not all the seats will be filled so straightforwardly, the person with the least votes is eliminated and their second preferences redistributed to the other candidates, some of whom may now make the quota. The surplus votes gained by those who make the quota are also reallocated if necessary. This process continues until all the available quotas are reached.

Complexity

Against: even STV supporters allow that the sorting of preferences is highly complex: if voters cannot understand the principles which underlie their system this could lead to cynicism and distrust.

For: the voter is asked to think – but not to the extent where confusion takes over: it is relatively easy to mark preferences on a

ballot paper. In 1968 moreover, a referendum on the voting system in
Ireland resoundingly endorsed it 3–2.

Party control

Against: it is likely that parties could still control candidate
selection even under STV.

For: it is possible, however, that voters would be able to choose
between candidates from different wings of the same party; STV
offers a virtual built-in 'primary' in this respect. The ability of individuals to attract personal followings would also help reduce party
domination of the political system.

Coalitions

Against: STV would almost certainly lead to coalition government
with all its attendant disadvantages.

For: voters are enabled under STV to register an opinion on
proposed coalitions between parties.

Small parties

Against: the smaller the number of seats per constituency the
larger the quota required to become elected. By reducing the number
of seats big parties can squeeze out or disadvantage smaller ones:
both Fianna Fáil and Fine Gael have tried to do this in the past.

For: the quota system is a guarantee against small party proliferation and since 1977 an impartial boundary commission has been set
up in Ireland which has removed political influence from the process
and which increased the number of five-member constituencies from
six to fifteen; four-member from ten to thirteen and reduced three-
member constituencies – the minimum size allowed – from twenty-six
to thirteen (Lakeman, pp. 91–2).

Proportionality

Against: STV is not truly proportional – some say that it is not a PR
system at all, e.g. in 1969 Fianna Fáil obtained 45.7% of first
preference votes but ended up with 51.7% of the seats.

For: anomalies notwithstanding, the overall result in Irish elections is usually pretty proportional and *much* more so than recent
British election results. Further, as the HSC pointed out, strict
proportionality is not that important, 'because the whole purpose of
STV is to allow later preferences to have an effect' and these do not,

of course, show up in first preference percentages. STV would, moreover, if adopted in Britain give reasonable representation to Labour in the south, Conservatives in the north, the Alliance all over the country and the Nationalists in their respective countries.

STV would also allow women and ethnic minority candidates to stand with a good chance of election especially where, in the latter case, the constituency included substantial number of immigrant voters.

MP–constituency link

Against: STV would produce cumbersome, unnatural constituencies of over 200,000 voters, where neither constituents nor their multiple members could develop a proper relationship.

For: many existing constituencies are unnatural creations, having been chopped and changed about with great regularity, and where the seat is safe, MPs have little incentive to be good constituency MPs. Under STV on the other hand there *are* no safe seats; a sitting MP can quite easily be defeated by a rival candidate from his own party. This would of course make it more desirable to be a local candidate but STV would in any case make it easier for candidates to stand in their locality rather than 'migrating' to areas where their parties had significant support. Moreover, under FPTP the majority of voters often have to seek the aid of an MP for whom they did not vote: under STV this would tend not to happen as a wider range of MPs would be available.

Both systems have their fervent advocates but the SDP–Liberal Alliance opted for STV in 1983 and 1987.

The barriers to change

Which of the two favoured systems suits Britain best? It is obvious that each would gain us different things at differing costs, the balance of advantage depending upon the value one places upon these changes; indeed, what is a gain for one person might be a loss to another. It cannot be denied that reforming the system carries with it political risks. Those who think the present system, despite its faults, produces acceptably stable and effective government will be disinclined to take such risks. But those like Professor Finer who 'fear the discontinuities, the reversals, the extremisms of the existing system and its contribution to our national decline' believe 'The time for change is now' (Finer, p. 32). However, politics is the art of the possible and whilst PR might appear desirable from many points of view it faces a number of major obstacles.

(1) Clearly it is not in the interests of the big parties to change the system and, whilst both have minorities who support PR, the majority are opposed either out of self-interest, conviction or a combination of both.

(2) The 'conviction' wings of the two big parties – Labour left and Tory right – do not wish to lose the chance of winning substantial legislative power, even on a minority vote, to do the things they believe necessary and right. In other words, Tony Benn is prepared to put up with a system which gives us Mrs Thatcher because he too wants for the left the kind of power it has given her.

(3) A MORI poll commissioned by *The Economist* (5 July 1986) suggested that the British people have 'a remarkable aversion to "coalition politics" '. When asked if the next election produced a situation in which no party achieved an overall majority, 50% believed it would be a 'bad thing' whilst only 28% thought it would be a 'good thing for the country'.

(4) Constitutional change is almost always a long drawn-out business with no guarantee of success: witness the abortive attempt to reform the Lords in the late sixties and the devolution saga which dominated the seventies and finally delivered the *coup de grâce* to the Callaghan government. Even when everyone agrees change is necessary – and this is rare indeed – no one can agree upon its precise nature and extended, bitter controversy is the invariable result. It will be a brave or overwhelmingly powerful government which re-enters an area so carefully avoided since 1931.

When will change come, if at all? Some reformers are optimistic and perceive a steady but inexorable process of conversion which will result in reform, possibly quite soon. Other are less sanguine and point out that winning the intellectual argument is not enough: foreign experience reveals 'that changes in the electoral system have all emerged from considerations of party advantage' (Finer, p. 31). Clearly the centrist parties will continue to campaign vociferously but the unseemly splintering of the middle ground into the SLD and the rump SDP in the wake of the 1987 election did not advance their chances.

The Charter 88 Movement, however, put some momentum behind the reform cause in 1988 and some perceived a strengthening of pressures for electoral reform in that year within the Labour party. Influential figures like Jeff Rooker and Austin Mitchell argue that Labour's declining electoral base and the reduced number of marginal seats make it unlikely that Labour will win the next election. Even if they did, argues Rooker, the activities of the Boundary Commission in the medium term would deny Labour any chance of a second election victory. If Britain is not to become a one-party state for the foreseeable future, they argue, electoral reform will need to be embraced by Labour. Once it has a major obstacle to electoral collaboration with the centre parties will have been removed. In the autumn of 1988 Neil Kinnock appeared to open a door to internal party discussion of the issue, but even if Labour formally agreed with the centre parties that electoral reform was necessary there would still be much to resolve if only because many Labour enthusiasts favour the Alternative Vote System and not STV.

Reading

D. E. Butler, *The Electoral System in Britain since 1918*, OUP, 1963.

Vernon Bogdanor, *What is Proportional Representation?*, Martin Robertson, 1984.

S. E. Finer (ed.), *Adversary Politics and Electoral Reform*, Wigram, 1975.

Peter Hain, *Proportional Misrepresentation*, Wildwood, 1986.

Enid Lakeman, *Power to Elect: the Case for Proportional Representation,* Heinemann, 1982.

Angus Maude and John Szemerey, *Why Electoral Change?: The Case for PR Examined,* Conservative Political Centre, 1982.

The Report of the Hansard Society Commission on Electoral Reform, June 1976, Hansard Society, 12 Gower St, London.

I am grateful to Geoffrey Roberts for some useful comments on this chapter, and to Michael Steed for some of the data.

6 *John McIlroy*

Trade unions and the law

If an employer gives a worker the month's notice to which she is entitled because he does not like the colour of her lipstick or because she has rejected his advances, should that be unlawful? It was not before 1971. It was, afterwards, when the law on unfair dismissal was introduced. Should trade unions have legal rights to recognition by employers? They did in a limited way until 1980. They do not today. Should sex discrimination be dealt with by the criminal law, as some feminists urge (and as it is in some Scandinavian countries), or by the civil law, as it is in this country? Should the law support the closed shop in industry, as it did in the 1970s? Or should the law make its existence more precarious, as it did in the 1980s? Should trade unions be able to take industrial action against the suppliers or customers of employers with whom they are in dispute, a tactic that, they argue, is essential to winning many disputes? Or should the argument of the secondary employers – they are not in dispute with the union and therefore should not suffer damage as a consequence – be accepted, so that they receive legal protection?

If you think about these issues, you can see they are complicated. And you can see that people's views as to how the law should deal with workers and management, employers and unions, depends upon value-judgements as to how industry should be organised and what role labour and capital should play in that organisation. Labour law is a secondary process. Its state at a particular point in time represents judgements about employers, workers, and unions filtered through the political process. But the shape it takes affects in turn the power relationships between the parties in industry. What the law says about trade unions is, therefore, intimately related to a government's economic policy and is usually highly-contested political terrain – witness the dramatic changes over the last two decades.

It is easy to state that the function of labour law is to regulate the power of unions and employers. The problem is that there is no agreement as to how that power should be ordered and balanced. Trade unions exist to improve the terms and conditions of their members. Laws which minimise the rights of workers and trade unions on economic grounds can be criticised on social grounds and will be opposed by unions. But we live in a society and an economy still based upon private ownership of the means of production, the market and profitability. There is a possibility, at times a probability, that – quite legitimately from its own point of view in protecting its members – trade unionism can blunt the operation of the market, erode profitability which affects investment and jobs, and ultimately drive employers out of business.

For example, some recent research tells us that strong union organisation pushes up wages and closes differentials. But it depresses profits and productivity and strongly organised companies are more likely to experience job losses. How do you balance the competing interests of employees, employers, the unemployed and consumers? Because of these conflicts a handful of people think that trade unions should be banned by law. At the other end of the spectrum, a minority believe that they should be completely unrestricted by law, free to play their part in ushering in an alternative society. The majority believe that there must be a legal framework balancing and ordering the relations between workers, unions and employers. The problem is, *what* framework?

This question has provoked the sharpest controversy because, whilst there is a consensus that trade unions should be free to organise, there is no agreed conception of how trade unionism should operate in practice, of its role in contemporary society. A Conservative might hold the view that unions should be severely restricted by law, as they have outlived their usefulness, and constitute a drag on economic growth: a boiler room for inflation. A Labour supporter may believe that unions need more legal rights – they have never been more essential and they should be represented in the boardroom, running the enterprise in partnership with the employer and in Downing Street, running the country in partnership with the government. We could find Labour or Tory supporters who believed none of these things. That is why this area is such a confusing battlefield.

In this short chapter we cannot resolve any of these problems but, by looking at how the law has developed historically in relation to unions and how the present position stands, we can perhaps encourage a more informed debate.

State paternalism

The earliest institutions which attempted to control the labour market were the feudal *guilds* which covered both the master craftsmen and their journeymen. With their decline many of their functions passed to *the state* which attempted directly to control the employment relationship. From the Ordinance of Labourers, 1349, a succession of statutes gave power to the local magistrates in the quarter-sessions to fix wages, the duration of employment, the hours of work, numbers of apprentices and the utilisation of machinery. From the Statute of Labourers, 1351, a series of laws totally outlawed associations of workers and laid down rules for the conduct of employees with criminal penalities for misconduct. State-sponsored wage fixing was not finally abolished until Acts of 1813 and 1824 but long before then it had ceased to have any practical effect.

Laissez-faire

The rising capitalist class opposed state intervention in favour of the freedom of new industrialists to use their resources as they wished and to follow only the dictates of the market in relation to prices, wages and the utilisation of labour. The free pursuit by individuals of their own economic interests would provide the best allocation of resources in the overall interest of society. The acceptance of this doctrine of *laissez-faire* was reflected in the legal sphere by the doctrine of *freedom of contract*. Employers and employees should be left to control fully their own relationship by voluntarily coming to legal binding agreements.

The breakdown of paternal state regulation as industrial capitalism developed at first led groups of workers to petition the magistrates to maintain wages. Increasingly, it gave a fillip to trade union organisation already stimulated by workers recognising that in reality there was little equality between employer and individual employee and that in practice freedom of contract, because of the imbalance of bargaining power, often meant dictation of the terms of employment by the employer.

Trade union organisation was anathema to the supporters of *laissez-faire*. It distorted the operation of the market, impeded freedom of contract and competition and sought to replace the individual with the collective. Its growth produced two responses.

(1) *Parliament*, fearing the impact of the French revolution, introduced the *Combination Acts*, 1799 and 1800. These measures outlawed unions and made all agreements for increasing wages or altering hours criminal.

(2) *The judiciary*, through the common law system which gives them the ability to make law, *developed criminal and civil liabilities*. Union organisation itself amounted to a 'criminal conspiracy', the judges decided. Unions were 'in restraint of trade', their activities involved crimes such as 'intimidation', 'molestation' and 'obstruction'. Industrial action involved also civil wrongs such as breach of contract.

Coming to terms with unions

If in 1806 unions were totally illegal, a hundred years later they had attained a fair measure of acceptance. The right of unions to exist, organise, bargain and take industrial action, was only recognised after a long process of struggle. The legal landmarks were:

(1) 1824–25 Repeal of the Combination Acts – legalised some union activities but set out a list of criminal offences which caused future problems.

(2) 1871 Trade Union Act – relieved unions from liability for 'restraint of trade' and gave them civil status and tax and administrative advantages.

(3) *1875 Conspiracy and Protection of Property Act* – removed unions' liability for criminal conspiracy in trade disputes.

(4) *1906 Trade Disputes Act* – protected unions against actions for civil conspiracy and for inducing breach of employment contracts and gave union funds protection against civil actions in trade disputes.

The change from total suppression to development of a legal framework giving some legitimacy to unions may be explained by:

(a) The already existing *tradition of co-opting* newly emerging groups witnessed by the interpenetration in Britain of the old

landed aristocracy and the new industrialists.

(b) The fact that it was *a gradual process*. For much of the century trade unionists faced strong disadvantages. In 1872 alone there were 17,000 prosecutions of workers under the Master and Servant Act repealed only in 1875.

(c) The fact that for most of the century *trade unionism remained weak*, limited to a small respectable elite of well under 10% of the working population.

(d) Concessions to labour could be made because of *the economic success of Britain*, the first industrial nation to dominate the world market and create a lucrative colonial empire.

(e) The granting of citizenship rights in the political sphere via the *extension of suffrage* to most urban male workers in 1867 created political pressure for the extension of rights in the industrial arena. However, it appeared to be *safe* and *limited* political pressure. The leaders of the working class in the 1860s and 1870s were not socialists and they did not fundamentally challenge the existing order. They did not have their own political organisation. In fact, they supported one of the two great parties of state, the Liberals, and deferred to middle-class radicals in the pursuit of industrial and political change.

Immunities

The *form* that the statues legalising unions took is important. Because of the common law's built in bias against collective organisation, a problem exacerbated by the social background of the judiciary, the unions did not seek a *code of positive rights* such as exist in most other countries. They sought *immunity from* legal doctrines which would impede their activities. This was the response of a cautious and pragmatic union leadership of conservative bent, operating in a society which, lacking a written constitution, gave major play through the common law system to a narrowly class-biased judiciary and which was soaked in *laissez-faire* values. It has been argued that the immunity form was the consequence of the fact that the working class lacked universal suffrage well beyond its formative period; and the failure of its own political party to frame a more specific and positive programme of rights for trade unions and trade unionists until the turn of the century. Britain was the first industrialised nation. Its working class, therefore, had little experience elsewhere to draw upon. In contradistinction, unions in other countries, developing in later and different conditions, secured a *right* to organise, a *right* to bargain, a *right* to strike.

But in Britain the method of immunity still governs today's Labour legislation. Once the mould was set it was not ruptured. No major social upheaval provided the opportunity for rethinking and restructuring trade union law. This system of immunities to exclude the judiciary did not give unions 'privileges' or 'place them above the law'. The system of immunities was simply the *method* by which unions were given basic rights without which they would not have been able to fulfil their social and economic roles.

The judges v Parliament

The system of immunities did not fully protect the unions. The common-law system was still there and could be developed by the judges. Unions were, for example, given immunity from civil wrongs when they were acting 'in contemplation or furtherance of a trade dispute'. It was left to the courts to decide *exactly* what that phrase meant. If they felt that union action did *not* come within the definition then there was no protection. The judges were able to limit union activities by interpreting existing legislation and thereby developing new liabilities.

British labour law became a battleground between the judiciary and a parliament reacting to pressures from labour. For example, the famous *Taff Vale* case (1901) which found that unions were responsible for the wrongs of their officers upset the protections the unions thought they had been finally given in the 1870s. Parliament then had to overturn the judgement in the 1906 *Trade Disputes Act*. Similarly in the *Osborne* judgement (1909) the right of unions to use their funds to support the Labour Party was struck down by the courts and the position on political expenditure had to be redefined by Parliament in the 1913 *Trade Union Act*. Judicial undermining of the unions often coincided with periods of sharp class conflict such as the Great Unrest of 1900–14. The courts reflected middle-class fears and public opinion.

Voluntarism

When in the 1950s the eminent Labour lawyer, Kahn-Freund, commented: 'there is perhaps no major country in the world in which the law has played a less significant role in the shaping of relations than in Britain and in which today the law and the legal profession have less to do with labour relations', he was expressing the orthodox view: the 1906 settlement represented the final paragraphs in a concordat accepting that unions and employers should regulate their own affairs. The unions, given the freedom to organise and act by the system of immunities, also wanted Parliament to set minimal rules on such issues as health, safety, welfare and social security. For the rest they preferred to rely on their own efforts through collective bargaining. They did not want laws on union recognition, let alone on unfair dismissal or the rights of shop stewards. The employers too saw collective bargaining as the optimal means of achieving equity and equilibrium. The state, having guaranteed the conditions for such self-regulation and under-pinned it by the *Conciliation Act*, 1896, and the *Industrial Court Act*, 1919, was prepared to leave well alone.

The British system of state abstention and self-regulation was seen as representing maturity in industrial relations, the product of an explicit philosophy of voluntarism or collective *laissez-faire*. Whilst there can be no doubt that historically, legal control of industrial relations in Britain has been slight in comparison with the USA, Germany, Japan, or France, and that primacy has been accorded to collective bargaining, not law, the orthodox view requires some qualification.

(1) In both world wars the state introduced a whole battery of measures to control unions and industrial action such as the *Munitions of War Act*, 1915, and *Order 1305*, 1940.

(2) The *Emergency Powers Act*, 1920 and the *Trade Disputes Act*, 1927, although used sparingly, gave the state extensive powers to intervene in industrial relations.

(3) For much of the inter-war depression, the weakness of the unions, particularly after the defeat of the General Strike, meant that they represented little challenge to management prerogative or state economic objectives. *There was little necessity for intervention.*

(4) The same was true while the post-war consensus on full employment, the welfare state and the role of union leaders in managing their members was underpinned by economic stability. When the beginning of the disintegration of Britain's post-war boom coincided with an escalation of aspirations by sections of the work-force, the fracturing of voluntarism and increased intervention of the law in industrial relations was on the agenda.

The 1964–70 Labour government

By the mid-1960s concern over inflation, strikes, labour efficiency and the inability of the state to plan (particularly through incomes policy) and increasing criticism of the overall impact of Britain's industrial relations on its economic performance in harsher international competition, led to attempts to change the voluntary system. All governments agreed on the necessity for change but there was disagreement on specific strategies of reform or repression.

The Donovan Report
The major justification of attempts to reconcile the continued existence of voluntarism with greater economic efficiency was the report of the Royal Commission on Trade Unions and Employers Associations published in 1968. Donovan saw the answer to what it analysed as the 'disorder' in industrial relations producing wage drift and unofficial strikes as *the voluntary reform* of industrial relations institutions. Industry-wide collective agreements had been undermined by local, often informal, bargaining by shop stewards. They should be replaced by comprehensive formal plant and company agreements. Areas such as discipline, redundancy and change at work should be the subject of formal agreements not custom and practice. There should be new efficient procedures and wage payment systems. There was a need to integrate shop stewards into the unions and provide them with more facilities and training. The Commission did suggest some sanctions against unofficial strikers. But the law as a *major means* of stimulating change was rejected. Laws against strikes, for example, would not work, would not be used by employers and would stir up resentment. Instead a new Commission of Industrial Relations would conduct investigations and *recommend* changes.

In Place of Strife
The purpose of Donovan was *gradually and through persuasion* to integrate workplace bargaining into the process of national determination of industrial relations by government, employers and unions, in the interests of incomes policy, manpower planning and more effective management. But the Labour party leadership, seeing legislation as electorally popular, produced a White Paper, *In Place of Strife*, which proposed measures to deal with inter-union

disputes, compulsory suspension of unofficial strikes while conciliation took place, compulsory ballots before official strikes and a
compulsory register of trade unions. In April 1969 a short Bill was
announced covering the 'penal clauses'. It was adamantly opposed
both by the TUC and by a large group of Labour MPs. Informed by
his whips that there was no majority for the Bill, Wilson withdrew it
on the basis of 'solemn and binding' assurances from the TUC that it
would take greater powers of intervention in strikes.

The Industrial Relations Act

From the late 1950s views very different from those propounded in
Donovan had gained ground in the Tory Party. Inflated union power
gnawed at management prerogatives, corroded efficiency and
tyrannised individual employees. A new comprehensive framework
of law was the main instrument in solving the problems. First enun-
ciated by Tory barristers in *A Giant's Strength*, 1958, these views
underpinned the Industrial Relations Act introduced in 1971 by the
Heath government. A most wide-ranging and revolutionary piece of
labour legislation, the Act covered:

(1) *Legally binding agreements:* written collective agreements
were presumed to be legally binding unless they specifically stated
otherwise. Strikes in breach of such agreements would be illegal. The
Commission for Industrial Relations could impose legally binding
procedure agreements where none existed.

(2) The Secretary of State for Employment could apply for an
order prohibiting industrial action harmful to the economy. There
could be a *cooling-off period* of up to sixty days and a compulsory
ballot.

(3) A series of *unfair industrial practices* limited union rights to
take secondary industrial action.

(4) A *Registrar* was established with wide powers to examine and
rewrite union rules. Those unions which failed to register lost tax
concessions and immunities.

(5) Registered unions could utilise a new procedure to gain *recognition and bargaining rights*.

(6) The *closed shop* was attacked by making pre-entry closed shop
agreements void and by giving rights to individuals not to belong to a
union.

(7) There were *individual rights* introduced for the first time: there

was a legal protection against *unfair dismissal* and a *right to belong to a union*.

(8) A new Labour court, the *National Industrial Relations Court* was established to hear cases and appeals from the industrial tribunals.

The Act was a singular failure. Its ambition, scale and new institutions focused opposition. Its objectives, seeking to pressure union leaders to discipline their members whilst at the same time attacking their institutional interests, for example, the closed shop, were to a degree contradictory. In a full employment situation union hostility was effective. There were one-day stoppages of one and two million workers before the Act was on the statute book. Employers collaborated in neutering the Act, ignoring its provisions on legally binding agreements and the closed shop. The Acts stimulated rather than minimised conflict and each confrontation intensified opposition. The government's one use of the cooling-off period provoked a six to one vote by railway workers in favour of their claim.

The use of the Act's penal clauses led to the imprisonment of five dockers in Pentonville for contempt. A major political confrontation with thousands of workers on strike and the TUC calling a one-day general strike, was only avoided by a hurried House of Lords judgement overturning the Court of Appeal. The government carried through a volte-face in its economic policies. From then on the Act was largely inoperative. This episode led many to conclude that in Britain a programme of legislation to restrict the unions simply would not work. In reality the dèbâcle had specific explanations in the weaknesses of the Heath government and crucially in the existence of full employment and the social power it gave the trade unions.

The Social Contract

The legislation introduced by the incoming Labour administration from 1974 was an essential part of the Social Contract; an attempt, given the deteriorating economic position, to involve the trade union leaders more closely than ever before in state institutions and the operation of the economy and ensure their co-operation and that of their members through incorporation rather than confrontation. The philosophy was to strengthen the Donovan approach by embodying some of its prescriptions in law. Against this background Labour's legal programme:

(1) *Restored trade union immunities to the 1906 position*, in the process overriding certain more modern judge-made liabilities.

(2) *Extended the legal rights of individuals*, for example, strengthening their position in relation to unfair dismissal; introducing guarantee payments when workers were laid off; introducing a system of maternity leave and maternity pay; and developing new rights in the areas of sex and race discrimination and health and safety.

(3) *Introduced a series of collective rights for trade unions and trade unionists:* a new recognition procedure was established; unions were given the right to advance notice and consultation when redundancies were declared. Employers were required to disclose information to trade unionists for collective bargaining purposes; compulsory arbitration awards could be made against employers not meeting the general level of terms and conditions in their trade or industry. And there were new rights to time off and facilities for union representatives and protections against dismissal or victimisation for union membership or activities.

This represented a dramatic change in union attitudes and an important qualification to trade union voluntarism. For the first time they had adopted a strategy of reliance on law and the state, starkly contrasting with the philosophy of independence they had outlined to the Donovan Commission. A point that should not be overlooked, however, is that many of the changes were required not simply by Congress House but by the need to meet EEC standards.

One reaction was to criticise the new 'corporatism' on the grounds that the unions were endangering their role of representing their members by becoming appendages of the state. Many of the rights, it was argued, were extremely limited, and difficult to enforce with inadequate remedies. For example, it was impossible for the tribunals or courts in a successful unfair dismissal case to enforce reinstatement or re-engagement. By 1980 the median compensation awarded by industrial tribunals remained well under £1,000. The provisions on trade union recognition were rendered inoperable and the scope of the protective immunities severely circumscribed by judgements in the Court of Appeal. Reliance on legal and quasi-legal procedures, some trade unionists felt, could cut across and immobilise more direct and potentially successful action.

The restrictions the unions accepted set the price of the legislation very high. The new structures could be built on in an anti-union way by a future hostile government. Another response was to argue that trade unions were running the country in defiance of democratic processes. In reality the TUC accepted some of the sharpest real wage cuts this century, rises in unemployment and cutbacks in welfare provision, in return for what amounted to influence, not power. Its policies on workers' participation, import controls and planning agreements were not implemented despite tight controls over industrial action and support for restrictive codes on the closed shop, picketing and industrial action. Rank and file resistance to TUC policies erupted in the 1979 'winter of discontent', when voters went some way with the Conservative manifesto's judgement that between 1974 and 1976 Labour had enacted a 'militants' ' charter of trade union legislation. It tilted the balance of power in bargaining throughout industry away from responsible management and towards unions and sometimes towards unofficial groups acting in defiance of their official union leadership.

Thatcherism and the unions

For many the 1974–79 Labour government represented the final failure of the reform–incorporation strategy. The post-war consensus, temporarily breached in 1970–72, must now, they argued, be laid to rest. The 1979 Conservative government was determined to succeed where Edward Heath had failed in establishing a detailed legal framework for trade unions. The repressive strategy – building on an attempt by the judiciary to circumscribe union immunities in a series of cases from 1977 – would be given a second chance.

This time it was part of a more rigorous economic perspective. The government declared themselves in favour of a monetarist strategy of removing artificial obstructions to the free play of market forces which involved increasing unemployment to inter-war levels and cutting back the welfare state. Legal changes were essential to transform trade unionism, reduce wages to productivity-related levels and end restrictive practices, to renovate Britain's economic base. The legislation therefore lacked the integrationist conceptions of Heath's Industrial Relations Act. It was intended to weaken union organisation; undermine efficient union methods; limit solidarity and integrate unions into a 'joint interest with the employer' perspective; curtail unions' political involvement; and mobilise the passive rank and file against the union activists; at the same time as coercing union leaders to police those activists. The government's purpose was not simply the diminution of trade union bargaining power and the reduction of its coverage of the labour force through the development of union-free zones in the new high-tech industries. The intention was to transform the *nature* of trade unionism on the lines of the model offered by US non-political business unionism and to stimulate a restructuring of industrial relations through more direct employer–employee communications; the introduction of new technology; increased flexibility at work; the eradication of traditional union controls over production; the extension of the part-time labour force; and the development of long-term 'no strike' collective agreements. In other words, legal policy was inextricably intermeshed with other aspects of the administration's industrial relations and economic policy.

The government's position was well thought-out and well prepared. During the period of opposition, groups under Lord Carrington and Nicholas Ridley analysed past mistakes, future possibilities and the likely union response. The now famous Ridley Report was a model of forward thinking in contrast to the lack of foresight of the TUC. The lessons learned from the 1971 experience dictated a cautious, step-by-step approach. The initial 1980 Act focused on electorally popular controls over picketing and the closed shop. These limited initiatives minimised opposition and allowed the legislation to develop in tandem with other aspects of government policies. When required, as in the 1981 confrontation with the miners over pit closures, Mrs Thatcher was willing to beat a tactical retreat rather than risk the consequences of a conflict she judged to be dangerously premature. The unions have been in a far worse position than in the early seventies with falling membership, dwindling finances, fears of redundancy, weakened workplace organisation and irresolute leadership limiting resistance.

The Conservative legislation

The three foundation pieces of legislation, the *Employment Acts*, 1980 and 1982 and the *Trade Union Act*, 1984, contain the following provisions:

(1) *Individual and union rights are limited:* it is harder to claim unfair dismissal or maternity leave, and the procedures for seeking union recognition and extending the terms of collective agreements have been abolished. The Fair Wages Resolution has been

rescinded.

(2) *The closed shop is weakened.* For employers to be protected against unfair dismissal proceedings the closed shop agreement must have been sanctioned by 80% of those covered by it in a secret ballot. Ballots must be held every five years. Existing employees are not bound by the ballot whilst even those employed later have a right not to be members if they can show genuine grounds of conscience. Compensation for those unfairly sacked in closed shop situations is dramatically increased and can total well over £20,000. Unions can be liable for damages if they seek dismissal of non-unionists.

(3) *Union members are given new rights* to claim unreasonable exclusion or expulsion from the union even if the rules are followed, if they work in a closed shop.

(4) *Industrial action is curtailed* by giving the courts new powers to strike down secondary boycotts and sympathy strikes, unless certain complicated and stringent conditions are met, and by removing immunities from those picketing at any workplace other than their own.

(5) *Union-labour-only contracts are made unlawful* by outlawing all agreements, tenders, lists of suppliers which require union membership as a condition of award.

(6) *Elections of union executives and executive officers must meet stringent balloting requirements* or they can be struck down by the courts.

(7) *Union immunities are removed if industrial action is called without a majority vote in a secret ballot.*

(8) *Ballots on whether a union can maintain a fund for political expenditure* must be held every ten years commencing in 1986. Unions will find it more difficult to use their ordinary funds for political campaigning.

(9) *The Taff Vale doctrine is re-enacted* so that unions as organisations are made responsible where members or officials commit civil wrongs unless the union denounces the action in question and polices the membership. Union funds are therefore at risk.

Conservative governments in the 1980s have, therefore, adopted the 'economic efficiency' as against the 'social responsibility' argument; the market and free employers, as against the incorporation of the unions at enterprise and state level as a means of running industry and the economic system. They have refashioned the legal framework in a way which favours the employer and weakens the rights of individual workers, as well as trade unions. But it has not been quite all one-way traffic. Because of EEC legal regulations, the Conservatives were forced to introduce pieces of legislation such as the *Equal Pay (Amendment) Regulations*, 1983, which made it possible for women to claim equal pay when they did work which was different but of equal value to that of men and the *Sex Discrimination Act*, 1986.

Having established a new core legal framework, the Conservatives were determined, given their continued electoral success and the continuing disarray of the unions, to continue adding to it piecemeal. In the wake of her 1987 electoral victory, Mrs Thatcher raised the question of abolishing the Wages Councils, the bodies which set minimum rates for poorly-paid workers. Young people under twenty-one had already been removed from the scope of Wages Council orders by the *Wages Act*, 1986. Employees leaving their jobs without 'good cause', or dismissed for misconduct, were subject to increased periods of disqualification from unemployment benefit. If lowering wage rates was one concern of the government's legislation, 'restrictive practices' was another. In 1988, after the unions in broadcasting had attracted the media's attention, previously reserved for the print unions, practices in the industry were referred by the government to the Monopolies Commission. A number of other ideas which would minimise individual rights, or make their realisation more difficult, such as a possible requirement for a £150 deposit before an Industrial Tribunal case could be pursued, were floated.

The main piece of legislation in the first part of Mrs Thatcher's third term, however, was the 1988 *Employment Act*, intended to tidy up and extend previous initiatives. The earlier provisions on balloting were tightened up so that, for example, union members as well as employers could demand a ballot before a strike and, in the case of ballots for union executive members and political funds, ballot voting was to be by the postal method only. Restrictions were placed on the powers of the union trustees, members were given enhanced access to union accounts and there were new limitations on unions' powers to indemnify officials who attracted legal action. The legal rights of employees on Training Agency schemes were clarified and curtailed.

However, the provisions of the Act which attracted most attention involved, as might be expected, the closed shop and industrial action. Having constructed, in the 1980 and 1982 legislation, a complex system of balloting over the closed shop, the government now at one stroke, and somewhat cynically, many felt, abolished it. In future, even if union and management had met the requirements of a ballot in which 80% voted for the closed shop, all dismissals to enforce it would be automatically unfair. The provisions on industrial action were criticised by the CBI and right-wing pressure groups. They stated that, even if a majority of workers had voted for action in compliance with the balloting requirements of the 1984 Act, it would now be unlawful for a trade union to take disciplinary action against members who failed to abide by that democratic decision. A third provision which provoked discussion was the establishment, despite the rhetoric of individual initiative and Conservative apathy or hostility to the Commission for Racial Equality and the Equal Opportunities Commission, of a Commissioner for the Rights of Trade Union Members. This official could assist and finance members who wished to take legal action against their trade union.

After a decade of government, the Conservatives had more than achieved their legal agenda of the 1970s. But for the first time there was a questioning by employers as to whether Mrs Thatcher was pushing things too far.

The union response

Throughout the late seventies and early eighties union leadership was unimaginative and marked by a lack of strategic thinking. It now seems clear that the union leaders miscalculated in their analysis of both the ambitious scale of Conservative policy aspirations and the determination of Mrs Thatcher to see things through. They were initially disoriented by the limited nature of the 1980 legislation and the fact that Jim Prior, Norman Tebbit's predecessor as Employment Minister, was a politician of moderation. More basically, their view that the administration would turn back from the consequences of its policies, particularly as unemployment soared, and do a 'U-turn' like Edward Heath illustrated a lack of understanding of Thatcherism.

The limited 'Day of Action' against the Conservatives' first set of measures gave way to a more orchestrated strategy at a time when the unions were already significantly weaker than in 1979. At a special conference at Wembley in early 1982 the TUC agreed a programme of action to immobilise the Conservative measures. Power was given to the General Council to call industrial action if an affiliate was brought before the courts.

However, in a series of small cases during 1981 and 1982 major unions accepted injunctions. Unions generally were on the defensive and little help was afforded by the TUC to unions such as the rail union, ASLEF, which had asked for support in their own disputes. At the 1983 Congress a policy of 'new realism' of seeking an accommodation with the government was adopted by the unions. When in the autumn of 1983 the Post Office Engineering Union was restrained by the Court of Appeal under the 1980 Act from boycotting attempts at privatisation of telecommunications, Len Murray informed them that the TUC was not interested in urging unions to break the law.

This approach was taken a stage further in 1983. The National Graphical Association locked in a dispute over the closed shop with a small employer, Eddie Shah, refused to comply with an order to restrain unlawful picketing under the 1980 Act. It refused to pay fines eventually totalling £750,000 and had its total assets sequestrated. The TUC General Council, strongly influenced by Len Murray, failed to support the union. This appeared to represent a watershed in relation to the early seventies. The union rank and file no longer had the ability to take action independently of their leaders as had happened in 1972. And the leadership were not prepared to initiate it from above.

The insistence of the government on banning trade union membership at the communication centre, GCHQ, and its inability to proffer even the smallest concessions to the unions severely inhibited the 'new realism', whilst the alternative, the Wembley principles, had been undermined by the TUC leadership itself and were increasingly seen as self-protective rhetoric related to internal union political processes, rather than a serious programme of action to derail the legislation.

The 1984–85 miners' strike was the most important industrial struggle in half a century. The defeat of the miners with their left-wing leadership removed a major obstacle from the path of Conservative policies. The new legislation was used only in the most limited fashion by the National Coal Board itself. Its use by companies which traded with the Board, however, led to sequestration of the assets of the South Wales NUM. But what marked the dispute and eventually produced a complete takeover of the national union's assets by the courts was a plethora of actions brought by working miners using long-established common-law rights. Nonetheless, the confrontation confirmed the lessons of the NGA-Shah dispute: under prevailing conditions unions were in no position to repeat the successful resistance of the early seventies. Its aftermath produced a 'new realism in practice' as unions took steps to ensure that their activities stayed within the law and obeyed injunctions when they were issued. The Austin Rover strike in late 1984 involved all of the unions represented, except the Transport and General Workers Union, in accepting the court's edicts on ballots. The TGWU, fined £200,000, decided, in its turn, to modify its stance. When, in the 1986 Wapping dispute between the print unions and Rupert Murdoch, SOGAT's assets were taken over because of their failure to obey court orders, the union's behaviour contrasted with that of the mineworkers: they apologised and purged their contempt.

The basic direction had been established as the 1980s moved to a close. Unions *were* adapting to the new legal framework. The methods utilised in industrial action reflected what unions thought they could get away with in relation to the law. When unions regarded a dispute as of vital importance they might, as the National Union of Seamen did in its dispute with P&O in 1988, court sequestration. But the successive back-downs of the NUS and their ultimate detailed compliance with the courts' requirements to instruct their members to call off picketing illustrated once more the strategic limitations of defiance.

A success story?

Mrs Thatcher's *tactic* of using the law to restrict the activities of trade unions because of their perceived contribution to Britain's economic decline represented nothing new. What *was* innovatory was its integration in a wider economic and political *strategy* centred on unemployment and privatisation; its cautious hard-headed preparation; its careful steering through; its emphasis on giving the unions back to their members; and its theme of non-political business–unionism.

By what criteria do we judge the success, or otherwise of recent legislation? It is on the Statute Book, it is being used, and the judgements handed down under it are sticking. By mid-1988 around 100 cases had been initiated, most brought by employers against unions arising out of activities by their own employees. Secondary action has been predominant in the cases, but primary action has not escaped and the legislation has contributed to a growing centralisation within the unions and an increased caution regarding activities which might attract legal penalties. In the context of the alarms and fiascos of the sixties and seventies *that* represents a specific success. But law is ultimately successful when those it is aimed at internalise and accept its values, when *coercion* gives way on a wide front to *legitimacy*. The trade union legislation does not as yet appear to have passed this test. From this broader perspective, it seems that Mrs Thatcher's success with the unions owes more to the disciplining impact of sustained unemployment, excellent prime-ministerial generalship and out-of-shape, short-sighted opposition, than it does to a significant change of attitude on the part of union members and activists.

The reform of balloting *has* struck a chord with members. But the legally required ballots have only been held in a small minority of cases of industrial action. Where they have been held they have, on the whole, produced 'yes' votes. A majority of the ballots on the closed shop – which again have embraced only a small proportion of union membership agreements – have returned impressive majorities in favour of its maintenance. The provisions of the 1984 Act requiring unions to ballot on the maintenance of their political funds backfired badly: in union after union the members affirmed that they wished their organisations to be involved in politics, rather than sticking exclusively to the industrial sphere. Indeed, in the aftermath of this pick-me-up, several unions were able successfully to ballot their members on establishing a political fund for the first time. Trade unionists, if they limit their picketing as the law demands to the primary employer, do so not because they have been *convinced* by the government that secondary picketing is illegitimate, but simply because they *fear* the consequences of their unions' funds if the law is utilised. Moreover, it might be argued that with large-scale unemployment interacting with a growth in average earnings far outstripping inflation for most of the eighties, most trade unionists have kept their heads down and the legislation has not received a rigorous testing. How successful would it be in a tighter labour market? The unions came back from the weakness of the twenties and thirties, so why shouldn't they bounce back with political and economic change in the nineties?

Conservatives can reply that the legislation was only ever intended to have a reinforcing back-up impact. And it was specifically intended to interweave with the government's economic and wider industrial relations policies. And, as jobs grow in service industries and the new and successful economy of small, high technology enterprise takes off – very different from the manufacturing-based war-based recovery of the thirties and forties and far less hospitable to trade unions – the legislation will finally be accorded a hard-won legitimacy. Look at the anorexic state of the unions today compared with 1979 and the related health of the employer. The unions have lost more than 3.5 million members since 1979. Unionisation of the labour force is dropping towards the 40% mark. Strikes and days lost through strikes are running at levels unknown in the last quarter of a century. The number of shop stewards in manufacturing is estimated at 40% below the figure a decade ago. The TUC is split and its political influence is derisory. Unions such as the expelled Electricians and the Engineers have eagerly embraced the new business model of trade unionism.

Against this, we have to weigh the evidence on earnings, the fact that workplace organisation has remained remarkably intact and spread to new areas, the fact that a majority of employers still involve trade unions in changes in the work process and the fact that the dramatic battles over the law which capture public attention have passed by the majority of managers and trade unionists. And as long as the changes which have undoubtedly occurred are underpinned by unemployment, high wages and legal coercion, the Conservative achievement in industrial relations generally, and in trade union law specifically, remains a fragile and potentially transient one.

Indeed, there has already been some reaction against present policies. Far from giving Mrs Thatcher a Falkland-style fillip her triumphalism during the miners' strike led to criticism. The Wapping dispute appeared to produce for the first time in many observers a realisation of the scope of the new legal edifice and its lop-sided nature: whilst the employer was able to obtain a variety of remedies to restrain picketing and boycotting of his product, the unions had no rights to recognition nor to contest the mass dismissal of their members. It was pointed out that it was as if the Conservatives had legislated for half of the system that operates in countries which have a strong legal framework for their industrial relations. The legal restraints and responsibilities on unions were nearly all now present in the UK: what was missing were the correlative protections and rights given to unions in such systems. The *degree* to which union activities had been fettered, employment protection rights cut back, institutional stimuli to collective bargaining removed and greater freedom given to the judges to develop common law wrongs against the unions in the absence of immunities, was much remarked upon. And the unveiling of the 1988 legislation led to concern amongst employers that the Conservatives were perhaps going a little over the top. Overall, the verdict must be that the introduction and operation of a new legal framework for industrial relations has constituted a success story for the Conservatives . . . but one or two qualifications must be made and one or two reservations remain.

The future

The policy of a future Labour government with regard to labour law has been the subject of much contention: widely differing approaches have been advocated. Labour has been struck in this, as in other areas, by the increasing difficulties involved in simply removing Conservative measures at one fell swoop. Labour's leadership have stated that employment protection rights would be restored to their 1979 position and developed beyond it. Part-time workers would be included in the protections and a Ministry for Women would consolidate and extend equal opportunity policy. A national minimum wage also appears to be on the agenda. Legislation would guarantee workers an extended role in company decision-making, although Labour has now formally forsaken the 'workers on the board' approach of the 1977 Bullock Report in favour of a development from below through workplace and company works councils.

Some sections of Labour and trade union opinion have favoured a break with the past in the regulation of collective industrial relations and have argued that the Labour movement should forsake the system of immunities. Rather than filling in the holes the Conservatives have dug, a Labour government should start over again by legislating a charter of positive rights for trade unions to associate, bargain and take industrial action. There are problems here: the issue is bound up with wider constitutional questions, in particular the debate about a broader Bill of Rights. The UK lacks a judiciary attuned to interpreting entrenched positive rights and supportive of trade unionism. Positive rights would entail limitations and correlative responsibilities: rights to take industrial action, for example, would be subject to qualifications and specific exceptions. This could create more legal involvement for the unions, not less. Labour has tended, therefore, to shy away from a full-blooded, radical, positive rights approach in favour of a mix of positive rights on recognition and bargaining and immunities on industrial action. What appears still unresolved is the degree to which the courts would continue to be involved in industrial relations and the extent, contrariwise, to which they would be replaced by specialist adjudicatory bodies. In at least one area the Labour leadership has no wish to simply repeal the Conservative legislation: the right to ballot on union elections and industrial action are perceived as electorally popular. Despite opposition from the left the suggestion is that a mixture of law and Code of Practice would regulate these matters.

The SDP–Liberal Alliance supported the creation of the new framework in broad terms. In some cases (the political levy) it wanted to go further but it emphasised the importance of complementing controls over trade unions with additional rights for workers, more participation, an extension of profit-sharing and employee share-ownership schemes and a strong incomes policy. As for the Conservatives, they are not resting on their laurels. They feel that if anti-union legislation is not the vote winner it once was, it does their pulling power little harm. We can expect further instalments, perhaps focusing on 'restrictive practices' and industrial action in essential services, a continuing whittling-away of individual rights, a fine tuning of recent reforms and, in contradiction to their general approach, a response to pressures from Europe for an extension of workers' rights.

What *is* clear is that the days of voluntarism have gone for ever. Whatever the immediate future holds it will leave Britain with an extended legal framework governing the relationships between union and employers and the ambit of union freedoms. It is the content of that framework which remains contentious and problematic.

Reading

G. S. Bain (ed.), *Industrial Relations in Britain*, Blackwell, 1983.

K. Coates and T. Topham, *Trade Unions and Politics*, Blackwell, 1986.

C. Crouch, *The Politics of Industrial Relations*, Fontana, 1979.

P. Fosh and C. R. Littler (eds.), *Industrial Relations and the Law in the 1980's: Issues and Future Trends*, Gower, 1985.

J. A. G. Griffith, *The Politics of the Judiciary*, Fontana, 1981.

R. Lewis (ed.), *Labour Law in Britain*, Blackwell, 1986.

J. McIlroy, *Trade Unions in Britain Today*, Manchester University Press, 1988.

K. Wedderburn, *The Worker and the Law*, Penguin, 1986.

7   *John McIlroy*

Television today . . . and tomorrow

The media play an important role in forming and sustaining our view
of social reality. They influence the way we look at the world and our
interpretation of what happens in it. Because of the potency of its
visual images, television can be a stronger influence than the press.
Our exposure to television has intensified over the last twenty-five
years, as the impact of the newspaper has declined and most of us
grant television a greater credibility – we tend to see the broadcasting
media as more truthful and reliable than the printed word. There are
television sets in over 95% of households and, despite the video
boom, we each spend on average over twenty hours a week watching
the 'box'. Children spend more time watching television than they
spend in the classroom. Television is, therefore, an important *political* medium. After a long period of consensus, controversy over the
role television should play in our society and how it should be owned
and controlled is once again hitting the headlines. This chapter
examines how television developed in the UK, its present organisation and its political impact. It goes on to review recent developments and considers the arguments for and against the reform and
deregulation of broadcasting.

Television and politics

In the last two decades television has become the main source of the
average citizen's information about politics. The 20% of television
programming devoted to news and current affairs plays an important
role in constructing the political agenda and determining which issues

are important and which are not, which issues should be prioritised for scrutiny and discussion and *how* they should be discussed. Other television programming, from advertising to documentaries and drama, influences political perspectives in more subtle fashion. The importance politicians themselves attach to television can be gauged from the degree to which they complain about its coverage. An ability to 'handle' television, to come across in a plausible and compelling manner, has increasingly been seen as a vital ingredient in political leadership. In his fascinating study *Live From Number 10*, Michael Cockerell claims that 'every modern Prime Minister has hated, loved or feared television – some have done all three'.

A poor television profile played a significant part in the removal of Sir Alec Douglas-Home as Conservative leader in the aftermath of the 1964 general election and this is often seen as the beginning of the 'tyranny of the box'. In contrast, television contributed strongly to the image and electoral success of Harold Wilson, a master of the medium, whose famous pipe was even taken up as a prop for his appearances. On the other hand, the Conservatives romped home in 1970, despite Ted Heath's lack of televisual charisma. But by the end of the decade the grooming of Mrs Thatcher by the ad-men and packaging specialists – including elocution lessons – and the fact that Neil Kinnock was widely seen as the first leader of the opposition to be created by television, paid tribute to the importance of the medium. It underlined the fact that television interviewers and pundits such as Robin Day, David Dimbleby and Brian Walden are themselves important political figures.

Television brought major issues of the 1980s, such as the Falklands War or the miner's strike, into our living rooms night after night and its reporting and analysis influenced how we thought about them. In a real sense television 'made' the SDP and turned it temporarily from a group of political notables, with no votes and no members, into a party possessing the support of a quarter of the electorate. And its influence on how we vote in elections seems to be on the increase. In one survey of the 1983 general election 63% of respondents cited television as their most important source of political information – as against 29% who cited newspapers and 4% who cited radio. Another survey asked voters in both the 1983 and 1987 elections how they learnt about the policies of the different parties. In 1983 43% and in 1987 50% of those surveyed ranked television coverage as their major source of information, compared with 37% in 1983 and 39% in

1987 who derived their information primarily from the press. People also preferred television coverage to press coverage but only one in five voters stated that television had helped them to decide how to cast their vote. This illustrates the extent and the limits of television's influence. We pay attention to what it says: we are still far from being its pliant creatures.

Bias in television

Television is often accused of trivialising complex problems, setting firm limits on controversy and projecting a bland centre position on most issues. Its claim to be impartial and objective has been challenged in recent years both from the left and from the right. For example, the Confederation of British Industry, the Institute of Directors and Aims of Industry all complained to the Annan Committee on the Future of Broadcasting which sat in the 1970s. They argued that television gave the activities of industrialists and employers a negative slant and provided far too much coverage for left-wing militants. Particularly influential, however, has been the critique proffered from the left by the Glasgow University Media Group in a series of books, including *Bad News* (1976) and *More Bad News* (1980).

These studies conclude that television news follows a very similar format across channels: decisions on what is news and how that selection shall be interpreted and presented are informed by built-in assumptions congruent with the world-view of those who control our society. In a study of twenty-two weeks of television news coverage the researchers found that reporting of industrial relations was superficial, unbalanced and misleading. Conflict and strikes were emphasised at the expense of harmony and other issues such as industrial accidents. The reporting of industrial action was 'clearly skewed against the interests of the working class and organised labour . . . in favour of the managers of industry'. Trade unionists were consistently portrayed, through the use of language and the presentation of events, as the aggressors – often the unjustified aggressors – in industrial conflict. Its real causes and management's contribution to problems went largely unexamined. Management were presented deferentially, seated in comfortable offices, and simply asked to state their position. Trade unionists were filmed at mass meetings and on picket-lines in more hostile fashion and were required to justify their position.

Reporting was focused on television – defined 'trouble-spots', such as the motor industry, in defiance of the statistical pattern of stoppages which showed other industries to be more strike-prone. In the case of British Leyland strikes were stereotyped as its major problem, despite the fact that government reports had discounted this explanation in favour of poor management and inadequate investment. The *Bad News* team documented cases of biased editing with speeches from politicians criticising workers *and* management being presented as if the main burden of the critique was addressed to the workers. They argued that biased coverage of industrial relations was only part of a slanted approach to wider economic issues which stressed wage inflation as the cause of the UK's economic difficulties at the expense of other plausible explanations. Television broadcasters, it is claimed, 'continually reinforce a managerially skewed view of industrial relations', as part of a wider conservative projection of current affairs supportive of the ideas of those who hold industrial and political power and the economic and social *status quo*.

These studies – the most detailed and extensive examination of television coverage mounted in the UK – have attracted support from a wide range of social analysts. In a more limited way the Annan Report commented that 'coverage of industrial affairs is in some respects inadequate and unsatisfactory'. But they have also attracted criticism. It has been claimed that whilst television news does tend to concentrate on negative situations and is often weak on examination of the causation and the broader context of issues, the Glasgow Media Group over-egg the omelette. Their research base was slender: twenty-two weeks coverage at most. At a time when industrial relations were generally perceived as a problem and when viewers were interested in its negative aspects, coverage of disputes only attracted 7% of ITN news time, a very small proportion of overall output. Most industrial coverage did *not* deal with strikes. The motor industry, too, was in the public eye during the period studied and British Leyland was of particular interest as it was in danger of impending collapse. An examination of the transcripts of the programmes studied by the *Bad News* group, it is claimed, demonstrates that their assertion that neglect of basic facts and explanations stereotyped strikers' behaviour as irrational is unjustified. Far from being systematically omitted, it is argued, the causes of disputes were often mentioned and sometimes analysed.

Workers were interviewed on picket-lines simply because that is where you will find them during a dispute. Moreover, critics claim, these studies sometimes ignore or underplay the evidence that management are underrepresented in industrial coverage and that trade unionists are often lacking in the PR that attracts favourable coverage. The situation has improved since this research was undertaken – look at Channel 4 News. Moreover, the defenders of television urge, impartiality does not necessitate that equal attention be devoted to all the different viewpoints in society. We have to weigh the degree of support that they possess and since mainstream views by definition attract most support they should be given more coverage. Finally, the view that television is simply a medium for the transmission of conservative messages ignores the contradictions within television coverage and its contradictory impact upon viewers.

Influencing attitudes

The argument about the *influence* of television – whatever the message it carries – is a complex and difficult one. Surveys of the 1987 general election campaign, for example, showed that there had been very little change in the percentage support for the Conservative and Labour parties from the start to the finish of what was an intensive media-documented campaign. Despite being widely credited with its most successful campaign for years, Labour only improved slightly on the position it held prior to the dissolution of Parliament. Was this because people had already made up their minds? And if so what role had the media played in this? What about those voters who *did* change sides, and was Labour's excellent campaign instrumental in saving it from an even worse drubbing at the hands of Mrs Thatcher? The 1964 and the 1983 elections were seen as strongly influenced by television compared with 1979 and 1987. Why the difference? We still know far too little about the extent to which television affects our political attitudes and behaviour.

Initially the conventional wisdom, based upon studies conducted in the 1940s and 1950s in the USA, held that the media simply *reinforced* our political views rather than creating or drastically changing them. These studies were later criticised on the grounds that they concentrated upon those who used the media most, who had a high degree of prior knowledge of issues, and who were least likely to change their positions. Moreover, it was claimed that they ignored or gave inadequate weight to the extent to which respondents had switched from their initial allegiances by polling day and that they exaggerated the degree to which change, when it did occur, was the product of personal contact and discussion rather than exposure to the media. Moreover, television at the time was still in its infancy. Later studies have emphasised the differential impact that the media had on different groups. They have suggested that reinforcement of already held attitudes is likely to occur with those whose exposure to the media is heavy but whose use reflects existing knowledge and attitudes which minimise its change impact. The frequency with which we discuss politics is another important factor. A change in attitudes is more likely to occur amongst those whose exposure to the media is moderate, who have more limited knowledge of the issues and who rarely discuss politics with friends and colleagues. Moreover, change is likely to take place over the long term rather than the short term. The influence of television is cumulative, not immediate.

Other studies have stressed that the impact of the message television sends out will vary as it will be received in different ways by different groups according to their class, social location and life experience. Researchers have shown that different groups watching the same television programme interpret it in different ways according to these criteria. This makes the point: it is unhelpful to emphasise the influence of television on politics isolated from other factors which influence us, such as our class position and our economic standing. The role of television needs to be located within wider explanations of political behaviour. Nonetheless, we need more evidence as to whether television educates us, deepens our understanding of the world we live in and helps us towards informed and autonomous choice. Or whether it sensationalises, de-educates and brainwashes us into seeing the world as others want us to see it. But it certainly seems clear that as our voting habits have become more fickle, as our allegiance to party has diluted, as our political activism has declined and our reading of newspapers has diminished, television has played a more active role in politics. This means that the politics of television becomes increasingly important. We need to know more about the impact of television on politics but also more about *the impact of politics on television*. How the medium is organised, how it is regulated, who makes the key decisions as to what does and does not go out, the power balance between the controllers of television and the government, these and other issues are today emerging as themselves important items on the political agenda. Before examining them it will be useful to outline how television developed in Britain.

Television past and present

Some understanding of the history of British television is important in order to grasp the challenges and choices which confront us today. Whilst developments have been continuous and complex we can divide the story of television into three main phases.

The birth of the 'Beeb'

From its inception broadcasting was seen as such a potentially powerful influence on individual lives and social development as to merit strong public regulation. The Sykes Report (1923) and the Crawford Report (1926) both saw the need to develop broadcasting in a planned and regulated fashion as a public service, rather than an arena for private enterprise. The BBC was established in 1926 as a non-profit-making organisation with the brief of covering the whole country and catering for all social groups. The BBC was insulated from market forces and direct government control. It was financed by a licence fee set by the government and run by an independent Board of Governors appointed by the Home Secretary. Nonetheless this attempt to combine autonomy and accountability opened the corporation to possible economic and political pressures. During the 1926 General Strike the first Director-General John Reith declared that 'since the BBC was a national institution and since the government in this crisis was acting for the people . . . the BBC was for the government in the crisis too'. Ramsay MacDonald, the leader of the opposition, was banned from broadcasting and such bans against Labour and trade union leaders, as well as against those who opposed government policies of appeasing the dictators, continued throughout the 1930s. Reith's attitude was 'one nation' and paternalist. The nation required education and was to be given what it needed – established culture – rather than popular entertainment. During wartime the BBC operated within tight limits and broadcasters such as J. B. Priestley, who were critical of government policies, were swiftly dispensed with. But the war years produced important developments in news and light entertainment.

Commercial television

BBC television was established in 1936. In the pre-war period it was limited to London and in 1939 was suspended for the duration. In the late 1940s, there was dissatisfaction at the BBC's failure to develop the medium. The Report of the Beveridge Committee (1951) criticised the BBC but reaffirmed the need to treat broadcasting as a public service. It compared the BBC's work to that of the universities and turned down plans for commercial television backed in a minority report from Selwyn Lloyd. Advertising interests, electronics firms and free marketeers in the Conservative Party began a campaign to implement Lloyd's proposals. The commercial lobby argued in terms of greater choice, the benefits of competition and what they saw as the disadvantages of the BBC's antiquated and fuddy-duddy approach. The defenders of the status quo argued that a duopoly and advertisements would trivialise and Americanise coverage and competition would drive down standards to the lowest common denominator demanded by the advertisers. The Labour Party's support for the BBC and the fact that its leaders Churchill and Eden had suffered at Reith's hands as anti-appeasers in the 1930s, swung the government's support.

In 1955 commercial television began. Over 20% of households now had television. But the system which emerged, although it represented a rupture with the past and a victory for private enterprise, fell far short of complete deregulation. In the new compromise a regulatory body, the Independent Television Authority (later the Independent Broadcasting Authority), appointed by the Home Secretary, awarded franchises (to be periodically renewed) to companies to broadcast in particular areas. They also policed the obligations laid down for commercial television in the 1954 legislation which were similar to those governing the BBC and which demanded impartiality in the treatment of controversial issues and balance in programming. Advertisers were not allowed to sponsor programmes and thus influence content, as in the American model. Nonetheless, there were criticisms of standards in the early days and by the end of the 1950s involvement in commercial television was widely seen as a 'licence to print money'.

British is best

Criticised by the Pilkington Committee in 1962 and faced with a levy on advertising revenue, the ITA's powers were extended and it subsequently developed a more active role. It reallocated franchises and intervened in programming to maintain provision for minority needs, ensure 'serious' programmes at peak viewing time and create some balance between education and entertainment. The second BBC channel was established in 1964 and by the 1970s the situation was one of regulated competition, with a rough if fluctuating audience-split of 50% ITV, 40% BBC 1 and 10% BBC 2. The system was rounded-out by Channel 4 coming into commission in 1982–83 with a brief to cater for minorities. It was seen even by its critics as amongst the best in the world.

Both the activities of the IBA and the existence of the BBC – particularly its requirements for a proportion of programmes on current affairs, education and for children, as well as its restrictions on imports – produced a marriage of commercialism and public service which was widely seen as providing a happy balance. British television was Coronation Street *and* World in Action, Beethoven *and* Chuck Berry, Panorama *and* John Wayne. The dual system of financing the BBC via the licence fee and ITV via advertising meant that the two arms of the system competed for audiences not for cash. This and the controls over advertising mitigated the worst excesses of the US system and constrained the plunge to lower standards and restricted choice which afflicted our transatlantic cousins and increasingly, as the 1970s developed, Britain's national press.

It was underpinned by the ultimate accountability of the television networks to Parliament. But the subtle arm's-length mechanisms of control were seen, despite periodic bouts of conflict, as avoiding the plight of broadcasting in many other countries where it is essentially an arm of state propaganda. If the ITV companies were essentially interested in profits and were interlinked with other media and industrial companies exercising a powerful political influence, they were, to a large degree, constrained by the overall regulatory framework and public service philosophy, happy to trade off excellence for reasonable profits and stand up to the advertising interests. British television, it was generally held, whilst not without blemish, represented a high-quality compromise which served the nation well.

Brave new world

In the 1980s, particularly since the Conservative victory in the 1983 election, this consensus has come under strain. British television has been the object of hostile attention from both commercial interests and from government.

The economic attack

The availability of new technology and, consequently, the opportunity to make massive profits have led private enterprise to mount a crusade to undermine the philosophy and organisation of public service broadcasting. Cable technology is efficient *and* cheap and can provide a wide range of services including a multiplicity of television channels. In accordance with their support for free market economics and privatisation the Conservatives insisted that cable technology should be developed by private enterprise, not the state. A stimulus for citizens to pay for linkage into the cable network would be the chance of access into a wide range of television channels available for a monthly fee. The 1982 Hunt Report supported this approach and the 1984 *Cable and Broadcasting Act* excluded the BBC and IBA and chartered a new Cable Authority which would award franchises but which was given no brief to control the quality and diversity of programming.

Cable, however, was far from even the small overnight success its supporters had hoped for. By 1988 only a quarter of a million households were 'cabled-up' and only ten out of twenty-five franchises awarded were operating. After four years Rupert Murdoch's Sky channel was still losing money. Big business was, by the second half of the decade, laying greater emphasis on direct broadcasting by satellite to houses equipped with a satellite dish. Here again the government accepted an emphasis on private enterprise, although the public bodies were to be involved. The IBA in 1986 awarded British Satellite Broadcasting – a consortium of multinational companies – a contract to beam four channels direct from space from 1989. Rupert Murdoch, already the owner of four national newspapers, announced his intention to start four new channels financed through pay TV, subscriptions and advertising from the same year. Robert Maxwell, W. H. Smith and British Telecom all bought up channels.

These developments were accompanied by a sustained campaign to deregulate broadcasting and discredit the BBC and IBA. In 1984 the advertising agency Saatchi and Saatchi, who ran Mrs Thatcher's first two election campaigns, published a hard-hitting statement, *Funding The BBC – The Case For Advertising*. This argued that the licence fee then standing at £46 was, because of its flat-rate nature, a regressive tax which bore hardest on poor households and which was expensive to collect. Advertising was a far better means of generating revenue and its introduction by the BBC would lower the cost of advertising on ITV. This was followed by attacks on the licence fee by Mrs Thatcher, who believed a boost for advertising was a boost for the economy. In her view, 'it was a sort of compulsory levy on the viewer irrespective of whether he watched BBC programmes a great deal'. The right-wing think-tank, the Adam Smith Institute, joined in claiming that the licence-fee system undermined consumer sovereignty by providing no link between the price of viewing and the rate of viewing.

Advocates of deregulation presented an idealised picture of the USA where viewers scanned mammoth TV guides to select from up to sixty different programmes and the diversity and quality of a UK press freed by recent developments in print technology. Advertising agency D'Arcy, McManus, Masius attacked the BBC for purveying the values of an aristocratic establishment whose attitudes had stimulated Britain's economic decline. The BBC was simultaneously stereotyped as a haven of left-wingers whilst the trade unions' activities in the ITV companies came under particular criticism from the newspapers owned by Rupert Murdoch's News International group. They mounted a sustained campaign against the status quo in broadcasting. BBC Director-General Alasdair Milne described the coverage of *The Times* as particularly 'malevolent. Every day – and it was every day – there was some distortion, some half-truth.' In the summer of 1984, Home Secretary Leon Brittan promised an unprecedented independent audit into the BBC's financial position and its management structure by consultants Peat, Marwick, Mitchell. In early 1985, he announced an increase in the licence fee below the BBC's claim and the establishment of a committee under economist Alan Peacock to investigate the financing of the Corporation, the introduction of advertising and the future of cable and satellite services. The idea was floated that BBC 2 and Channel 4 should be sent via satellite vacating their existing channels for private enterprise. The *Sunday Times* commented: 'The free-market Thatcher government has helped create the climate in which the BBC – ITV duopoly could be bust.'

The political attack

Conservative governments established both the BBC and the IBA, as well as Channel 4. But Mrs Thatcher, despite what many criticised as increasingly obsequious treatment from interviewers, has, according to Michael Cockerell, found television's handling of politics 'not just an irritant but an affront. Any fear in her has long since turned to loathing.' Conflict between television and governments is nothing new – witness the Conservatives' fury over Suez in 1956, Harold Wilson's incessant railing against the BBC and the long-running conflicts over the war in Ireland. But no administration has locked horns in such a sustained bout of attrition as those led by Mrs Thatcher. The BBC has been the main object of hostility. In the early 1980s the BBC refused to transmit Open University material, refused to allow CND campaigner and distinguished historian E. P. Thompson to deliver the Dimbleby Lecture and pulled several plays on the Falklands from the schedules. In December 1981, the Corporation refused to allow the Campaign For Free Speech on Ireland to appear on the *Open Door* programme (specifically intended for groups whose viewpoints were unpopular or underrepresented) to discuss the forty-plus TV programmes on Ireland banned, delayed or altered in the previous decade. Nonetheless, the Conservatives were far from happy with coverage of the Falkland affair. Relationships were further strained by an ultimately successful libel action brought by Conservative MPs over a *Panorama* programme linking them with extreme right-wing groups. The middle of the decade was punctuated by a series of bitter encounters between the government and the BBC.

Real Lives   In July 1985 a forty-five-minute film looking at the lives and views of Sinn Féin Leader Martin McGuiness and hardline Loyalist Gregory Campbell of the Democratic Unionist Party was scheduled for transmission as part of a BBC documentary series *Real Lives*. On hearing of the film Mrs Thatcher had reacted unfavourably and Home Secretary Leon Brittan had written to Stuart Young, Chair of the Governors, requesting them to ban the programme even if it was hostile to the IRA. Brittan had not seen the programme and it was also pointed out that Sinn Féin, the political wing of the IRA, was not a proscribed group and had regularly and successfully stood candidates in national and local elections. In the absence of Director-General Alasdair Milne, the Board of Governors, departing from past traditions in the BBC, insisted on seeing the programme. They rejected Milne's advice and insisted that it should not go out. This unprecedented overruling of the Editor-in-Chief produced what the *Guardian* termed 'the greatest constitutional crisis in the history of British Broadcasting'. The BBC's independence from government was widely questioned, particularly the role of the Governors led by Conservative supporters Stuart Young and William Rees-Mogg. Many saw the issues as one of censorship and an attempt to turn the corporation into an instrument of government propaganda. There was almost total support for a one-day strike called to oppose the governors' decision by the National Union of Journalists on 7 August and such was the strength of feeling that they were joined by colleagues from ITV and radio. The programme went out with small agreed changes in October 1985.

The BBC and Norman Tebbit The spectre of government censorship and the political role of the Governors was raised in relation to what most viewers felt on seeing it was a relatively innocuous programme. In the past the BBC had accepted restrictions on reporting the situation in Ireland but had asserted the need for evenhandedness between the two communities in the north-east – and Sinn Féin had the support of around 40% of the Nationalist Community. In this situation Leon Brittan's 'request' to ban the *Real Lives* programme was widely perceived as attempting to draw new limits. Matters were not improved by the disclosure in the *Observer* that MI5 had been for many years vetting BBC staff and in eight documented cases this had prevented staff being employed or promoted. But the Conservative government was equally annoyed at the BBC's response. By making Martin McGuiness appear to be an ordinary human being the BBC, they felt, was providing 'terrorists with the oxygen of publicity'. Conservative Party Chair Norman Tebbit began to take a closer interest in the BBC. A unit was created at Conservative Central Office to monitor the BBC's political and current affairs coverage. In April 1986, the unit studied television news coverage of the American bombing of Libya. They reported that 'News at Ten (ITV) was able to preserve an impartial editorial stance while the BBC took a number of decisions the effect of which was to enlist the sympathy of the audience for the Libyans and to antagonise them towards the Americans.' In the summer of 1986 Norman Tebbit wrote to the BBC enclosing a copy of the twenty-one-page dossier and stating that BBC coverage of this issue was 'a mixture of news, views, speculation, error and uncritical carriage of Libyan propaganda'. The BBC issued a statement denying the allegations and noting that 'the complaint could suggest that the Conservative Party is attempting to intimidate the BBC'. Mr Tebbit, however, returned to the attack, questioning the number of libel actions the BBC was attracting, ringing the Chair of the Board of Governors to insist that Cecil Parkinson appear on *Breakfast Time* over the opposition of the programme's producers and demanding clarification of the BBC's position on apartheid. When BBC Assistant Director-General Alan Protheroe stated that the BBC was opposed to apartheid Mr Tebbit demanded a public correction from the Director-General. When this was not forthcoming he suggested an independent report on the issue. By the end of 1986 relations between the BBC and the government were at an all-time low.

The Zircon Affair   In January and February 1987 the government ordered police raids on BBC Scotland, the *New Statesman* and the homes of journalists, seized the tapes of the entire BBC 2 *Secret Society* series, applied for a spate of injunctions against journalists and banned MPs from viewing one of the films in the series. The well-known *New Statesman* journalist Duncan Campbell had been commissioned to produce a series of six thirty-minute investigative films, one of which dealt with the Zircon project – government plans to put a spy satellite into space at a cost of £500 million. The film's central allegation was that this had happened without the knowledge of the Commons Public Accounts Committee which had been given categorical assurances that it would be informed of such defence expenditure. During the summer of 1986 the Ministry of Defence and GCHQ got wind of the existence of the Zircon film and began informal pressure to have it banned. Nonetheless, in October and November the film was viewed by BBC lawyers and the Assistant Director who pronounced themselves satisfied that it would not damage national security. However, political pressures were now mobilising the BBC governors, several of who inquired as to why 'a destroyer' like Campbell had ever been employed. He was 'not the sort of person the BBC should consort with'. In December 1986 Alan Protheroe, the Assistant Director-General, changed his mind and recommended that the Zircon film should not go out. On 17 January, the *Observer* broke the news that the Director-General had agreed to pull the film from the schedules. When the *New Statesman* ran a story about the project and copies of the film began to circulate the government leapt into action. All the evidence suggested that the banning of the programme stemmed from the judgement and pressure of the Ministry of Defence, rather than the judgement of the BBC that national security was at stake. And it also suggested that national security was not, in fact, at stake. This view appears justified by the fact that in the end no prosecution occurred and the programme went out with minor changes in the autumn of 1988. Campbell himself felt that the furore which occurred *after* the decision had been taken to ban the programme was motivated by the Cabinet antipathy to investigative journalism and a desire to pursue its vendetta with the BBC. A final casualty of the affair was BBC Director-General Alasdair Milne, who was asked for his resignation on 29 January.

By that time it was possible for Jeremy Isaacs, former head of Channel 4, to note that 'The Government regards itself as having "sorted-out" the BBC and it is now looking for ways of "sorting-out" ITV.' The BBC was widely seen as having been subdued by sustained attrition. As attention turned to ITV in 1988, Channel 4 dropped an edition of *After Dark* after objections to the appearance of Sinn Féin MP Gerry Adams. A prize-winning film, *Acceptable Levels*, about media self-censorship over Ireland, was dropped because the verdict in the Birmingham Six appeal had just been announced. Geoffrey Howe phoned Lord Thomson of the IBA to try to stop a *This Week* programme, *Death on the Rock*, dealing with the SAS shooting of IRA activists in Gibraltar. When the IBA refused to bow to pressure and doubts were raised about evidence in the programme Thames Television instituted an inquiry. To the fury of the government Thames TV were also completely exonerated by an inquiry led by Lord Windlesham, an ex-Conservative minister. Finally, in autumn 1988, the government announced a ban on broadcasts involving Sinn Féin.

The most important impact of these well-publicised assaults on television's autonomy is the extent to which they undermine public confidence in broadcasting and the fact that by putting down markers for acceptable limits to coverage over the longer term, they encourage self-censorship. As the producer of the programme *Yesterday's Man*, which came under fire in 1970s for its criticisms of politicians commented, 'I would never try to do it again . . . Better to be safe than imaginative', or as producer Elaine Morgan put it in 1988, 'Anodyne crap makes for a quiet life . . .'

Peacock and after

By the second half of the 1980s concern was growing amongst
supporters and even critics of British Broadcasting at the range and
intensity of the assault from government and private enterprise.
They took some comfort from the fact that the report of the Peacock
Committee failed to give the supporters of deregulation all they
wanted. It was a 'hold your horses' report. It disappointed the
government by rejecting advertising on the BBC 'while the present
organisation and regulation of broadcasting remains in business'. Its
immediate introduction would drive the BBC into a ratings war with
ITV and, by putting financial pressure on the ITV companies, undermine the regulatory power of the IBA, with deleterious consequences for consumer choice and programme quality. But the
present organisation and regulation of broadcasting should not
remain in business for much longer. There should be, Peacock
urged, a planned and phased move 'towards a sophisticated market
system based on consumer sovereignty. That is a system which
recognises that viewers and listeners are the best judges of their own
interests which they can best satisfy if they have an option of purchasing the broadcasting services they require from as many alternative sources of supply as possible.' But a move towards the market
should be limited because 'There will always be a need to
supplement the direct consumer market by public finance for programmes of a public service kind . . . supported by people in their
capacity as citizens and voters but unlikely to be commercially self-
supporting in the view of broadcasting entreprenuers.' There should
be a greater injection of market forces into the broadcasting system
but that injection should be policed so that the public service philosophy was complemented and not eroded. Peacock represented a
compromise which specifically rejected hard right comparisons with
the press: '. . . there is a pervasive abuse of market power within the
publishing and printing markets'.

Nonetheless, the moves towards the market that the report
recommended were real and important ones. In order to encourage
pay TV and a greater use of cable and satellite, Peacock prescribed
that all new sets should be fitted with peritelevision sockets and
associated equipment interfacing with decoders to pick up encrypted
signals. All restrictions on 'pay per channel' and 'pay per programme' should be lifted, although Peacock favoured the former
system. Franchise contracts for ITV operations should in future be

put out to competitive tender and, if the IBA did not accept the highest bid, it should have to explain why. Franchises should be awarded on a rolling review basis with a formal annual review of performances by the IBA and consideration should be given to extending franchise periods to ten years. Channel 4 should be allowed to sell its own advertising time rather than being funded by the ITV companies. DBS franchises should also be put out to competitive tender.

The BBC licence fee, Peacock suggested, should in future be pegged to the annual rate of inflation and the corporation should collect the fee itself. Both the BBC and ITV should be required over a ten-year period to increase to 40% the proportion of programmes made for them by independent producers. British Telecom and Mercury, Peacock felt, should be allowed to deliver television programmes, the restriction of cable franchises to EEC companies should be lifted and non-occupied time on BBC and ITV wavelengths should be sold off to independent broadcasters. Finally, as regulation was gradually phased out, general legislation on obscenity, defamation and related areas should be widened to cover broadcasting.

Opinions on Peacock and the degree to which implementation of its recommendations would or would not leave broadcasting in a public service mould varied. The government's first response was to leave the report to gather dust. It then began to look at the proposals piecemeal. The recommendation on indexing the licence fee was accepted in 1987, despite the critics' contention that this would reduce the BBC's income and impair its efficiency as television costs rise faster than the general rate of inflation. The government also informed the BBC and ITV that in future 25% of its programming should come from independents – critics saw this as a Trojan horse for privatisation. Small independents often applied poor working conditions and were vulnerable to takeovers from big companies. The government was also torn two ways by Peacock's proposal that broadcasters should be as free as publishers, subject only to the general law of the land. In the end its authoritarianism won out over the libertarian side of its philosophy. In 1988 the establishment of a Broadcasting Standards Council, chaired by Sir William Rees-Mogg, with powers to preview and vet programmes was announced. This was again loudly condemned by critics as taking the already pervasive if *ad hoc* tendency towards censorship a stage further. The

government was seen as divided into two camps regarding broadcasting reform. The deregulators, centred on the market-minded
Department of Trade and Industry, wanted to trust big business and
make a bonfire of controls. The authoritarian group, centred on the
Home Office, and represented by the Standards Council innovation,
were worried as to the impact of market liberalisation on sex and
violence on television and on programme quality. Would television
end up looking like the *Sun?*

The White Paper: Broadcasting in the 90s: competition, choice and quality

To hammer out future strategy and reconcile differences, a cabinet
sub-committee, chaired by Mrs Thatcher, who took a hawkish line on
deregulation and involving Lord Young from the DTI, Douglas
Hurd from the Home Office, and Nigel Lawson, giving the Treasury's viewpoint, met through 1987 and early 1988. Key issues were
progressed at the weekend 'Silchester summer seminar' where Hurd
and Lord Young, counselled by Mrs Thatcher's adviser Brian
Griffiths and free-market enthusiasts such as P&O chair, Geoffrey
Sterling, attempted to meld their differing emphases. The resultant
White Paper, unveiled in late 1988, contained a package of measures
which represented a compromise between the DTI's thrusting
market line and the Home Office's rearguard action.

ITV was in the firing line. The IBA would be replaced by a new
Independent Television Commission. It would supervise all independent television services, terrestial and satellite, and take over the
work of the Cable Authority. It would, however, apply 'lighter, more
objective programme requirements'. The Broadcasting Standards
Council was also earmarked for an important regulatory role.
Henceforth, ITV franchises – to be awarded for ten years – would be
knocked down to the highest bidder and the existing restrictions on
stock-exchange takeovers of successful companies would be relaxed.
However, bidders would still have to clear a quality standards hurdle
prior to being cleared by the ITC for competitive bidding. There
would also be ill-defined controls to avoid undue concentration of
ownership. ITV would be renamed Channel 3. Channel 4 would
retain its existing distinctive remit but would be separated from the
ITV system, with its advertising sold separately and Channel 5,
financed by advertising, would come on stream in 1993. The possibility of a sixth channel would be examined. With British Satellite

Broadcasting launching three DBS channels in 1989, the two remaining DBS channels should be sold off in the same year. There would be a new enabling framework for local services, utilising both cable and microwave, to provide over thirty channels using local high-frequency transmitters.

An important proposal, buried in the White Paper, suggested that future franchise holders would have to pay a levy based on advertising revenue throughout the period of the franchise, instead of as now, a levy on profits which creates an incentive to reinvest profits in quality programmes, rather than handing the money over to the government. The BBC did not escape unscathed. The licence-free system would continue and until 1991 would be linked to the Retail Price Index. Thereafter it would be linked to the Index, minus an unspecified percentage. One of the BBC's night-time frequencies would be transferred to the ITC and the Corporation would only retain the second night-time channel if it was utilised to launch a subscription service – charging viewers to watch its programmes. A greater use of subscription television was envisaged as a means of minimising reliance on the licence-fee system. The White paper was seen by Mr Hurd as nudging the BBC in the direction of direct Charges and away from the licence fee. Discussions would be held with both BBC and ITV on the privatisation of broadcasting transmission and a further theme of the White Paper was the need to inject a greater element of independent contracting into programme production.

The White Paper, Mr Hurd declared, promised 'a substantial liberalisation . . . and greater reliance on the viewer, rather than the regulator to sustain range and quality'. Yet essential safeguards would, he claimed, be maintained. The White Paper would be the forerunner of legislation – a new Broadcasting Act would reach the statute book in 1990 – and would increase standards, choice and popularity. The White Paper was condemned by the Labour Party as 'a giant retreat from the concept of public service broadcasting. Its result will be less diversity and lower standards.' The Democrats felt that it would result in 'inferior programming and a narrowing of choice'.

Contemporary perspectives on television

Different positions on the future of television share certain common orientations and at times overlap and shade into each other. But they also disclose internal conflicts and different emphases. It is, however, possible to outline three main perspectives, although more refined analysis would produce a more complex typology.

Traditional – pluralist
In this view there have to be limits on the autonomy of the broadcasting media. Internal violence and external subversion requires that a degree of control and self-censorship should be exercised. Exactly *what* degree depends on the circumstances, but the national interest in security must always be carefully weighed against the public's interest in having sufficient information to make educated judgements as citizens of a democracy. Television in Britain possesses a large degree of freedom and independence from government although we must be vigilant over recent governmental incursions. Television has, on the whole, acted as a responsible trustee for the national interest. At times this involves the IBA and BBC accepting government demands and at other times rejecting them. In the long run the arm's-length bodies have taken a balanced approach and their evenhandedness with government has been reflected in the service they have provided to the public. British television has provided access for the views of a wide range of competing opinions including significant minority views, whilst justifiably limiting access to those who wish to violently undermine or overthrow the social order. It has strengthened our sense of national community and played at least a small role in educating aware and responsible citizens. Because it is publicly-owned or controlled, television in the UK has contained commercialism and its attendant dangers – low standards, bland conformity and crippling conservatism. It has provided a varied balanced diet of programmes. In this lies the justification for the present system of regulation and the mixed system of financing. Its virtues are such that Britain leads the world, as demonstrated by a glance at the television screens in other countries, the piles of prizes British-made programmes garner annually in international competition and the fact that the daily cost of the licence fee is, at 16p, cheaper than buying the *Sun*.

We would be foolish to risk all this by handing our airwaves over to the profiteers. The analogy the supporters of deregulation draw with newspapers is a false one. Television is a far more intrusive and powerful medium than newsprint and television channels, despite the potential for expansion new technology holds, will remain in relatively limited supply. And look at the recent concentration of ownership and decline of standards in the press. It is difficult to think of *less* suitable bodies than the multinational conglomerates, led by the Murdochs and Maxwells, to entrust with our high-quality television inheritance.

High-quality is, of course, associated with high-cost programming and regulation. With a balanced duopoly and guaranteed large audiences the existing system generates the revenue to make good programmes. Current affairs programmes or quality drama costs ten times as much to make as game shows or soaps. The new satellite companies will spend less on programmes than BBC and ITV. They will not have the same obligations to produce quality programmes and restrict imports. Pressed by the need to attract advertising and the advertiser's demands for big audiences, they will race down-market. The audience will be split and the existing channels will consequently lose revenues and be pushed into competition with the new stations for ratings. ITV, in particular, will be pressurised by the new competition and by its need for advertising into removing quality and minority programmes from prime-time slots. The danger then is that low quality and smaller audiences on the established channels will legitimate a further drive by private enterprise for deregulation of television. More will mean worse, and if things go the way the deregulators want them to go, we will be in for a television diet of tabloid news, yuppie hedonism, repeats and soft porn.

Modern market
From this perspective the traditionalists are viewed as elitist and paternalist. It is difficult to understand how they can have the arrogance to try to dictate what other people can and cannot watch on television. A minority should not have the rights the existing system gives them to mould others' lives in their own image. The majority must have their freedom to choose restored and there is little to gainsay the view that they will exercise it judiciously, once 'the great and the good' are put out to pasture. Britain is not the USA, Italy or Japan. The British tradition is different and the British viewer is more discerning. With deregulation people will watch more selectively. Deregulation *will* produce more bad programmes but it will also produce more good programmes. It will create a market where television *Guardian*s and *Independent*s flourish as well as

television *Sun*s and *Star*s. Because, in the end, broadcasting is no different from any other form of publishing. The idea that advertisers are the ogres who will debase standards and cut out minority programmes is pure fantasy. Advertisers do not simply want to get their hands on *big* audiences. They want to reach a *range* of different groups with different needs for different products. Quality minority programmes will, therefore, still be produced.

There will be less censorship as government will have less control and the broadcasters will be less vulnerable to financial pressure from the state. The IBA has suffered less interference than the BBC because it has more control over its own revenues and deregulation will represent a further step forward. When 'the great and the good' talk about standards they are really talking about censorship in the broad sense of the term – stopping people watching what they want. The Broadcasting Standards Council is a questionable innovation in this perspective because broadcasting should simply be governed, like the press, by the ordinary law of the land. Finally, many of the ills of broadcasting have stemmed from the insulated duopoly enjoyed by the BBC and ITV. Greedy trade unionists have conspired with flabby managements to jack up wages and perks, and hence production costs, to unbelievable levels. The broadcasting media have also provided a safe resting place for radicals whose views are out of joint with the bracing 1980s. The move towards a new market, facilitated by the government's reference of the broadcasting unions' restrictive practices to the Monopolies Commission, will create a new access for hitherto excluded groups and will have a salutary impact on dead wood, drones and dissidents. A weakening of union power will also mean a chaper service for the consumer.

Radical–Marxist
This perspective covers a variety of positions but there is general agreement that the traditional–liberal perspective gets it wrong because it overestimates the degree of independence from the state that broadcasting has enjoyed. The legislation gives the government clear powers, if it appears 'necessary' or 'expedient', to *require* the BBC or IBA to broadcast any item or to *prevent* them from broadcasting any item. The structure of the BBC and ITV is elitist and undemocratic. Its controllers are carefully vetted and are drawn from the upper classes. Of the eighty-five governors in the BBC's first fifty-years, fifty-six had a university education, forty went to

Oxbridge and twenty to Eton, Harrow or Winchester. Its producers internalise what is or is not acceptable in programme-making, what will or will not reach the screen, what will and will not help them up the organisational ladder. Balance operates within a restricted range of viewpoints roughly from right-wing Conservative to right-wing Labour. This is clearly illustrated by the growing censorship of the Irish issue where the government is preventing the people understanding the real roots of the conflict by censoring one side's point of view. Television is acquiescing in the elimination of the difficult questions and the concealment of the inconvenient facts. And if the broadcasters do not play the game then the job Mrs Thatcher has done on the BBC illustrates how they can be forced into line. Overall, broadcasting reflects and reinforces existing power structures and critical messages partake of mild reformist dissent rather than any substantial challenge to the status quo. The compromise the traditionalists defend was an inadequate one. The views of oppressed groups were inadequately attended to, the views of the powerful were dominant. Women, blacks and trade unionists had far less access to broadcasting than businessmen, mainstream politicians or press magnates. The system urgently required liberalisation by, for example, electing the IBA and BBC governors and limiting the trivialisation of important issues which brainwashed viewers and sitcoms, soaps and talk shows which acted as 'bread and circuses' to divert them from more important political questions.

But despite its limitations, the traditional system *does* require defence against the new marketeers. Once deregulation gets going – the Broadcasting Act is just a start – its momentum will become unstoppable. In the words of an American pundit, the collapse in standards will be so great that we will recall Benny Hill as a major intellectual! If there are no restrictions on companies which are awarded franchises being gobbled up by other companies there can be no quality control. The fragmentation of the national audience will affect political coverage and relegate serious political analysis – increasingly limited to BBC 2 and Channel 4 – even further – to the detriment of our already inadequate political education. In one way trivialisation will operate as censorship. Programmes like *Death on The Rock* or *Real Lives* are unlikely to be made, or be seen if they do. In another way the Broadcasting Standards Council is the foot in the door for more drastic formal controls. The new satellite and cable channels will have no obligation to be impartial. They will not be accountable to Parliament. We are likely to end up with a broadcasting system as overwhelmingly politically conservative as our national press. The idea that advertisers will protect minorities is laughable. It will protect *rich* minorities. The pressure for deregulation has nothing to do with more choice or more quality. It has everything to do with more profits. That is why the big multinational conglomerates who control the print media in the UK and broadcasting abroad are trying to bust open our present system. And all this is happening despite any persuasive evidence which demonstrates that anywhere near a majority of viewers are pressing for this kind of change.

Television's big bang
In the immediate future there is a strong likelihood that ITV as presently constituted will be broken up and its basis as a public service weakened. The existing companies will find it difficult to compete with the giant multinational predators who will enter the new franchise auctions and whose essential motivation will be profit, not quality. The BBC licence fee, if present tendencies continue, will be gradually replaced by direct payments by the viewers. The DTI and the marketeers have won out over the Home Office and the regulators as architects of the new deal. Privatisation has replaced quality control as the major imperative of government policy. But the market revolution in television is likely to develop in a more gradual fashion than some critics believe and its impact is likely to be more limited. The growth of cable TV has been undramatic and seven out of ten Britons say they would not be prepared to pay any extra money to receive satellite teleivision channels. Compare this with the USA, where cable reaches 50% of the TV market. The spread of the video recorder is also a countervailing factor and the new Broadcasting Act involves cautious deregulation rather than a bonfire of controls. Nonetheless, the move towards a greater role for market forces appears irresistible and if government fails to use its regulatory powers to maintain standards and guarantee real choice the important achievement that British Broadcasting, for all its failings represents, could be at risk. At the moment the betting is that the kind of changes proposed will encourage change for the worst. Television can enrich or impoverish the quality of our lives. That is why the debate about its future is so important for us all.

Reading

M. Cockerell, *Live From Number 10: The inside story of Prime Ministers and Television*, Faber & Faber, 1988.

J. Curran & J. Seaton, *Power without Responsibility: The Press and Broadcasting in Britain*, Routledge, 1988.

Glasgow University Media Group, *Bad News*, Routledge, 1976.

Glasgow University Media Group, *More Bad News*, Routledge, 1980.

M. Harrison, *T.V. News: Whose Bias?*, Policy Journals, 1985.

A. Milne, *DG: The Memoirs of A British Broadcaster*, Hodder & Stoughton, 1988.

T. O'Malley, *Switching Channels: The Debate over the Future of Broadcasting*, Campaign For Press and Broadcasting Freedom, 1988.

Adam Smith Institute, *Omega Report: Communications*, Adam Smith Institute 1984.

ECONOMIC ISSUES

8 *Geoffrey Lee*

Privatisation

This chapter considers the political and economic arguments for and against privatisation. It begins with an explanation of the terminology and a list of past, present and future candidates for transfer of economic organisations from the public (government-owned) to the private sector.

Terminology

'Privatisation' is used to cover several political initiatives.

(a) Denationalisation – this term was employed before 'privatisation' came into fashion. While some industries, such as British Rail and British Leyland, could be returned whence they came, most concerns in this process were never in the private sector.

(b) Sale of 100% of the shares of a newly-created (but still publicly-owned) company; either on the stock market, e.g. Amersham International, Enterprise Oil and British Gas, or to management and work-force, e.g. the National Freight Corporation, Leyland Bus and Unipart.

(c) Issue of 51%, i.e. a majority of shares in a newly-created public company, e.g. British Aerospace, Britoil and British Telecom.

(d) Issues of 49%, i.e. a minority of a public company's share, e.g. Associated British Ports.

(e) Placement of shares with investors, e.g. 24% of British Sugar, and Rover with British Aerospace by waiting for a suitable bidder and arranging transfer.

(f) Hiving off and outright sale of profitable concerns – Sealink, Travellers Fare and hotels (from BR), Jaguar (from BL), warship yards (from British Shipbuilders).

(g) Sale of shares and removal of custodianship/aid, e.g. through the National Enterprise Board (Ferranti, ICL).

(h) Joint ventures with the private sector – Hoverlloyd and BR hovercrafts, Allied Steel and Wire (British Steel and GKN).

(j) Permitting competition in place of former monopoly – Mercury in telecommunications (25% government-owned), private generation and sale of electricity, and coach companies.

(k) Permitting and stimulating private contractors to tender for public services. Southend and Wandsworth Councils led the way on refuse collection. By September 1984 all but thirty-five of the 223 district health authorities had complied with the circulars requiring them to put catering, cleaning and laundry out to tender.

(l) Introduction of private finance into large projects, e.g. road-building (Civil Engineering Economic Development Council), and the December 1987 Eurotunnel share issue.

Some of the categories above were interlinked: often the sale of a majority of shares was the first stage in selling off the whole; private-sector takeovers occurred as worker–management buy-outs failed (BR hotels) and the government directed who could and could not own industries (RTZ's share of Enterprise Oil, and that Thorn-EMI and not AT&T should buy Inmos).

Main sales to date

1979/80	*£ million*
BP (5%)	276
ICL (25%)	37
Suez Finance Co.	57
1980/81	
Ferranti (50%)	55
Fairey (100%)	22
British Aerospace (51%)	195
Automation & Technical Services, etc.	91
Prestcold (100%)	9
Motorway service stations (to THF)	28

1981/82
British Sugar (24%)   44
Cable & Wireless (50%)   182
Amersham International (100%)   64
National Freight Corporation (100%)   5

1982/83
Britoil (51%)   225
Associated British Ports (49%)   46
British Transport Hotels (100%)   40
International Aeradio   60

1983/84
Britoil   293
BP (7%)   565
Cable & Wireless (25%)   260

1984/85
J. H. Sankey   12
Scott Lithgow   12
Lye Tinplate   16
Enterprise Oil (100%)   392
Wytch Farm Oil (50%)   215
Associated British Ports (48.5%)   51
Inmos   95
Jaguar Cars   295
Sealink   66
British Telecom (51%)   3,700

1985/86
Britoil (48.8%)   450
RO Factory, Leeds   11
Hall Russel shipyard   —
Cable & Wireless (22·7%)   558
Trustee Savings Bank   1,000
Warshipbuilding yards
     (Vickers, Yarrow, Swan, Hunter, Vosper)   140
British Aerospace (48.4%)   400

1986/87

National Bus Company	250
BA Helicopters	13.5
Unipart	52
Leyland Bus	4
Royal Ordnance	190
Leyland Trucks (40% holding new venture with DAF)	—
DAB	7
Istel	26
British Gas	7,720
British Airways	900
British Technology Group (ex NEB)	—

1987/88

Rolls-Royce	1,080
British Airports Authority	1,275
BP (31.7%)	7,240
Dockyard management	—
Ship repair yards	20

1988/89

Travellers Fare (from BR to management)	20.6
Govan Shipyard (to Norwegians)	—
Rover Group (to BAe)	150
Short Bros (offers invited July 1988)	
Professional and Executive Recruitment (first civil service activity to be privatised)	
British steel	2,500
Girobank (from Post Office)	300
Water authorities	5,000
Total	
	36,315 million

Planned, under consideration or being advocated
British Telecom (49% – £7 billion)
British Coal (pledge to Tory conference, October 1988)
Land Registry
NHS hospitals opting out (White Paper January 1989)
Nature reserves
Parts of prison service (remand centres early 1989)

100 Government agencies over 3 years (report July 1988)
Management of Civil Service
Civil weddings (report December 1988)
Tote (study September 1988)
Tourist industry funding (study July 1988)
Property Services Agency (by 1993)
British Rail
Roads (11 toll projects under consideration)
Post Office (letter monopoly retained after investigation and strike in 1988, but 1,500 offices downgraded to private sub-post offices)
British Nuclear Fuels
London Transport
Civil Aviation Authority
Crown Suppliers (from PSA)
Electricity industry
  (i) Area boards £5–6 billion
  (ii) National power (70% of CEGB) £10–12 billion
  (iii) Power generation (30% of CEG B) £4–5 billion
  All in 1990 = total £20 billion

In addition to any further sales, more NHS and local government services would be contracted-out. Plans were implemented to commercialise hospitals with restaurants, private health-screening and shops, and in 1986 the government speeded up tendering of cleaning, laundry and catering services to save more than the current £40 million – even if that meant using existing staff rather than improved methods. Social service departments were to make more use of voluntary agencies and charities and the DHSS sold twenty centres for homeless people. In July 1986 the DOE revived its plan to compel tendering for refuse collection, school meals, vehicle fleet maintenance and street cleansing. New town asset sales had brought £700 million by 1987 with £1 billion more to sell, and councils were even thinking of selling 480 playing fields to raise money. The radical right were reported in March 1986 to have proposed tendering for packages of schools, urban and rural.

Meanwhile central government continued to hive off or contract out – Treasury computer operations, and army pay corps, dental and medical services (the last group being part of a reorganisation to free 4,000 soldiers for front-line duty). The Cabinet Office report of July 1988 revealed that 100 agencies were to be hived off – a quarter of the civil service by the next election, and 75% of it within a decade.

Government could more easily press for privatisation leading to competition in local authorities, rather than in its own bureaucracy – hence provincial airports come into focus, with Luton likely to be sold first in 1989 for £30 million.

The impetus for privatisation

The arguments for nationalisation had consisted of an intermeshed set of factors: economic ones such as economies of scale, co-ordinated investment and the public control of monopoly power; political–economic impulses to preserve key industries such as Rolls-Royce and British Leyland; socio-political reasons such as the provision of uniform services and safeguarding regional economic development; and political determination to ensure the public ownership of key industries.

A similar mixture is to be found in the rationale for privatisation.

Political

(a) *Ideological underpinning* It has long been a central tenet of Conservative political philosophy that the role of the state should be minimised, and the government which came into office in 1979 was clearly committed to rolling back the frontiers. In particular there was little liking for the nationalised industries; the eighteen largest employed 1.6 million workers, in protected or monopoly markets, with strong unionised work-forces, and large debts. These 'dinosaurs' were said to increase the scale of public borrowing, increase taxation and cause unemployment. In the House of Lords Lord Beswick noted the 'sick language' used by the Prime Minister and her colleagues in describing them as 'horrific, poisonous, debilitating, voracious and a haemorrhage' (*Hansard*, 4 February 1981).

(b) *Policy formulation* Yet while the political inclination may have been there, no radical programme of privatisation existed. In April 1977 John Biffen had called for the introduction of some private-sector resources into nationalised industries but the Conservative policy study group had reported in 1978 that denationalisation 'must be pursued cautiously and flexibly, recognising that major changes may well be out of the question in some industries' (*Sunday Times*, 9 October 1983). The Conservatives were slow to reject completely the thirty-year Butskellite agreement on the boundaries of the public sector. For their 1979 manifesto they adhered to the so-called 'BP solution' of selling just under a half-share in a few industries. Intellectual respectability and guidance began to be added – from the Institute of Economic Affairs, the Centre for Policy Studies, the Adam Smith Institute and Professors Beesley and Littlechild.

When the government had to channel hundreds of millions of pounds into loss-making industries such as British Steel and British Shipbuilders, and as some of their manifesto sales were thwarted by economic and technical problems, it seemed the process would falter. An article, 'Whatever happened to the great sell-off?', in the *Observer* concluded of privatisation, 'The word hasn't yet made its way into any dictionary. Whether it will now do so is increasingly doubtful' (23 November 1980).

(c) *Policy commitment* A radical change in policy was signalled, however, by Sir Geoffrey Howe in 1981 with the declaration that the postal services, British Telecom, BNOC and even gas and electricity were under consideration. Sir Keith Joseph has stated that in so attempting to deal with the problem and clear their desks, privatisation was a product of government, not opposition. It was very much in keeping with 'the resolute approach'. The 1983 manifesto promised to continue the process, and only as an afterthought were nationalised industries unsuitable for privatisation mentioned. It was said that ministers were competing to bring industries to market as proof of their political virility. Having sold off assets worth £3·6 billion since 1979, the Cabinet 'E' committee agreed to sell a further £10 billion over five years – it was clear that privatisation had become a central and distinguishing policy of the Thatcher government. Mr John Moore, Financial Secretary in the Treasury and in reality the minister for privatisation, attacked the failure of the concept of public corporations and warned that 'no state monopoly is sacrosanct' (*Financial Times*, 2 November 1983). By 1983/84 the scale of the shift in the debate was astonishing – groups were then calling for the privatisation of the railways, coal, gas, electricity, the universities, the BBC and more of the NHS. In response to the question what would be left at the end of a third Thatcher government, Mr Moore was said to have replied, 'the Treasury'. Stockbrokers Grievson Grant identified a package of £28.5 billion assets in 1984 and went on to suggest another available £55 billion which the government could sell.

The proof of ideological commitment is the willingness to privatise for nil gain; the introduction of private management into the two royal dockyards would have cost as much as it would save over 3½ years and selling Rolls Royce would involve writing off debts of £372 million, injecting another £100 million and yet still giving state support. The latter has the symbolic political attraction of reversing the Heath Government's 1971 'lame-duck' takeover.

(d) *Public opinion* Bolstering the government's case is a public opinion far from hostile to privatisation. A MORI poll in 1983 showed 39% favouring privatisation against 21% wanting more nationalisation (*Sunday Times*, 9 October 1983). £40 billion had been spent on nationalisation and write-offs since the war, but it has shown to be a vote-loser. An ORC poll in 1978 showed that 71% of respondents (against 19%) thought it to have failed, and 78% (against 13%) believed Labour should abandon the policy (*Times*, 10 July 1978). And in times of high unemployment, the unions' defence of jobs and index-linked pensions was muted.

(e) *A share-owning democracy* Just as the Conservatives have sought to strengthen property-owning democracy (e.g. by council house sales), fostering a share-owning democracy is a political ambition. Share-ownership in Britain has been rising – trebling from 1979 to reach eight million small shareholders in 1979 (six million of those holding privatised shares. By contrast, in the USA 42·5 million citizens own shares, with most Western countries ahead of the UK. The growth in Britain has been replicated in Europe.

Small investors have been favoured in sales such as British Aerospace – of the 158,000 initial investors, 150,000 held less than 1,000 shares. In the Britoil sale small investors were offered a loyalty bonus whereby after three years they would receive a free share for every ten held.

The major effect came with the sale of British Telecom when a £7·6 million advertising campaign was launched by the government in the press and on television to persuade people to buy shares and so share in BT's future. The simplicity of the procedures was stressed, booklets on the city and shares and investment were provided, and incentives were offered in the form of £18 vouchers to offset rental payments and a 1 for 10 scrip issues. Application forms could be taken to banks and post offices. In offering free shares and other incentives to BT employees the government was dealing with nearly ¼ million potential investors. The floatation of BT in November 1984 was hailed as a triumph for the government as two million people bought shares, many for the first time (small investors being favoured in the allocation of shares). Of BT's 233,000 employees, 96% ignored union advice and applied for free shares. Its Annual General Meeting is a twice-daily roadshow in five centres, preceded by 60,000 telephone calls and replies to 10,000 letters after a mailing of 1·5 million annual reports. The sale of British Gas cost £20 million in advertising (twice BT's) to reach small shareholders – the 'tell Sid about it' campaign was known to 90% of the population and spawned jokes and cartoons galore.

(f) *Workers as shareholders*   The idea of workers becoming share-holders in their own company is not new – Sir Alfred Mond, the founder of ICI, advocated this. Unlike co-operatives, worker shareholding leaves control undisturbed and has been advocated as the answer to socialism, in making workers 'capitalists'.

During the process of privatisation, worker shareholding has obvious attractions – it weakens opposition, particularly if free shares are offered, and may impede renationalisation later. In the longer term, it may motivate staff and increase productivity – Keith Stuart, Chief Executive of Association British Ports, was convinced that staff awareness of the business had increased since workers had taken 8% of the shareholding. Between 1979 and 1986 some 600,000 workers were transferred from the public to the private sector, over half had become shareholders and the proportion of state industry had fallen by 40% from 10·5% to 4·2% in 1988. Besides weakening the trade unions, it has been argued that worker shareholding, in producing lower wage claims, will assist the economy. In November 1983 British Airways, as preparation for its privatisation, offered its 36,000 workers low wage rises for two years in return for a profit-sharing bonus plan, with money held in trust for share purchase. The frequently cited example of worker shareholding success is the National Freight Corporation, where management took the initiative in 1981 and organised the biggest buyout in British industry. Eighty-two per cent of the company is now owned by employees, families and pensioners. When the company was floated on the stock exchange in February 1989 the average £600 investment at the time of privatisation was worth £60,000.

Workers in the six unions of the Yorkshire Rider bus company pushed for employee share ownership in 1988 and the electricity privatisation split the unions – while the NUM and NUR opposed the sale, the eight unions most closely involved pressed for the best ownership deal for their members and consulted City experts.

The management of the Vickers and Cammell Laird warship yards worked to persuade employees and local residents to invest to the extent that 80% of the work-force subscribed, with the whole over-subscribed twice.

Profit-sharing schemes have been encouraged by the 1978 and 1980 Finance Acts which conferred tax benefits on employees and companies. Nigel Lawson's 'Popular Capitalism' Budget of 1986 was well received by 58% of people – it offered tax incentives to buy shares, employee share schemes (7% of workers now covered), and outlined a profit-sharing plan that would link 20% of wages to those profits.

A survey of firms involved with share ownership reported that all of them had experienced a significant improvement in industrial relations (P. Burns, *Industrial Relations Review*, November 1988).

(g) *Public borrowing*   Between 1979 and 1988 privatisation revenue totalled £17 billion and the sale of council houses £5.5 billion. These sales of assets reduce the Public Sector Borrowing Requirement (PSBR – or the amount government has to borrow each year to balance income with expenditure). Additional expenditure is therefore possible by allowing a higher PSBR when these sales are added. In 1983/84 the asset sales brought £3·1 billion which was 30% over the intended PSBR target of £10 billion. For 1985–86, if the proposed sales were subtracted, the PSBR of £7 billion or 2% of GDP would have to be halved. Privatisation thus enables the government to cling to the monetarist claims of expenditure control and sound finance, while continuing to spend with a large deficit – keeping pressure off ministers.

By 1986 the central issue was whether the Chancellor could generate enough revenue for tax cuts and/or public spending to ensure a suitable approach to the election. Though the government minimised the fact, the £4·5 billion a year in 1986–88 from asset sales was important, going into the 1987 election. Overshooting its 1987–88 target of £5 billion by £1¾ billion began to be embarrassing for the Treasury, as it encouraged spending departments.

(h) *Civil service interference*   Nationalised industries have always had to submit their investment and borrowing plans to the Treasury and report to their 'sponsoring ministry'. But beyond the formal controls there have been the 'lunchtime directives' to chairmen and informal pressures – to set an example on pricing, wage settlements and to favour British manufacturers, e.g. or aircraft or computers. The chief executive of National Freight described privatisation as 'breaking out of a strait-jacket' and the chairman of Cable and Wireless of an end to the 'psychology of restraint' – C&W had seen the 'dead hand' of the Tresury delay its plans and veto a vital project. The idea of being free to make commercial decisions and being rid of constant meetings with officials has proved attractive to corporation boards, and serves the government's purpose of reducing the role and size of the 'bureaucracy'.

Commercial

(j) *Expansion*   In freeing the corporations the government believes they will be able to invest more, expand and meet international competition.

In 1981 BT lost customers as it raised prices to keep its £1 billion self-provided investment going. The Treasury had withdrawn the chance of raising a £360 million bond and BT had to be helped twice by raising its borrowing powers. Privatisation is intended to avoid this constraint and enable BT to compete with the privately-owned communications company, Mercury, and its backer Cable and Wireless (C&W), Standard Telephones and Cables and the formerly state-assisted ICL and with international competition. Once privatised, BT began to expand overseas, particularly in North America, through joint ventures (DuPont and McCaw cellphones) and takeovers (Mitel, CTG and Dialcom). Similarly, British Gas intended to re-enter the spheres of oil exploration and production, and begin joint ventures, especially in the USA.

Similarly, the government believes it has no place in the dynamic, competitive environment of oil exploration and production – so hiving off Britoil from the regulatory functions of the British National Oil Corporation (BNOC). In August 1984 Jaguar Cars, hived off from BL, announced plans to expand production by 4,000 cars a year and employ 530 extra workers, to meet demand and German competition. Here was evidence, claimed government supporters, that privatisation works.

(k) *Efficiency* Nationalised industries' accounts have been poor measures of their performance, for in addition to problems of inflation and depreciation, governments have altered prices or levied profits. Supporters contended that the threat of privatisation so concentrates the mind that efficiency improves dramatically. British Steel's productivity rose 60% over the ten years to privatisation in 1988 while its work-force was cut by 70% – from a loss of £1·7 billion in 1979 to a profit of £500 million.

Rover's newest plants approach Japanese standards, and government spokesmen commented favourably as BT created and then reorganised its divisions, introduced profit centres, revolutionised its accountancy away from monopoly capitalisation, and began to install two digital exchanges a day and lay 370,000 miles of high-quality optical fibre cable, including a network in the City. Mercury launched a 12–25% cheaper service for some phone calls, and both they and BT lost their exclusive rights to computer communication by phone network. Nor has OFTEL taken a low profile, as many have predicted, as it stopped BT linking with IBM, obtained interconnect terms favourable to Mercury, ended the pay-phone monopoly in 1988, imposed new metering standards on BT and re-negotiated the tariff/pricing structure in the customers' interest – from RPI minus 3% to 4·5%. In the summer of 1987 BT came under immense pressure, following an engineers' strike in February and a National Consumer Council report, naming it the worst public service. By reallocation of resources and new standards, pay-phone availability rose from 75% to 92%, new business lines installed in six days rose from 28% to 60%; faults cleared in two days rose from 74% to 90%. It accepted that compensation should be paid for delays in repairs and installation.

(l) *Customer satisfaction* By increasing efficiency and introducing new services the customer benefits: from British Rail's special offers; from BT's struggle to modernise and its 2½-year price freeze on main services to March 1989; from lower rates bills where refuse services have been privatised; from a choice of airline services on UK routes; and in towns like Hereford, where competition on bus services was introduced – more frequent services and lower fares.

The promotion of efficiency and removal of 'take it or leave it' attitudes became central to the advocacy of privatisation.

The government could also claim to have taken steps to safeguard the public. In its Gas Bill it strengthened safety provisions – requiring a response to leaks within twelve hours (half the time required before) the BGC will be responsible for leaks on the customer side. For water privatisation, the second proposal in 1988 contained provision for a National Rivers Authority to take over regulation, pollution control, fisheries and care of the environment. This separation of paocher and gamekeeper had not been in the 1987 proposals and had been opposed by the chairmen of the water authorities, the latter being among the main polluters with sewage. Committed to tough EEC standards and 'green policies', the government began to advocate the sell-off as an expensive but long overdue clean-up – needing £3.5 billion for beaches, drinking water and sewage works.

The government learned from the BT and Gas experiences – not merely did it break up the electricity industry, but it included a money-back scheme for bad service from the start.

The case against privatisation

General
(a) *Confused objectives*   it was unlikely that the factors described above would weave together into a coherent strategy. The main inconsistency has proved to be between the ideological drive for liberalisation and competition and the Treasury-led demand for maximum sales revenue.

This was exposed most clearly in the privatisation of British Telecom and British Gas (BGC), monopolies capable of generating annual profits in excess of £1 billion. Having decided against breaking up BT on either a regional or product basis so as to maximimise income upon flotation and create an international 'heavy weight', the government had to institute a regulatory quango in the form of the Office of Telecommunications (OFTEL). Instead of creating bureaucratic controls which critics doubted would be effective, many Conservatives demanded competition. In this respect ministers were also faulted for safeguarding the fledgling Mercury at the expense of would-be leasers and resellers of BT lines.

When the BGC's oil assets were sold off as Enterprise Oil and only one-sixth of the shares were wanted by ordinary investors, the government were placed in the embarrassing position of blocking Rio Tinto Zinc's bid for 49%. While this was consistent with aims of promoting competition (RTZ has oil interests) and safeguarding small investors in an independent company, it alienated free-market Conservatives and the City. The gas and electricity industries presented a similar dilemma – whether to break the production and distribution monopolies radically or simply sell the shares and apply regulation. The industrial customers, who provided 30% of British Gas's income, were so angry at the differential pricing that they won a verdict against the privatised giant from the Monopolies and Mergers Commission in October 1988. The users were soon lobbying to break its monopoly. Learning from such experiences, electricity was split up on the generating side as well as from the distributors. But again free-market principles were shelved to safeguard nuclear power – making the boards buy up to 20% of power from non-fossil fuel. And a special share was inserted into water privatisation to stop merger or takeover for five years.

The Civil Aviation Authority's recommendation in 1984 that over thirty major routes be taken from British Airways and given to competitors produced uproar. BA hotly opposed the plan as producing no competition or benefit to the customer, and retarding privatisation. In becoming efficient for flotation BA had become more of a threat to competitors. Privatised, it would start to remove them.

When privatising Jaguar the government were accused by the all-party trade and industry committee of rendering BL and its privatisation less viable, and the government had to turn down a management–worker buyout of some of BR's hotels in order to try for a better price. A bitter dispute occurred over Britoil's capital structure, as the company tried to obtain government funds while the Treasury pressed for a sale of assets to save money. The result was a Britoil perceived to be weak with insufficient reserves while the government was still accused of wasting money.

Inevitably, others pressed the cause of privatisation to logical conclusions with demands for the break-up of monopolies, buy-outs and decentralisation (CBI, October 1983), and widespread ownership of capital by giving away shares (Samuel Brittan, the *Financial Times*, the SDP, and the Stock Exchange chairman). At times the government was trapped between its own inclinations towards market forces and political expediency. After secretly negotiating with Ford to take over Austin–Rover and having invited General Motors to discuss the Trucks and Land Rover part of BL. it found itself assailed by angry Tory MPs led by Ted Heath and Michael Heseltine. Having followed orders to privatise BL, directors now began to bid for Land Rover and other offers, having been spurned, were welcomed. All negotiations were eventually dropped. Similarly, in deciding between state-owned Harland & Wolff and newly-privatised Swan Hunter for a £130 million order the government was squeezed between Harland's cheaper bid under 'competitive tendering' (and appeasing Loyalists), and yet not wishing to see a new company go bankrupt in the north-east (where there were marginal seats) after it was virtually promised the order before flotation. Both yards were given work.

(b) *The wrong problem* Changes in ownership do not necessarily bring improved performance. Indeed, transferring ownership to pension funds and unit trusts, away from civil servants and politicians, may actually diminish accountability.

It has been argued that privatisation is desirable because all governments interfere with nationalised industries and only severance will provide a solution. This view discounts past proposed reforms such as the Select Committee on Nationalised Industries' 1968 report recommending a ministry for the corporations and the 1976 National Economic Development Council's advocacy of policy councils to direct them. Ironically a post-privatisation measure to rationalise controls over the public corporations was dropped in 1984 because of their opposition.

It overlooks too the major successes achieved in public ownership. BP thrived irrespective of majority or minority government shareholding, while Cable and Wireless have enjoyed steady success before and after privatisation. BL as a private sector company went bankrupt, while it improved dramatically in the public sector – against competition and, under Sir Michael Edwardes, it operated at a distance from government. British Steel's dramatic revival came in the public sector, and the Post Office raised productivity 17% in the five years from 1981. Ironically, the government seemed to have been making a success of the corporations, in their terms, by their board appointments. A report by the Centre for Policy Studies in July 1984 showed that chairmen were increasingly sympathetic to government policies but prepared to challenge outside interference. It was the combination of uncompromising management under chairmen such as Lord King (BA) and Mr McGregor (BS), plus competition which produced major improvements in performance. Electricity prices are lower in the UK than most of France, and the main problem for energy corporations have been Treasury-demanded price rises as chancellors sought to levy revenue, fattened them for privatisation and provided a self-fulfilling prophecy of interference. Ownership is less important than competition and good management in terms of responding to customer needs. Cost reduction to avoid takeover or bankruptcy will not apply to huge companies like BT and BGC. In exposing these inconsistencies, left-wing critics and crusading privatisers found a common theme – if it is such a good idea, why only sell off profitable concerns?

Political factors

(c) *Management opposition* Three board members of BT and BNOC resigned over the privatisation issue. Nevertheless, management has largely concentrated on obtaining the best terms – resisting attempts to break up the corporations (BT, BL, BGC, BR) or minimising regulation (the degree of control allowed BT for pricing). The most open opposition came from Sir Denis Rooke, to the selling of BGC's showrooms, North Sea Oil and Wytch Farm oilfield in Dorset, and from Lord King and the BA board who mounted a powerful campaign against ceding routes. Critics argued that these supposedly sympathetic chairmen had not only delayed privatisation but impeded competition. The Institute of Directors also alluded darkly to key enemies in the civil service.

After the British Airways sale had foundered several times over Lake anti-trust lawsuits, Jumbo defects, arguments over restructuring its balance sheet and a downturn in business, Nicholas Ridley postponed the 1985/86 sale because of impeding renegotiation of transatlantic flights. In anger and frustration, Lord King organised a management buy-out in March 1986, but this was blocked after a public row. It was speculated that Ridley had wanted to restructure BA into three or four airlines to promote competition and increase the sale price. Far from this happening, the powerful Lord King organised a takeover of BCal – winning a Monopolies and Mergers inquiry (giving up on 3·3% of the latters' routes) and beating off SAS airline competition in December 1987.

(d) *Union opposition* Unions have good reason to oppose privatisation; over nine-tenths of workers in nationalised industries are union members, many in closed shops, while three-quarters of manual and one-third of white collar workers in private manufacturing are unionised. Whilst some workers in successful enterprises such as Amersham have been unaffected, others in hotels have seen their pay, working conditions and security suffer. Unions have taken a strong anti-privatisation stance – at the 1982 TUC ten motions were submitted with demands for renationalisation without compensation, except in cases of hardship. Action taken so far has included:

(*i*) Days of action – by the gas and other unions (e.g. NALGO) against the sale of showrooms, and by 180,000 BT employees in six unions against privatisation in October 1982.

(*ii*) Alliances – NALGO contributed £1 million to a fund and agreed to work with NUPE in the campaign.

(*iii*) Campaigns – NUPE and SCAT (Services to Community Action and Tenants) organised local campaigns against contracting out services. The BT unions initiated a publicity and parliamentary campaign, the latter included a 11¾-hour filibustering speech by POEU-sponsored MP John Golding. NUPE produced education packs, and the unions turned from generalised defences to critical analysis of efficiency, costs and consequences.

(*iv*) Education of the membership against buying shares, e.g. TGWU in National Freight Corporation and POEU in BT.

(*v*) Prolonged industrial action. This has been most bitter against loss of jobs through contracting out at several hospitals and councils. In BT the POEU escalated their action in 1983, refusing to connect the rival Mercury, targeting government departments and Mercury's backers (Barclays, BP and C & W). By October 2,500 engineers were suspended and ¼ million a week was being paid in strike pay. The High Court at first ruled in the POEU's favour as job security was at stake but the Appeal Court reversed this in Mercury's favour in November. Despite a TUC attempt to raise funds to help the POEU, the action was called off. Industrial action does not deter a determined government with a renewed mandate, but it airs countervailing arguments and may make contractors or investors hesitate. The NCU's (ex-POEU) strike in 1987 helped lower BT's performance to the extent that critical doubts were expressed over future privatisations.

(e) *Labour renationalisation*   Labour's original policy was one of renationalisation without compensation but this was modified for the 1983 manifesto. Given the sums of money involved, a future Labour government would have to resort to a combination of partial and selective reacquisition, co-operatives and employee involvement in decision-making. Roy Hattersley's 1984 paper on new forms of public and social ownership highlighted this. In 1986 Labour explained that 'social ownership' would entail a public sector able to work outside cash limits with corporations able to develop commercially beyond their standard roles. Employees would collectively hold shares and would have board representation. Shares in key privatised companies could be exchanged for the original price or kept as bonds with a rate of interest. They promised to give local control and more power to consumers. A holding company and an investment bank would co-ordinate. Health service contracts would be cancelled and private schools taken over. Though Labour could briefly affect the share price of privatised companies – as when it published its 1987 election plans, the time had come for even clearer definition to be effective in the changed environment. As part of the policy review, at the 1988 Labour conference Bryan Gould rejected Morrisonian nationalisation completely and won acceptance for regulation in the interests of consumers and workers rather than buying back.

(f) *Public opinion* Labour renationalisation could well be impeded by public opinion. But that same opinion can be cited against privatisation, which polls have shown to be a low priority. Indeed a CBI–British Institute of Management survey in October 1983 revealed that only 6% of managers agreed with the government policy – privatisation ranked seventeenth on their list of priorities. The anti-privatisation of BT campaign succeeded at least to the extent that 46% thought it a bad idea in October 1983, compared to 37% in December 1982 (those who favoured it fell from 43% to 39%) according to a Gallup Poll. A BBC/Marplan poll of January 1988 found 57% wanting privatisation postponed or abandoned and only 25% wanting continuation. And a MORI poll eleven months later confirmed the views from three years before – there was a five to one majority against water being sold (75% to 15%) and a three to one majority against electricity privatisation (*Sunday Times*, 4 December 1988).

(g) *Dubious motives* Initially it was said that government was diverting attention and right-wing criticism from aid to 'lame-duck' industries such as BL and British Steel. The privatisation connections of Conservative MPs were condemned – twenty-one owned shares in cleaning, catering or laundry firms or were part-time directors or consultants, and the Labour Research staff traced the ninety-one Tory MPs with BT shares and identified multiple applications. In October 1987 former MP Keith Best was imprisoned for four months and fined £3,000 for making six applications. The City too was criticised as it was paid over £660 million by 1987 in fees, expenses, commissions and underwriting – the non-executive directors of TSB 'mutinied' over the 3·8 million to be paid to Lazards. The City received more than £128 million for the sale of BT, and auditors subsequently found £1 million illegal multiple applications. The government found that the rules were too indefinite to take action against profiteers buying 'institutional' shares. But by the time of the BP sale in October 1987, with twenty-three outstanding prosecutions from the BA, BGC, BAe and TSB sales, the 'forensic' accountants were using a computerised tracking system.

The Public Accounts Committee had criticised the lack of control in 1986 and a year later condemned the £281 million perks (vouchers and loyalty bonuses) offered since 1981. It was noted that £15 million speculative profit was made on the first day of trading of C&W Shares and that TSB shareholders doubled their money on the first day. At the TUC conference in 1984 Mr Bickerstaffe of NUPE concluded, 'wherever public need is met by private greed, corruption is not far behind . . . For privatisation read profiteering, expense account lunches and sweatshop wages' (*The Guardian*, 7 September 1984). (In fact there were complaints in the City that the government was using its influence to force down fees to an unrewarding level.) A study by the London Business School in November 1988 showed that salaries of chief executives rose by an average 78% in the year after privatisation and by 250% in real terms since 1979. The Labour party analysed the donations to the Tory election funds, including £50,000 from Rolls Royce in 1987.

(h) *Shareholding*   The ideal of a wide shareholding seems not to have been realised, for after initial interest small investors sell for a profit. Of 65,000 Amersham buyers, only 7,717 were left by October 1983. Ten per cent of BAe's work-force did not apply for their £50 of free shares. C&W shareholders reduced from 157,000 to 26,000 in a year, and BAe from 158,000 to 26,000 at the end of 1982. The number of BT shareholders fell from 2·3 million at the time of the floatation to 1·58 million in March 1986, with the big institutions controlling 62·5% of the non-government shares. By the end of 1988 British Gas was losing 10,000 'Sids' a month as its shareholding fell from 4·5 to 2·8 million, TSB lost 700,000 in six months, a third of the Rolls Royce shares changed hands in a ninety-minute scramble as profits were taken and individual shareholders were left owning only 16% of BA after the other two-thirds of the buyers took their 83% profit. To avoid setting fixed prices too low the government was increasingly turning to the tender, on which city institutions bid low, meaning that the temptation of big gains for individuals was missing. By offering low prices for monopoly shares, it was argued that a false impression of risk capitalism had been given, and these large institutions were unwilling to take necessary risks or bring accountability to companies. After the 1987 stock market crash there was talk of British Gas and BT being UK-based 'defensive stock'. Despite the increase in absolute numbers, the proportion of shares held by individuals has continued to decline since 1979 – most of them are held by the older and more prosperous citizens.

Socio-political

(j) *Decline in service* In October 1983 the chairman of the publicly-funded National Consumer Council warned of the dangers to consumers in privatisation, that less information would be available and that loss-making parts of the business – rural telephone boxes and bus services – would wither. The Labour Party and the TUC thought their fears were justified when BT began to rebalance its tariffs to the advantage of long-distance and international callers and to charge for 999 repairs. Deregulation of bus services under the 1985 Transport Act left one-fifth of routes with no bidders, with 35% less rural mileage compared to an 8·5 cut in urban areas. Weekend, evening services and children's reduced fares all suffered and fourteen rival companies in Strathclyde helped bring traffic to a standstill in Glasgow in 1986. Studies also suggested that bus privatisation would cost £3 for every pound saved and raise rates by 22% (*Guardian,* 3 December 1984). Nevertheless, pressure for more public authority bus companies to be sold off was increased in September 1988. Two months later it was reported that BR was considering closing more than 1,000 miles of track and substituting buses on rural and provincial routes to prepare for privatisation.

The National Consumer Council warned that gas prices would rise because the regulatory OFGAS would be unable to prevent cross-subsidisation of industrial contract customers with profits from tied domestic householders. The BT – like price formula of Retail Price Index minus x%, plus 'y' to reflect additional costs in buying North Sea gas, was not deemed to be strong enough. Water privatisation raised social issues; metering would be to the disadvantage of those in dirty jobs or with large families, and would commercial pressure mean disconnections? The introduction of meters would cost £2 billion (£200 per household). There were fears that pollution controls were being lowered, that control would be insufficient – fears heightened by the December 1988 revelation of 6,000 times the aluminium level in some Cornish waters. Their 435,000 acres of land came into focus as a possible sell-off after water privatisation to the detriment of the countryside and ramblers.

The Gas Consumers Councils showed disconnections to have risen sharply since privatisation – the MMC condemned the 'uncaring attitude'.

Councils and public complained that privatised refuse services were inefficient and poor performance penalities were imposed (*Sunday Times*, 31 July 1983). Similar complaints arose over NHS contracting – checks at a Cheltenham hospital revealed 73% to 85% rejection rates on sheets and pillows, against a NHS target of 5%. Trust House Forte withdrew from tendering in September 1984, claiming the conditions imposed were detrimental to patients and staff. Rodney Bickerstaffe, for NUPE, said that the government had let in 'the Sewer Sharks' (7 September 1988). Hereford & Worcester in 1987 was found to be offering poor school meals, according to heads and teachers, as private caterers were used. Auctions for TV programme companies under 'quality, choice and competition' in December 1988 were predicted to lead to lower quality programmes.

(k) *Prices*

Besides the question of value for money for Gas and Telecom services, it became increasingly doubtful whether the consumer would benefit from later sales. Fears over water rate rises were confirmed by authorities' raising prices up to 30% in 1989, to ministers' fury. Selling electricity could cost £1 billion or 5% and the nuclear waste was a £4 billion problem. Labour predicted a 25% rise, especially because of the 'nuclear tax'.

(l) *Job losses*   Privatisation was said to be costing jobs; 3,000 in the

NHS where contractors had been told they could abandon standard terms of employment and had cut members and used part-timers; 4,000 in BR's engineering division, and up to 9,000 bus jobs due to deregulation, abolition of metropolitan authorities and break-up of the National Bus Company into seventy units. Rover's takeover by BAe in July 1988 led to two plant closures and 4,900 job losses and BAe then moved on to rationalise Royal Ordnance. The sale of Govan shipyard in April 1988 and their encouragement of a millionaire bidder for Holland & Wolff gave rise to fears that the government was pulling out of, rather than privatising, British Shipbuilders. In December 1988 it closed North-East Shipbuilders with 2,000 job losses.

Legal-political

(m) *Ownership*   The right of the government to sell public assets has been challenged, beyond the basic political objection to 'giving away' public investment.

The Trustee Saving Bank's floatation in 1985 was postponed when Scottish depositors claimed it belonged to them and were upheld in the Court of Sessions. After acrimony with the Bank the Treasury pushed an act through Parliament in 1985 saying that the TSB belonged to no one and established ownership with the successor companies. The Law Lords, however, in August 1986, published their decision that these had been state assets and the Treasury had given away £1 billion from the sale and £800 million assets. The £5 million campaign to sell to a million shareholders had been started in July, and the Opposition called for the Minister to be sacked for 'gross incompetence'. The Treasury maintained its position that this was a normal flotation, not privatisation. When the proposals to privatise the water authorities were published, Conservative MP Robin Maxwell-Hyslop asked what compensation ratepayers would receive given that they had paid most towards the assets. The union quickly promised a legal challenge as these had never been nationalised resources. It was partly this time-consuming and controversial prospect that led to postponement until after the 1987 general election.

Ownership encompassed the problem of privacy – should private contractors be allowed to handle military data, including medical records (a leaked proposal of September 1988)?

The government also had to accept defeat and delay at the hands of

Lord Denning and his colleagues in the Upper House. Dispensing
legal advice to the unions, Denning blocked the Dockyard Services
Bill to privatise management in Rosyth and Devonport because a
trade union consultation process had not been observed.

Political–economic

(n) *National interest*   It is contended that economies of scale dictate
that some industries are organised on a national scale, and that
bringing competition into the telephone, gas or electricity systems
simply produces duplication and waste.

Some industries were acquired for the public sector because of
their strategic position, particularly the oil industry – beginning with
BP before the first world war. Selling Britoil caused the loss of future
profits and its cash flow into the Treasury. It had taken a 'golden
share' in that company to prevent takeovers and monopoly, and the
Treasury indicated it would block BP's £2·27 billion takeover in late
1987. But two months later it had changed its mind and the absorp-
tion went ahead. Yet the national interest did require the
government to step in through the Monopolies Commission, and
order the Kuwaitis to reduce their BP stake (acquired in the crashed
privatisation) from 21·6 to 9·9%. Relations were strained until
£2,000 million were bought from Kuwait – by BP!

The imperative of control can also be claimed for British Nuclear
Fuels and the Royal Ordnance Factories. There was political uproar
when it seemed that the state-funded microchip company Inmos
would be sold to American Telephone and Telegraph (AT&T) for a
mere £50 million. Claims that the government had undervalued state
concerns to ensure sales led to accusations that they were 'mortgag-
ing the future' and 'selling the family silver' (Lord Stockton, 1985).

Some 18·6% of the BT shares went to foreigners and over £100
million was taken as immediate profit.

The greatest furore met the secret talks to break up and sell BL to
American companies, especially in the wake of the Westland affair.
£2·4 billion had been put into recapitalising BL since 1975 and
attempted explanations that BL could not thrive were rebutted by
the charge that BL exported £1 billion a year, while GM and Ford
had negative balances of trade of £656 million and £501 million
respectively. Complaints of anti-Americanism were swept aside as
critics accused the government of 'dogma and defeatism' (Ted
Heath), of reducing Britain to an offshore assembly operation and

jeopardising hundreds of thousands of jobs in motor and parts manufacturing. Opponents claimed the government was not acting in the national interest by reneging on its promise to keep 25% of BAe; being pushed by Vickers' managers into privatising before awarding the Trident order to its monopoly supplier; and by allowing gas and oil companies to deplete reserves without effective control.

The sale of Rover and Royal Ordnance to British Aerospace ended with calls for a judicial enquiry into its 'mismanagement'. Losses at Rover of £2·7 billion were written off in 1988, on top of £560 million the year before. As BAe took over and shut two plants, shareholders were offered only a quarter of what they wanted. It then transpired that BAe could make over £1 billion on the land sales of Rover and RO (the two had cost £340 million). Opposition and the public accounts committee criticised this collusion in asset-stripping.

Financial problems
The mechanics of selling state assets often proved to be difficult and politically embarrassing.

(o) *Capital structures and controls*   It often takes public industries time and money to bring their accounts into line with private companies. BT's treatment of fixed assets led to qualifications on its accounts, a long argument took place over Britoil's capital structure, and BNOC's agreements with other oil companies were difficult to untangle.

One particular problem is the cost of honouring pension arrangments. £49 million of the £52 million raised by selling National Freight was used in paying off the pension scheme deficit, and to do the same for the Royal Ordnance Factories would entail the government paying out £100 million more than the sale would raise. To cope with the problem BA closed its scheme to pay off the £1·25 deficit (but running the scheme will be a charge on profits). While BAe did not present such problems and was attractive to the market, the huge writing-off of debts in the case of industries such as BA and the Docks Board (ABP) opened the government to attack.

The government was in the difficult position of honouring commitments (down to concessionary travel for BR hotel staff), exercising control in the public interest (e.g. through OFTEL), and still trying to convince the market to buy – in BA's case this led to a government promise not to exercise their influence as shareholders.

The Government has had to write off vast sums of public investment/debt, e.g. £3 billion on Rover, £5 billion on steel, and probably £5.2 billion for water.

(p) *Timing*   The government found it very difficult to 'get it right'. The Amersham issue was twenty-four times oversubscribed, 75% of Britoil was left with the underwriters, Associated British Ports, BA and Jaguar were thirty-five, thirty-five and four times oversubscribed respectively, and five-sixths of Enterprise Oil was unwanted. The all-party Public Accounts Committee twice looked at and criticised the government's record, recommending phased sales.

Analysis of the sale of NFC, BP, Amersham, ABP, BAe, C & W and Britoil showed that by June 1984 the shares had risen to the extent that £799 million had been lost – to speculative gains in a rising market. BAe's shares had risen 143%. Critics pointed out that this 'rip-off' or 'shambles' was an opportunity-cost worth sixteen NHS hospitals. The *Daily Mirror* dubbed it 'jumble sale politics' (28 June 1984).

Problems in this respect worsened as the market, which doubled in Mrs Thatcher's first five years, went down – wrecking the Enterprise flotation.

The ultimate disruption came in October 1987 when the stock market crashed in the middle of the huge £7.2 billion BP sale – the Bank of England had to offer a buy-back facility.

After the sale of BT the Labour Opposition claimed that the five times oversubscription and the 45p (or 90%) premium when the marked opened meant that the government had wasted £1·3 billion, in addition to spending £320 million on the sale and was guilty of 'criminal incompetence' (House of Commons, 4 December 1984).

Occasionally, however, the government gets it just right. Labour attacked the British steel sale as underpriced but the financial pundits predicted a bigger flop than BP. In fact it was 3·3 times oversubscribed – proving a market for water and electricity – yet it opened at a 2p premium and there were no quick gains.

(q) *Investment*   Floating huge concerns like BT and BGC created fears that a 'crowding out' of other investment – in gilts, industry, and building societies – would take place. Experts warned that higher interest rates and an appreciation of sterling would follow, putting pressure on companies' profit margins.

Summary

The Conservative government almost 'happened' upon the policy of selling public assets. Despite many obstacles, inconsistencies and embarrassments it persisted and enlarged the process until privatisation not only came to be one of its main claims to success and its distinguishing feature but also a primary means of survival. By 1987 Treasury officials had advised twenty countries about privatisation and, appropriately, in 1989 they embarked on a venture with the US to sell the expertise to the developing world.

Reading

Adam Smith Institute, *Omega Project* reports.

Centre for Business Strategy, London Business School, 'Does Privatisation Work?', London, 1988.

CIS Report, *Private Line*, 1982.

Roger Hall, 'Privatisation and British politics 1979–86', *Teaching Politics*, September 1986, pp. 460–76.

S. Hastings & H. Levie (eds.), *Privatisation?*, Spokesman, 1983.

K. Newman, *The Selling of British Telecom*, Holt, Rinehart & Winston, 1986.

NUPE Education Pack, *Keep Your Services Public*, 1982.

J. Tivey, *Nationalisation in British Industry*, Longman, 1971.

J. Vickers & G. Yarsow, *Privatisation and the Natural Monopolies*, Public Policy Centre, 1985.

9 *John McIlroy*

Unemployment and the economy

In a society whose citizens have been taught that there is both a right and a necessity to work, large-scale unemployment throws up a myriad of problems, from the role of the state to the nature of human dignity. In the 1980s, unemployment re-emerged in Britain on a scale unseen since the Depression of the 1930s. As in the inter-war years, it failed to act as a radicalising agent: in 1983 Labour failed to attain a majority amongst unemployed voters and, in 1987, only scraped through with 52%, in the context of a high abstention rate. As in the inter-war years, there has been a growing acceptance by the voters of unemployment levels thought intolerable in the fifties and sixties. Mrs Thatcher has found, like Stanley Baldwin before her, that unemployment does not lose elections. Whilst unemployment has remained one of the major political issues of the 1980s – it topped the list of key issues in surveys of voters during the 1987 election – the employed majority have not been prepared to translate their concern for the jobless minority into action at the polls.

The dimensions of the problem

Between 1974 and 1978 unemployment rose from 600,000 to just under 1·5 million. In the first three years of the 1979 Conservative government, it rose to over the three million mark (see figures 1 and 2). It first stayed at this post-war record level, and then, in Mrs Thatcher's second term, exceeded it, touching 3·4 million, or 14% of the working population, by January 1986.

From the late summer of 1986 unemployment began to fall,

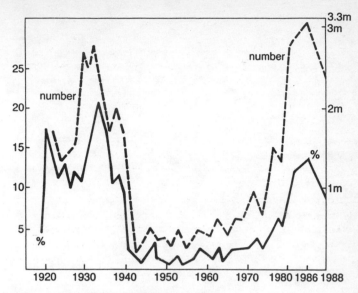

Figure 1 Unemployment in the UK, 1920–88
Source: Department of Employment *British Labour Statistics: Historical Abstract;* Central Statistical Office *Annual Abstracts of Statistics* (updated).

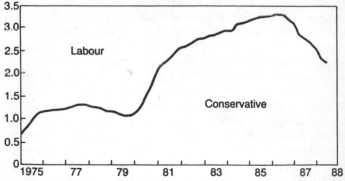

Figure 2 Unemployment: Labour and Conservative, 1975–88
Source: Department of Employment Gazette.

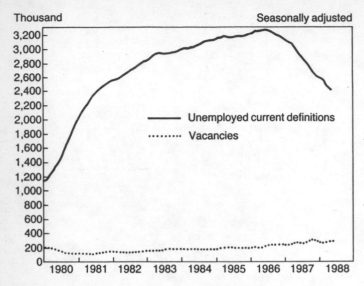

Figure 3 Unemployment and vacancies: UK, 1980–88
Source: Department of Employment Gazette.

dropping to 3,299,167 by the end of the year, and the position
continued to improve significantly throughout 1987. By the end of
1987 government figures showed the numbers unemployed standing
at 2,685,583, or 9·7% of the working population, more than half a
million below the November 1986 figure. Six months later the official
count had dropped to 2·34 million, or 8·3% of the working population (see figure 1 and 2). Throughout the first part of the 1980s, the
average length of unemployment also increased: by 1983 nearly 60%
of unemployed men had been out of work for more than six months
and the position worsened thereafter. Again, there was an improvement in the second part of the decade and, in mid–1988, the number
of long-term unemployed fell below a million for the first time in five
years (see table 1).

These figures have aroused controversy and there can be little
doubt that official statistics, based since 1982 on those claiming
unemployment benefit, underestimate the degree of unemployment.

Table 2 Unemployment – duration at April 1986 and April 1988

Male and female	Proportion of number unemployed		Male	Proportion of number unemployed		Female	Proportion of number unemployed	
	1986	1988		1986	1988		1986	1988
Up to 2 weeks	6·0	5·4	Up to 2 weeks	5·4	4·9	Up to 2 weeks	7·2	6·3
2–4 weeks	3·9	4·8	2–4 weeks	3·6	4·5	2–4 weeks	4·7	5·3
4–8 weeks	6·7	7·2	4–8 weeks	6·2	6·8	4–8 weeks	7·6	8·2
8–13 weeks	7·6	7·8	8–13 weeks	7·3	9·1	8–13 weeks	8·9	9·2
13–26 weeks	15·0	15·2	13–26 weeks	14·2	14·2	13–26 weeks	16·8	17·7
26–52 weeks	20·0	19·1	26–52 weeks	18·4	17·6	26–52 weeks	23·6	22·5
Over 52 weeks	40·8	40·6	Over 52 weeks	45·1	44·9	Over 52 weeks	31·3	30·8

Source: Department of Employment Gazette, July 1986, August 1988.

There were no less than nineteen changes in the basis of assessment of the jobless total between 1979 and 1988. A significant proportion of unemployed women do not claim benefit, neither do more than half a million 'employed' in the limbo of job creation schemes. The government has eliminated unemployed men over sixty and youngsters under eighteen from the figures, ended half and three-quarter rates of unemployment benefit for those leaving employment without 'good cause'. There have been changes in the way the rate of unemployment is calculated, with the self-employed and the armed forced being added to the category of employees to deflate the jobless percentages. Tighter availability-for-work tests have been adopted which pilot schemes have found disqualify applicants for benefit at twice the previous rate. Evidence from the *Restart* scheme introduced in 1986 suggested that around 10% of unemployed workers stopped claiming as a result. It has been pointed out that the more reliable *Labour Force* survey shows a drop in unemployment in the late eighties much smaller than that suggested by the government's monthly statistics. And the *Unemployment Unit*, which calculates the total on the still imperfect 1982 basis, estimates that by the summer of 1988 2·8 million, or 10·1% of the working population, were unemployed.

The government's main defence to the charge that it is fudging the figures to minimise political embarrassment is to call upon international criteria for aid. Conservatives claim that the official count, despite recent changes, gives a higher figure for the jobless than if the number of unemployed was calculated using international measurements. The International Labour Organisation and the Organisation for Economic Co-operation and Development count only those who state in official surveys that they are available and have actually sought work in the previous four weeks. By counting all those claiming benefit, the British government gets an unemployment figure some 70,000 higher than would be arrived at if international definitions were adopted.

These figures represent, despite improved welfare provision, 'a return to the thirties'. During the inter-war years, unemployment was rarely under a million. For three years, it was over 2·5 million, 20% of the work-force (see figure 1). The position is highlighted, as during the twenty-five years after the war the problem was held to be solved. Between 1984 and 1968 unemployment averaged 1·7%. A prominent Labour economist, Michael Stewart, could comment in the sixties, 'Other economic problems may threaten; this one at least has passed into history.'

Unemployment is usually analysed in three categories. *Frictional* unemployment represents workers who spend a couple of months between jobs owing to problems of interchange and can occur when there is full employment. *Cyclical* unemployment is directly created by the economic cycle of boom and recession. *Structural* unemployment is the product of decline in industries or processes. Britain's present problem is the product of the last two categories.

As well as economic recession there has been a significant erosion of the country's manufacturing base, a process called *deindustrialisation*. In the mid-sixties nearly 50% of the work-force worked in manufacturing, mining, construction, gas and electricity. Ten years later it was only 40%. Today, it is heading for 30%; this decline has not been compensated for by job growth in other areas. But if Britain's recent employment has been cyclical and structural, these factors have been exacerbated by the policies of the present government.

Unemployment has a *regional* as well as an industrial dimension. Government figures showed unemployment in mid-1988 standing at 17% in Northern Ireland, 12% in the North of England, 9% in the West Midlands, 5·3% in the South-East and 5% in East Anglia. These factors mask *intra-regional* differences – in parts of Northern Ireland and, indeed in parts of Liverpool and Manchester, unemployment in the eighties has been well over 25%. The regional dimension has become more serious in recent years so that people now speak of a 'North–South divide'. An increasing amount of evidence shows a growing disparity in terms of jobs, wages, housing, share of gross domestic product, indeed quality of life, between the prosperous southern part of England and the rest of the UK.

Unemployment also has an *international* dimension: the higher unemployment in Britain in the late seventies and eighties was also experienced in the USA and most European countries. Today, there are eleven million unemployed in the EEC countries. However, the general tendency for unemployment to grow in the Western economies masks special differences. In the USA and in Finland the graph is falling – in Switzerland unemployment has been under 1% whilst in Spain it has reached 20%. In Britain, the problem is particularly severe because of the historical weaknesses of the British economy and the solutions governments selected to deal with these.

The Impact of unemployment

(1) *Cost to the state and the economy*
This is difficult to calculate with precision. Factors involved include
the cost to the state in unemployment pay, supplementary benefit
and redundancy payments; part of the expenditure on the special
employment schemes; loss of income tax, national insurance
payments, VAT and other indirect taxes on foregone spending, as
well as tax refunds, and the overall losses in terms of spending and
production.

In 1980, Showler estimated that total tax losses added to benefit
payments represented £4,128 million in lost public expenditure,
7·6% of the government's total budget. Two other economists, Glyn
and Harrison, estimated that unemployment lost 20% of potential
production in nine different industries. In 1985, Glyn estimated that
full employment would have permitted production of around £52
billion extra goods and services a year which he calculated, allowing
for extra consumption, could represent a trebling of council house
building, a doubling of manufacturing investment and a 50%
increase in pensions and in government spending on health and
education.

In the 1983 election, Labour argued that prevailing unemployment
figures represented a loss of £17 billion in tax revenue and increased
benefit payments and a cost in lost production of over £30 billion per
annum. Mrs Thatcher claimed the loss was only £6 billion. There can
be little doubt that unemployment on today's scale is economically
wasteful.

(2) *The economic cost to the individual*
Unlike the thirties, we have a welfare state, but poverty and deprivation can be *relative*. Living on supplementary benefit long-term
means living in officially defined poverty. In 1979, Townsend found
that those out of work for ten weeks or more were two and a half
times more likely to be living in poverty than those who had not been
unemployed, and if they got jobs they were likely to be poorly paid.

For a married man previously on average earnings, with two
children, life on supplementary benefit means a 45% cut in gross
earnings, a position unchanged in the last fifteen years. If he is living
on unemployment benefit he loses around a third of his average
earnings and this cut has increased recently, particularly with the

abolition of Earnings Related Supplement in 1982. The average redundancy payment of a little over £1,000 held only marginally. A recent Department of Employment study of 2,000 unemployed men found that for almost half those surveyed state benefits gave them less than half of their previous earnings.

(3) *The social cost*
A wealth of evidence shows unemployment breeds shame, guilt, frustration and a sense of worthlessness. A 1980 Manpower Services Commission study of the long-term jobless saw unemployment as producing depression, anxiety and illness. In 1984 a report for the government's Office of Population Censuses and Surveys by Professor John Cox showed death rates among unemployed men seeking work at least 21% higher than expected and death rates among their wives 20% higher. Unemployment was to blame for the death of more than 1,800 men and 1,000 wives *per annum*. The research showed that, by 1981, unemployed men, compared to others of the same age, were more than twice as likely to have committed suicide, 80% more likely to have had a fatal accident and 75% more likely to have died of lung cancer. The report may understate the problem.

Another survey from the Nuffield Centre at Leeds University commented that 'The evidence of an association between unemployment and suicide is overwhelming.' This accords with US research which shows that for every hundred thousand whose lose their jobs, mental hospital admissions increase by 6,000, deaths increase by 5,000, and prison intake increases by 1,900. And in 1988 a government-sponsored report, *The Nation's Health*, confirmed 'a twofold higher death-rate from suicide among the unemployed'. It concluded 'There is strong evidence that the deprivations associated with unemployment are damaging to health'. Some of the social consequences of mass unemployment were evident in the inner-city riots of the 1980s.

(4) *The inequality cost*
Unemployment hits the poorest hardest. Particularly vulnerable are the unskilled manual workers, the young, the old, the disabled, those in poor health, women and black workers. As we have seen, unemployment also hits certain regions' industries and communities harder than others. *Unemployment is socially and economically divisive* and creates a barrier between the workless and those in jobs. The

1984–85 miners' strike has highlighted how unemployment produces resistance in threatened communities which has implications for social stability and law and order. However, as the situation has deteriorated there has been a levelling effect in relation to regional unemployment. Although disparities remain, the rates are closer together than they were during the thirties.

Theories of unemployment

The market economy
The classical economists thought *laissez-faire* (freedom of the market to operate) would tend to produce full employment. J. B. Say (1767–1832) and David Ricardo (1772–1823), two of the few economists who referred to the issue, argued that supply would create its own demand: the production of commodities would generate adequate purchasing power. Overproduction could only ever be temporary as it would be solved automatically by a fall in the market price and a return to natural equilibrium and full employment.

Marx
In contrast, Karl Marx (1818–83) saw unemployment as inherent in the workings of capitalist economy. He attributed the cycle of boom and slump since the Industrial Revolution to the attempt of capitalists to *compete* to expand their share of production. Wage costs rise as unemployment decreases and the 'industrial reserve army of the unemployed' which exercises a downward pressure in wages, becomes depleted. To increase productivity and lower wage costs, capitalists reduce the number of workers employed relative to the machinery and raw materials they work.

The first contradiction Marx saw was that reducing wages and replacing labour by machinery meant a smaller market for the goods produced. He wrote of the periodic crises of overproduction. 'The final cause of all real crises always remain the poverty and restricted consumption of the masses.' Moreover, profits, in Marx's model, came only from the exploitation of workers. With relatively few workers and a greater amount of machinery over which to calculate the rate of profit, the resultant growth in productivity was insufficient to stem the fall in the rate of profit. The result was a failure to invest and an increase in unemployment. As the slump produced bankruptcies, prices would fall, purchasing power would recover and a new boom would be stimulated.

Marx did not suggest policies to control unemployment. The answer was to get rid of the anarchic, wasteful system that produces it and replace the market with a planned economy where it would disappear. His predictions that the crises would get progressively worse and provoke unpheaval have not been fulfilled. Booms and slumps continued. So did capitalism. Marx took some account of countervailing tendencies. His theory underestimated the ability of the system to adapt and adjust but it has been developed and applied to today's society by economists such as Mandel and Kidron. Varieties of Marxist solutions are still advocated by some on the left of the Labour party, the Communist party and the small revolutionary groups.

Keynes

Looking at inter-war unemployment, John Maynard Keynes (1883–1945) realised the inadequacy of the classical view but, unlike Marx, he wanted to make the existing system work. He saw that the conventional cures to recession, cut-backs on spending and reduction of imports, led to a contraction of world trade and a diminution in purchasing power and therefore made the patient worse. A vicious circle set in: falling demand created unemployment, that unemployment further diminished purchasing power and, in its turn, created further unemployment.

Keynes saw the central problem as 'an insufficiency of effective demand'. He argued that the free operation of the market might lead to an equilibrium between sales and purchases but all the evidence suggested that this might not be at a level which ensures full employment; the total sum of money available to spend on goods and services and total sum available for investment might together fall below the level needed to provide jobs for everybody.

In this situation, the state should prime the pump. It should reverse its normal policies and, if the problem of the free market is the reluctance of the private investors to invest, the state should revive effective demand by spending money itself. *It could thus manage effective demand: expanding it in slump; curtailing it in boom.* Full employment and economic growth could be launched by governments resorting to deficit budgeting: spending more than they collected in taxes; directly investing in public works such as schools, roads and hospitals which would not compete with private commodities; generating purchasing power through increased welfare payments; and influencing interest rates downwards to encourage private investment through expanding the money supply.

Keynes also stressed the need for some form of international co-operation in an increasingly interlocked and interdependent world economy if problems like mass unemployment were to be controlled. His ideas were influential in the Bretton Woods agreement which established the International Monetary Fund, the World Bank and the US dollar as a world currency, and were vital in generating the long post-war boom. Though particularly attractive to social democrats who welcomed the elements of state management, they appealed to a wider spectrum and became the new conventional economic wisdom in the forties and fifties. They increasingly came up against the problem of inflation and were complemented by some form of incomes control. However, the full employment they helped to generate means that such policies were only of temporary efficacy. In Britain the increasing necessity to put up taxes, borrow more money and expand the public sector to maintain full employment as the industrial structure developed towards high productivity sectors with less demand for labour, led to pressure on profits and wages in a context of sluggish growth. Large monopolies were able, to a degree, to insulate pricing, investment and employment policies from central government strategies. In particular, the power that full employment gave shop stewards who were relatively independent of union leaders limited the success of state intervention on wage cuts. Intensified state involvement proved unpopular. The results – a drop in investment, increasing unemployment, declining profits, static real wages and inflation – led many to argue that, in the end Keynesian remedies had failed.

Monetarism

The most influential proponent of monetarism has been Professor Milton Friedman. Monetarists argue that there is no painless or simple way out of the unemployment problem. Jobs will only be available when a nation's products are competitive in the world market. This means attacking not only inflation but union power. For monetarists, unemployment is caused by mismanagement of the money supply – the notes and coins in circulation as well as money in short-term deposits, in transit, in deposit accounts and public sector deposits. This is called M3. Monetarists believe that if there is too much money in circulation bidding for relatively scarce goods and services – 'too much money chasing too few goods' – prices will go up. In response, wages will go up and ultimately industry will be uncompetitive.

If the *growth of the money supply is controlled* through higher interest rates credit becomes more expensive and more difficult to arrange. Fewer goods can be purchased on credit so sales fall and bankruptcies occur. The less competitive and efficient companies, fighting to avoid going to the wall, are forced to resist the demands of trade unions, impelled to push down wages to real economic levels and pressurised to reorganise work more efficiently. As the most inefficient go under, increasing unemployment makes workers more willing to accept change. Trade union controls are thus weakened and the unemployed are willing to take jobs for lower wages and on different terms.

Government spending must also be slashed as it has increasingly been financed by borrowing and printing money, speeding up M3. This involves cutting state employment, privatising some nationalised industries and placing the rest under tight monetary discipline. Subsidies to private industry must be removed, ending feather-bedding, stimulating productivity and removing artificial insulation against the market. As trade unions have become monopolies, able to interfere with the operation of the market, there may be need for legislation to limit many of the practices such as picketing and the closed shop on which their artificial power to interfere with the economy is based. Monetarists see their policies as *creating* unemployment. As it increases so wages, which they see as the main ingredient in inflation, will fall. As the inflation rate declines so will interest rates. Growth can now recommence. But this time it will be based on healthy 'slimmed-down' highly productive companies, freed from union power and reliance on the state and able to compete effectively in the world market. Whilst Friedman stresses the need to free the market from inefficient government bureaucracy and social welfare, a strong state is essential to guarantee the rules of competition, to defend society and to administer certain essential industries such as electricity.

Keynesian economists have questioned whether the increase in the money supply causes the increase in cash incomes. Kaldor has argued that it is in fact the other way round and has claimed – with some justification – that the money supply theories are simply cosmetics for classical deflation: reducing demand and attacking the unions. Other problems are the scale and planlessness of the monetarist experiment. Vast levels of unemployment may be required, confidence may collapse and push recession into depression. Both economic and social costs may be too great. Powerful business monopolies may be able to successfully circumvent attempts to stimulate greater market competition. Strong unions may be able to resist strategies to increase productivity. There is no guarantee of what kind of market you will be left with. There may be tension between economic liberty and political freedom so that the strong state required to guarantee the free market becomes a dictatorship. In Chile – advised by Friedman – monetarist policies increased both unemployment and inflation on an enormous scale. In Britain inflation has decreased but unemployment remains significant.

The political economy of jobs

(1) *Politicians become committed to full employment*
Sir William Beveridge's White Paper, *Full Employment In A Free Society* (1944), was strongly influenced by Keynes's theories. It argued that the state should take responsibility for employment just as it did for defence or for internal policing. Beveridge defined full employment as a situation where 'those who lose jobs must be able to find new jobs at fair wages within their capacity without delay'. This break with the past and with the market was influenced by the following factors:

(a) A strong leftward move in politics which combined with a mood of national unity to create opposition to any return to the divisions, social turmoil and suffering of the inter-war period.

(b) Wartime planning and controls showing what could be done if the state played a more active role; a role required for post-war reconstruction.

(c) The war had halted the UK economy's slide in the world market. Reversion to peacetime production created an acute shortage of labour. Not only Labour but the Tories were committed to a greater degree of intervention.

Initial expectations of full employment – Keynes thought it meant less than 6% jobless, Beveridge around 3% – were soon exceeded in practice: under the Attlee government it hardly rose above 2%. This created further pressure on the Conservatives. In the 1950 and 1951 elections both major parties were commited to full employment policies.

(2) *The politics of full employment dominate*

The boom was helped by Keynesian measures. But also important were technological advances made in wartime; the weakening of unions in many countries such as the USA, Germany and Japan; the need for reconstruction based on large reserves of labour. Britain was helped by the weakening of pre-war competitors and demand for manufactured goods from a devastated world.

The fifties saw the era of Butskellism; both parties committed to Keynesianism competed in the priority they accorded to the jobs issue. Before the 1959 election an increase in unemployment towards over half a million was widely seen as pressing a Labour victory and its eventual decline as a vital factor in the Tories' success. The prevailing orthodoxy was:

(a) It was possible to maintain full employment *and* control inflation.

(b) Any party which questioned demand management to achieve this would lose votes as the opinion polls and attitude surveys showed the issue was crucial to the electorate.

(c) That unemployment involved hardship and stigma and only a tiny minority did not want to work.

(d) That incomes policies could be developed to handle the increasing problem of inflation.

(3) *The commitment to full employment begins to disintegrate*

As the sixties developed, the guarantee of full employment began to be seen as a problem in relation to inflation, international competition and pressure on profits. The boom began to fray at the edges as Japan and Germany challenged US dominance and the stability of the dollar; as US military spending, particularly in Vietnam, fuelled inflation; and as full unemployment shifted power to Labour movements. The historic weaknesses of the British economy once more became evident.

(a) The deflationary policies of the 1966 Labour government have been seen by some as a watershed. Unemployment not only increased from 1% to well over 2% and stayed there: but it was seen by Labour Chancellors Callaghan and Jenkins as a weapon in curbing inflation.

(b) The 1970 Heath government, elected on a programme of a reduction in government intervention and planning, pushed up unemployment from 2·7% to 4% within eighteen months. Heath then did a 'U-turn' which provided a renewed test for Keynesian policies. He attempted to stimulate slow growth and curb rising unemployment by increased public spending and government aid to industry. The 'dash for growth' collapsed in the government defeat at the hands of the miners, a growing balance of payments deficit, and increasing inflation.

(4) *The commitment to full employment disappears*
The failure of the Heath government led many to conclude that attempts to increase production by simply increasing demand will not succeed. Rising unemployment seemed to be a symptom, not of deliberately weakened demand but of major firms being unwilling to alter long-term expectations of production and profitability in response to increased overall demand, so that the increases in public spending simply funded increased imports and diverted investment into property speculation. Whilst the price of property rose, industrial profits declined. This produced important changes in political policy.

(a) In September 1974 Milton Friedman delivered an important lecture in London. Tory economic expert Sir Keith Joseph, in his Preston speech, declared his conversion to monetarism and a new view of full employment *as a problem*. 'We are dominated by the fear of unemployment. It was this which made us turn back against our better judgement . . .'

(b) Sir Keith was soon supported by Margaret Thatcher. Her election as Tory leader in early 1975 was crucial for the monetarists. By 1977 other leading economic figures such as Sir Geoffrey Howe had been converted and former Heath supporters such as Prior were carried along with the tide. A year later Sir Keith was telling the Bow Group, 'Full employment is not in the gift of government. It should not be promised and it cannot be provided.' The Tories went into the 1979 election committed to the new strategy.

(c) The new climate was strengthened by the policies of the 1974–79 Labour government. The Wilson and Callaghan administrations ditched the ambitious 1974 manifesto which had promised expansion, wealth redistribution and a move to a planned economy. Its practice can be described as 'moderate monetarism'. It attempted

to control the money supply, cut public spending and the welfare state, transfer resources to private industry and boost profits. Callaghan stated that the Keynesian option of spending your way out of a recession no longer existed and announced the disappearance of 'the cosy world . . . where full employment could be guaranteed by the stroke of the Chancellor's pen'. Unemployment, under 600,000 in 1974, was just under 1½ million in 1978. It was, ironically, Labour who had in practice broken the full employment consensus.

(d) The new climate produced diminishing public concern. Unemployment levels undreamed of in the fifties, when half a million jobless occasioned horror, preceded not only the return of the Tories in 1979 and 1983 but to a reassertion of the myths of 'scroungers' and 'work-shy social security fiddlers'.

(5) *Mass unemployment becomes normal*

The break with full employment philosophy, then, was a central ingredient in the break with the 'welfare compromise', based on the social philosophy of Beveridge and the economic philosophy of Keynes, whose writ ran from the forties to the seventies. Politicians were no longer prepared to risk what they saw as the social costs – enhanced aspirations, increased dependence, the 'nanny state' – and the economic costs – inflation, depressed profits, industrial decline – which they saw the commitment to the welfare state and full employment as engendering. Changes in technology – labour-saving equipment – and demography – the entry of the products of the post-war 'baby boom' into the work-force – were minor factors in what was essentially a *political* turn. As Britain's monetarist experiment got under way, the abandonment of full employment as a major political objective was trumpeted by Ministers such as Nicholas Ridley who commented: 'The high level of unemployment is evidence of the progress we are making.' For most of the 1980s unemployment was around the three million mark. Conservative governments succeeded in engineering a change in expectations both as to what a satisfactory level of unemployment was and the degree of control the state possessed over changes in employment levels.

Thatcherism, jobs and the economy

How do we assess the Conservatives' record after a decade with Mrs Thatcher at the helm?

(1) *Inflation*

The greater control attained over inflation is undoubtedly an achievement. By 1986 the annual rate of price increase had fallen to under 3%, half the figure of twelve months before and the lowest figure since 1968. On the other hand, it must be recalled that inflation was around 10% when the Conservatives came to power in 1979 and that is more than doubled in the early days of Mrs Thatcher's first administration. Further, the position even in the mid-eighties compared unfavourably with that of our key economic competitors, particularly Germany, Japan and the USA. Moreover, by 1988, inflation was once more accelerating.

(2) *Economic growth*

Further bright spots in Conservative economic policies, their supporters have argued, were the increased rate of profit, enhanced productivity and the acceleration of economic growth. Sustained economic growth had eluded previous governments. Yet from 1982 the British economy was growing by more than 3% a year, whilst the improvement in output per person meant seven years of productivity growth at almost 6% in manufacturing, depressing unit wage costs, the central factor in inflation and international competitiveness. Moreover, increased profits meant increased investment, whilst for most of the decade average earnings ran well ahead of price increases.

On the other hand, it is argued that this way of looking at things ignored the cataclysmic and enduring impact on the economy of the deep recession of 1980–81. In 1988, manufacturing output and investment was only just approaching pre-1979 levels. Growth over the Thatcher years *as a whole* averaged under 2%. In 1988, the regular review of the British economy by the Paris-based Organisation for Economic Co-operation and Development felt that Britain's productivity growth under Mrs Thatcher was largely a 'once and for all' gain, rather than representing an enduring transformation in underlying performance. It was a manufacturing phenomenon – service industries had performed less well – and based in the 1980–81 shakeout of Labour. Productivity in the UK was 30% less than that in the USA and 25% less than that in the EEC. Moreover, the levels of increase in average earnings were perceived by the government not as a triumph, but as an urgent problem.

(3) *Employment*

High unemployment in the first half of the decade, Conservatives argue, was necessary to galvanise an ailing economy and a complacent society. But look at the success story from 1986! Government policies needed time, and from the spring of that year they began to work. And, reinforced by the imaginative efforts of Lord Young in developing the 'New Workers' and 'Job Training Schemes' and increasing the places on the Community Programme, they removed 600,000 people from the unemployment rolls, created more than three-quarters of a million new jobs, and thickened the ranks of the self-employed.

In their turn, the critics insist that this is to view the world through rose-coloured spectacles. The *real* unemployment statistics show around three million still out of work – an intolerable figure. If that represents economic success after ten years' effort, what would economic failure look like? The jobs that are being created are part-time, often temporary and largely low-paid. Even within their own terms, the Conservatives' policies on unemployment have inhibited other aspects of their strategy: for example, the increase in social security payments has impeded plans to cut public expenditure. The contradictions in Thatcherism are demonstrated by the fact that, having initially sliced more than £170 million from the job creation and training programmes of the Manpower Services Commission that it had inherited from Labour, the Conservative administration presided for the rest of the decade over a massive expansion of the schemes.

(4) *Balance of payments*

Mrs Thatcher's opponents claim that even if we accept that the waste and deprivation eighties-style unemployment entails is justified by the pursuit of other economic objectives, the failure of Conservative economic strategy is already becoming apparent. Following a healthy balance of payments surplus in the early eighties, the artificial expansion of the economy and the boom in consumption stoked by Nigel Lawson's 1988 Budget, cutting taxes, particularly for the rich, has already led to a re-emergence of balance of payments problems. And the consequent credit squeeze can only prime inflation, depress investment and slow down the growth of jobs.

(5) *Economic philosophy*

Where most commentators agree is that the economic theories on which Thatcherism is supposed to be based have played only a limited role in all this. As unemployment soared, the pure milk of monetarism prescribed by Sir Keth Joseph in pamphlets such as *Why Britain Needs a Social Market Economy* curdled, to be replaced by more traditional deflationary policies. Between 1979 and the 1983 election, M3 – the broadly defined money supply – rose significantly faster than government targets allowed for. Between 1984 and 1988 the money supply rose at around 20% per annum. The government increasingly turned to fiscal means to limit inflation by exercising control over the Public Sector Borrowing Requirement. It was not, for example, monetarist controls exercising downward pressure on wages that produced the drop in inflation but the fall in world commodity prices – 10% between 1985 and 1986 – and, in particular, the fall in the oil market. Moreover, state expenditure on job creation was accompanied by continued financial and technical support for industry, again in flat defiance of monetarist tenets. What happened in 1987 looked very much like the traditional reflationary pre-election spree indulged in by Mrs Thatcher's much despised predecessors. The rhetoric on cutting taxes could not be said to have been implemented until 1988. By that time, the government seemed to have deserted reliance on monetarism in favour of direct control over public spending and an increasing reliance on an expanded privatisation programme. The growing gap between the theorising of the 'new Conservative' ideologies and the practice of the Conservative government has led many to criticise estimations of Thatcherism which emphasise its novelty and coherence. It has been observed that the continuities between this and previous administrations and the pragmatism with which the Cabinet has tempered principle must also be taken into account.

To sum up: how you look at Conservative policies depends on your focus, values and philosophy. *Theory A* asserts that Thatcherism is a disaster. It represents a failure for the disciplines of economics and politics. The price of tentative, transitory and partial successes has been too high. It has created a dual economy and two nations, alienation, conflict and an unbalanced casino economy. The unemployed and low paid have financed the artificial prosperity of just a sufficient proportion of the electorate to keep Mrs Thatcher in power. In the end, her views on economics stem from her social philosophy – or lack of it – summed up by her statement that 'there is no such a thing as "society".'

The decline in the unemployment figures in the late eighties leaves the problem on the political agenda and at least to some degree relies upon fiddled figures and the cosmetic and palliative approach of the Manpower Services Commission/Training Commission Schemes. A reliance on large-scale unemployment is not only a wasteful, primitive, uncivilised way of regulating a modern economy; it is an unnecessary one. For if there is the political will, the economic means for reconciling employment levels with growth and price stability lie ready at hand.

Theory B denies that what success Thatcherism has had has been minor, purchased at disproportionate cost and delivered in defiance of its own theories. Other ways were tried in the thirty-five years of consensus and welfare state. They simply did not work. They produced rampant inflation, union militancy, a throttling of the enterprise spirit and a spiral of economic decline. Large-scale unemployment does not stem from social irresponsibility. It has been a necessary evil, a means justified by the end – the restoration of economic health. And the Conservative approach *is* working. From 1986 the figures *did* begin to fall. Whatever the mode of calculation that fact is undeniable. And the MSC/Training Agency Schemes have made an important contribution to bringing down unemployment and providing a more flexibile, skilled labour force. At the end of the eighties more people than ever before own their own homes, own shares, own cars, telephones and videos. The *majority* are better off. The problems we face now are problems of success. With the reforging of entrepreneurialism and an enterprise culture that the short-term and well-cushioned suffering of the employed has facilitated, that deprivation will be repaid a thousandfold. The fruits of success, as yet confined to a section of the nation, will trickle down to all its citizens.

Commentators are, therefore, split in their estimations of the Thatcher experiment. But there must be serious doubts as to whether the increase in inequality and relative deprivation is justified by the economic results. With Mrs Thatcher's third term well under way, Britain's underlying social and economic problems still, stubbornly, seem to be there. How do the different parties view unemployment and future economic strategy today?

Party responses to unemployment

(1) *The Conservatives*
The Conservatives are standing firm on existing policies. To reflate
excessively now might be electorally popular but would increase
union power and endanger reduced inflation and increased profitability. The Tory leadership is gambling on the minimal impact that
unemployment had on its fortunes in 1983 and 1987 and the fact that,
with wage increases well ahead of price increases, those *in work* have
had small but relatively important increases in living standards. In
Mrs Thatcher's phrase, 'There is no alternative.' It is a time for
gritting teeth and simply waiting until the medicine works and the
figures fall further. The flavour of the Conservatives' public posture
throughout this period is given by the statement in the 1983 election
manifesto: 'We shall maintain firm control of public spending and
borrowing. We shall continue to set out a responsible financial
strategy which will gradually reduce the growth of money in circulation.' The failure of government strategy has thrown up various
opponents from Sir Ian Gilmour ('Almost all the tenets of monetarism have been destroyed') to Francis Pym who, in 1985, launched
the anti-Thatcher grouping *Centre Forward* and who participated
with other Tory MPs in the cross-party 'Charter for Jobs', and that
hardy perennial Edward Heath. From time to time, Tory 'wets' have
clamoured for a moderate reflation. They never achieved any strong
organisational expression and from 1986 they were outflanked by
Nigel Lawson's more expansive policies and the fall in
unemployment.
     Despite the significant downturn in the government's popularity in
the opinion polls and in by-elections, an increasing number of
débâcles, such as the Westland affair, the resignation of important
Cabinet Ministers and the apparent exhaustion of the administration's radical impetus, no individual or grouping which could act as
an important internal opposition to Mrs Thatcher has emerged.

(2) *The Labour party*
The Labour party essentially advocates a *very limited* return to
Keynesianism. Its 1983 programme, under the heading *Ending Mass
Unemployment*, stated: 'We will expand the economy by providing a
strong and measured increase in spending. Spending money creates
jobs . . . we shall borrow to finance our programme of investment.'

There were two striking points about this otherwise classical statement: it spoke of reducing unemployment to below a million *over five
years* and there were few specific details with vague references to
'back up' import controls 'if these prove necessary', 'a radical extension of industrial democracy' and 'negotiation' of development plans
with companies. Even an almost certain commitment to incomes
policy was veiled as 'a national economic assessment'.

The problem was that the manifesto, which many voters found far
too vague, represented a compromise between different viewpoints
in the party. In the immediate aftermath of the electoral defeat, it
was possible to distinguish different views within the party:

(a) *The Labour right*, represented by Denis Healey, Roy Hattersley and, most articulately, Peter Shore, believed in a cautious
Keynesianism. They opposed moves to protectionism as likely to
isolate an export-dependent nation in a trade war and were concerned that too full-blooded an expansion would collapse in rampant
inflation. Incomes policy, employers and unions working together in
tripartite harness with government was, therefore, essential to this
approach.

(b) *The 'soft' left* had a far firmer view of an 'alternative economic
strategy'. This involved not only expansion but – and here there are
different emphases – a firmer commitment to import controls; the
introduction of a thirty-five-hour week; selective nationalisation;
public control of the financial institutions; workers on the board and
compulsory planning agreements. There were again different views
on the central question of wage controls.

(c) *The 'hard' left* – these views were given public voice by the
Campaign Group. They saw the various alternative economic strategies as no real alternative to Thatcherism: although left forms of
Keynesianism, they still suffer from its central defects. Expansion
would lead to higher pay and less profitability as full employment
approached and stronger trade unions pressed for wage increases.
Price controls tight enough to avoid evasion would squeeze profitability and lead to a collapse in investment. A thirty-five-hour week
would put employers' costs through the roof. Channelling more
funds to capitalists does not necessarily make them invest. Import
controls would lead to higher prices and retaliation. Capitalism must
be replaced by a move towards a planned socialist economy and
involvement of the workers in democratic planning.

In 1985–86, in the backwash of the miners' strike, the leadership of

Neil Kinnock and Roy Hattersley consolidated control of the party
on the basis of a centre-right approach, leaving only the Campaign
Group in serious opposition. The keynote was realism. Labour, it
was stated, would be unlikely to re-establish full employment in one
term: the creation of a million new jobs would be no mean achievement. In the words of Neil Kinnock, change would not produce 'the
full employment of the 1950s, 60s, or even the early 70s – we know it
is not coming back in that form'.Labour went into the 1987 election
on a programme of controlled reflation to be primed with increased
borrowing money from a reversal of the Tories' tax cuts from pension
funds, insurance companies and overseas assets and to be centred on
a refurbishing of the infrastructure, house building and increased
expenditure on education, the NHS, and industrial training. Final
strategy would be determined at a National Economic Summit
involving government, CBI, and TUC. Progress in counteracting
unemployment would be contingent on success in restraining inflation and would, in all probability, although this was left unsaid,
involve a TUC-policed incomes policy. There were plans for more
workers' participation and extended employee shareholding. Local
authorities, in particular, would be given an enhanced role in job
creation. Whilst in 1988 Labour commenced a National Policy
Review, it seemed likely that the essentials of this approach would
endure into the 1990s.

(3) *The third parties*
In both 1983 and 1987, the Alliance argued for carefully selected
increases in public spending and reductions in taxation. In classical
Keynesian fashion investment would be concentrated on railways,
roads, hospitals, housing and transport whilst tax reductions would
focus on reducing prices by, for example, removing the National
Insurance Surcharge. Job creation programmes would be expanded
and particular attention would be paid to youth, with firms being
given financial incentives to take on the long-term unemployed. The
Alliance saw their proposals as realistic and having a limited impact,
reducing unemployment by one million after two years in
government. They would, it was acknowledged, stimulate some
inflation. This would be avoided by a formal pay and prices policy.
An Alliance government would set up a Pay and Prices Commission
to monitor pay settlements in large companies, introduce a counter-
inflation tax to penalise those who went beyond the range of

settlements laid down after negotiations between employers, unions, consumer groups and government; similar arrangements would apply to nationalised industries whilst they would establish an independent Assessment Board for public service settlements.

There were, of course, differences between the two components of the Alliance. Whilst the Liberals and sections of the SDP tended to be firmly located within the above framework, David Owen and his supporters were oriented towards the Tories' 'wet' support and emphasised social 'market' and 'modified monetarist' positions. Although it was strongly arguable that Alliance policies in this area were compatible with those of Labour and a spur to some sort of electoral arrangement, the subsequent split in the Alliance took this off the agenda and left the economic policies of the former partners in a state of some uncertainty.

The future

Britain's unemployment problem has been related to the world economic picture but has had its own specific characteristics. The UK has had sluggish growth, low investment, poor productivity and a powerful labour movement compared with its competitors. These factors are in turn related to the UK's history as the first industrialised country, past failures to innovate and reconstruct its industrial base, the privileged position given to finance capital and relatively large defence expenditure. Neither Keynesianism or monetarism have thus far solved these underlying problems. The years since 1979 have seen important changes in the employment picture: an intensification of the movement from manufacturing to service industries; the introduction of new technologies; a weakening of union power; a growth of peripheral part-time employees. They have also witnessed the emergence of apparently enduring large-scale unemployment. The fall in the jobless from the mid-eighties cannot be ignored but whether, and for how long, it will continue remains unclear. And looking at the alternative: if the policies advocated by Labour and the Alliance did not work in 1964 and in 1974 – despite differences in nomenclature and emphasis they are in the same mould as those implemented by the Wilson and Callaghan administration – why should they work in the 1990s when firmer versions such as those of the Mitterand government in France have faltered? Whilst a future non-Conservative administration would inherit a weaker trade union movement, they would also inherit a weaker economic situation. Although there is evidence that countries which take a corporatist approach, involving unions and employers directly in economic strategy, achieve higher levels of employment, these arrangements are prone to eventual breakdown and, in Britain, would entail a difficult solution to the problems of incomes policy and the decentralised trade union structure. Doubts must remain about the success of neo-Keynesian strategies and, indeed, any return to the full employment of the post-war years.

Finally there are those, such as Gorz, who argue that we should abandon that goal and look beyond the Protestant ethic that we need paid labour to fulfil ourselves. Such an emphasis seems likely to find little resonance in the programmes of the major parties in the foreseeable future. That future appears likely to involve a slow continuation of a stabilisation of Britain's economic decline and an acceptance that full employment is no longer an immediate political goal. The people may be willing to tolerate unemployment on today's scale on the basis that 85% are not affected. On the other hand, increased industrial decline and intensified social conflict may see a turn to as yet untested left strategies. Certainly, with giant strides in new technology, the whole question of the future of work urgently demands political discussion.

Reading

D. N. Ashton, *Unemployment Under Capitalism*, Wheatsheaf Books, 1986.
S. Fineman (ed.), *Unemployment, Personal and Social Consequences*, Tavistock Publications, 1987.
M. Friedman, *Free To Choose*, Penguin Books, 1980.
Sir I. Gilmour, *Britain Can Work*, Martin Robertson, 1983.
A. Glyn, *A Million Jobs A Year*, Verso, 1985.
A. Gortz, *Farewell to the Working Class*, Pluto Press, 1982.
J. Keane & J. Owens, *After Full Employment*, Hutchinson, 1986.
R. Layard, *How to Beat Unemployment*, OUP, 1986.
F. Pym, *The Politics of Consent*, Hamish Hamilton, 1984.
P. Riddel, *The Thatcher Government*, Basil Blackwell, 1985.
S. Williams, *A Job to Live*, Penguin, 1985.

SOCIAL POLICY

10 *Paul Wilding*

The debate about the welfare state

Until the mid-1970s there was no real debate about the welfare state. Certainly, there had been sharp questions about it from the 1950s – for example from the Institute of Economic Affairs in its many publications – but there was little debate. Critics were seen as eccentrics, people who had failed to come to terms with the post-war world. Supporters of the welfare state felt sufficiently confident and assured not to engage in debate.

In fact, supporters of the welfare state were its strongest critics through the 1950s, 1960s and 1970s – for example Richard Titmuss and Peter Townsend – but their criticisms were about the quantity and quality of provision. They wanted more, more quickly; they did not question the idea of the welfare state itself.

The consensus about the welfare state which existed from 1945 to 1975 can easily be overemphasised. There were differences between the main political parties about what should be done and how quickly, but there was near universal acceptance of the major role of the state in welfare which had emerged in the years between 1945 and 1950. There was little questioning of that principle.

The collapse of consensus

What has become quite clear is that consensus about the desirability of a major role for the state in welfare broke down in the 1970s for a variety of reasons. These are some of the reasons put forward:

(1) The consensus was never more than superficial. The welfare state in Britain has suffered from two damaging associations – with

socialism and with austerity – and this had inhibited its wholehearted acceptance as a fact of late twentieth-century life.

(2) The era of painless financing out of economic growth ended in the mid-1970s. As long as the economy was expanding, private consumption and welfare spending could expand simultaneously. In the 1970s for the first time it was much more either one or the other.

(3) Paying for the welfare state had come to rest more heavily on those with average and below average incomes because the income at which people started paying tax had fallen. This gave greater credibility to politicians talking about 'the burden of taxation' caused by the welfare state and broadened concern about welfare expenditure.

(4) The welfare state has been blamed for Britain's economic difficulties. The high taxes which are required to sustain it have, it is alleged, fuelled inflation and reduced incentives, so weakening the economy. The welfare state is also charged with absorbing labour which would be better employed in productive enterprises rather than in the provision of social services.

(5) The welfare state has come under strong criticism for its ineffectiveness in achieving its aims. It has not, even its supporters agree, abolished poverty, achieved equality of opportunity in education, or equality of access to health services. In many services, e.g. higher education, the middle classes are clearly the main beneficiaries.

(6) Public confidence in welfare state services has been weakened by the continuous deafening chorus of complaint about lack of resources and low standards of services which arises from those who work in them. As Enoch Powell pointed out many years ago, to secure more resources, those in the services feel they have to denigrate them. People therefore came to think that services were substandard – and therefore not worth paying for or supporting.

(7) Welfare state policies depend on faith in experts, the belief that there are people who know how to solve the problems of poverty, ill health, bad housing, urban redevelopment, juvenile delinquency, and so on. The reputations of the key welfare professionals have gone down the skittles in the last few years – and the welfare state has suffered in consequence.

(8) The belief that public action is the appropriate way to deal with social problems was a basic building block in the consensus. This has been weakened by the emergence of new and more complex problems which no one is confident they know how to tackle – the problem of the inner city, the problem of order in society, the increasing

numbers of very elderly, for example.

(9) From all sides, the welfare state is attacked for what it is alleged to do to *people* and to *society*. The New Right talk of 'the nanny state' destroying independence, initiative and self-respect and fostering dependency. Feminists accuse it of contributing to women's subordination. Marxists see it as propping up capitalism and disciplining the working class. The romantics talk of the 'schooled', 'medicalised' society.

(10) The essential underpinnings of the welfare state were provided by Keynesian economics. What Keynes did was to make legitimate high levels of government activity and spending. The eclipse (temporary or permanent) of Keynesianism means the removal of a basic philosophical prop to the welfare state.

Most of these points are contestable. They are clearly of varying degrees of importance but they make up the background to the debate about the welfare state.

Positions in the debate

It is difficult briefly to characterise the various positions in the debate on the welfare state without seeming to caricature them. The sketches which follow can do no more than indicate the broad lines of the different perspectives.

The New Right position
The New Right critique of the welfare state is the contemporary expression of anti-collectivism. It draws on the work of two distinguished academics – Milton Friedman and F. A. Hayek. It stresses certain values – freedom, individualism and inequality. It stresses the creative possibilities of the free market economy. It emphasises a range of doubts and anxieties about government action. It makes a number of general and particular criticisms of welfare state policies.

(1) The welfare state is a threat to freedom because
    (a) it gives people little or no choice about the type or quality of service which is provided:
    (b) services are not subject to effective democratic control.
(2) State provision of welfare is fundamentally inefficient because it is monopolistic. There is no competition between providing bodies and it is only through competition that efficiency is achieved.

(3) In a welfare state system what is provided is not what consumers want but what professionals and bureaucrats *think* they want. Public provision is therefore inevitably unresponsive to individual needs and wishes.

(4) Although designed to help, in fact the welfare state damages people. It creates dependency and weakens individuals' sense of responsibility for themselves and their families.

(5) A welfare state leads to the view that the state is the main source and provider of welfare services. Other sources and systems of welfare – the family, the community, the voluntary sector, the market – are neglected and weakened and, in time, perish.

(6) Welfare state policies weaken the economy because they depend on debilitating rates of taxation which fuel inflation, destroy incentives and damage investment. The real sources of welfare – a healthy economy and economic growth – are therefore undermined.

(7) As well as weakening the economy, welfare state policies also weaken the authority of government. Governments become the focus of interest group activity as groups fight for the recognition and protection of their particular needs. Governments committed to particular welfare programmes all too easily become the creatures of particular groups.

Underlying the whole critique is one vital belief – *private provision is always better:*

(a) *economically* because it is not damaging to the economy and because it will be more efficient;

(b) *politically* because it does not make government the creature of particular interests; and

(c) *socially* because it does not make people dependent and because it offers choice and makes providers accountable to consumers.

The Marxist position
The Marxist critique has not become part of current political debate as has that of the New Right. The most obvious reason is that what Marxists say is of little or not immediate political importance. It is also difficult to talk about a Marxist critique because 'Marxist' is a loose category embracing a rich variety of opinions. It is, however, possible with this warning to sketch a Marxist position.

(1) Marxists see the welfare state as shaped by three forces:

(a) the needs of capitalism;

(b) class conflict;

(c) the ideology generated by capitalism.

Capitalism needs healthy, educated and contented workers. It needs systems which maintain workers in times when the onward march of economic progress is temporarily checked. It needs a state whose authority is seen as legitimate, and the provision of welfare can contribute to such legitimacy. The capitalist state is characterised by the conflict which Marxists see as the essential characteristic of the relationship between capital and labour. This conflict produces concessions by capital and/or victories for labour – and sometimes these take the form of welfare services.

Marxists are therefore ambivalent about the welfare state. It is both a prop to capitalism and a symbol of victories won by the working class.

(2) Marxists lay much stress on the social control functions of the welfare state – i.e. its contributions to inculcating and reinforcing the values and patterns of behaviour required by the capitalist system.

(3) An important strand in the Marxist critique is the argument that many of the problems with which the welfare state seeks to deal are the direct product of the particular nature of the capitalist system. They are not therefore amenable to solution by social services.

(4) Marxists also stress the limited possibilities of social services. They are not, they argue, a tool for changing society. The most that can be achieved through welfare state policies is, in Miliband's words, 'a certain humanisation' of the existing order.

(5) An anxiety which Marxists have is that, providing tangible and immediate goals, welfare services will have a deradicalising effect on the working-class political movement. Workers will become content with the half loaf of the welfare state rather than striving for the whole loaf of socialism.

Marxists cannot, therefore, be optimistic about the possibilities of welfare provided by a capitalist state. On the other hand, they recognise the real benefits accruing to the working class from such provision. They contest the New Right arguments but they do not want to see welfare services become an alternative to radical social reconstruction.

The Fabian position

In many ways the welfare state represents a triumph of Fabianism – the belief that the amelioration or removal of social ills is possible by modest institutional change within a mixed economy. The group of thinkers has, from a fundamentally supportive position, produced a variety of criticisms of the welfare state which have been part of the raw material of the debate.

(1) This group supported the welfare state as a means of reducing social inequality. Their researches however, show that this has not happened. In health, housing and education, for example, there are still striking inequalities between class, sex, region and ethnic groups.

(2) They have come to accept that more resources are not necessarily always the best answer to unmet needs.

(3) They accept that state services can be bureaucratic, inefficient, inflexible and so complicated that people get lost in a welfare maze.

(4) They accept that the welfare state gives many professionals who work within it a degree of power which is problematic because they are directly answerable to no one for its exercise.

(5) They agree that the welfare state has made some pretty awful mistakes – e.g. some local authority housing developments.

(6) More and more supporters of the welfare state would agree that the concentration on services is bound to bring failure because the achievement of particular goals, for example, for health and education, cannot be achieved without taking account of factors which go way beyond the purview of the health or education service. What is needed, Fabians argue, is a broad health or education *policy*, not just health and education *services*.

The Fabian critique has contributed to the dissatisfaction with the welfare state. The group saw criticism as the rational way to improvement. The New Right, however, have used their work as ammunition in the struggle to destroy the credibility of welfare state policies and 'roll back' the state.

The feminist position

Feminists have developed a powerful critique of the welfare state based on an exposure of its sexist assumptions, implicit and explicit, and their impact on the lives of women. They point out that:

(1) Social policies are based on certain unstated assumptions

about sex roles. In the British welfare state those assumptions contribute directly and indirectly to the continuance of women's unequal position in society.

(2) Those assumptions – e.g. about women as carers – trap women, whether they like it or not, in a traditional female role.

(3) The welfare state is a living witness to women's inequality. They are the main clients of many services, they staff many of the services. But they have few of the top jobs, they contribute little to the decision-making and they are treated badly when they need help, for example when using ante-natal care of when suffering from depression.

Feminists are not (as a generalisation) hostile to the principle of the welfare state. They are, however, keen to point out how good (male) intentions can have unfortunate even if unintended implications for women.

The romantic position

This is the group for which it is most difficult to find a suitable title. The position is occupied both by genuine romantics like Ivan Illich and by people whose arguments are much more pragmatic and hard-headed. Essentially, it represents a reaction against the welfare system of the late 1960s and early 1970s and three of its salient characteristics – its size, its powers and its typical organisational forms.

(1) The romantics worry about the increasing size of organisations because for them it spells remoteness and bureaucracy, and the inability to respond swiftly, sensitively and flexibly to individual needs.

(2) They are concerned about increasing professionalisation because they see this as involving costs as well as gains for clients – social distance, dependency, and a neglect of people's capacity for self-help on an individual or collective basis.

(3) The failure of the state welfare system to involve consumers of services in decisions about the shape and nature of current and future provision seems to the romantics both a reason why the welfare state has developed as it has and a result of such trends.

(4) Romantics worry, too, about the failure of the state services to take sufficient account of other systems and sources of welfare – family, neighbourhood and voluntary – and to work sensitively with

them.

What romantics want is a small-scale, local, less bureaucratic, decentralised, deprofessionalised, participative system of welfare. They see the welfare state as developing in the opposite direction, as becoming alienated from, and alienating, those who use its services.

Warnings

(1) The debate about the welfare state is an ideological debate. Positions are not adopted on the basis of a scientific assessment of evidence and argument. Attitudes to the role of the state in welfare depend on social values, beliefs about society, beliefs about the role of government, and beliefs about the right ordering of economic and social relationships.

(2) Do not forget the achievements of the welfare state. Even its supporters spend more blood and ink on criticism than defence. Criticism is easy – so too is defence, but we are at a point when the welfare state looks a bit middle-aged and unappealing. Users had come – until the early 1980s at least – to take it for granted. The politicians and the media are only interested in its shortcomings. Stress is on costs and cuts – not on what is provided – and achieved. Since 1945 the real value of social security benefits has vastly increased, so have the number of seventeen and eighteen-year-olds continuing their education, so has the number of students in higher education. We have made an enormous improvement in the physical standards of our housing stock. We have a national health service which gives a better service at a cost of 6% of gross domestic product than the United States gets for an expenditure of 11% of a relatively larger GDP.

(3) The debate is also carried on at a level of generalisation which, while it may be satisfactory to politicians, is little help to the careful student. The welfare state, it is said, for example, is a threat to freedom. All kinds of questions have to be asked and answered before such a statement can be evaluated. What is meant by the welfare state? What freedom? Whose freedom? And so on.

(4) Certainly there are sharply distinct positions in the debate. There are those who believe that a market system with a modicum of residual state provision could provide all the welfare needed in our kind of society. On the other hand there are those who believe that

only the state can provide what is required.

Between these extremes there is a considerable area of muddy middle ground inhabited by large numbers of people who would agree about a good number of things – that the pure doctrine of state welfare (i.e. the state does all) *has* collapsed, that there *is* a real role for a properly supported voluntary sector, that private provision *has* a role, that self-help groups can make a valuable contribution, that decentralisation and more participation *must* be developed.

Conclusion

The debate about the welfare state is important because it is about the kind of society we want. It is real because it raises fundamental questions about individual and social responsibility. It is about economic and political issues, about the broad nature and pattern of social development, and about the more effective and efficient organisation, administration and financing of particular services in particular places.

The debate is confused. Therefore it can be unhelpful. But if policy-makers listen attentively there is much to be learned.

Reading

M. & R. Friedman, *Free to Choose*, Penguin, 1980.

V. George & P. Wilding, *Ideology and Social Welfare*, Routledge & Kegan Paul, 1987.

R. Hadley & S. Hatch, *Social Welfare and the Failure of the State*, Allen & Unwin, 1981.

M. Loney, *The Politics of Greed*, Pluto, 1986.

R. Mishra, *The Welfare State in Crisis*, Harvester, 1984.

A. Seldon, *Whither the Welfare State*, Institute of Economic Affairs, 1981.

P. Wilding (ed.), *In Defence of the Welfare State*, Manchester University Press, 1987.

11 *Geoffrey Lee*

The politics of housing policy

It is inevitable that government should be closely involved in such a basic human concern as the availability and quality of the houses in which we live. This chapter examines the background and current issues in housing policy and places them in the context of the party political debate.

Development

(1) *Post-war activity*

During the second world war Britain had 200,000 houses destroyed and a further half million severely damaged. Demand was rising as demobilisation took place and marriage and birth rates rose. As in other policy sectors the solution was an extension of wartime state control and direction. Procedures for compulsory purchase were streamlined, subsidies were increased and local authorities were empowered to build prefabricated houses on public open land. As during other periods of Labour government, local authorities assumed greater powers. Besides increased requisitioning, they built 80% of houses and controlled repairs and private building. Central government still determined design and materials through an increasing stream of circulars. This cash programme came to an end in 1947 as building materials and fuel ran low and Britain suffered a balance of payments crisis.

During this period, planning was revolutionised with the passage of the Distribution of Industry Act, New Towns Act, the National Parks and Access to the Countryside Act, the Town Development

Act and, most significantly, the Town and Country Planning Act 1947 which gave local authorities the responsibility of producing development plans and the power to control the whole process.

At the same time the potentially damaging separation of housing staff and planners, who looked to different ministries and underwent different training and career paths, was consolidated.

(b) *Conservative disengagement*

Macmillan's promise during the election of 1951 to build 300,000 houses a year made a significant contribution to the Conservatives' success.

Under the Conservatives, the private sector was actively encouraged. Licensing was abolished in 1954, rent control eased and the purchase of council houses forwarded. This was gradually formulated into a positive policy direction, heralded by the White Paper, 'Housing: the next step'. As local authorities were guided from building towards slum clearance (a public health problem) the private sector was stimulated by legislation on rents, subsidies and improvement grants. From 15% of houses built in 1952, those for owner–occupation rose to 63% in 1963 (figures from Donnison and Ungerson).

Deliberately eschewing 'planning', the Conservatives appeared to be driving towards a residual role for the public sector which would look after only those in need. Planning concentrated on green belts and conservation, and any compulsory purchase had to be for a 'fair market price'.

(c) *Intervention resumed*

Demographic changes ensured that disengagement would not continue. A rise in the birth rate, more marriages and a reduction in family size all began to increase demand. At the same time slum clearance, emphasis on ownership and the steady decline of private rented accommodation created stresses at the poorer end of the market, and these began to surface as 'human interest' and scandal stories in the media.

Labour   As a result, Labour could use housing policy to good effect in the 1964 election by concentrating on empty office blocks, tenants rights, rents and building. Their National Plan of 1965 contained a proposal to build half a million houses a year and, following the

Parker Morris Committees, council house size and standards were improved, Rent rebates were introduced and 'fair rents' established. Control was clearly re-established with the advent of the Land Commission which could buy land and encourage development.

Pressure groups Forces on government to act on housing were increased by pressure groups at this time. The problems of the homeless were highlighted by the television programme *Cathy Come Home* and in its wake, Shelter was founded in 1967. The Skeffington Committee had advocated public involvement in planning, and the middle class increasingly resisted road-building programmes and city-centre redevelopment, especially in 'gentrified' London boroughs.

Inner cities Richard Crossman had turned the attention of the Labour government from large clearances to rehabilitation, and the Conservatives continued this 'total approach' to areas of special need by co-ordinating services. Labour attempted to press further in 1975 with the Community Land Act which enabled authorities to acquire land for development and draw revenue through a tax on transactions. But while some progress was made, Britain's economic problems impeded any real solution. Approximately 10% of inner-city land was unused and the social deprivation was severe. Perhaps one of the last major interventions on behalf of the disadvantaged was the Housing (Homeless Persons) Act which was created and processed in 1977 by coalitions of Lib–Lab leaders, allied pressure groups, backbench MPs and DOE civil servants.

Finance The Housing Finance Act, 1972 sought to rationalise debts, rents and subsidies to best advantage. It caused disruption and opposition, notably at Clay Cross, Derbyshire, where councillors were surcharged and barred from office, and it was repealed by the 1974 Labour government. It did, however, leave a system of allowances for private tenants.

(d) *Thatcherism*
The Conservative government which came to power in 1979 was committed to free-market principles. In seeking to 'roll back' the state and cut public expenditure, local authority housing programmes fared badly. The 1980 Housing Act also gave private

landlords powers to raise rents and evict tenants, and provided a system whereby council and housing associations tenants had the right to buy their homes. Far from allowing impetus to be lost as the rate of sales peaked in 1986, the Conservatives mounted a second radical initiative as they went into the 1987 general election – to increase the roles of the private rented sector and housing associations and to reduce that of local authorities to a minimal and residual one.

Ideology and housing Labour's extension of wartime controls and increased local authority powers were to turn into a ideological commitment. Such constraints were to prove increasingly unacceptable as Britain moved into the 1980s, and in the long term identified the party with bureaucratic restriction of tenants' freedoms, epitomised by the prohibitions on painting their own front doors. At the same time Labour exuded hostility to private landlords by retaining rent controls, and did little to encourage owner–occupiers.

As we have seen, the Conservatives adopted the contrary stance of relaxing controls and encouraging the private sector. In equating Labour policy with identity cards and food rationing they derived considerable benefit in the 1950s, and in a similar way seized the advantage in the 1980s by emphasising freedom of choice in line with publicly-expressed wants. In large cities, the Conservatives accused Labour administrations of 'social engineering' and bureaucratic incompetence while Labour warned its tenants of rent increases and deteriorating standards if they lost power. Here is to be found the bedrock of Labour support, for while 30% of the electorate are council tenants, over ninety constituencies have a majority of people living in council houses.

Deriding Labour's 'rearguard action' against council house sales the Conservative government made good use of their pursuit of a 'property-owning democracy' in the 1983 election. In her five-year anniversary statement in April 1984, Mrs Thatcher extolled the virtue of the wider spread of home ownership 'than at any time in our history; this is the way to become "One Nation" '. The opinion polls at that time gave the Conservatives a 6% lead over Labour, and significantly they had a 2 to 1 lead among homeowners while Labour led 2 to 1 among council tenants.

The Conservatives are on firm ground – the preference for home ownership is strong, particularly among young people, where 65% of

16 to 19-year-olds want to buy. Britain has also seen an unparalleled rise in ownership – from 31% in 1951 to 66% in 1987, with the Building Societies Association predicting 75% by the year 2000. With this in mind, in May 1986 the Housing Minister, John Patten, could begin to suggest limiting the proportion of council ownership to force matters in areas such as Tower Hamlets (82% public-owned), and to propose giving tenants the right to vote on switching to private agents or to take over their own estates' management. Extolling the latter as 'exciting' as peoples' attitudes changed in such cooperatives, he set out the Conservative thinking on 'social housing' in terms of such 'diversity' and 'flexibility' and advocated co-operatives as an alternative to 'mass municipal ownership and management' for the three million who might not want to buy. He referred to the rest of the free world where no one else had followed our bureaucratic path (*Guardian*, 30 January 1987).

The Conservatives also developed a 'right to rent' policy to complement the right to buy – scrapping fair rent laws which had 'distorted' the market and seeking an injection of new funds. Their 1987 manifesto was the most radical, if not doctrinaire, – besides co-operatives and the right to transfer ownership, Housing Action Trusts would take over and renovate run-down estates and then sell them.

There was no evidence cited of how or why private-sector management would be more efficient. The ideological underpinnings of the new policies could be identified in the first speech of William Waldegrave, the new minister, as he challenged 40-year assumptions: he intended to bring the 'Prime Minister's' radical Conservatism to bear on the 'sclerotic housing institutions which brought you the Hulme housing estate, cardboard city, billions of pounds worth of badly-maintained state-owned houses and the £50,000 broom cupboard' (*Independent*, 29 August 1987). The right to housing where one lived was dismissed as 'nonsense' and 'half-baked', and the right to buy mitigated against further generalised building by councils. Where co-operatives were not possible, housing associations were closer to the people and could manage better than councils. Ministers redefined councils' role as 'essentially strategic – identifying housing needs and demands, encouraging methods of provision by other bodies to meet such needs, maximising the use of private finance and encouraging interest in the revival of the independent rented sector' (Marion Roe, *Sunday Times*, 27 December 1987). As part of this retrenchment the government made it as difficult as possible for councils to take over the 60,000 houses in new towns – inserting amendments into the 1986 Housing and Planning Bill and considering new legislation in 1988 when ballots went in favour of council tenancy (94% in Peterborough). These manifesto proposals, which would lead to the Housing Act of 1988, were only the first phase – a second bill in 1989 would prevent councils subsidising rents from rates and change the annual investment programme.

Labour response   Aware that they have been pushed on to the defensive, the Labour Party has had to re-examine its policies and beliefs. David Griffiths of the Labour Housing Group (LHG) took issue with the routine conference reaffirmations of 'the right of everyone to a decent home at a price they can afford' for its lack of egalitarian commitment and paternalistic omission of any reference to rights. What has been lacking in the past was any real equality of tenure and a new comprehensive approach was now required:
   (1) The overall level of investment for both sectors should be determined by central government but thereafter Whitehall controls over local authorities should be removed.
   (2) Local authorities could take responsibility for supply in both sectors, free to buy and sell.
   (3) Standards should be raised to meet the expectations of tenants.
   (4) Democratic rights should be extended to facilitate accountability and eliminate what Frank Field called 'serfdom'. Co-operatives and collective control would be encouraged, rather than ignored or discouraged (as in Riverside, Liverpool).
   These policies, first seen in the 1977 report, 'The assessment of housing requirements', of the Labour government's Housing Service Advisory Group, were seen as restoring some vision. The Labour Housing Group was scathing about the party's past 'hypocrisy' of restricting public-sector investment and pretending that the huge concessions to owner-occupiers did not exist, or that they could be offset by the one-year rent freeze proposed in the 1982 Programme.
   The Labour Party continued to respond to the Tory agenda – the 'right to rent' had been an LHG response to right to buy – but on behalf of councils, not to their exclusion. The 1987 manifesto also included tenant co-operatives, consultation on rents and repairs, security of tenure for private tenants and a right to repairs and a

house 'log book' of history and condition for buyers. By June 1988 Neil Kinnock was accepting tenants' voting to change to private landlords as part of the 'new realism' of a diversity of provision.

The Alliance   The nature of this debate is anathema to the Alliance. The SDP's 'A strategy for housing' begins with the words: 'The characteristics of British housing today reflect, with awesome accuracy, the failure of the two party system. The polarisation of tenure between owner-occupiers and council tenants is socially divisive and offers insufficient choice.' The Alliance called for increased investment coupled with increased rights and devolved control. There have been some problems and dilemmas in their decentralisation and subsidy policies which will be reviewed later.

Current issues

(1) *Housing shortage*
In 1975 households exceeded dwellings by 800,000 but by the mid-1970s this deficit had turned into a surplus of 500,000. The Labour Housing Group delve beyond this figure, however, to discount empty properties, second homes and necessary vacancies. Even without concealed households they estimate an actual deficit of 421,000 in 1976, of 188,000 in 1981 rising to 362,000 in 1986. By 1988 the Conservative controlled Association of District Councils (ADC) was reporting a deficit of 50,000 homes a year to cope with homelessness and rising waiting lists (Study by Bristol University, School of Advanced Urban Studies).

The 1977 Housing Green Paper had outlined a requirement for 300,000 new homes every year to meet problems and projected trends. In fact completions fell short, as is shown in Table 3. At the same time private sector completions fell from 153,000 in 1975 to 120,000 in the slump of 1981 and then began rising steadily towards 200,000 as the economy revived in the mid-eighties.

(a) *Public sector decline*   The clear decline in public sector housebuilding, caused by public expenditure cuts which fell most heavily on capital spending and particularly on housing, is an obvious focus of political dispute. The Commons' Environment Select Committee, measuring against the 1977 Green Paper, foresaw a shortfall of 300,000–350,000 by the mid-1980s.

Table 3   *Homes built*

Year	Council	Housing association
1975	140,000	19,600
1979	58,000	16,000
1981	26,000	12,000
1983	36,000	13,500
1985	22,600	12,000
1987	16,000	10,000

Source: Sunday Times, 15 June 1986; *Guardian*, 24 November 1988.

In November 1984 it was reported that Patrick Jenkin had reduced the Treasury's attempted £600 million cut in the public housing investment programme to £65 million. But the Treasury sought what were described as 'revenge' cuts of £1 billion by cutting from 40% to 20% the proportion of receipts from the sale of council houses which authorities were entitled to invest in new housing. The announcement in December sparked a major Conservative back-bench revolt from groups opposed to government policy on the economy and/or local government, and from those wanting some capital spending especially on housing and in the inner cities. Thirty MPs abstained and three voted against the government. In 1985 a cut of £185 million was imposed, and 1979 and 1986 capital and current spending on housing fell by 60% (£6,870 million to £2,612 million). In this respect it fared worse (see Table 4).

Table 4   *Public spending = real change 1979/80 to 1984/85 (%)*

Law and order	+ 29·1
Social Security	+ 28·4
Defence	+ 22·8
Industry and employment	+ 17·8
Health	+ 16·7
Education and science	+1·0
Housing	−54·6

Source: 1985 Report of the National Federation of Housing Associations.

In the 1986 debate on tax cuts versus public spending, housing was still not seen as a priority compared to education and the Health Service, and on becoming Environment Secretary Nicholas Ridley cut his predecessor's proposals by £250 million.

(b) *Government strategy* As economic recovery made further investment possible this was redirected – political steering rather than fiscal restraint came to the fore. The £451 million increase in 1986/87 was targeted on renovation and maintenance rather than on building and the housing associations were singled out for generous funding. The following year it was proposed to cut investment grant contributions from 40% to 25% and increase the amount for reno- vating estates (possible sell-off targets) from 31% to 55%. Increasing the housing association funding in 1988 by 80% over three years, Mr Ridley foresaw them overtaking council building.

Council building was deliberately held back. With 80% of councils running estates at a profit, with only £25 billion of debt charges on stock of £100 billion and holding £6 billion from house sales – they could have resumed building by 1986. Even pressure from Tory back-benchers in April 1987 did not move the government from the 20% of sale receipts rule. Concerns over inflationary pressures were matched by a dislike of municipal power and perceived misma- nagement. Successive reductions in gross capital spending were planned to 1990.

The government therefore devised alternative sources of supply to cope with shortages. In February 1987 councils were given powers to go into partnership with private enterprise to provide rented accom- modation – up to 30% of the cost. At the same time they supported the deal between North Housing Association and City stockbrokers James Capel to build 2,000 homes for rent in towns, and saw it as a way of building thousands more. In March 1988 cash incentives were offered to council tenants to encourage them to move and buy homes, releasing council homes – £100 million to £200 million over two years to 50,000 households. Empty property also came into focus: the Empty Property Unit (sponsored by Shelter) estimated that there were 700,000 empty dwellings in England in 1986 – 112,000 belonged to councils, 15,000 to housing associations, 19,000 to public-sector bodies and 552,000 were privately-owned. To exert pressure Lord Scarman launched an Empty Property and Com- munity Aid Bill to put buildings into residential use for five years. In 1988 government said it required statements of policy to reduce empty council properties before investment money was released. Meanwhile, to bring the empty private housing into use the Housing Act of 1988 replaced fair rents by 'assured tenancies' at the market rate while 'shorthold' tenancies were intended to encourage the letting of spare rooms. This was also designed to stop the selling off of 200,000 private rented homes per year and expand it beyond its current 8% of stock.

(c) *Regional shortages and mobility* Shortages contributed to house price inflation (30% per annum in 1988) and the effects were disproportionately severe in the south and east. In London, where average prices passed £100,000, there was a black market in council housing with cash being paid for unauthorised tenancies. The enthusiastic selling of council houses in the south and south-east had rendered the problem more acute – a third of all households there had an income too small to enter the housing market with a mortgage – double the number of five years previously (G. Bramley, *Housing Needs in Non-metropolitan Areas*, 1987). Complaints were now coming from Conservatives, whose children were affected.

Problems of lack of mobility were said to be costing business £500 million per year and British Rail had recourse to providing subsidised housing on its sidings in 1988/89. The government worked with the CBI to promote company homes, alone or by shared ownership or subsidy. As early as 1986 they had changed the law on rents and leasehold to foster shared ownership so that a purchaser could buy part of a house and rent the rest – enabling a move to a more expensive region by 'reinvestment'. The Nationwide Anglia Building Society's move into the rented sector in 1987 was welcomed and encouraged.

(d) *Opposition criticism   The Labour Party* referred to a 'crisis' in their 1982 Programme caused by cuts at a time of accelerating demand as the 'baby boom' of twenty to thirty years ago created more new households. In England they claimed there were 500,000 households sharing a home and 300,000 married couples and single parents living 'concealed' in other households.

For the *Alliance*, the Liberal Party too criticised the failure to meet house-building targets, even during the Macmillan years, and the SDP sought to puncture the complacency on housing. In their 'Strategy for Housing' they described the structural changes in population: decreasing household size as people live longer, more marriages end in divorce and young people leave home earlier. The increase in the number of households is running at about 165,000 *per annum*. Add to that annual number of houses demolished (around 35,000) and we can see the inadequacy of the country's new construction programme' (pp. 2–3).

(e) *Consequences* The opposition pointed to resulting inadequate temporary accommodation, the worst problems being faced by single parents and women whose marriages had broken down, enforced entrapment in tower blocks for families, fewer transfers to sheltered flats for the elderly and tenants on older estates suffering inadequate amenities. Local authority waiting lists held 1–2 million people.

(f) *Opposition solutions* Both the Labour Party and Alliance proposed a major housebuilding programme by allowing councils to spend the £6 billion from sales. The Alliance promised a national mobility scheme (extending it beyond the public sector) to abolish Stamp Duty for first-time buyers, introduce a Home Loan Scheme, reduce taxation on rents from spare rooms, and to extend the 'partnership' of private renting with government subsidies.

(2) *Decay*
According to the DOE's 'English House Condition Survey' of 1988 there were 1·2 million unfit homes (6·3% of the total, compared to 5·6% in 1981); 564,000 lacked basic amenities such as indoor lavatories and hot and cold water (3%, down from 5% in 1981); 5% needed urgent repairs of £2,900 or more and 4·7 million homes needed £2,200 of repairs. The country's four local authority associations were less optimistic and in 1986 said that £75 billion was needed – £1,500 for every man woman and child, and that 83% of council homes needed repairs on average of £4,900, while the private sector was worse. The problem particularly affects the elderly – 206,000 of the 480,000 in unfit homes in a government survey were pensioners. And more than 80% of the bed-sits, student lets and hostels (housing 2·6 million people) lack fire-escapes, half need major repairs and only a quarter are adequate.

This deterioration is a function of:

(a) *Age* In 1979 30% of the housing stock was built before 1919 and 22% between 1919 and 1944.

(b) *Public expenditure constraints* Grant-aided expenditure was restricted in the 1970s to prevent speculation and to save money. Slum clearance fell from 72,000 in 1971 to 20,000 in 1983. The imposition of VAT on building alterations in 1984 accelerated the decline as public sector spending was halved.

(c) *Building errors* Much post-war housing was substandard. Of council homes, 1·2 million suffer from damp, a third from damp or condensation and 300,000 homes are 'difficult to let'. Some authorities, such as Liverpool and Manchester, have had to blow up flat blocks on which interest is still being paid, while Birmingham is contending with the colliery shale used in the foundations of defective system-built houses. In such overspill dwellings the kitchens and bathrooms are too small, heating systems outdated and expensive, constructional faults have been discovered and their environments have become vandalised. The Association of Metropolitan Authorities in 1985 estimated that it would cost £5 billion to repair the defects in system-built housing, particularly deck access, in the next ten to fifteen years.

Opposition proposals The political response of the opposition parties is to deplore this state of affairs, the impact of government cuts and to demand action. The Labour party believed a threefold increase in the level of building and renovation to be necessary, and given the failure of the private sector this would have to be public-sector-led investment. Standards would be reviewed and low-energy housing provided to avoid past errors, and a rolling programme to improve problem areas begun. Local authorities would be allowed to improve for sale, the renovation grant would be simplified and extended and in action areas they would be given compulsory improvement powers. The Alliance offered simplification of grants, renovation areas and building programmes.

Conservative response Increasing public expenditure and more public sector control are not the panacea for the government elected in 1979. Instead, the remedies have included:

(a) *Improvement for sale*   The 1980 Housing Act made grants available to local authorities and housing associations to improve run-down dwellings for sale. By the end of 1982, 6,000 houses were being so improved by 100 authorities and ninety associations.

(b) *Homesteading*   By 1982 4,400 unimproved homes had been sold at low cost to would-be home-owners who would make them habitable.

(c) *Priority Estates Project*   Three 'difficult to let' estates in Bolton, Hackney and Lambeth were being systematically upgraded as an example, the process being reinforced by a report, film and seminars. The Estate Action team had a budget of £75 million for 1988 and gave advice on removing walkways, taking off storeys and creating 'defensible space'. Another £38 million was announced for inner-city estates in 1987 – coupled with talk of a change of management.

(d) *Housing Defects Prevention Unit*   Established in 1981, this unit analyses problems, disseminates technical information, and has produced sixteen Defect Action Sheets for public and private sectors.

(e) *New improvement grant system, 1980*   Grants became available for pre-1919 properties, as well as phased payment, applicable to both the public and private sectors, with high rates for Greater London. In 1982 the rates were raised to 90%, and a special scheme was introduced to buy old prefabricated houses. Whole street improvement or 'enveloping' was extended. In producing a rise in spending from £200 million in 1979–80 to £900 million in 1983–84, the government claimed to be at last 'doing something' about the improvement problem. But by October 1981 officials were doubting the value of giving local authorities improvement grant funds which they would have otherwise found themselves, and in August 1984 the government was expected to halve available cash for the second year running. In 1985 the government declared that it was never intended to continue this indefinitely and moved to introduce loans and means-testing in order to reduce the expenditure to £250 million.

Some repair grants were increased slightly – in 1986 those for structurally defective 1960s homes, but the trend was downward. Funds for repairing system-built houses were cut from £30 million to £14 million in 1986, home insulation grants were similarly reduced, and in 1989 even improvement grants to private landlords were cut from 75% to 20% of the work. Environmental Health officers were soon reporting the deterioration.

(f) *Right to repair*   The Housing and Building Control Act 1983 confers a statutory right on council, new town and housing association tenants to carry out their own repairs and claim reimbursement of at least 75% of the cost from their landlords.

(g) *Building control*   The 1983 Act attempted to remove bureaucratic controls. Supervision passed from local authorities to inspectors who issued certificates. Guidance through regulations could be provided by the Ministry. These measures were attacked by the opposition as centralising at the expense of local authorities, likely to diminish quality and as being palliatives given the size of the problems. The Labour party promised to reintroduce Parker Morris standards to increase room size.

It should be remembered that the Building Societies Association in 1987 reported that 88% of people were very or quite satisfied with their housing (83% in 1975), including 77% of council-home dwellers.

(3) *Responsibility*
(i) *Government policy*   Withdrawing rapidly from housing project control and funding, the Conservatives have sought to reduce central government's role. This is evident with the housing benefit scheme which passed from the DHSS to local authorities for administration. Unfortunately lack of preparation in the form of staffing, training and publicity led to chaos – at least 100 of the 500 councils in England and Wales were unable to cope, tenants suffered hardship and rent arrears among housing association tenants doubled to £10 million in August 1983. The confusion was criticised by the Public Accounts Committee in 1985. The system covers eight million households, or one in three of the population, and led to a doubling of administrative staff to 9,700.

When the DHSS changed the rules again to tighten control in 1987 it provided £25 million and a year's notice. The controls imposed penalties for councils who broke the regulations, reduced benefit back payments to 25%, cut the subsidy on overpaid claims and for councils with unreasonable rent levels (by penalising high-rent property in the public sector it could try to force people to move). The government had to pull back from its attempts to only reimburse 80%, rather than 97%, of housing benefit – an attempted shift of £600 million on to local government.

The huge sums of money involved have ensured continuing government involvement. The DOE has tried to make councils tackle the problem of £200 million rent and £100 million rate arrears and considered cutting grants to force rent rises in 1985. However the government contributed to a 37·5% increase in rent arrears by cutting £68 million off housing benefit in April 1986 – stopping all payments to a million tenants and reducing it for five million. But the Minister dismissed all other reasons than mismanagement in November of that year and threatened legislation. Meanwhile the DHSS cut back on the initial six-month benefit to pay mortgage interest, but in 1986 had to abandon proposals to make rate payers find 20% of rent rebates. The most contentious subject is the frozen cash from council house sales – to control inflation and council building but also to avoid awkward questions of redistribution (the wealthier areas with 60% of the cash have only 30% of the need). Some councils, notably Liverpool, turned to accounting devices to avoid such restrictions and were threatened with central government vetoes.

In 1986 the Audit Commission criticised both sides, calling on central government to give more cash to urban areas (as did the Church of England report, 'Faith in the cities') and to allow councils to spend all their sales cash. At the same time local authorities were urged to double their rents from £15 and tackle arrears, and to streamline their reletting rules and use hostels.

The government had to accept that increased spending on housing benefit was a consequence of pursuing its politicial aims of restructuring the housing sector and increasing mobility. Housing benefit was planned to rise to £4·4 billion in 1990–91 but the full effects of the 1988 Act in removing rent controls was likely to add a further £3 billion as poorer tenants in the private sector were protected. In addition, the Local Government and Housing Bill, 1989 was designed to force councils to increase rents, with a single 'housing revenue account subsidy', and, by ring-fencing housing finances from other funding, to stop subsidies from the rates. It was intended that higher rents would make up more of the rebates. The government declined to define the 'affordable' rents they foresaw.

In this situation a conflict of responsibility arose between government departments. The DHSS was keen to lose housing benefits to the Department of the Environment, believing it to be a housing responsibility rather than social security. In turn, the DOE would have welcomed control to press the policy changes outlined and would have argued that increases were a new burden not to funded by cuts elsewhere. For the Treasury, however, the very success of the Housing Act would mean open-ended rising spending. It therefore blocked the transfer in Cabinet committee to reserve the right to recoup by cuts in the main social security budget.

(ii) *Housing associations*   One sector that had more responsibility thrust upon it was that of the housing associations. They received more discretion to provide low-cost housing and, in 1982/83, more funds to do so (£690 million). Particularly attractive to the government was the example of Thamesmead, which voted to run its own affairs when the GLC was abolished.

The associations have 500,000 homes (5% of stock) and let 20,000 new homes a year. As noted, the government steadily increased their funding and in the Housing Act of 1988 they were given the power to raise funds privately – half in the city. This was not welcomed wholeheartedly as it was feared higher rents would damage inner-city developments.

(iii) *Blame*   As in other aspects of central-local government relations, shared responsibility could be useful in the appointment of blame. When the DOE revised house-building in the south-east downwards by 50,000 in June 1988, under intense political pressure, the ministers could blame the 85% of councils with no approved plans for generating speculative development applications.

(iv) *Opposition*   The Labour party regards it as an essential to reassert control – to stimulate investment, impede unrestricted council house sales, regulate private landlords and plan whole areas. There is, though, an ambivalence about the extent to which local authorities will determine their own investment and council house allocation under 'guidelines'. Housing associations are seen as useful to 'fill gaps' in Tory local authorities which are disinclined to build. Co-operatives would be likely to receive more encouragement, and Labour dislikes private tenancy where 80% is unsatisfactory accommodation and where harassment takes place (4% of London's

350,000 tenants).

The Liberals always favoured local control by councils or preferably co-operatives and neighbourhood committees, while the SDP
offered local neighbourhood trusts while still wanting a National
Housing Bank to channel funds.

(4) *Council house sales*
The Conservative government of 1979 gave council tenants, new-
town tenants and those of non-charitable housing associations the
right to buy their houses or flats at discounts of between 33% and
50%. Over 700,000 or 11·5% of the housing stock were sold between
1979 and September 1984. The 1983 Housing and Building Control
Act extended the scheme by:

(i) Giving a discount of 60%, to 400,000 tenants of thirty years'
standing.

(ii) Reducing the qualifying period from three to two years.

(ii) Giving 50,000 leasehold tenants the right to buy.

(iv) Giving new rights to buy or shared ownership to the elderly
and least well-off.

By May 1984 the government was encountering opposition from
councils who were terminating tenancies and from the House of
Lords who exempted university land and homes for the elderly. In
September, government launched a £1·4 million publicity campaign
which was quickly condemned as 'political advertising'.

By the end of 1986 the millionth council house had been sold (20%
of the 4·6 million English tenants) and in 1987 mounted a £¾ million
campaign to sell council flats – the 40,000 already sold were deemed
to be too few. The Housing and Planning Act of 1987 made flats an
attractive buy, with 70% discount and the right to resell in three
years. Councils were to be given the power to evict tenants to sell or
to turn over management to private landlords. To protect the 'right
to buy' policy a Housing Defects Act was passed, obliging councils to
repair defective prefabricated concrete dwellings (PRCs) or buy
them back.

To facilitate sales even more the government wrote further
measures into the Housing Act, 1988 – letting councils use the
proceeds of sales for administrative costs, increasing discounts on
recently-improved homes and blocking councils' transferring
ownership to a trust while keeping control. After a delay of three
months the Housing Minister won from the Secretary of State the

policy initiative for 'social landlordism', with a charter of protection to persuade tenants of the safe nature of transferring out of council ownership. In January 1989 the Housing Corporation published its criteria for approving potential landlords, with a right to take out an injunction for breaches of the criteria. Incentives could also be of a negative nature – while tenants could stay with the council after the majority of an estate had voted to move to the private rented sector, their rent level would be at that set by the private landlord. Under secondary legislation in 1989 landlords would have to show they had the support of 10% of tenants before applying.

Chiltern District sold its stock of £31 million to a housing association after a majority vote by tenants. But early moves were not trouble-free: the Conservative-controlled ADC advised against transfer; Anglesey dropped its plans when only 4% of tenants were shown to be favourable; the vote in Torbay, which showed 387 in favour, 2,210 against and 2,209 abstainees who were supposed to count as being in favour, could not be sustained – after many accusations of vote-rigging, the government had to concede there was insufficient evidence of support.

When the 'run-down' estates left the control of housing action trusts tenants would also be given the chance of buying their homes or transferring to private ownership (as well as returning to the council).

One option being considered in a Cabinet committee chaired by the Prime Minister at the end of 1988/early 1989 was to allow conversion of rent payments into mortgage payments. The government was hoping for £3 billion over three years from sales resulting from its housing legislation.

Labour opposition   Labour opposition is based on the premiss that the best council housing is being lost, thus depriving authorities of revenue and flexibility. The first 'knee-jerk' reaction of the 1980 Conference was to pass a motion requiring resale to authorities at the same discount, i.e. below market price, despite NEC opposition. By 1982 the policy had changed to repurchase (when available) at market price, no statutory obligation to sell, outstanding options to be cancelled and future sales at market price. After the June 1983 election there were suggestions that Labour should simply abandon its opposition to 'right to buy'. The Labour Housing Group (LHG) vociferously opposed this as inegalitarian, divisive and socially damaging. The 1984 Conference agreed that controlled sales would be allowed, and in May 1985 a consultative document from the leadership was advocating the right to buy but with the reservations that inner-city tenants might have to be given grants to buy elsewhere, that tentants could buy from absentee private landlords and that owner–occupiers could sell to councils and remain as tenants. Labour could point out that the ease of 'right to buy' schemes had led to council mortgage arrears of £14 million by April 1986, and repossessions up from 2,500 in 1979 to 12,000 in 1986. Those homeless as a result of repossessions had risen from 5% in 1979 to 12% in 1988.

But the extent of Labour's shift in attitude on the issue was demonstrated in 1986 when their spokesman proposed discounts 10% higher than the Tories – to their delight and his colleagues' astonishment.

The Alliance believed in sales, but with qualifications such as no sales of empty houses, temporary waiver in areas of social need and reduced discounts.

(5) *Subsidies*

The *Conservatives*, as we have seen, have altered the pattern of subsidy distribution – cutting local authority expenditure in general, but providing funds for homesteading, discounts for housing associations and for improvement grants. Life for home-owners was made easier by the changes to stamp duty and an end of conveyancing monopoly but they had to circumnavigate the MIRAS changes on mortgage payments, 15% VAT was imposed on building alterations and in 1984 came the abolition of life insurance premium relief for endowment mortgages. Nevertheless owner–occupiers receive £3·5 billion in tax relief on mortgages (a 29% repayment subsidy) plus 2·5 billion in capital gains tax relief. The inquiry set up by the National Federation of Housing Associations and chaired by Prince Philip condemned this system in July 1985 as expensive, unjust in favouring those with larger mortgages and doing nothing for the elderly or first-time buyers. The report went on to advocate phased reduction (like Labour), with a new rent-fixing formula and means-tested housing allowances. Mrs Thatcher quickly moved in to assert that tax relief would stay as long as she did. There was some support within the party and in the Treasury for an assault on 'middle-class dependency on the state' and the government did push back relief from home improvements and mortgages over £30,000. But grass-roots opinion could be seen as it attacked notions of a capital gains tax or property tax to slow down the prices spiral and credit boom in late 1988. Indeed there were trends the other way with attempts to cut mortgage payments of essential groups, such as nurses and teachers, in the south-east.

Labour believes that if the wealthy are to benefit from mortgage tax relief (MTR), it should be at the standard, not the higher rate. In general Labour believe in subsidies as a means of freezing rents and dislike means-testing. The LHG go further in demanding a housing wealth tax, parity of rent at the 1979 level, universal housing allowances based on cost and size, and mobility through 'housing on demand'.

A feature of *Liberal* policy in its local 'grass-roots' campaigning was to channel money into renovation and repair. Like Labour, they advocated equality of opportunity for women and racial minorities. The SDP 1984 Housing Green Paper reaffirmed that they believe in subsidies based on need (using means-testing) rather than type of housing and in greater equity between owner–occupation and rented housing.

One policy proposal which surveys showed to be controversial among their own middle-class membership was the long-term intention to reform mortgage tax relief so it related to income rather than size of mortgage. During the 1987 general election it was revealed that the Labour and Alliance policies to curb tax relief would put another 100,000 people into the higher tax bracket.

(6) *Green belt and planning policies*

In July 1983 the government issued two draft circulars. The first gave the minister power to override local authority plans and allow developers to build on greenfield sites. The second announced the relaxation of green-belt cordons. It was quickly revealed that developers had five mini-towns in mind. The announcements were made after the election and during a parliamentary recess. Nonetheless there quickly grew a mixed alliance of opponents – the Country Landowners' Association, National Farmers' Union and Conservative MPs oppose such development on grounds of self-interest and food imports; the Council for the Protection of Rural England and Civic Trust bring environmental arguments to bear; and Labour councils and their associations see a loss of population from the forgone regeneration in the inner cities.

As a result the Secretary of State, Patrick Jenkin, backed down in December 1983, reaffirming green-belt status and in February applied relaxations only to interim green-belt land. Nevertheless the pressure was sustained and during 1985 there were moves to cut into the 4·5 million acres of English green belt and the 277,000 in Scotland. The major problems were always likely to be in London's 1–2 million acres where Hertfordshire county council intended to build 4,000 homes, and Consortium Development Limited (representing the major companies building 30% of UK homes) proposed a series of small, carefully landscaped mini-towns of 15,000 people each. Developers claimed the lack of land had pushed up house prices (land forming 40% of the cost). The government gradually developed its policy of not upholding a 'green-belt museum' in which piecemeal development went on anyway, of deciding planning applications 'on merit', trying to resolve housing shortage problems, and easing the pressure on green-belt land by forcing the release of unused land. Under the 1980 Local Government Planning and Land Act authorities are required to register such land and can be forced to auction it off – 110,000 acres were identified and 30,000 released by early 1986. They also claimed to be reclaiming 3,500 acres a year – the size of Bath.

Under Nicholas Ridley government policy fluctuated amid controversy. In January 1987 the *Observer* first reported that a new package of policies was being developed in an interdepartmental group on the countryside and in the following month it was stated that Mr Jopling, Minister for Agriculture, had won the DOE's acceptance to 85% of farm land being freed from building restrictions and the attraction of small firms to the countryside. This seemed to be confirmed by a draft circular from the DOE which did not seek to conserve except for green belts and National Parks.

With attacks coming in from all directions and Labour gibing that having sold the family silver they were gambling away the turf – Mr Ridley and Mr Jopling were soon contradicting each other and were reprimanded by the Prime Minister. Mr Ridley had to give reassurances about strict scrutiny of plans but reassert that more homes were still needed. By 1988 eight Tory MPs had formed a pressure group (SANE) to oppose the crumbling of the countryside and their majorities – they wanted the 'new prosperity' directed to urban areas or the poorer regions. Mr Ridley hit back at them in May 1988 – for 'not giving a damn', 'selfishness' and of suburbs now under pressure so people could have a 'nice view in their windows' (*Sunday Times*, 8 May 1988). His earlier critique of Nimbyism ('Not in My Back Yard') had been undermined by the revelation of his own opposition to some.

By late 1988 the political climate had changed, however, with the Prime Minister espousing green policies, and with Mr Ridley and the DOE centrally involved. The counting of new housing was extended beyond greenfield sites to include redeveloped and smaller 'windfall' sites. Larger-scale development was rendered extremely unlikely.

(7) *The homeless*

It seems appropriate to conclude by looking at the other end of the social scale. Here in the housing sector we find teenagers, battered wives, ethnic minorities, groups unfamiliar with the social services, alcoholics and travelling people wanting only temporary resting places. While the numbers are undertain, it is clear that the economic recession has worsened the problem. The DOE's 1981 report, 'Single and Homeless', revealed that most homeless single people become so after marital or family conflict and that one-quarter are women. Professor Greve, commissioned by the GLC, found that the official homeless total had risen by 700% in the capital since 1970 so that one in ten people lacked a proper home. It was going up more rapidly in the suburbs among black families and among the disabled (*Freedom to Lose* (Dr Jenny Morris, Shelter)).

Claimants were being priced out of 90% of the cheapest bed and breakfast hotels and the £4 billion housing benefit bill increased as councils transferred families from the rates to Social Security.

The number of households officially 'homeless' was 128,345 in December 1988, meaning 370,000 people. But Shelter, in its report, 'Raise the Roof', estimates that the true figure was in millions because many did not apply to councils. The bill for bed and breakfast accommodation in London would be over £100 million in 1988, with wide variations in interpretation of the rules by councils – 29% accepted those looking for work as homeless, while 55% rejected them as intentionally homeless. Faced with shortages, councils turned to using caravans and redundant ships.

Social Security payment changes in April 1987 removed urgent needs payments and replaced supplementary benefit payable in advance with income support, which was available two weeks in arrears. Young people were unlikely to qualify for the new crisis loans and, unable to obtain bed and breakfast, often had to sleep rough, move into squats or try to get into overflowing night shelters. The government had to meet lobby groups in July 1988 to discuss the problem and emergency support. The government was determined to pass applications for accommodation elements of charges to councils by 1989 and the ADC wished to close loopholes on abuses – allowing councils not to give security of tenure, making applicants prove homelessness, and extending the residential qualification from six to twelve months.

In this sector the sub-system of pressure groups is very different from the above, comprising Shelter, SHAC, Campaign for the Homeless and Rootless, the Gypsy Council and the Campaign for Civil Liberties. The process whereby they pursue their cause is difficult. It usually consists of a study of the particular problem, mobilisation of change agents inside parliament and government and, crucially, exposure of the problem by the media.

As the 1977 Act showed, however, legislation does not secure implementation. The opposition parties have offered measures directly to address the needs of the homeless, extending provision and relaxing qualification controls. The government seeks to address the matter by general policy on extending the private rented sector and boosting housing associations

Conclusions

Housing is not a policy area which attracts attention with the constancy of economic, education or defence matters. At times its measures can attract all-party consensus and support – as with the Landlord and Tenants Act of 1987 which attacked excessive service charges, neglect and defective leases. But nor is it sufficiently neutral that anyone could proclaim 'Keep politics [i.e. the politics of change] out of housing', as the Duke of Edinburgh ingenuously suggested in February 1987. As we have seen, this is one of the most polarised, interest-based policy sectors in British politics.

Reading

G. Bramley, *Housing Needs in Non-metropolitan Areas*, 1987.
Conservative Research Department, *Politics Today*, 13 February

1984.

D. Donnison & C. Ungerson, *Housing Policy*, Penguin, 1982.

R. S. Forrest, 'The politics of housing', *Teaching Politics*, September 1986, pp. 426–45.

Labour Housing Group, *Manifesto for Housing*, 43 Anson Road, London N7.

Labour Housing Group, *Right to a Home*, Spokesman, 1984.

B. Pitt, 'Liberal Action on Housing'.

SDP Green paper no. 12, 'A strategy for housing'.

12 *Lynton Robins*

Issues and developments in education

Education has developed into an extremely controversial political issue during the last twenty years. The optimism that stemmed from the passing of the 1944 Education Act which influenced thinking during the 1950s and 1960s has been replaced today by a sombre mood resulting from both pessimism and uncertainty. The political consensus on the aims and methods of education has crumbled under attacks from left, right and centre. Right-wing critics argued in the *Black Papers* that 'disastrous mistakes are being made in modern education' and the socialist and feminist left made its most articulate attack in *Unpopular Education*. But the most damning blow came in 1976 when the Prime Minister of the day, James Callaghan, delivered a much publicised speech in which he suggested that educational standards were falling and that schools were failing to serve Britain well.

The education system, which has enjoyed many years of public confidence, was now the subject of doubts and reservations in many minds. Scandals such as the William Tyndale affair did nothing to allay public fears that education was indeed in deep trouble. By the late 1970s it had become clear that in education too 'the party was over'. The years of post-war expansion had come to an end, to be replaced by stringency and educational cutbacks.

This chapter examines reasons why education has moved to the centre stage of party politics in Britain. This will involve considering the purposes which lay behind the growth of mass education and the role that education plays in shaping society. We shall see that different philosophies or ideologies about education come into conflict from time to time, and that these ideologies are particularly powerful when they are disguised as being 'scientific' in nature. The conclusion attempts to understand the significance of some recent educational issues by setting them in the context of the ideological struggle.

The growth of mass education

In his analysis of educational developments in the nineteenth century, David Glass revealed that two fairly distinct sets of considerations influenced schooling; one related to the middle class and the other to the mass of the population. The main concern regarding secondary education was that it should be effective in procuring wealth and maintaining or enhancing social status. The professions were raising their standards of entry and university education was acquiring new meanings for the old and new middle classes alike. Elementary education for the working class, on the other hand, was designed to elicit four major responses:

(1) To 'gentle' the masses.
(2) To instil discipline.
(3) To obtain respect for private property and the social order.
(4) To provide the kind of instruction which was necessary for an expanding industrial and commercial nation.

Some argue that the objectives of the educational system remain basically unchanged towards the end of the twentieth century.

Before 1870, the provision of schools was left to private individuals and churches. The Elementary Education Act of 1870 empowered local authorities to 'fill the gap' and provide schools where voluntary church schools did not exist. The Act established school boards which were elected by ratepayers, and which could build and maintain elementary schools with money from rates, government grant and school fees. The expansion of schools was rapid and by 1876 it was realistic to make attendance compulsory for children who lived within two miles of school. At this time it was felt that elementary schooling was sufficient for the majority of children, and the responsibility of school boards ended when a child was ten years old. Secondary education was the responsibility of parents and independent schools.

The Education Act of 1902 led to a major reorganisation, with

2,559 school boards being replaced by 330 local education authorities. The new LEAs had power to provide not only elementary education but also secondary and technical education. The years that followed saw a great expansion in secondary education with a variety of schools being built. Some were purpose-built and referred to as 'high schools', others were senior elementary schools which usually took the form of annexes built on to existing elementary schools. The special place examination (known later as the 'scholarship', then 'eleven-plus') and free places at grammar schools became general after the 1907 Education (Administrative Provisions) Act. In large towns, junior technical, junior commercial and junior art schools took pupils from thirteen to sixteen.

The next major development was the 1918 Education Act, sometimes referred to as the 'Fisher Act', which raised the school-leaving age to fourteen. It was intended that children over fourteen should attend part-time 'day continuation schools' but this reform was not compulsory and consequently not widely implemented.

Education for all
In 1926 the Hadow Report recommended that there should be a formal break in children's education at eleven. Elementary education should then be divided into primary and secondary stages. In 1938 the Spens Report considered the curriculum of grammar and technical high schools. The Norwood Report was published in 1943 and developed further the then current idea that children could be divided into three different types:

(1) Those who loved learning for its own sake.

(2) Those who delighted in applied science and applied art.

(3) Those who dealt more easily in concrete things than ideas.

The report suggested, therefore, that there should be three kinds of secondary school:

(1) Secondary grammar schools of the type that existed already for child type 1.

(2) Secondary technical schools, to be developed from existing technical schools, for child type 2.

(3) Secondary modern schools, to be developed from senior elementary schools, for child type 3.

The committees which produced these reports were impressed by recently developed intelligence-testing, which could be used to identify the 'brightest' and 'dullest' pupils so that they could be educated separately from 'average' pupils. The majority of LEAs followed Norwood thinking and set up a *tripartite* system of grammar, technical and modern schools. In practice, however, a *bipartite* system emerged in most areas after 1944 since few technical schools were built.

The 1944 Education Act – referred to as the 'Butler Act' since R. A. Butler was president of the Board of Education – reorganised education into a national system based on three successive stages; primary, secondary and further. Elementary education was replaced by 'secondary education for all'. The Act reduced the number of LEAs to 146, made religious education compulsory, raised the school leaving age to fifteen, and established the first Minister for Education.

New directions

During the 1950s and 1960s there was a growing awareness that the new system of education was flawed. Criticisms were numerous:

(i) Secondary modern and grammar schools were never seen by parents, teachers or pupils as being equal. Grammar schools had acquired high prestige because of the strong links with higher education and the professions.

(ii) There were not enough grammar school places for all who wanted them. Only 20% of eleven-year-olds would go to a grammar school, leaving many parents disappointed.

(iii) An education system which 'fails' 80% of its pupils each year was seen as undesirable.

(iv) There was much geographical unfairness in the system since the number of grammar school places available varied from one authority to another. For example, in 1962 11·9% of Bootle's eleven-year-olds went to a grammar school whereas the figure was 40·3% in Merthyr.

(v) The examination which pupils had to pass in order to go to a grammar school – the eleven-plus – became a crucial, often emotionally-charged event for pupils and parents. The exam had a bad effect on many primary schools which were geared to preparing children for the eleven plus rather than developing all aspects of ability and personality.

(vi) Free access to grammar schools had not benefited working-class pupils. Those working-class pupils who were selected for grammar schools tended to do less well, once there, than their

middle-class peers.

(vii) Educational theorists began having doubts about the possibility of measuring intelligence in the way the eleven plus attempted. Some feared that intelligence tests could not identify the three types of Norwood child because they did not in fact exist. It was believed that the whole education system was based on a psychological fallacy.

The 'ideological comprehensivists', once seen as having radical ideas about common schools, began to win support as more and more people felt that graded schools were intolerable in a democratic society. It is hard to believe that in 1960 there were only 130 comprehensive schools, given their preponderance today. Depending upon its political masters the DES has blown both hot and cool on this expansion. Circular 10/65 invited LEAs to submit plans for reorganising secondary schools into a comprehensive system. Circular 10/70 removed this invitation but Circular 4/74 again applied pressure. Vacillation such as this created a climate of uncertainty in which local authorities could defy ministerial advice. The opposition of Tameside LEA to the policies of a pro-comprehensive Labour minister is the best documented of several cases.

Changes were not confined to the secondary stage of education. Innovations also took place in the establishment of middle schools which straddled the 1944 division between primary and secondary schools.

Education's internal struggle

As we have seen, the work of educational psychologists during the 1930s influenced the structure of post-war education. Intelligence-testing was associated with pioneering psychologists such as Cyril Burt. Intelligence was seen as the ability to perform abstract thinking, and intelligence tests measured this ability. Psychologists felt that intelligence was an innate ability which led them to believe that *intelligence was inherited*. This was an assumption which had enormous social and political implications.

If dull parents produced dull children, bright parents produced bright children, and if the social system rewarded people according to ability and merit then the existence of different social classes was based on genetic factors. Educationalists expected children from working-class homes to perform less well at school. Because they believed intelligence was inherited, educationalists thought it natural that schools should reflect and reproduce the stratifications which already existed in society.

Computer analysis has revealed that the data used in many of Cyril Burt's studies were fictitious, and it is now generally agreed that any differences between social classes is not genetically determined. Some critics argued that IQ tests are not 'culture-free' and this accounted for much of the difference between classes. In other words it should be of little wonder that working-class pupils did less well in tests the design of which favoured middle-class pupils. Indeed, it has been argued that IQ tests really measure social class membership and not intelligence.

Sociologists challenged psychologists' view of education and introduced new insights into how the education system might work. They rejected genetic arguments and stressed the *importance of the environment* on how well pupils would do at school. Educability depended on factors such as: (i) parental attitudes which could influence pupil's motivation; (ii) provision for general learning in the home – the availability of space, privacy, books etc.; (iii) language development. Since humans think in words, it was argued that the quality of thought depended heavily on the quality of language.

Social class categories seem a crude yet useful way to summarise many aspects of the home environment which influenced educability and attainment. Also studies revealed that an unconscious class bias often held by teachers influenced the way pupils were streamed at school. Well-clothed, clean pupils were often placed in higher streams than their ability would justify. Pupils of poorer appearance tended to be put in lower streams than their ability justified. And once there, these pupils deteriorated. Indeed, streaming in schools acted in the same way as a self-fulfilling prophecy. Pupils placed in the 'A' stream were expected to succeed and generally lived up to this expectation. In contrast, 'D' stream pupils were expected to do poorly, and inevitably this proved to be the case. Sociologists argued that in many schools, streaming by presumed ability was reinforcing the process of social selection. Just as streaming *between* different types of school became discredited, so too did streaming *within* schools.

It was argued that the school was itself a micro-political system and the distribution of scarce resources within it reflected the inequalities found in society at large. In this context the school timetable could be viewed not as a neutral or technical document but as a bill of rights.

Ken Shaw has argued:

If a smallish group of pupils gets regular contact with highly paid, experienced, high status teachers not overburdened with disciplinary problems or
marking, in expensive specialised facilities, they are advantaged and they
know it . . . Other younger less successful children are taught in groups of
more than 30, by newly qualified staff in overcrowded general purpose rooms.
Most option systems present a real choice to able pupils; the less able are
steered into what is left, so that choice for them is very restricted . . . Who are
the beneficiaries, who are the losers when the timetable is analysed from this
point of view? And how does this match up with winning and losing in the
world outside? There is plenty of evidence to show that the answer is: pretty
closely.

Harold Lasswell once defined politics as 'who gets what, when and
how'. Some sociologists were defining education in identical terms.
They felt that schools were bound to reflect the divisions that existed
in wider society. In other words, education could not lead to change
in society but could only reproduce and legitimate the sort of society
that already existed. Within a free-market economy schools were
bound therefore to serve the interests of capitalism, namely the
creation of profit and stability. The efforts of well-intentioned
liberals to make schools the agents of social change were seen as
having failed in the past and being bound to fail in the future. It was
argued that schools will only change *after* the economic system that
they serve has changed. Neither the introduction of comprehensive
education nor innovations to humanise the conditions of schooling
such as mixed-ability teaching can alter the basic purpose of education, and that remains much the same as David Glass's analysis of
education in the last century.

Education policy has therefore been shaped by 'scientific' arguments which have contained highly political ingredients. The arguments of traditional psychologists were attractive to right-wing
individuals who saw the existence of social classes as natural and
desirable. Sociological research lent support to liberal and left-wing
individuals who wanted social change. Various studies identified
much infairness in the way some pupils were treated and encouraged
measures leading to greater equality of opportunity, which it was
hoped would eventually lead to a less class-based society.

The deschoolers
The notion of deschooling has been with us since 1971 and is

associated with Everett Reimer, Ivan Illich and John Holt. Their basic argument was that schools had failed and should therefore be abolished. In particular, schools had:

(i) Failed to teach the basic skills, and had consumed more and more resources in order to achieve less and less in terms of knowledge and skills taught.

(ii) Imposed a 'hidden curriculum' that indoctrinated pupils into accepting the status quo and the materialistic values of a technological society. Pupils were taught to conform in order to survive, to know their place, and to accept the judgements of others about what is worth doing and knowing. Schools, it was argued, actually damaged pupils.

(iii) Employed many 'qualified' teachers who were poor teachers whilst failing to employ many gifted teachers who were not qualified.

According to the deschoolers, learning is in fact inhibited by schools. One solution proposed was that all members of society should receive 'edu-credit' cards. These would be spent following whatever courses people wished with whatever teachers (qualified or not) they chose, whenever they liked. Ideas associated with deschooling have proved attractive to some on the political extremes. On the left, some were attracted by a form of education which promised to act as an ineffective instrument of social control. On the right there were those who favoured the idea of ending compulsory education. Also something akin to 'edu-credit' cards, 'education vouchers', have been considered by Kent LEA in order to introduce market forces into education. Parents would be able to spend their vouchers on schools of their choice, private or maintained. Popular schools would prosper, with unpopular schools having to improve their reputations or face the prospect of withering away. The Conservative-controlled Kent Authority failed to implement the scheme on the grounds of cost.

External political influences

The education system has also been shaped by the ideological struggle which takes place in wider society and which influences other institutions. The main ideologies are:

(i) *The aristocratic ideology* which produced schools giving a classical education to the children of the social elite. The emphasis was on character-building and was deliberately non-vocational in character. This ideology is still associated with the traditions of a public school education.

(ii) *The bourgeois ideology* championed by the merchant and professional classes influenced the establishment of schools which provided specialist education for high-status positions. One of the central concerns of grammar and independent schools has been the preparation of pupils for entry to higher vocational and professional courses.

(iii) *The democratic ideology* of the early reformers was concerned with 'education for all'. It influenced the 1944 Education Act and the creation of the Open University in 1969. Within schools this ideology has resulted in mixed-ability teaching and informal teaching methods.

(v) *The proletarian ideology* was held by those who felt that the children of the working class should be provided with a utilitarian education which was practical in nature. The proletarian education aimed at limiting the aspirations and political demands of the working class. The secondary modern school, with its low prestige and non-academic curriculum, is a manifestation of this ideology.

(v) *The manpower planning ideology* recognises pupils as 'human capital' who will eventually fill roles in the economy. Education is seen as the key to Britain's economic advance, and schools and colleges should supply the type of people needed by the labour market. The establishment of technical schools and colleges represented the presence of the 'economically useful' within education. In the past most universities have been suspicious of applied courses, and the CNAA was set up to validate vocational courses to prepare students for the world of work run by the new polytechnics created in the late 1960s.

There is a complex web of relationships between these ideologies with different ones dominating the minds of decision-makers at different times. The aristocratic and democratic ideologies are diametrically opposed to one another, with the former associated with an exclusive education and the latter with universal education. The aristocratic and proletarian ideologies are congruent with a society divided into 'well-rounded gentlemen' and 'drawers of water and hewers of wood'. The eleven-plus and the Assisted Places Scheme represent links between the bourgeois and proletarian ideologies with the most able pupils from working-class homes receiving an academic education on the basis of merit.

Educational developments in the early years of this century were influenced by a combination of the aristocratic and bourgeois ideologies. The democratic ideology was at its height during the 1960s with the expansion of comprehensive schooling. But it was not all-out victory for the ideological comprehensivists since the private sector still exists and even within the maintained sector comprehensive provision is not universal. The 1970s and 1980s have seen the manpower planning ideology in the ascendancy, with education increasingly concerned with the provision of the technical skills required by industry.

Areas of controversy

(i) *The private sector*
The existence of a private sector in education has long been at the centre of party conflict. Most Conservatives agree with Sir Ian Gilmour's view that the egalitarianism which would result in everybody having to use the same school service would also mean that citizens would be increasingly regulated by state monopolies and be at their mercy. For Conservatives, freedom is associated with the absence of coercion (particularly by the state) and is best promoted by the expansion of the market. In other words, competition maximises the freedom of the individual to satisfy his or her needs. It is argued that parental choice between the state and private sector, and within the private sector, ensures individual freedom within education.

This view is challenged by the Labour party, which is committed to the eventual abolition of the private sector. Labour also opposes the Assisted Places Scheme which strengthens private schools with public money at a time when many state schools cannot afford to buy sufficient textbooks. Labour also rejects the 'freedom of choice' argument and Roy Hattersley has argued that for ordinary parents there is no choice between Eton or the local secondary modern for their children's education. The private sector is seen as bolstering privilege and thus contributing to a divided society, and having little to do with protecting freedom and democracy.

(ii) *Teaching methods*
Arguments about which teaching methods are the most efficient inevitably develop into political disputes. This is because different methods are concerned not only with teaching particular subjects –

geography, English, maths – but also with moulding different types of pupils. Basically, traditional teaching methods tend to be authoritarian, associated with hierarchical social relations within the school with pupils playing a largely passive role and relying on the teacher as the expert. The 'closed' classroom encourages pupils to conform and not to expect to participate in decision-making within the classroom. In contrast, the 'open' classroom is characterised by a friendlier and more libertarian atmosphere in which there is not such a sharp distinction between teacher and pupil. Teaching will involve 'discovery' methods in which the teacher manages the learning process rather than expository methods in which the teacher directs the process. Teaching, then, can be an elitist or participatory affair and it should not be surprising that it is the subject of political conflict.

The progressive/traditional debate erupted in the mid-1970s over the very progressive methods used in the William Tyndale junior school. Inquiries and surveys into the efficiency of different forms of education are difficult to conduct because of all the other variables that have an influence in addition to that being measured. Publication of research findings are customarily accompanied by accusations of cheating, bias, muddled thinking, or distortion being directed at the authors. For example in *Teaching Styles and Pupil Progress*, Neville Bennett suggested that progressive methods were less effective generally in teaching traditional skills. Other social scientists were highly critical of his research methods and one likened his conclusions to a zoologist on finding that all elephants are bigger than mice, except for one mouse which was bigger than all the elephants. In 1980 a survey published by the National Children's Bureau, *Progressive Secondary Schools*, claimed that pupils in comprehensive schools 'did as well and as badly as if selection had still operated and some had gone to grammars and the rest to secondary moderns'. Such a claim was predictably challenged in a Centre for Policy Studies report, *Real Concern*, which attacked the research for using dubious data and drawing the wrong conclusions.

(iii) *Control of the curriculum*
The 1944 Education Act said little about the content of the curriculum apart from the inclusion of religious education. The Act did, however, establish an informal partnership between central government, local authorities, teachers and the churches which would act as the decision-making structure. The working of this

partnership has often been described as the 'mystique of English education'. Within it the DES played a rather limited role. Indeed, within Whitehall the DES was viewed as a very weak department with little direct control over the service it ran. For example, the curriculum was decided at school level. Teachers, together with the head and influenced by parents, examination boards, etc., decided curriculum issues and could only be sanctioned if they performed below approved standards. However the publication of the Crowther and Newsom reports focused attention on the curriculum and the DES hinted that central (or state) control of the curriculum was worth considering. In his Ruskin speech James Callaghan hinted at teacher inefficiency in this area and gave further support to the idea of more centralised control of the curriculum. A little over a decade later the Education Reform Act provided centralised control over some 70% of the school curriculum.

(iv) *The Thatcher revolution in education*
The Conservative government has had to confront the uncomfortable fact that for the first time in the post-war period educational standards have fallen. Using 'O' level (now replaced by GCSE) and 'A' level results as measures of standard, 1983 is the year when patterns changed for the worse. For example, the percentages of pupils leaving school with at least one 'O' level, five 'O' levels, or one 'A' level rose steadily from the 1950s until 1983, when the improvement either tailed off or turned into a decline. Viewed another way, the percentage of pupils leaving school with no qualifications fell steadily from 65% in the early 1950s to 10% in 1983, thereafter remaining static. Comparative surveys have also revealed Britain's relatively low educational standards with pupils in rival industrial economies such as Japan being more academically skilled than their British counterparts. The 'great debate' on education initiated by James Callaghan assumed a more urgent nature in the 1980s as the decline became more acute.

Critics of the government argued that its policies, notably cutting back on public expenditure in pursuit of a monetarist economic strategy, had resulted in inadequate funding for the educational system and in the low morale of the teaching profession. Government supporters argued that the decline in standards could be blamed on the poor performance of pupils in certain left-wing-controlled education authorities. Whilst one lobby called for more cash to be spent on education, the other demanded less local authority power over education and more parental choice.

The latter solution to the problem lay in the thinking behind the Education Act of 1986. This Act provided for increased numbers of parent governors to serve on schools' governing bodies which, with other changes, reduced the number of local authority governors to a minority. However, the Act has encountered a number of difficulties in operation. Firstly, although many parents are very interested in their children's education, surprisingly few are keen to stand for election on to the governing bodies. Secondly, a loophole in the Act has allowed councillors to remove their political opponents from governing bodies. In Manchester, for example, Labour sacked all Conservative governors, whilst in Barnet, Conservatives removed all Labour governors.

The Education Reform Act of 1988 (sometimes referred to as the "Gerbil") pursued the logic of the 1986 Act as well as including many other important changes throughout the education system. Designed in part to limit local authority control and release the working of market forces within education, it also represented a considerable centralisation of power to the DES. The Education Reform Act was the government's conclusion to the 'great debate' and it stands alongside the 1944 Act as a landmark in educational development.

The Bill consumed a massive amount of parliamentary time, being debated for over 200 hours by the Commons alone with another twenty-two days in committee. The Lords rejected a number of provisions in the Bill but despite its wide scope and controversial contents, it emerged from the parliamentary process basically unaltered.

The Act specifies that a *national curriculum* be taught to pupils until they reach the age of sixteen. It will contain three core subjects – Maths, English and Science – together with seven foundation subjects which will include a foreign language. The national curriculum will be accompanied by national testing of pupils at the ages of seven, eleven, fourteen and sixteen.

The Inner London Education Authority (ILEA) will be abolished on 1 April 1990, with its powers being transferred to thirteen inner London boroughs. The Act also provides the possibility of state schools 'opting out' from local authority control to DES control. Under the Act school headteachers and governors will have power under financial delegation to take more independent decisions on issues such as the length and timing of the school day.

Within *higher education* two important changes included the ending of academic tenure for university staff and the establishment of English polytechnics and some of the larger colleges as corporate institutions outside local authority control.

Naturally such a large bill as this generated a wide ranging debate, but it is also the case that one issue in particular – that of schools *'opting out'* – emerged in the public debate as the most significant of all the changes. Some feared that increasing parental choice would result in schools in middle-class catchment areas being the ones which voted to opt out, leaving local authorities with the 'sink schools' of the run-down inner cities. Others feared that once having opted out, schools would then be free to charge fees or operate other forms of selection. The fear was voiced that Britain's various communities might each pursue an ethnic preference, resulting in all-white, all-Asian and all-Afro-Caribbean Schools. Members of the House of Lords were concerned about the way in which a decision for a school to opt out would be reached. Should a majority of parents who actually voted in the ballot be enough, or should there be a majority of all parents eligible to vote? It was originally proposed that a simple majority would be sufficient, but the Minister agreed to amend the bill so that if turn-out was less than 50% in a vote then a second ballot must be held within fourteen days. The decision reached in the second ballot will be binding whatever the level of turnout.

Reading

D. V. Glass, 'Education and social change in England' in A. H. Halsey, J. Floud & C. A. Anderson (eds.), *Education, Economy and Society*, Free Press, New York, 1961, pp. 391–413.

Maurice Kogan, *The Politics of Educational Change*, Fontana, 1978.

Lynton Robins, 'Political socialisation in British Schools: some political and sociological approaches' in Lynton Robins (ed.), *Topics in British Politics*, London, 1982, pp. 221–43.

Brian Salter & Ted Tapper, *Education, Politics and the State*, London, 1981.

K. E. Shaw, 'The timetable: a Bill of Rights?', *Teaching Politics*, 9, 1980, pp. 111–20.

Ted Tapper & Brian Salter, 'The politics of secondary education' in Lynton Robins (ed.), *Politics and Policy-Making in Britain*, London, 1987.

13 *John McIlroy*

The politics of racism

A broad definition of *racism* would run: racism is a set of ideas and practices which asserts that:

(a) Human beings can be divided into a series of distinct groups or races on the bases of identifiable physical features most obviously skin colour.

(b) These unalterable physical types are inherited.

(c) Those who belong to the group or race also share a relationship between their inherited external appearance and other allegedly inherited characteristics such as intelligence; personality and culture are also the products of race.

(d) Some groups or races are naturally inferior to other groups or races.

(e) These groups, therefore, require different and in practice less favourable treatment and we should encourage action on this basis.

As you can see, this kind of racism which has influenced domestic policy in many countries at different times – Germany during the National Socialist era, Britain and America in the days of slavery and South Africa today – asserts that racial differences are genetic and inherent. Others have argued that different groups can be arranged in a superior–inferior hierarchy according to their culture and customs, rather than their physical differences. People who hold this view and who see their own group or nation at the top of the tree are sometimes termed *ethnocentric*. Action against allegedly inferior groups on this basis is sometimes termed *ethnic* discrimination.

Whilst traditionally racists have argued in terms of biological inheritance, it has been pointed out that theories which use social, historical or cultural factors to distinguish between one group and another and to justify discrimination, operate in the same way as if they utilised biologically based arguments. Today we hear less about biology, more about 'culture' and 'nation'. Moreover, most racists do not have clear-cut theories but a confused 'common-sense' jumble of ideas which sees one group as more stupid, dirty, lazy, greedy than another, possessing strange, alien customs against which the habits of one's own superior group must be defended.

Some writers today distinguish between *racism* – the institutionalised practices in the social system which generate disadvantage for certain groups – and *racialism* – the specific acts of *discrimination* visited by one group upon another on the basis of the belief that the latter are racially distinct and consequently inferior. Whilst not in general use, this distinction could be useful as it draws our attention to the fact that the ideas, feelings and attitudes of individuals are usually related to wider structures of power and social organisation and that trying to change the individual without trying to change wider structures may be ineffectual, even counter-productive. The attitude which can produce discrimination against particular groups is termed *prejudice*. Prejudice is seen as being based upon *stereotypes*, broad mental views based on partial or distorted information: all Irish people are drunks, all Jews are mean.

The myth of race

Today racist ideas are generally accepted as possessing no scientific validity.

(1) It can be shown that the idea of race is a relatively recent one. The word first appears in English in 1508; it was only in the 1770s that it took on its present meaning. Moreover, it is only during the last three centuries that racism has developed its present political importance. In the more distant past differences between or within societies were not articulated in such terms. The culture and achievements of particular groups are not natural or pre-ordained but socially produced. Civilisation has not been the prerogative of the 'white race' but has arisen at different times in many different parts of the world.

(2) Physical differences do exist between human beings but they shade into each other on a spectrum. To decide which are important and which constitute dividing lines between different groups requires

a selective value-judgement. The way we are taught to look at the world, our political moulding and our material interests influence that judgement and may lead us to stress or exaggerate one difference above another. To divide or classify people in a racist way is to make a social, not a biological, judgement.

(3) There are still scientists today – Jensen and Eysenck and their followers – who defend the idea of inherited differences. The vast weight of scientific evidence, however, indicates that genetic differences between individuals within the same 'race' may be greater than the differences between one race and another. Scientists believe that over 90% of all the difference can be found within a given 'race' rather than between races so, biologically, a white Londoner is likely to be just as similar to or different from, his or her white neighbour as he or she is to a neighbour from Jamaica or Kuala Lumpur. Racism is scientifically discredited, but still grips people's minds and influences their behaviour. In the past Jews and Irish people were victims of racism in Britain. Today it is primarily black people.

(4) There are not many races but one human race. As the world's most prominent scientists gathered under the aegis of the United Nations Educational Scientific and Cultural Organisation, it was concluded: 'all men everywhere belong to a single species. As is the case with other species all men share their essential hereditary characteristics in common having received them from common ancestors . . . race is not so much a biological phenomenon as a social myth. The myth of race has created an enormous amount of human and social damage.' Today, there are few who describe themselves as racist. This does not mean racism does not exist, but that its extent is sometimes minimised or ignored and racist policies justified by pleading other considerations.

The black British

Blacks have lived in this country since the time of the Romans and were the object of immigration control as early as Elizabethan times. Our present black population, however, is largely the product of post-war immigration from the New Commonwealth – the West Indies, Bangladesh, India, Pakistan, Sri Lanka, parts of Africa, notably Kenya, Nigeria, Uganda and parts of Asia, such as Malaysia, Singapore and Hong Kong.

The heyday of immigration was the fifties and early sixties. In 1951 only 0.2 million people in the UK were from the New Commonwealth. Twenty years later the figure had increased to 1·2 million. Today Britain's black population is over 3 million and, though often still referred to as immigrants, half were in fact, born here. By the year 2000 it is estimated that there will be nearly 3·5 million black Britons, making up nearly 6% of our total population.

The largest single group is of West Indian origin; the other significant groups coming from the Indian sub-continent. The black population is concentrated in certain areas of the UK, following the immigration pattern. Blacks responded to the need for labour generally in the south-east; to the requirements of the metal manufacturing industries in the West Midlands; and the textile industries in Lancashire and Yorkshire. Outside the south-east, they are concentrated in Wolverhampton, Birmingham and Coventry, West Yorkshire, particularly Bradford and Greater Manchester. Different communities still live in distinct areas with, for example, a majority of Pakistanis compared with other groups in Bradford, and a majority of West Indians in Leeds.

Why they came

(1) *Shortage of labour* was a major economic problem for postwar Britain. A Royal Commission in 1949 estimated that 140,000 immigrants annually would be required. The black British came to answer shortages in transport, the hospitals, textiles, clothing and foundries. In the absence of an internal reserve army, Britain's 1950s boom was fuelled by immigration.

(2) *Citizens of the Commonwealth had the right to enter the UK and settle here* This was confirmed by the *British Nationality Act*, 1948. Many, particularly the West Indians, looked to Britain as the 'mother country'. They had fought in the British armed services during the war, they spoke English and identified to some extent with British culture.

(3) *The black British came from areas of traditional emigration which were blighted by long-term underdevelopment* Long before the first 400 came on the *SS Empire Windrush* in 1948, West Indians had migrated to the USA as cheap labour to build the Panama Canal, just as Indians had found it necessary to emigrate to South and East

Africa to work on the railways. Unemployment and population growth constituted 'push' factors. From 1952, entry to the USA was controlled by the McCarren–Walter Act, whilst in the Punjab, for example, increasing agricultural competition was a factor.

(4) *The system seemed to suit everybody*   The British were getting labour for on the whole, low-paid, socially undesirable jobs. The newcomers were leaving even worse jobs for better conditions and the possibility of saving for a return home. The mechanism of immigration was happily self-adjusting from the viewpoint of the UK: a fall in the number of advertised jobs led to a fall in the number of immigrants. However, few of the immigrants became self-sufficient enough to return home. Once here they encountered disadvantage and discrimination.

Blacks and disadvantage

(1) *Blacks are disadvantaged in housing*   In the 1970s more than 70% were concentrated in districts which contained nearly three times the national average of households, which had to share or altogether lacked basic amenities and were overcrowded. While, for example, only a quarter of white households lived at a density of over 1·5 persons per bedroom, and only 2% had 2·5 persons per bedroom, 54% of West Indian households and 65% of Asian households had more than 2·5 persons per bedroom.

A decade later there was no dramatic change. The 1984 survey by the Policy Studies Institute stated: 'Among owner–occupiers and council tenants black households are more often found in older property than the white households and less often found in detached and semi-detached houses; in the council sector, blacks are twice as likely as whites to be in flats. Black households have higher densities of residence in both the main tenure sectors.'

(2) *Blacks are disadvantaged in employment*   A Department of Employment Survey in 1976 stated that blacks were 'concentrated in conurbations where the pressure of demand for labour has been relatively high and in some skilled and unskilled jobs to which it is difficult to attract other workers because of such features as low earnings, a need to work unsocial hours, and/or unpleasant working conditions'. Blacks are less likely to be in white collar jobs, and more likely to be in unskilled manual work and whilst 15% of white men

worked shifts, this was true of 31% of black males. 79% of whites with degrees were in professional jobs but for blacks with the same qualifications the figure was only 31%. Earnings of non-manual workers were significantly higher among whites than among blacks. In the case of skilled manual workers, they were far higher. Only amongst semi-skilled and unskilled grades was there parity.

As unemployment generally increased between 1973 and 1980, total unemployment doubled: amongst blacks it is quadrupled. A survey published in 1987, in the *Employment Gazette* showed that whilst cultural differences contributed, unemployment amongst white workers was 10% but amongst black workers it was almost 20%. More specifically, 17% of workers of Indian backgrounds, 21% of those of West Indian extraction, and 31% of those connected with Pakistan and Bangladesh were out of work. Unemployment rates for young people were even higher – 34% for West Indians and 48% for Pakistanis and Bangladeshis.

(3) *Blacks are disadvantaged in education* In 1972 West Indian children constituted 1·1% of all children in state schools but 4·9% of children in special schools. Black children are more likely to be perceived by teachers as inadequate and/or stupid.

The Rampton Report (1981) argued that racism, and specifically, the stereotyped attitudes of many educationalists played an important part in the underachievement of West Indian children. It also questioned research which found West Indian youths between twelve and sixteen surpassing their white counterparts. Other ethnic minority groups also underachieve. The 1985 Swann Report, 'Education For All', stressed that no single factor explained this situation. It recommended various changes – more black teachers, better teacher training, more English language programmes – but concluded that the best way to change the inadequate school performance of black children would be by improving the social and economic circumstances of their families.

(4) *Blacks are disadvantaged in society* Whilst certain of Britain's black citizens have achieved prominence in fields such as entertainment and sport, their exclusion from the centres of power is symbolised by the fact that there are no black Cabinet ministers, only four black MPs, no black High Court judges and no black senior police officers. The appointment of Bill Morris as Deputy General

Secretary of the Transport and General Workers Union in 1985
highlighted a similar position in the trade unions. Blacks exist in what
the Commons Home Affairs Select Committee termed 'a complete
fabric of social and economic disadvantage'. The crudest index of this
is illustrated by the densely detailed documentation of the physical
violence blacks have to endure culminating in the Home Office
Report of 1981. The 1984 report of the Policy Studies Institute
(formerly PEP) argued that overall, the difficulties of black citizens
had intensified with the recession. There was a clear need, it concluded, for firm action by central government if further deterioration
was to be avoided.

Racist discrimination
Whilst cultural factors are at work, racist discrimination played a
significant role in blacks' continuing disadvantaged position. There
were racist strikes and threatened strikes on the railways, buses and
the hospitals in the fifties and sixties against the initial employment of
black workers. Trade union bodies, fearing undercutting of wages
and conditions, created colour bars. The Notting Hill riots of 1958
drew attention to the seriousness of the problem. As the first major
research on the subject in the mid-sixties commented:

after these three surveys all but those with closed minds must accept the fact
that in Britain today discrimination against those coloured members of the
population operates in many fields. In the sectors we studied, different
aspects of employment, housing and provision of services, there is racial
discrimination, varying in extent from the massive to the substantial. The
experience of white immigrants such as Hungarians and Cypriots leaves us in
no doubt that the major component is colour.

The 1976 PEP Survey found some improvement. Since 1967 discrimination in the field of housing had decreased although they still
found, for example, discrimination against blacks in 27% of applications for rented accommodation. Discrimination against applicants
for unskilled jobs still occurred in nearly 50% of cases, and for white
collar jobs there was no improvement.
    In the late seventies and early eighties a series of studies showed
continuing discrimination in housing, education and all aspects of
employment. The 1984 survey by the PSI documented a further
worsening of unemployment rates for black workers. Surveys
charted widespread racism within the police force and characterised

black–police relationships as 'disastrous'. The Scarman Report on the Brixton riots saw the disturbances as most immediately an outburst against the police. At the same time as blacks were being portrayed in the media as 'muggers' there was, in reality, increasing violence *against* black citizens. In March–June 1981, for example, Coventry Community Relations offices logged sixty incidents of violence against blacks, including what they regarded as two racially influenced murders. The situation continued to worsen throughout the decade. Metropolitan police figures for 1987 disclosed an increase of 26% in reported 'racial incidents' – up from 1,733 in 1986 to 2,179. The general economic situation, large-scale unemployment and the changing pattern of industrial change found black citizens trapped in urban decline. Liverpool provides a good case study. Prior to the 1981 riots black unemployment was estimated at 50%. Out of 1,738 people employed in the Liverpool Environmental Health Department only eleven were black. The Social Services Department employed 3,840, but only thirty-five blacks. There were 30,000 blacks in the city but only 169 were numbered amongst the 22,000 council employees. As the 1984 PSI report stated:

We have moved over a period of 18 years from studying the circumstances of immigrants to studying the black population of Britain only to find we are looking at the same thing . . . racialism and racial discrimination continue to have a powerful impact on black people . . . the position of black people remains largely geographically and economically that allocated to them as immigrant workers in the 1950's and 1960's.

Race and class
But how do we specifically characterise the social position of black people in Britain? Should we see blacks as a distinct group in our society, essentially characterised by their ethnicity and by racism? Or should we ultimately relate ethnic groups to the class structure? Two points need to be made here. We have referred to those of Afro-Caribbean and Asian extraction as 'blacks' because the composite term appears to be favoured by a majority of community activists as a means of asserting a common experience of past oppression and a common identity in relation to contemporary racism. But this should not blind us to the *heterogeneity* – in terms of culture, religion and political attitudes – of the black communities. And against this background there are, quite clearly, black capitalists, black managers and black professionals as well as black white collar and manual workers.

Despite this, the evidence shows that black capitalists and black members of the middle class suffer discrimination because of their ascribed racial or real ethnic identity. And that the large majority of blacks are members of the working class who, again, encounter particular oppression compared with their white counterparts. One of the big arguments amongst activists and commentators is whether – and to what degree – we should give pre-eminence to 'race' over class, or class over 'race' in analysing the current position. The best view appears to be that it is important to relate racist oppression to class oppression. The latter provides the essential context for the former. The majority of Britain's black citizens remain today a specific grouping within the working class, suffering double deprivation because they are workers and because they are black. As the experience of Liverpool City Council, who tended to reduce everything to class demonstrates, there is a need for specific struggle against special deprivation. But this, in turn, should always be seen in the context of wider working-class organisation and related to wider working-class action.

Explanations of racism

How do we explain the existence of racialist attitudes? A number of possible explanations are considered below.

(1) *The importance of ideas*   particularly the ideas of scientists who argued for the existence of races based on genetic inheritance. The problem with the explanation is that whilst these ideas may have had some influence, they were trying to explain and sometimes justify racist behaviour and structures that existed before the ideas were produced. The theories were developed in a particular social and economic context initially, for example, where slaveowners in the West Indies and southern states of the USA were being challenged and European powers bent on colonial conquest needed to justify themselves.

(2) *Racism is a problem of individual psychology*   This explanation is a popular one today and many analyses and prescriptions are informed by this approach. Much of the Scarman Report, occasioned by the riots in Brixton, viewed racist problems in terms of subjective feelings and attitudes, whether of the police or the black community.

Much of the race relations training which takes place is based upon individualistic psychology and partakes of therapy. But an individual's racial prejudice is learned within social structures in which racial discrimination already occurs. Such attitudes do not exist as part of an immutable human nature. There is no racial prejudice in some societies, while in South Africa racism is a mark of normal adjustment to society. This is not to argue that psychological attitudes, neuroses and anxieties are not imporant in understanding the particular forms racism takes in particular situations.

(3) *To understand racism we need to look at the overall social, economic and political context in which it develops* This kind of explanation provides us with the best means of coming to grips with the problem. We have to look for explanations to today's racism in terms of both the historical development of our society and the practical problems people face today. 'Nation', 'slavery' and 'empirc' are key words here. Britain's development as a nation, its central involvement in the slave trade and its later accumulation of a vast empire of what were viewed as primitive inferior people took place at the same time as the equality of all men was being asserted in Europe. Racism usefully excluded 'savages' from the family of man, whilst the treatment meted out to blacks made them inferior in a very real way. Colonialism contributed to Britain's position as a great power and thus nourished chauvinist and racist ideas amongst all sections of the population. We also have to look at contemporary external factors such as the performance of former colonies since independence. But a crucial internal factor was the sudden appearance of a relatively large number of people of perceived inferior race within Britain, just as its role as a major power was ending and not very long before economic decline set in. The fact that immigrants not only had black skins but were brought here as cheap labour, worked in the worst jobs in the declining industries and lived in the worst housing, reinforced racist stereotypes among British workers. And the fact that they could be seen as competitors for jobs and increasingly scarce resources provided these hostile opinions with a cutting edge and led to 'scapegoating' – blacks were blamed for the problems facing whites.

The theory that material conditions prompt racist ideology leaves many questions unanswered. We still need to know more about the specific links and exactly *how* racist ideology is generated, reproduced and rendered redundant. A whole host of questions – why racism exists in one society but not another, whether racism existed in ancient societies or is purely a product of capitalism – remain the subject of intense and impassioned debate.

We now need to turn to look at the reaction of politicians to the development of racism in post-war British society.

Immigration legislation

Breaking the ice

The initial response of British politicians to the post-war immigrants was cautious and contradictory. Both the Attlee and Churchill administrations explored but rejected restrictions on entry. Initial numbers were small, there were real manpower needs and there was a desire not to offend the Commonwealth. But neither government was prepared to will the resources and give the political leadership which might have minimised later problems. As the fifties developed the policy reaction was not to attack racism but to try to limit the problem and the consequent social disruption, by managing its victims and controlling the inflow into Britain of black workers. Pressure from right-wing constituencies and MPs to reduce black immigration in the wake of the Notting Hill riots led the Conservatives to introduce the 1962 Immigration Act. This measure was also prompted by a rise in the numbers entering Britain and the fact that the polls showed control was electorally popular. British citizens from the Commonwealth could now only enter if they were dependents of residents or students or possessed an employment voucher: Category A for those with a specific job, Category B for those with a scarce skill, Category C for other applicants. The Act was a temporary measure requiring periodic renewal. It was not *overtly* racist, applying to all Commonwealth citizens, but it did not apply to the 60,000–70,000 Irish citizens entering annually. 'The Bill's real purpose was to restrict the influx of coloured immigrants. We were reluctant to say as much openly' (Minister William Deedes in 1968).

Labour strongly opposed the Bill on the grounds that the government was succumbing to racist pressures. They promised the speedy repeal of an act they claimed was anti-Commonwealth and unjustified economically. But the Commonwealth was becoming decreasingly important, economically and politically.

Establishing consensus

The two election defeats of Labour's chosen Foreign Secretary, Patrick Gordon Walker, apparently on the racist issue, impressed the incoming 1964 Labour government. There was a desire not to appear 'soft' and consequently lose votes to the Tories, to create a bipartisan approach and 'take race out of politics'. Labour renewed the Act and in a White Paper in 1965 promised to strengthen it. The 1968 *Commonwealth Immigrants Act* was introduced in the wake of another right-wing campaign opposing the rights of Asians expelled from Kenya to enter a Britain 'bursting to the seams'. The Act removed the right of entry from all British citizens who did not have a parent or grandparent born in Britain. Instead, they could apply for special vouchers: 7,500 would be issued annually.

The ancillary 1969 *Immigration Appeal Act* allowed an appeal to those refused entry but required all intending immigrants to obtain an entry certificate following an interview and production of birth and marriage certificates. In many areas this led to obstruction and long delays for those with rights of entry.

Those from Australia, New Zealand and Canada who would, on the whole, have the *patrial* connection and who were overwhelmingly white, had the right to enter whilst British passport holders from the New Commonwealth who would, on the whole, not have the patrial connection and were overwhelmingly black did not. The Act, therefore, appeared to be not about numbers but about colour. Its passing was accompanied by a series of speeches from Tory Shadow Cabinet member, Enoch Powell, who spoke in terms of the destruction of 'nation' and 'culture' by black immigrants and eventual civil war. Given the mass media coverage, these speeches articulated, extended and made respectable racist attitudes. Powell's widespread resonance was illustrated on 23 April 1968 when London dockers went on strike and marched to Westminster to support him.

Labour's patrial distinction was taken up by the Conservative *Immigration Act*, 1971, designed to replace all existing legislation. The 'right of abode' was given to patrials or those resident in the UK for five years or more; those born to or adopted by those born in the UK; and spouses. All aliens and all non-patrial commonwealth citizens needed permission and a work permit to enter Britain, although those already resident retained the right to bring in dependants. There continued to be no control over nationals of the Republic of Ireland and the EEC. Introduced to put an end to further large-scale

immigration, the Act actually increased the numbers of those eligible
for entry from the old Commonwealth. However, where Labour had
succumbed to pressure not to admit the Kenyan Asians, the Tories in
1972 stood firm against pressure from the media and right-wing
politicians and allowed British citizens expelled from Uganda to
enter the country.

Labour opposed the legislation although its opposition was undermined by the fact that it was based on its own 1968 Act. Labour
spokesperson, Alex Lyon, promised its repeal, but this pledge was
not redeemed. Labour did increase the number of special vouchers
available for those with no rights of entry from 3,000 to 5,000 a year.
It allowed entry to husbands and fiancés of women living in Britain, a
right it had originally removed, but later tightened these provisions.
It also halted the virginity tests on women seeking entry which had
been openly carried out in the previous period.

Breaking the consensus

In 1977 Mrs Thatcher argued the necessity of 'holding out a clear
prospect of an end to immigration'. A year later she claimed 'the
British character has done so much for democracy, for law and done
so much throughout the world that if there is a fear that it might be
swamped, people are going to react and be rather hostile to those
coming in'.

This clear articulation of sentiments close to those expressed by
Enoch Powell a decade earlier presaged a move to the right by the
Conservatives. Mrs Thatcher was responding in 'authoritarian populist' fashion to what she saw as the real anxiety and concern of the
majority. The Conservative new turn was accompanied by a significant improvement in the opinion polls; the fact that it was seen as
stealing a march on Labour reinforced its momentum. Moreover,
Britain was now in the years of surplus labour. The British Nationality Act, introduced in January 1981 (when primary immigration
had slowed to a dribble), was intended to bring the law on nationality
into line with the now consolidated system of immigration law based
on patriality. There would now be three categories of citizenship:
British citizens, broadly, those with full rights of entry; *British overseas citizens* (New Commonwealth); and *Citizens of the British
dependent territories* (e.g. Hong Kong, Bermuda). The latter two
categories would now have restricted nationality as well as immigration rights.

The Thatcher Years

The Thatcher administrations also tightened up on the rules ancillary to the legislation. In 1986, the use of 'genetic' fingerprinting to establish the bona-fides of prospective immigrants was authorised. In the same year visa requirements were introduced for visitors from five 'black' countries – India, Pakistan, Bangladesh, Ghana and Nigeria. The government took a firm line in refusing sanctuary to Tamil refugees whilst the *Carriers Liability Act*, 1987 imposed fines on airline and shipping companies bringing passengers to Britain without proper accreditation. After a brief pause, perhaps occasioned by the fears of civil disorder the urban riots prompted, the Conservatives had returned to a restrictive line.

This was confirmed by the *Immigration Act*, 1988. Justified by Home Officer Minister Timothy Renton by the dangers of continuing 'mass immigration on a vast scale', the Act reached the Statute Book as it was reported that 46,000 had been accepted for settlement in the UK in 1987, the lowest annual figure since 1962, and as the government prepared for the removal of immigration controls between EEC countries in 1992. The 1988 Act removed the automatic rights of those who had settled before 1973 to bring their dependants into the country (those settling later than that year had no such rights). In future they would have to establish that they were able to house and support their families. Where previously, action against those overstaying their proper periods of entry had lain with the immigration authorities, the police would now be involved. Immigration officers were given new powers to refuse entry without any right of appeal to those claiming to be British who could not produce a valid passport. Home Office decisions on deportation would no longer be subject to appeal to an immigration adjudicator. And there were new restrictions on the rights of those involved in polygamous marriages to enter the country – despite the fact that this had never been an issue. The 1988 Act was, therefore, a further small addition to the restrictive framework developed since 1962, despite statistics which showed an overall population loss through emigration and immigration of 700,000 between 1962 and 1982.

The Thatcher years saw the Labour Party recanting on its own contribution to that framework. A 1980 National Executive statement, *Labour and The Black Electorate,* argued that the party's past policies had failed black people. Labour now pledged itself to repeal the existing 'racist' immigration laws; to convene a

Commonwealth conference to discuss their replacement; to establish rights to free entry for all British citizens; and to appoint a special minister to lead the fight against racial inequality. Labour spokesperson Roy Hattersley specifically criticised his own past positions. And Labour promised to repeal the Nationality Act, opposed Mrs Thatcher's further restrictions on immigration in terms of human rights, and sought an answer to the urban riots of the 1980s in terms of social and economic deprivation as against the Conservatives' law and order approach. However, the statements in the Party's 1983 and 1987 manifestos were a good deal more coy than many of its leaders' utterances.

The policies of the ill-fated Alliance in this period were close to those of Labour. They opposed the Conservative legislation, promising to restore the right of all those born in Britain to citizenship and re-establish rights of appeal. Immigration law would be remoulded on a non-racist basis and controls would operate in non-discriminatory fashion. Policy in this area would be related to the introduction of a Bill of Rights. Thus, by the end of the 1980s, the consensus between the parties on immigration forged in the immediate post-war period had undergone at least a partial disintegration.

Anti-discrimination legislation

The initial response to the arrival of the post-war black immigrants has been termed 'colour blindness'. There was a refusal to accept that discrimination was taking place on a significant scale and, consequently, a refusal to accept that there was a necessity to take specific measures to deal with it. The government argued that legislation against discrimination would *introduce* distinctions which did not exist. In similar fashion, the TUC claimed that workers were *workers* regardless of pigmentation, and legislation would disrupt the existing unity of the working-class movement. It was only in the face of mounting irrefutable evidence that distinctions were already being applied against black citizens and that solidarity and unity did not exist, that action to assimilate the new citizens was reluctantly taken.

In 1965 Roy Hattersley argued: 'Without integration limitation is inexcusable; without limitation integration is impossible.' To this end successive Labour governments have taken initiatives in the area of combating racism. The position of the Conservatives has basically been one of grudging aquiescence, their hesitant acceptance of ameliorative measures contrasting with the vigour with which they have pursued the control side of the strategy.

The *Race Relations Act* 1965 established conciliation machinery to deal with complaints of discrimination which was to be unlawful on grounds of 'race, colour, ethnic or national origin' in public places such as hotels, restaurants and transport. The Act was criticised on the following grounds:

(1) It did not apply to crucial areas such as housing or employment.

(2) Enforcement methods were inadequate.

(3) Its impact was limited, judging by the small number of complaints.

Its successor, the *Race Relations Act,* 1968, introduced in the same year as tighter immigration control, also covered housing, employment, the provision of goods, facilities and services and the publication or display of advertisements. The Race Relations Board was revamped and given a duty to investigate complaints of discrimination. It had to resolve disputes initially by conciliation and it had the power to take a case only if all else failed. It also established the Community Relations Commission to promote community relations and oversee the work of local community relations councils. By 1975 the Labour government argued the need for tighter legislation as:

(1) The 1968 Act had not succeeded in significantly improving the position.

(2) The definition of discrimination was too narrow and did not cover cases where *the impact* of rules and regulations, intended or not, was discriminatory.

(3) Enforcement methods were still inadquate. The Race Relations Board was inhibited by the need to examine every complaint, its powers were inadequate, individual cases were handled too slowly and the obligation to investigate denied more effective individual access to the courts.

(4) Compensation awards were very small and court orders difficult to obtain.

The *Race Relations Act,* 1976 built on this analysis. The definition of discrimination was extended to include indirect discrimination 'where unjustifiable practices and procedures which apply to everyone have the effect of putting people of a particular racial group at a disadvantage' (such as language requirements not necessary for a job). The individual can now proceed directly to an industrial tribunal or county court without awaiting a decision of the Commission for Racial Equality. This latter body replaced the Race Relations Board and the Community Relations Committee and was given new powers, for example, of serving non-discrimination notices and enforcing them by injunctions. There was also a new clause on racial incitement.

The Race Relations Acts have also been complemented by a series of measures to deal with urban deprivation with an anti-discrimination dimension. The Home Office has been responsible for the Urban Programme (1968), the Community Development Project (1969), the Urban Deprivation Unit (1973) and the Comprehensive Community Programmes (1974).

Section 11 of the Local Government Act, 1966 allowed local authorities to claim grant aid to employ extra staff in the event of substantial numbers of 'immigrants' in their area whose language and customs were different from the rest of the community. A local authority qualifies for assistance by showing that 2% of its schoolchildren have parents born in the New Commonwealth and resident in the UK for less than ten years. The Department of Education and Science has been responsible for Educational Priority Areas (1967), the Education Disadvantage Unit (1974) and the Centre for Information and Advice on Educational Disadvantage (1975). The Department of Environment has been responsible for the Housing Action Areas and the Inner Area Studies and, since 1977, the Urban Aid Programme.

The anti-discrimination approach remained open to criticism. Through the eighties the funds available to the CRE declined in real terms. Despite the publication of a Code of Practice on equal opportunities policies, industrial tribunals were, in 1987, dealing with under 300 cases, with only forty applicants achieving success. This was due to inherent weaknesses in the legislation and its remedies. In 1987, successful applicants in the majority of cases were awarded less than £1,000. It was also related to the attitude of the courts to the issue which reflected the resistance of many key social institutions to change. The judges were active in restricting the powers of the CRE, Lord Justice Oliver referring in one case to the Commission as 'an engine of oppression' and Lord Denning opining in another, 'you might think we were back in the days of the Inquisition'.

Equal opportunities policies

In the seventies the enduring nature of black disadvantage and racism, together with a greater degree of self-assertion by black communities, produced a move from 'assimilation' and 'integration' to 'multi-culturalism'. The new approach stressed the importance of the black cultures and their right to parity of esteem in a pluralist society. The white community should understand and respect them. This approach was criticised on the grounds that greater understanding did not necessarily produce greater toleration. It was combined with a growth of equal opportunities policies, particularly in local authorities and in the education system with a stronger emphasis *on combating racism* and recruiting black workers. Multi-cultural education and Racial Awareness Training (RAT) aimed at bringing white people to an understanding of their own racism became fashionable. These tendencies were strongly represented in the municipal socialism of the early eighties – which particularly sought to channel funds to minority groups as part of an 'enabling' strategy – and accelerated in the aftermath of the riots. To some degree this kind of positive action became part of the right's carricature of Labour in local government as the 'loony left'. It was erroneously reported in the press that children of Islington were being taught to sing 'Baa baa greensheep'. But the new approaches were also given a stimulus by the publication of the Swann Report. However, there was some evidence that the application of these policies was alienating the white working class and doubts even amongst certain sections of the left as to their efficacy.

In the wake of the 1985 Honeyford affair, where a Bradford headmaster agreed to early retirement after protest by parents about articles criticising anti-racism he had written in the right-wing *Salisbury Review,* the suspension, of Maureen McGoldrick, a Brent headteacher, for allegedly refusing to take a black teacher on to her staff, focused controversy. The action of Brent council and their fierce pursuit of the matter through the courts appeared draconian in relation to a popular teacher who, in contrast to Ray Honeyford, had an excellent anti-racist record. It appeared as if some councillors were in danger of succumbing to the obsessional view that racism was everywhere and McGoldrick was only fully reinstated after intervention by the Minister of Education and Neil Kinnock. Further critical scrutiny of anti-racist policies were prompted by the report of a panel of inquiry into the murder of thirteen-year-old Ahmed Iqbal Ullah by a white fellow pupil at Burnage High School, Manchester. The report, suppressed by Manchester City Council, criticised the school's anti-racist policy as failing to involve white pupils and parents and viewing racism as an individual white problem, to the disregard of the influence of the wider material environment. It went further and argued that

The basic assumption behind many policies is that, since black students are the victims of the immoral and prejudiced behaviour of white students, white students are all to be seen as 'racist' whether they are ferret-eyed fascists or committed anti-racists. Racism is thus placed in some kind of moral vacuum and is totally divorced from the more complex reality of human relations in the classroom, playground or community.

This approach, which implies that, because there is racist ideology in society, all whites are equally infected, takes no account of the class dimension and suggests that whites have little or no function in overcoming racism. Rather than feeling that they were involved in fighting racism, white children at Burnage felt that their aspirations were being neglected and that anti-racism was operating at their expense. Similar criticisms have been made of RAT which, it has been argued, is concentrated myopically on individual feelings and attitudes, fails to relate them to state and social structures which generate racism and is fuelled by white middle-class guilt. A prominent black left-winger, Sivanandan, bitterly criticises recent approaches:

The ensuing scramble for government favour and government grants (channelled through local authorities) served, on the one hand to deepen ethnic rivalry and, on the other, to widen the definition of ethnicity to include a variety of national and religious groups – Chinese, Cypriots, Greeks, Turks, Irish, Italians, Jews, Moslems, Sikhs – till the term itself became meaningless (except as a means of getting funds).

Critique

We have to disentangle the true from the false in criticism of anti-racist policies. In some cases criticisms are based on the erroneous view put forward, for example, by Russell Lewis in his book *Anti-Racism: A Mania Exposed* that 'There is no institutional racism in Britain', that what white hostility there is will simply wither away through increased contact with blacks and that anti-racism is a bigger problem than racism itself. This view ignores, or downplays the evidence on the extent and density of racism. There is a need for an anti-racist approach in education and equal opportunities policies in employment, commerce, and housing. The demand for a pure English education, for example, is in the tradition of cultural imperialism and a recipe for the alienation of minorities. On the other hand, there are real fears that increasing fragmentation will produce a more divided society, with each minority following their own path. The recent controversy has been useful in raising the question of whether it is possible to talk of a unifying culture in our class-divided society and the degree to which we need a unifying culture. It is also sobering to note, as a CRE report did in 1988, that only 50% of local authorities had introduced equal opportunities policies.

There can certainly be no doubt that bureaucratic anti-racist approaches imposed from above, with an easy over-reliance on rhetoric, discipline and a faulty analysis of the problems, can intensify the disease they seek to eradicate. A particular criticism of the policies developed by some Labour local authorities is the weight they give to dealing with the superficial effects of racism rather than its material causes. A harsher view would see in the approach of the municipal anti-racists, which attacks the problem largely on its ideological fringes, an attempt to provide an easier substitute for the more difficult assault upon racism's material roots. Certainly there are many who would now agree that the GLC's £20,000 anti-racist space fantasy video game, the renaming of streets on the grounds that appellations such as 'Cecil Rhodes House' were racist, and the similar criticisms aimed at a variety of literary characters such as Huckleberry Finn or Rupert the Bear, taken in their overall context, trivialised both racism and anti-racism. The emphasis placed by largely middle-class radicals on such *symptoms* paid little attention to the real problem of racism, or to the prevailing consciousness of the electorate, or to the overall political balance in the country, particularly between central and local government. Moreover, a number of surveys in Liverpool, London and Manchester showed that municipal anti-racism was not working: the number of blacks in local authority employment continued to be disproportionately low.

There must be a middle ground between doing nothing – a policy which can only strengthen racism – and an ill thought-out counterproductive approach. For example, in a situation of cutbacks in overall resources in local authorities, earmarking of funds for blacks will have an opportunity-cost in terms of white workers. Preferential treatment for blacks in relation to jobs or housing *will* be at the expense of whites. Training courses which focus on the ideas in people's heads, failing to relate them to lack of jobs, poor housing and inadequate incomes *will* be ineffective. It may be possible to overcome some of these problems. But success demands careful thought, discussion and negotiation, rather than the zealotry of principle.

The black communities and the parties

Until recently, the black voter was a Labour voter, although surveys demonstrated that, despite a close attention to particular issues, such as immigration and law and order, black voters generally shared a similar political agenda to their white counterparts. Whilst figures are not entirely reliable, CRE surveys showed 8% of the black electorate voting Conservative in the 1979 general election, 5% voting Liberal and 86% voting Labour. In 1983 the figures were 7%, 11% and 81% respectively. However, there are differences between Asian and Afro-Caribbean voting and there is some evidence that this monolith is flaking, with class identity rather than 'race' identity becoming a stronger motivator. Harris polls showed 23% of Asians voting Conservative in 1987 compared with 9% in 1983 – a significant figure in the context of a general small swing *towards* Labour. Labour attracted only 67% of Asian voters compared with 81% in 1983, whilst the Alliance proportion stayed the same. However, the Afro-Caribbean vote remained steady. According to Harris, 6% voted Conservative in 1987 compared with 7% in 1983. The figures for Labour were 86% compared with 87% and for the Alliance 7% compared with 5%. There was also some evidence that the general swing away from Labour in London was connected with its policies in this area.

This move to the Conservatives requires further scrutiny, but, contrary to public perception, this is the party which has made particular arrangements for black activists. In 1976, a Community Affairs Department was established to relate to previously neglected groups. The Conservatives established Anglo-Asian and Anglo-West Indian societies, open to both white and black voters, the former growing to over thirty branches. However, in 1986, plagued by feuding between Sikh activists, it was dissolved and the following year the experiment gave way to a new One Nation' advisory forum.

In the 1987 election six Conservative candidates were black, compared with two in 1979; although running in strong Labour constituencies, none were successful.

In the early 1980s, agitation developed for constitutional representation within the Labour Party for a black section, open exclusively to black members. A motion to the 1983 Conference was remitted to a working party which, after two years and heavy defeats for motions supporting black sections at the 1984 conference, came down in their favour. The party leadership refused to accept this verdict and gained conference support for a Black and Asian Advisory Committee embracing both black and white representatives. This was condemned as 'Uncle Tomism' by advocates of the black section who challenged it unsuccessfully at successive conferences. The issue provides a good illustration of the problems concerning the relationship of the general interest and the specific interest, of unity and autonomy in undermining racism.

Opponents of the black section, which include not only Labour leaders but some black activists, argue that all Labour Party members have an interest in, and a commitment to, anti-racism. It is not the special property of blacks. Although blacks must play a leading part, white members too have an important role: our politics are not dictated by our personal identity as female, gay, black or Irish. To support demands for sectional representation is to tend towards the disaggregation of the party into a range of groups and thus undermine its coherence. Black section supporters are not representative of the black community and are often those who will most benefit from sectionalisation. Blacks will not become more but less integrated into the party via a black section and are quite capable of making their way through the party's existing mainstream institutions.

Advocates of the black section point to Labour's poor record of anti-racism. This has been related to the white domination of the party and the lack of black representation at every level. Because they are the recipients of racism, blacks must play the leading role in combating it. They cannot wait on the sluggish wider labour movement to get to grips with the issue, and they thus require a degree of autonomy to provide leadership for the wider party. Black sections do not increase separation – it already exists because black members are *already* marginalised. Black sections, their supporters insist, are an essential means by which blacks can develop the confidence, the strategy and the organisation to change the Labour Party and the wider political picture. It is hypocritical to oppose separate organisation in the party for blacks when it already exists for women and a variety of other groups such as Poale Zion.

This issue has been confused by the identification of black section supporters with the 'hard left', the desire of the party leadership to present a moderate profile to the wider electorate and their some-times insensitive attitude towards black members. The removal of Sharon Atkin as a candidate in the 1987 election, after her statement that the Labour Party was racist, increased bitterness. But the return of four black MPs in the 1987 election – the first since Saklatvala in the 1920s – demonstrated that progress was being made. By 1988, with war-weariness setting in, there were signs that some of the leadership of the black sections were willing to seek a compromise solution.

The Liberal/SDP Alliance, in its limited lifespan, avoided such controversial experiments. Despite its small proportion of black voters, the SDP established a Campaign for Racial Justice which tried to hold meetings in areas with concentrations of black voters and produced several documents such as *Racial Justice – an SDP Approach to Equal Opportunities*.

The Liberals argued that 'the principle of racial equality is at the very heart of liberalism' and in 1985 David Steel established a Com-mittee of Inquiry to investigate the lack of black involvement in the party. In 1983 there were eight and, in 1987, seven black Alliance candidates. However, the shine was to some degree taken off these initiatives by the disclosure, in 1987, of the role played by the Liberal-controlled council in Tower Hamlets in cutting off benefits to Bangladeshi families who faced eviction from bed and breakfast accommodation on the grounds that by coming to this country, they had intentionally made themselves homeless. In 1988 a CRE Report stated that Tower Hamlets' Housing Department had been guilty of discrimination in its allocation policies.

The politics of extremism

The National Front (NF), Britain's premier fascist organisation, was formed from a number of small racist sects in 1967. The Front projected an electoral strategy based on 'law and order', opposition to the EEC and, crucially, the compulsory repatriation of all black 'immigrants'. Their ten candidates in the 1970 election received only

3·6% of the vote. Their fortunes improved after the Conservative decision to admit the Ugandan Asians and as the economic pressures nuturing working-class racism intensified. A year later they were reported to have 14,000 members and received 16% of the vote in the West Bromwich by-election. However, despite growing publicity, their candidates polled only just over 3% of the vote in the two 1974 elections.

After a split (giving rise to the British National Party) in 1976, membership declined to around 9,000 and there appeared to be a move away from the respectable strategy of parliamentary democracy to street politics. The NF appeared to benefit from these tactics in 1976 and 1977, obtaining over 10% of the vote in twenty-five local elections. In two areas their vote was over 20%. Despite more publicity through running battles with the Anti-Nazi League, the NF met electoral disaster in 1979, their candidates collectively polling around 1·3% of the vote. Handicapped, perhaps crucially, by the tension between an inner circle embracing fully-fledged Fascist philosophy and recruits won in the 1970s from conservatism who were right-wing nationalists pure and simple, the National Front declined into congeries of warring sections. Some observers explained this downturn in terms of the Conservative move to the right in the late seventies, itself possibly a response to the earlier vigour of the NF. The fascist groupings are today of minor political significance, although a split in the National Front in 1987 was seen as presaging a new development through a regroupment of the majority with the breakaway British National Party.

Black organisation and resistance

The black British have long-established community organisations such as the three Indian Workers' Associations – all with a strong left-wing bias – and the various Pakistan Welfare Associations. Moulded by the influence of Asian politics they have, nonetheless, acted as effective pressure groups in Britain. The experience of racism appears to have brought the different communities closer together. In 1980, there was an attempt to establish a National Co-ordinating Committee of Afro-Caribbean and Asian organisations. Asian youth movements have also been prominent in Southall and Bradford. There are long-standing collectives such as *Race Today* and the Institute of Race Relations based *Race and*

Class. Prior to the 1979 election, a standing conference of Afro-Caribbean and Asian Councillors was set up and published a Black People's Manifesto for the campaign. And in the wider sense of anti-racism we must not overlook the activities of the Anti-Apartheid Movement.

There are many examples of blacks organising self-defence against white violence, but the most successful campaigns, those of the Anti-Nazi League and Rock Against Racism, were in fact inspired by the sectarian Socialist Workers' Party, although they did involve wide support. They proved ephemeral and declined in tandem with the National Front. Official organisations have done little – witness the moribund TUC/Labour Party campaign against racism of 1976. But black workers have become more active in the trade unions and been involved in a continuing series of struggles of which Mansfield Hosiery, Imperial Typewriters, Grunwick and Chix are only the best known.

In 1983 a Black Trade Union Solidarity Movement was established whilst several unions such as NALGO have strong, if unrecognised, black sections. Campaigns against deportation of individuals under the immigration legislation have also mobilised support. The future political trajectory of black citizens is to some degree contingent on wider political initiatives.

In the context of an overall turning towards activity in mainstream institutions, the three main responses today would seem to be:

(1) Black self-organisation to turn traditional institutions, specifically the Labour Party and the unions, to the purposes of the black communities.

(2) A turning inwards to compensatory creeds such as Rastafarianism and Pan-Africanism which in themselves lack a practical political dimension.

(3) Militant semi-spontaneous resistance to draw attention to the plight of the communities as in the riots in Bristol in 1980, in most major British cities in 1981 and in Handsworth and Broad Water Farm in 1985.

Racism as a political issue

Throughout the sixties and seventies, despite different emphases and rhetoric in opposition, there was a broad consensus on the 'control and integrate strategy'. This has been criticised as a strategy for combating racism on the grounds that:

(1) The immigration legislation involved appeasing, legitimising and encouraging the racism of the electorate by identifying black people, not white racism, as the problem and by practising racial discrimination at the point of entry.

(2) This state institutionalisation of discrimination led to a system of internal surveillance of black residents. Every black was a potential criminal, as could be seen most graphically by the six police raids on workplaces in early 1980 in search of illegal immigrants.

(3) Successive governments, far from seeking to educate the electorate, have succumbed to the lowest common denominator. A high-profile anti-racist campaign plus a determined attempt to provide more resources to support the new settlers in the fifties and sixties could have limited the problems we face today. The failure to grasp the nettle has helped its luxuriant growth.

(4) The anti-discrimination legislation was not only a case of too little, too late. It was contaminated by the laws on exclusion. If the government was refusing to admit people on the grounds that their skin colour would cause problems, why shouldn't a factory owner do exactly the same?

(5) A harsher analysis depicts the race relations legislation, central and local government funding, and the recent vogue for equal opportunities and anti-racist policies and RAT as co-option intended to inhibit black self-organisation and as tokenism intended to create a 'black middle class' and suppress conflict without redressing injustice. Most critics, however, accept that the 1976 legislation and the increased role or the CRE represented a passing-over from half-hearted education to more vigorous enforcement and that the legislation has some role to play in an anti-racist strategy.

In this context Labour local authorities at least attempted to deal with the problems whatever the inadequacies of their approach. Moreover, the debate over anti-racist policies and education at least has the advantage of focusing attention on this area – necessary if not sufficient for progress. But there was evidence that at least some of the motivation in the controversy was racist and other pessimistic portents – witness the saga of the white Dewsbury parents who, in 1987–88 successfully boycotted a largely black school and the fears that the 'opting-out' provisions of the 1988 Education Reform Act could lead to 'all white' and 'all black' schools. In the late eighties, there were signs – a surprising 32% of Labour voters in the 1986

British Social Attitudes survey admitted to racial prejudice – that a more explicit racism was re-entering the political mainstream.

The last decade has seen a rupturing of the previous consensus on race relations between the two main parties. In one sense, the Conservatives seem broadly satisfied with the status quo. They are firmly opposed to further moves in the direction of positive discrimination and pessimistic about the role of state intervention. But they possess a keen awareness of the dangers of civil disorder. And they are prepared to devote more resources to 'crisis' situations and areas of particular disadvantage and to turn aside pressures from the right for the abolition of the CRE or schemes for repatriation.

The cynical might observe that the Conservatives do not have the black vote and they do not need it. They have, moreover, passively benefited from the lampooning of anti-racism, the failings of municipal socialism and the white working-class backlash. But Mrs Thatcher wants to conquer the inner-city electorate and Thatcherism does have a black dimension. Conservatives believe that, as Sir George Young put it, 'We've got to back the good guys, the sensible, moderate, responsible leaders of ethnic groups.' Blacks must be given a stake in society which will stimulate the adoption of enterprise values and self-help. The aftermath of the riots, therefore, saw increases in central government spending through the Urban Programme and the inner-city Task Forces, support for private enterprise in carrying through urban regeneration and attempts to develop black businesses and strengthen the black middle class. But the failure rate of small enterprise is high. And it is difficult to see how this strategy will provide a way in or up for more than a small minority of blacks.

Labour is presently stranded on the rocks of the black sections – anti-racist controversies. It is losing black votes at a time when it needs all the votes it can get. Key areas where it remains in control at national and local levels are areas of high black concentration. On the other hand, the activities of black members, filtered through the media, intensify public perception of a divided party. And the party leadership wishes to win over skilled workers and middle-class voters who, it feels, may be alienated by a firm anti-racism. In this situation, it has produced no new compelling and convincing initiatives. Certainly a botched anti-racism will not do. Nor will the encouragement of sectionalism and autonomy as positive aims in themselves rather than as reluctant, grudging means to an end.

It seems unlikely that Labour will make progress until, whilst acknowledging the importance of ideology, it asserts the centrality of changing material conditions, for both the black and white deprived, in strategies for undermining racism. Without changes in the social situation, more houses, more jobs, more money at the bottom end of society, the race relations industry will remain an important and token substitute for a real strategy. The present impasse in Britain represents a failure of political nerve, political strategy and political action.

There is a crying need for new policies, as race relations suffers from the more authoritarian political climate. It is also clear that the implementation of any such policies will have to take account of the growing activism of the blacks themselves and their increasing impatience with their continued standing as second-class citizens.

Reading

Martin Barker, *The New Racism,* Junction Books, 1978.

C. Brown, *Black and White Britain,* PSI, 1984.

E. Ellis Cashmore & Barry Troyna, *Introduction to Race Relations,* Routledge & Kegan Paul, 1983.

Marian Fitzgerald, *Black people and Party Politics in Britain,* Runnymede Trust, 1987.

Peter Fryer, *Staying Power: The History of Black People in Britain,* Pluto Press, 1984.

Charles Husband, *'Race' in Britain,* Hutchinson, 1987.

Zig Layton Henry, *The Politics of Race in Britain,* Allen & Unwin, 1984.

Zig Layton Henry & P. B. Rich (eds.), *Race, Government and Politics in Britain,* Macmillan, 1986.

Russell Lewis, *Anti-Racism – A Mania Exposed,* Quartet Books, 1988.

Robert Miles & Annie Phizacklea, *Racism and Political Action in Britain,* Routledge & Kegan Paul, 1979.

Ron Ramdin, *The Making of the Black Working Class in Britain,* Wildwood House, 1987.

A. Sivanandan, *A Different Hunger,* Pluto Press, 1983.

A. Sivanandan, 'RAT and the degradation of black struggle', *Race and Class,* XXVI, 4, 1985.

14 *Karen Hunt*

Women and politics

Women are virtually invisible in textbooks on politics. Voters, MPs, even prime ministers are assumed to be male and are discussed as though it is not important to ask why politics remains a 'man's world'. But to ask such a question – as this chapter seeks to do – raises the much broader issue of women's position in the wider society and challenges our understanding of what politics is about

The vote – exclusion from politics

Until sixty years ago the denial of the right to vote effectively excluded women from participation in formal parliamentary politics – only women over thirty were granted the vote in 1918 and it was not until 1928 that universal suffrage was achieved. Many women saw winning the vote as the key to their emancipation. Once women had access to the system they believed that they would be able to end inequality and change the male political agenda.

The suffragists (constitutionalists) and suffragettes (militants) were not alone, for women have been arguing for women's rights and challenging men's power for centuries. But the voice of Mary Astell in the seventeenth century and even Mary Wollstonecraft in the eighteenth century have been distorted, ignored and even silenced. Women therefore have very little sense of their own history and the reasons why women were willing to sacrifice so much – their health and even their lives – to get the vote.

Separate spheres – public and private

The traditional divide between the public world of politics and work and the private world of the home and the family has been used to justify the exclusion of women from the political process and remains a strong barrier to women's equality. What does this mean for women's political participation?

(1) In the past, it was argued that the two spheres were separate but equal (rather like apartheid). Women had their own responsibilities and participation in the public sphere would 'unsex' them, making them unfit for their primary duty of motherhood and the family. Although the physical divide between public and private is not as sharp now as it was in the nineteenth century, its power persists at the level of ideas: politics is not a 'feminine' pursuit but a man's world.

(2) Psychologically, the effect of the division is to undermine women's confidence in their own abilities. The attributes which are popularly associated with politicians are seen as male: aggression, ambition, self-confidence. There is little for a woman to identify with as women's skills and abilities are undervalued.

(3) The stereotype of woman at the heart of the public/private split is that women are *only* mothers and carers; they are emotional rather than political. Some women accept this as natural and make a virtue of it. These arguments are used very differently by Conservative women (e.g. pro-family, anti-abortion) and by some of the women's peace movement: as mothers, women have a particular responsibility to ensure a world for future generations free from nuclear war.

Women's under-representation

Women make up 51·4% of the population yet only a fraction of that number hold positions of power in formal politics. The 1979 general election on the one hand resulted in the election of Magaret Thatcher as the first woman Prime Minister but it also saw the smallest number of women MPs (nineteen) elected since 1951. Although this number increased to twenty-three by the end of the Parliament, the 1983 general election did not produce an increase in the number of women MPs. In contrast, the number of women MPs nearly doubled in the 1987 general election to a total of forty-one. However, the House of

Commons still has the fourth lowest representation of women in Europe, behind countries such as Portugal and Italy. In Britain, 94% of MPs are male; a clear picture of the under-representation of women. The achievement of one woman in becoming Prime Minister has obscured the fact that there are actually very few women in Parliament, no women in the Cabinet and only one woman on the Opposition Front Bench. Her role is somewhat ambiguous as she does not shadow an existing minister, but would head a Labour government's proposed Ministry of Women.

The comparative picture in Europe is varied. It ranges from countries where women are poorly represented, e.g. Greece, where only 4% of their MPs are female, to Scandinavia, where women form between a quarter and a third of their parliaments. Although the general trend in European elections since 1986 shows an increase in women MPs, women remain significantly under-represented.

Why are there so few women in politics?
If challenged on women's under-representation in politics, men often complain that the problem lies with women themselves: not enough put themselves forward. But the issue is not as simple as this.

(1) *Attitudes*

  (a) As girls grow up they are not encouraged to be assertive and they learn very quickly that they have to be much better than a boy at any task if they are to be taken seriously. Women therefore learn not to put themselves forward.

  (b) Men's beliefs about women's capabilities reinforce women's perception of themselves. The belief persists that women are not up to the job and that they should stick to what they are good at, i.e. being wives and mothers.

  (c) Political parties, particularly their constituency selection panels, reinforce these attitudes by a firm, if not proven, belief that the voters do not like women candidates and that votes will be lost if the standard issue male, white, middle-class candidate is not adopted.

  (d) The media's approach to women in public life reinforces stereotyped attitudes, e.g. the destruction of Maureen Colquhoun's career as an MP because she came out unashamedly as a lesbian or the criticism of Helene Hayman for breastfeeding her baby in the House of Commons.

(2) *Childcare*

Domestic responsibilities, particularly caring for children at home, are a huge obstacle to the equal participation of women in the 'public' world, including politics. This is, of course, because such responsibilities are generally regarded as women's.

(a) This is reflected in the tendency for women MPs to be single or married/divorced without young children. Of the twenty-seven women MPs elected in 1974, only two had children under ten years old.

(b) By the time children are old enough, women themselves are relatively rather old to embark on a political career. This has ramifications for what women can then achieve and can affect women's decisions on the best ways to use their skills and energies.

(3) *Paid work but no time*

Women's increasing involvement in paid work outside the home has to be combined with their domestic reponsibilities. They therefore, literally, have little time for politics, with its endless meetings. In 1985, 66% of women of working age (16–59) and 62% of married women of working age were in the labour force. Although participation in the work-force can increase women's political awareness through breaking their isolation, it is much more likely, because of the practical and ideological constraints on women, to result in grass-roots and community political action rather than parliamentary politics.

(4) *Unlikely to fit the model of an MP*

For the same reasons – discrimination and the division of labour, the occupational segregation of the work-force – it is harder for women to have the same occupational background as male potential MPs; specifically the professions. Moreover women cannot rely on the 'old school tie' or brotherly sponsorship in the way that men now take for granted.

(5) *The cost*

Women's reticence in putting themselves forward for political office may, in fact, be a rational anticipation of the obstacles involved. The costs may just be too great.

The barriers to selection as parliamentary candidates

Many women who would be eligible because of their political experience, occupation and educational background do not put themselves forward because of the constraints just discussed. But even those who are undeterred face a daunting set of obstacles.

(1) *Approved candidates* The political parties have lists of approved candidates. The Labour Party has an A list (trade union nominated) and a B list (constituency party nominated). Those candidates with trade union sponsorship are more likely to succeed, yet because of women's under-representation in the trade union hierarchy, there are very few women on the A list, e.g., only one woman was on the A list announced at the 1988 Annual Conference while the B list contained 17·7% women. The Conservatives, similarly, had only 15% on their list of approved candidates for 1979.

(2) *The shortlist* Having made the list of approved candidates, women then have to get on to the constituency shortlists. Here women have a better chance inasmuch as the need for a 'token' woman has become widely accepted. Indeed, the 1988 Labour Party Conference resolved that there must be one woman on every shortlist.

(3) *Selection* Then, the problem is actually to get selected as a prospective parliamentary candidate. There is still some prejudice that women are an electoral liability despite the dearth of evidence to prove it and much to show that gender is not a factor in the political outcome.

(4) *A safe seat* Although the overall number of women candidates is increasing at general elections (from 212 in 1979 to 325 in 1987), the number elected, as we have seen, is a small proportion. Most of those women were standing either in unwinnable seats or in marginals. In 1979, of the fifty-two women Labour Party candidates, fifteen were standing for re-election, one had been selected to fight a safe seat and four were standing in marginals. Only eleven were elected, five incumbents lost and none of the women's marginal seats were won. Of the eight Conservative women elected that year, seven were standing for re-election and one out of the three women standing for a marginal was successful. Because so few women are selected for safe seats, the probability of women becoming MPs under the present electoral system remains slight. However, a reformed voting system, based on multi-member constituencies and proportional representation, might increase women's chances (see Ch. 5).

(5) *Re-selection*

(a) In the 1970 Parliament, over two-thirds of male MPs had been elected on the first occasion they stood for Parliament whereas less than a third of women had succeeded at their first contest. So as women are less likely to win at their first attempt, it is important that they get re-selected, as that increases their chances. But only 20% of those women defeated at the 1974 elections were re-selected to fight in 1979. There is therefore a high wastage of women candidates and the length of the odds against election, combined with the practical constraints, must deter them from putting themselves forward.

(b) Even if a woman gets elected for a marginal seat, which may be her best option, she is then as vulnerable as any other MP sitting for a marginal seat.

In the House of Commons

The obstacle course just described ensures that few women get elected. But even when safely elected, there are limitations on women's participation.

(a) *A male institution* It is not for nothing that the House of Commons is claimed to be the 'best gentleman's club in Europe': its traditions, atmosphere, concerns and most of its members are male.

(b) *High office* The relatively precarious nature of women MPs' careers means that their chances of being in Parliament long enough to become a Cabinet member are less than for men. Up to 1979, of the seventy women Labour MPs elected since women first became eligible (1918) only 7% became Cabinet Ministers, whilst for the same period, of the forty Conservative women MPs only 5% have achieved Cabinet rank. Of course, this is not the only reason for the lack of promotion of women MPs either by male prime ministers or indeed, by a woman prime minister (who now has no women in her Cabinet). Women have never held the high status office of Chancellor of the Exchequer or been Home or Foreign Secretary. Women who do succeed are therefore seen as exceptions or as Margaret Thatcher is often described, 'the best man for the job'.

Taken together there is little official, and negligible practical, aid or incentive for women to overcome their under-representation in politics.

But there's more to politics than MPs!

Politics is not just about electoral bodies and political parties. Unfortunately the picture of under-representation is as true for public bodies and for the trade unions as it is for Parliament and the parties.

(1) *Public bodies*

In terms of public bodies, whose members are appointed by ministers, only 19% of their membership was female in 1987. In keeping with the sexual division of labour, women are to be found in far greater numbers on 'caring' bodies and on those concerned with consumer affairs than on those responsible for agriculture, defence or transport. So women constitute 32% of Home Office appointments but none of those made by the Department of Energy. Many public bodies either have no women ministerial appointees (304 in 1981) or just one (159 in 1981). The 'Women into Public Life' Campaign which started in 1986, has led to an increase in the number of women known to the Public Appointments Unit at the Cabinet Office. Women now make up 27% of the names from which appointments to public bodies are made.

(2) *Trade unions*

(a) There was a large growth in women's membership of trade unions in the sixties and seventies as the number of women in the labour force rose. Of the total increase in trade union membership between 1960 and 1978, over half (55%) were women, the largest growth being in the public sector. By 1988 45% of the work-force was female and a third of these were TUC members. Women's unionisation has not suffered as much as men's in the recession of the eighties which hit traditionally male industries, such as coal and steel, much harder than traditional female sectors such as light engineering, the public sector and part-time work. Yet this has not resulted in greater female participation in the leadership of trade unions. From shop steward upwards there is little correlation between women's membership of trade unions and their representation within the union hierarchy.

Even unions with a predominantly female membership such as NUPE (66% are women) have a disproportionate representation of women, although this has improved more recently. In 1981 women made up 23.5% of NUPE's executive and only 4.7% of their full-time officials: by 1987/8 they made up 50% of the executive and 9% of full-time officials.

As for the largest union (the TGWU) with their 224,506 female membership in 1986 (15%), women only constituted 5% of their executive in 1987/8 and there were no full-time officials.

This under-representation can be explained in the same terms as women's under-representation in formal politics.

(b) Traditionally women's concerns, for instance working hours, part-time workers' rights and childcare provision, have been low on unions' lists of priorities when it comes to collective bargaining. This is exacerbated when the unions themselves are under attack and are losing members as jobs are lost.

Some unions are now beginning to realise that women workers, particularly part-time workers, are a growing part of the work-force. To be representative and effective, unions will therefore have to target the traditionally marginal workers, hence the TGWU's Link Up campaign and GMBATU's drive to recruit women. But these campaigns can only be successful if the unions are seen to be responsive to the particular needs of women and part-timers, not merely in their publicity but in collective bargaining and in the ways in which they conduct their business.

(3) *Local government*

(a) There is an increasing interest among women in local government. By 1985 19·2% of all local councillors in Great Britain were women, compared to under 4% of MPs in the House of Commons. Participation in local politics is not so disruptive to domestic responsibilities and family commitments as parliamentary politics can be, but a sample survey of local councillors in England in the mid-seventies found that 91% of women councillors were house-wives, retired or employed part-time. Generally the age of women councillors is appreciably older than women in the population as a whole, with a ratio of almost two to one in the 55–69 age group. Local government is also concerned with questions of housing, welfare and education, for example, at a local level where the links to women's experience within their community are much stronger. Yet, once again in terms of the hierarchy, very few women become chair-persons of council committees.

(b) One development which has affected both a general and a feminist perception of local government is the advent of Women's

Committees, e.g. within the now abolished GLC, various London boroughs, Sheffield, Leeds and Manchester. These have involved women in local government in an unprecedented scale and pushed higher on the agendas of full councils a series of pressing issues. These include childcare, continued institutional sexual discrimination in the council's employment policies and also in the areas for which the council is responsible, e.g. education, transport, discrimination against lesbians, facilities for women with disabilities, the needs of black women and low-pay campaigns. Many of the Women's Committees were formed because of outside pressure from women and all represent an attempt consciously to involve women in the local decision-making process. But they and their work are also vulnerable to shifting political priorities and to the general cutbacks in local government.

To summarise the chapter so far: the popular assumption is that the under-representation of women in many of the bodies mentioned is evidence of women's lack of interest in politics, that women are apolitical and through their own choice have low levels of participation in politics. It is hoped that the foregoing has disposed of this myth: the practical and ideological constraints on women's participation are enormous.

Women's conception of politics – where do women choose to put their energies?

Clearly there are other kinds of activity seeking to influence the making of public policy and the distribution of resources which are beyond the narrow definition of politics as Parliament and political parties. It is when these less conventional political arenas are examined that the limitations of the apolitical stereotype of woman are exposed.

(1) *Women have always been politically active*

(a) For example – women were prominent in seventeenth, eighteenth and early nineteenth-century food riots, and the anti-Poor Law demonstrations (1837). These were local and immediate concerns for women and their families which prompted direct action as a protest.

(b) Women have always organised as women in campaigns to change the conditions of women's lives, e.g. agitation for the repeal

of the Contagious Diseases Act, for access to education and the professions, for the vote and for equal pay. Women have shown in the past that they are able to develop organisations for themselves with their own forms – such as local suffragists networks – using imaginative and often disruptive tactics. To publicise the demand for the vote, for example, women disrupted meetings, held the first mass women's demonstrations and sent themselves as human protest letters to the Prime Minister.

(2) *Women and community action*
Many of women's concerns in the past focused on the community, dealing with issues of immediate need where practical organisation could be based around the many demands on women's time. Today women are very active participants in tenants' groups, childcare campaigns, health campaigns, anti-poverty lobbies, anti-nuclear groups, Women's Aid, and other campaigns. Such campaigns, prompted by women's own experience, often combine self-help projects with pressure group activity.

(3) *Women's associations*
There are many organisations of women which usually define themselves as 'non-political' (accepting the narrow party-political definition) but which nevertheless seek to influence the determination of public policy, e.g. Women's Institutes, Townswomen's Guilds, the National Women's Register, the WRVS. About three million women in Britain are involved in these organisations, where women organise as women. They have been involved in campaigns relating to taxation policy, the payment of Child Benefit, local planning decisions and the closing of local facilities. Women's associations often act as a springboard for participation in formal politics, particularly local government.

(4) *The Women's Movement*
  (a) Women continued to organise (on a much reduced scale) after the vote was won, keeping up the pressure for equal rights and campaigning on issues which directly affected the condition of women's lives. But in the late 1960s the Women's Liberation Movement blossomed, with a new generation of feminists.
  (b) Women are self-consciously organising as women to support one another through battered women's refuges, Rape Crisis Centres,

Women against Violence against Women: together organising to combat male violence. The Women's Movement has also focused on a women's right to control her own body and thus her own life, campaigning for free contraception, against attacks on abortion rights, for the extension of abortion facilities and well-women clinics.

(c) Women have become involved in a broad range of issues, some of which have mobilised those previously untouched by politics. Examples are the Women's Peace Camp at Greenham Common and its support network throughout the country, and Women against Pit Closures as part of the support for the 1984 miners' strike. The latter appeared in the heartland of working-class masculine culture: the mining communities. Women came together, valuing their own experience and supporting one another, to recognise and mobilise their potential collective strength. But it has proved hard to sustain these women's groups since the defeat of the miners' strike.

(d) The Women's Movement thrives on its lack of conventional political organisation – you cannot join; there are no leaders. The campaigns and groups of which it is composed are characterised by women organising autonomously (where only women are welcome), non-hierarchically (rotating tasks within groups and nationally using networks rather than centralised structures) and where each woman's voice should be equally valued. The intention is to live your politics: as the slogan says, 'the personal is political and the political is personal'.

But the Women's Movement remains ambiguous about politics as conventionally defined. Different types of feminism would emphasise different approaches to this question:

Liberal feminists are principally concerned with women's rights, believing that under the current system women's inequality can be rectified principally through legislation and education.

The *Sex Discrimination Act* (1975) and the *Equal Pay Act* (passed 1970, into force 1975) were therefore important breakthroughs although they and the Equal Opportunities Commission (set up in 1975) have disappointed women in key respects. The lack of teeth for the enforcement of both Acts and the weakness of the EOC has meant relatively little progress in any absolute measure of equal rights. One problem is of definition particularly over equal pay, for given women's occupational segregation – i.e. women are concentrated in low-paid, low-status jobs, often with no direct comparison with male workers – the initial concept of equal pay for equal work proved ineffective in achieving its goal. Women's average pay is still less than 75% of men's average pay. Yet the government only bowed to EEC pressure in 1984 when the Act was amended to the wider definition of equal pay for work of equal value. It remains very hard to win equal pay cases and even harder to enforce their payment. For example, despite being the first woman to win equal pay for work of equal value (1985), Julie Hayward, a cook at Cammel Laird's shipyard, had to fight through a further three years of protracted appeals to get the award enforced.

Using tne law depends upon persuading sympathetic men and women to frame legislation but it also depends upon the courts to interpret and enforce that law in women's interests. Therefore liberal feminists are also concerned to change sexist attitudes in the media, in education and to promote genuine equal opportunities throughout society.

Socialist feminists believe that women's oppression can only end with the end of the capitalist system. In the meantime, however, demands can be made of the state, whilst recognising that it embodies both class and male power. Socialist feminists organise inside mixed organisations, such as the labour movement, by building their own support networks (women's sections and caucuses) as well as organising in autonomous women's groups, depending on the nature and requirements of the issue. Issues of concern to socialist feminists include statutory childcare provision, women's rights and working conditions and cuts in the welfare state which particularly affect women. They are very critical of male-defined politics but choose to become involved over particular campaigns to build broader support, to gain access to resources and influence the system without becoming enmeshed in it.

Radical feminists believe that the fight is against institutionalised male power in all its forms. They argue that essentially men as a group benefit from the oppression and exploitation of women as a group. As change can only come about through women's collective action, the convincing of men of the need for feminism is not a priority. Key issues for women to organise around in women-only groups include: male violence, pornography, sexuality and the building of a woman's culture.

Radical feminists are opposed to involving themselves in conventional politics except on a very limited basis, where their own terms can be set: in order to gain government grants, local authority support for Women's Aid, Rape Crisis lines, lesbian support groups, and so forth.

This is inevitably an over-simplified analysis and such is the richness and diversity of feminism that many women would not define themselves as belonging to any particular brand, preferring to be described as 'just a feminist'.

What can be done to involve women in politics?

(1) *Positive action*
If the under-representation of women in political parties, parliament, public bodies and the unions is to be reversed then the barriers to their participation have to be removed.

(a) Some women are demanding that men make space for women, that some of those safe seats have to be handed over. The 300 Group has been formed to promote the election to Parliament of at least 300 women (irrespective of political party).

(b) It is argued, particularly by women in the Labour Party, that parties have to make good their stated commitment to women's equality and consciously recruit them to higher office with all that that may entail – for example, meetings and Parliament at social hours, with childcare provision.

(c) Most importantly, attitudes have to change – women have to be welcome not just as tokens or as proxy men but as themselves.

(d) Women are also demanding power, e.g. the campaign in the Labour Party to empower the Women's Conference to bring forward five resolutions onto the full conference agenda and that women should elect the five women's representatives on the party's National Executive Committee.

(e) There is also a debate on whether more seats should be reserved for women on the executives of unions and political parties, for it seems that only by women being seen to do the work, can other women's confidence be raised and an example be set to remove prejudice.

(2) *Valuing women's issues*
(a) The stereotype of women as carers means that women tend to be given responsibility for education, social services, and consumer issues. These are therefore regarded as 'soft' and have less status than the 'hard', masculine issues of finance and foreign affairs. So, it is

argued, the identification of politics with maleness alienates many women and reinforces a belief that politics do not relate to their experience, life and immediate concerns.

(b) It has also been suggested that the small number of women MPs should not be seen as a failure of women's nerve: the large number of women involved in community politics, pressure groups and voluntary bodies indicates that women are consciously choosing *not* to get involved in Parliament. There is a cynicism amongst these women about MPs – their lack of real power, their isolation from the grass-roots, their conception of politics as compromise and committees. A valuing of women's issues and a commitment to real change for women is needed, it is argued, to end this possible abstention by women and their clear under-representation.

(3) *Domestic responsibilities*

(a) A practical demand now made by women is for statutory provision of childcare for both pre-school and school-age children, in and beyond school hours. Women would then have far wider options in terms of paid work and political participation. Current demographic changes mean that this issue may have to be taken more seriously across the political spectrum. For the falling number of school-leavers means that in the near future more women will be needed in the work-force. In order to enable women to return to work the practical provision of childcare will have to be addressed. Equivalent support would also be needed for women caring for other dependants, e.g. elderly and handicapped adults.

(b) As challenging is the observation that unless domestic work ceases to be women's prime responsibility, despite 'help' from men, then paid work continues to be a second job for a woman and politics a third. The key point in this argument is that women will not have enough time unless men give up some of theirs.

Together these changes could alleviate a woman's perennial choice between family and career, and allow her to make real choices about what she does with her life.

Concluding comments

This chapter has argued that women's position in society, specifically the division of labour, fundamentally inhibits women's participation in formal politics. It is therefore suggested that only major changes in society will allow women to participate equally. At its most challenging, some women are now arguing that women have to get men to give up some of their power and make space for women. So women have to be organised and although some women are self-consciously choosing not to participate in parliamentary politics that does not mean that they are not political. Women *are* actively organising, particularly in grass-roots and community politics, over issues which directly affect their experience as women. When formal politics deals more with women's concerns and priorities and rids itself of the structural barriers to women's participation, then we may see something approaching equal representation of women and their interests. Of course, this would transform politics itself.

Reading

Beatrix Campbell, *The Iron Ladies: Why do Women Vote Tory?*, Virago, 1987.

Jill Hills, 'Britain' in Lovenduski and Hills (eds.), *The Politics of the Second Electorate,* Routledge & Kegan Paul, 1981.

Vicky Randall, *Women and Politics*, Macmillan, 1982.

Barbara Rogers, *52% – Getting Women's Power into Politics,* Women's Press, 1983.

Margaret Stacey & Marion Price, *Women, Power and Politics,* Tavistock, 1981.

15 *Peter Byrd*

Northern Ireland

This chapter traces Britain's involvement in Ireland and examines various explanations of the 'Irish question'. It reviews a number of the proposed solutions to the question that have been discussed since the issue became acute at the end of the 1960s and concludes by discussing the impact of the latest major British initiative, namely the Hillsborough Agreement with the Irish Republic of November 1985.

Britain in Ireland: an historical overview

The first military intervention in Ireland was initiated by Henry II in 1172. During the Middle Ages the deployment of English power in Ireland was part of a complex process of expanding the realm of the Crown and defending the English state from internal and external subversion. The Reformation in England added a new dimension because the people of Ireland remained staunchly Catholic and henceforward potential allies for England's continental Catholic enemies. Catholic uprisings against the state provoked a more systematic reaction in the form of English and Scottish Protestant 'plantations', concentrated in the northern province of Ulster, designed to maintain a Protestant ascendancy. Renewed Catholic resistance in the 1640s led to further military intervention by the Crown followed by Oliver Cromwell. The crisis of the English state in 1688 encouraged another phase of Irish rebellion, again with strong continental support, and following its defeat at the Battle of the Boyne in 1689 a new regime was instituted in Ireland. Penal laws against Catholics were introduced and a Protestant Parliament was established in Dublin; Ireland became a quasi-colony governed through its Anglo-Irish Protestant 'collaborators'.

In 1800 this form of indirect rule from London broke down and a formal union with Great Britain, the United Kingdom of Great Britain and Ireland, was established with an enlarged Parliament at Westminster. However, despite the emancipation of Catholics in 1829, integration failed to meet the growing demands of Catholic nationalists who demanded Irish Home Rule. In 1886 Prime Minister Gladstone decided to concede Home Rule but this split his Liberal party and led to two decades of Conservative domination in government – the Conservatives championing the cause of 'Unionism' with Ireland. When Asquith's Liberal government resurrected Home Rule in 1912 it faced political crisis in Ireland and in Britain. The Ulster Unionists or Loyalists, descendents of the sixteenth and seventeenth-century planters, demonstrated their absolute opposition to Home Rule under the skilful leadership of Edward Carson. In March 1914, units of the British Army based at the Curragh near Dublin demonstrated their sympathy with the Unionists. (The Unionist community had become and remained thereafter a major element in the British Army.) Nevertheless, the legislation on Home Rule slowly progressed through Parliament.

With the outbreak of the First World War, the Irish question was put on ice. But in 1916 the Easter Rebellion in Dublin revealed the strength of a new and more extreme nationalist movement, Sinn Fein. The government mishandled the situation and at the end of the war was confronted with totally incompatible demands from the Unionists of Ulster on the one hand and from Sinn Fein, which had displaced the moderate parliamentary nationalist party, on the other hand. The Government of Ireland Act in 1920 offered a compromise: two Parliaments in Ireland each enjoying Home Rule, one in Dublin and one for the Unionists in Belfast, together with a Council of Ireland, all operating within a looser United Kingdom in which London's control was confined primarily to foreign and defence policy. The Unionists reluctantly conceded but Sinn Fein refused and launched an armed insurrection against British rule.

In 1921 the government conceded to Sinn Fein a treaty giving virtual independence for Ireland under the Crown along the same lines as that enjoyed by the 'White Dominions' of Canada, Australia, etc. However, the six counties of Ulster with a Protestant majority were to remain within the United Kingdom. The 1921 treaty split

Sinn Fein and a bitter civil war within Ireland followed. The moderates won and the treaty was implemented. In 1932 one of the defeated extreme republicans, Eamonn De Valera, came to power as leader of a new party, Fianna Fáil. While on the one hand he outlawed the old rump of Sinn Fein and its military wing the Irish Republican Army (IRA), on the other hand he exploited the ambiguities of dominion status, especially in the 1935 Constitution, which laid territorial claim to the whole of Ireland. In the Second World War he remained neutral. In 1949 full legal independence under a republican constitution, including withdrawal from the Commonwealth, was agreed by Britain, reflecting Dublin's *de facto* independence. The 1949 agreement continued however to give Ireland a privileged legal status in, for instance, the right of its citizens to settle in Britain and enjoy full political and social rights.

The six counties of Ulster with a Protestant majority remained within the United Kingdom and, in return for having agreed to the 1920 act, the Unionists retained the devolved powers and the Parliament in Belfast (at Stormont). The London government, exhausted by Irish affairs, allowed Stormont great autonomy and the Unionists enjoyed almost complete freedom to act outside the usual conventions of British politics. The objective of the first Prime Minister of Northern Ireland, Lord Craigavon, was 'a Protestant parliament and a Protestant state'. The Catholic third of the population of Northern Ireland was treated as a potential enemy of the regime. Laws discriminated against Catholics and were enforced by a largely Protestant police force and a wholly Protestant paramilitary force, the B Specials. These arrangements, reinforced by economic discrimination, were both massively unjust and surprisingly stable so long as the Catholic minority was too weak to offer any effective challenge.

In the 1960s the Northern Ireland political system began to unravel. The prosperity of the Protestant working class, based on old declining industries such as textiles and shipbuilding, faltered, while enough Catholics gained middle-class status to demand political reform. The Catholic-led campaign for civil rights culminated in a major demonstration in 1968 with the inevitable Protestant backlash. The Prime Minister, Terence O'Neill, pursued a moderate policy of attempting to modernise the political system. He even opened up a dialogue with Dublin but inevitably failed to satisfy either community, and in 1969 he resigned. His successor James Chichester-Clark could maintain order only by requesting military assistance from London. Harold Wilson's government sent in the troops which were at first welcomed by the Catholics as protection against the Protestants. The British government was drawn in politically and it demanded reforms from the Unionist government in Belfast to establish proper civil rights. Two consequences followed. Firstly, conflict grew between the London and Belfast governments over the pace of reforms and the control of security policy. A crisis developed and in April 1972 Prime Minister Edward Heath suspended Stormont and governed Northern Ireland directly from London ('direct rule'). Secondly, the IRA exploited the unrest to renew its campaign against British rule. Catholic opinion was turned against the British military presence and the IRA conducted a terrorist and guerilla war against Britain. The war began, and has continued, mainly in Ireland but with periodic campaigns on the British mainland. The IRA factionalised. In May 1972 it split into the 'Officials' who called off the armed struggle against Britain and the 'Provisionals' who intensified the campaign and conducted a series of bomb outrages in Britain against innocent civilians (most notably perhaps the Birmingham bombing in 1974).

The Army has remained in Northern Ireland; its strength reached a peak of about 22,000 but it has since stabilised at about 10,000. Occasionally the government has deployed 'special units', particularly the Special Air Service, to undertake covert missions against the Provisional IRA.

Explaining the Irish question: six languages of analysis

The nature of the Irish question can be discussed in distinct 'languages of analysis' which, taken together, help explain some of the complexity of the issue.

(1) *Religion*

Church attendance, and religious identification, is very high in Northern Ireland and religion is a major aspect of social life. Religious leaders are drawn into politics and some, though by no means all, self-professed Christians appear to most British people as bigoted, intolerant and generally unpleasant. Protestants denounce the privileged status of the Catholic church in the Republic and the religious traditions perceive themselves as expressions of political traditions. The communal conflict in Northern Ireland does therefore have a religious dimension which has persisted for four centuries. The religious separation of education reinforces the two traditions. But religion alone does not explain the conflict. Some Christians are able to coexist and when removed from the particular *political* context of Northern Ireland to, say, Liverpool or Glasgow, relations between apparently similar communities are much less conflictual. Nevertheless, religion certainly legitimises the conflict and gives religious leaders political influence. Exhortations from Great Britain of Christian reconciliation are fatuous and irrelevant.

(2) *Nationalism*

The conflict in Northern Ireland can be seen as a clash of two competing nationalisms, each claiming exclusive control of the same territory. This explanation is relevant not only to Irish nationalism but also to a Protestant Ulster nationalism. This Ulster identity has strongly espoused the union with Britain (Unionism or Loyalism) but it also emphasises Ulster standing alone. For some Protestant politicians, therefore, Ulster separatism is an alternative to the union and perhaps a sounder platform for re-establishing a Protestant ascendancy based on Stormont.

A nationalist perspective or explanation does not lead to an easy solution of the problem. Protestants argue that their two to one majority in Northern Ireland justifies their rejection of a united Ireland on the basis of self-determination. Nationalists in Northern Ireland and the Republic emphasise the natural unity of the island of Ireland, reflecting a common belief of nationalists that islands form natural political territories, with self-determination to be decided therefore on an all-Ireland basis. However, not all Catholics in the north who support the nationalist political tradition actually favour Irish unification – nationalism is in large part an expression of opposition to the power of the Protestants and the tradition of British rule. It is in fact difficult to establish how many Catholics in Northern Ireland favour unification, just as it is difficult to measure support for unification from the citizens of the Republic.

The IRA draws interesting analogies between its struggle against 'colonial rule' and that of nationalist movements in the Third World, particularly the Algerian and Palestinian cases where nationalism confronted a settler population. The IRA sees the struggle of the Algerian nationalists in the 1950s against the French state and the French settlers, the *pieds noirs,* as similar with its struggle against the

British state and its settler population, the Ulster Protestants. However, two contrasts can be drawn. Firstly, the *pieds noirs* were outnumbered seven to one by the Algerians and, even on an all-Ireland basis, the Protestants of Northern Ireland are outnumbered only about three to one, with a two to one predominance in Northern Ireland. Secondly, the *pieds noirs* arrived in Algeria only in the mid to late nineteenth century and they continued to view France as their spiritual and political home, unlike the Ulster Protestants who have settled in Ulster for four centuries and for whom Ulster is their real home. In Israel/Palestine, the IRA strongly supports the Palestine Liberation Organisation and views the Jews as alien settlers with no legitimate claim on the territory. However the Jews can claim settlement back to the time of Abraham, interrupted by an enforced diaspora but even then with a continuous thread of some settlement. Another interesting analogy is with South Africa where, the IRA argues, British liberals would be shocked by a political settlement which allowed self-determination for the whites where they enjoyed a *local* majority in the towns and countryside, just as Protestants constitute a local majority in part of Ireland. In any case self-determination cannot be resolved solely by historical claims (unless the political legitimacy of the United States, Australia, etc., is to be challenged) or without reference to such factors as economics or political geography.

In short, while the conflict in Northern Ireland can be viewed from a nationalist perspective, that in itself does not point unambiguously to any particular solution. In the remainder of this chapter the Protestant/Unionist/Loyalist majority community in Northern Ireland will be referred to as the Unionist or majority community (although we have already seen that Unionism does not imply unequivocal commitment to the union with Britain) and the Catholic/Republican/nationalist minority community will be referred to as the nationalist or minority community (although we have already seen that not all nationalists necessarily favour unification with the Republic).

(3) *Marxist analysis*
There are several strands to Marxist thinking on Ireland. The chief advantage offered by each of them over, say, the religious or nationalist explanations, is that they focus on the relationship between Britain and Ireland as well as on politics within Ireland.

Dependency analysis explains the development of capitalism in terms of economic 'cores' and 'peripheries'. The core or metropole exploits the periphery and builds political power around its economic strength. Relations between core and periphery are indirect, with conflict between them mediated through 'semi-peripheries' or local metropoles which are exploited by the core and, in turn, exploit their periphery. While most dependency analysis has concentrated on Latin America, the Belfast area can be seen as a local metropole, exploited from the capitalist core in London and exploiting in turn its own periphery. Within this theoretical approach the prosperity of the semi--periphery is crucial to the stability of whole system; as we have already seen, in the 1960s the prosperity of the traditional Unionist-dominated industries declined.

Internal colonialism is a variant of dependency analysis, arguing that within a metropolitan power there would be core and periphery. In the case of the United Kingdom Michael Hechter made popular the view in the 1970s that the English had established 'internal colonies' over Scotland, Wales and Ireland. Political, cultural and economic domination ensured the subordinate position of the peripheries. Economically the emphasis within the theory was on the subordinate position of the peripheral economy within the larger external and imperial-orientated economy dominated by England. The decline of the larger economy thus affected particularly sharply the prosperity of the periphery and produced political instability.

Uneven development is a theory of nationalism associated with the work of Ernest Gellner and, in the case of the United Kingdom, with Tom Nairn. Nairn is an unorthodox Marxist who is very sympathetic to peripheral nationalist movements. Within the United Kingdom he argues that uneven economic development has produced two varieties of nationalism: firstly, that associated with relative under-development and deprivation, such as Welsh nationalism, nationalism in the deprived west of Scotland, nineteenth-century Irish nationalism and contemporary Irish nationalism in Northern Ireland; secondly, that associated with relative economic over-development *vis-à-vis* a political core, such as the rich east coast of Scotland. Nairn sees Ulster Unionism as fitting, awkwardly, into this second category in terms of relations with Dublin and the withdrawal of political power from Stormont. Unlike most Marxist analysts, Nairn regards the Unionists as, at least potentially, a historically 'progressive' force whose bourgeois values are a necessary precondition for eventual proletarian emancipation.

Each of these closely related Marxist analyses helps make the link between the re-emergence of the Irish 'troubles' in the late 1960s, and the revival at that time of peripheral nationalist movements elsewhere in the developed world – France, Spain, Canada, Yugoslavia, etc. – at the very moment when many commentators had assumed that nationalism outside the Third World had lost its potency. However, most of these nationalist revivals, with the exception of the Basque and Yugoslav cases, tended to decline in the late 1970s.

A crude Marxist view might regard the state in Northern Ireland simply as an agency of British imperialism protecting the interests of British capital. However, from any calculation of economic interests, Northern Ireland appears as a major drain on the British state and economy and it is difficult to imagine British capitalists conceiving of advantages from a continuation of British rule.

(4) *Political and social modernisation*

The argument here is simple. Traditional societies are relatively stable. They possess clear hierarchies, exhibit little social dynamism and have strong centres of power. Modernised societies are also stable. They are pluralistic, secular and affluent. But *modernising* societies are unstable as the old order gives way painfully to the new. This thesis, derived from the study of modernising societies in the Third World, seems to fit Northern Ireland. The stable Unionist domination from 1921 to the early 1960s continued the pre-modern Protestant ascendancy, suitably adapted to incorporate some industrial development. Catholics were badly treated but were powerless. Their response was a sort of 'political abstentionism'. In the 1960s society changed. A nascent nationalist middle-class demanded civil rights and thus inadvertently offered a covert route for the IRA to re-establish itself. The Unionist middle and working-classes suffered from industrial decline. From 1963 Prime Minister O'Neill pursued an ambitious policy of modernising Northern Ireland. In a society as deeply divided as Northern Ireland, these social changes, together with O'Neill's policies, produced complex conflicts both within and between the two communities.

(5) *Liberal analysis*

Liberal analysis of Northern Ireland has two main foci. The first is that modernisation will soften old antagonisms, develop new cleavages in society, lead to the triumph of secular values and ultimately produce a more integrated society. From this perspective, drawing on the same analysis as the modernisation thesis, high unemployment exacerbates the conflict because it slows down modernisation and allows minds to concentrate on old and irrelevant struggles. Industrial development on a cross-communal basis is thus an important goal. The second emphasis is to stress the importance of political institutional reform. Establish sound liberal institutions and the rest will follow. Certainly after 1969 the British government forced liberal reforms on to the Stormont government, the worst civil grievances of the Catholics were resolved, but peace did not follow.

The classic example of the application of a liberal analysis and prescription is the institutions established by the Heath government in 1973. Firstly, there was to be a regular referendum on Northern Ireland's continued union with Britain in order to meet the fears of Unionists that Irish unity would be forced on them. Secondly, there was to be a new assembly at Stormont, elected by proportional representation and hence fair to the nationalist minority. Thirdly, a new political executive to exercise devolved powers in Northern Ireland would be drawn from the Assembly on the basis of 'power-sharing' (or 'consociationalism'), to include the nationalist opposition. In December 1973 a conference was held at Sunningdale attended by the British government, the Irish government, the Unionist party headed by Brian Faulkner and the newly formed Social Democratic and Labour party representing the nationalist minority. Sunningdale confirmed the new power sharing arrangements and added another dimension to the governing of Ireland, a Council of Ireland which would bring together all the parties to discuss issues of common interest on an all-Ireland basis. In January 1974 the Unionist–SDLP executive took office.

Power-sharing and the Council were unacceptable to many Protestants. By a stroke of bad luck the general election followed almost immediately. In Great Britain the great issue was 'Heath versus the miners'; in Northern Ireland the only major issue was the new constitutional system. The Unionist Party split and Brian Faulkner's grouping was humiliated. The legitimacy of the new system and of the executive were weakened. In May 1974 a political strike organised by Faulkner's opponents demonstrated the power of the Protestant working class and the new institutions collapsed. Harold

Wilson's government condemned the strike but did not intervene to save Faulkner.

Despite the 1974 fiasco British governments have continued to support new liberal institutions in Northern Ireland. In 1975 Secretary for Northern Ireland Merlyn Rees held elections for a new convention, designed to prepare new power-sharing institutions. The convention collapsed because forty-five of its seventy-five seats were held by Protestant parties opposed to power sharing. In 1979–80 the same fate befell a similar attempt by the Conservative Secretary for Northern Ireland, Humphrey Atkins. In 1982 Jim Prior finally re-established an assembly, although with very limited powers and no executive. This assembly was boycotted by some Protestant parties and by the SDLP. More seriously for the British government, the Provisional Sinn Fein gained five seats (10% of the vote) to the SDLP's fourteen (19%). By this time security policy in Northern Ireland had dissipated the goodwill engendered within the minority community by the bold steps of 1974.

Security policy has been a constant problem for the British government and the successful pursuit of a containing operation against the IRA raises severe problems for a government committed to liberal institutions in Northern Ireland. Four major elements of security policy can be identified.

The first is the extent to which the Army maintains a 'hands off' policy of supporting the Royal Ulster Constabulary without directly intervening in operations. A particular problem concerns covert operations against the IRA which have been undertaken by the Special Air Service. After Rees's unsuccessful tenture, Roy Mason's strategy was dominated by a promotion of security as the major objective with political initiatives firmly deferred until the IRA had been defeated. The SAS was given much freer rein during this period.

The second issue in security policy has concerned the treatment of IRA terrorists or alleged terrorists. In 1971 Secretary Willie Whitelaw introduced two new measures: suspected terrorists would be interned without trial and convicted terrorists would be treated as 'political prisoners' (Protestant terrorists were treated similarly but in practice the move was directed mostly at the IRA). Internment ended in 1975 but, following the abolition of the special political status in 1976 by Rees, there were a series of demonstrations and hunger strikes which culminated in a major hunger strike in 1981 when the leading hunger striker, Bobby Sands, was also elected as MP for the border constituency of Fermanagh and South Tyrone. The government refused to yield and ten prisoners died before the campaign was abandoned. It was the bitterness precipitated by the hunger strikes which was exploited so successfully by the IRA/Sinn Fein during the 1982 elections for the new assembly when the SDLP's hold on the minority community appeared to be gravely shaken.

The third element in security policy has involved the administration of justice. Trial by jury became, in practice, impossible as juries were placed in a hopeless position when confronted by dangerous terrorists. The British government responded in 1972 by establishing trial by a senior judge sitting without a jury (the 'Diplock courts'). Diplock courts fall outside the normal British convention of trial by jury and their acceptability to the minority community was further weakened by reliance on so-called 'supergrasses' – IRA terrorists who give evidence to the courts in return for a degree of immunity for their own serious crimes.

Fourthly, the British government has relied since 1974 on the Prevention of Terrorism Act to give it additional powers to deal with suspected terrorists throughout the United Kingdom. The PTA has to be renewed annually and at first enjoyed bipartisan support although the Labour Party, which introduced it, now opposes its renewal on the grounds of its ineffectiveness and unacceptability within a liberal state.

From the perspective of liberal analysis two general conclusions may therefore be drawn. Firstly, successive attempts to establish liberal institutions have failed because there is simply no consensus for such institutions. Moderate nationalists prefer power-sharing as the best short-term policy but most Unionists would prefer a revival of the old Stormont. Both groups probably find direct rule a tolerable second best but one of the objectives of British policy is to reduce the burden of direct involvement in Northern Ireland. Direct rule can of course be justified from a liberal perspective, especially since the increase in the number of seats in Parliament from twelve to seventeen in 1979. The twelve seats had reflected Northern Ireland's representation at both Westminster and Stormont. The seventeen seats fairly reflected the post-Stormont situation although the increase was promoted by Prime Minister James Callaghan in order to maintain Unionist support for his minority Westminster government. Secondly, the maintenance of order in Northern Ireland and the defeat of the IRA demand security measures which are difficult to reconcile with the normal requirements of a liberal state. However, the British state is confronted by a terroristic enemy of fanatical determination which almost succeeded in 1984 in murdering the Prime Minister and most of her Cabinet and which has repeatedly carried out appalling bombings against innocent civilians. In these exceptional circumstances normal standards of behaviour by government inevitably fall.

(6) *The territorial politics of a 'dual polity'*

In *Terrority and Power in the United Kingdom* Jim Bulpitt argues that the United Kingdom has always been a 'dual polity' – two relatively independent political systems coexisting alongside each other. A London-orientated political elite, which includes both major parties, controls the High Politics of the state, defence and foreign affairs in particular. A quite distinct set of local elites has managed the Low Politics of the periphery. The implicit bargain underlying the dual polity was that of mutual non-interference, allowing each partner a high degree of autonomy within its own sphere.

When the English state incorporated the Celtic peripheries within the realm it preferred to do so informally, relying on the existing local elites which collaborated with the new regime. Formalisation of state power with a constitutional political union and an enlarged Westminster Parliament was costly and unnecessary. It was implemented only when informal collaboration broke down or a severe external crisis of the state threatened to destabilise the ambiguous political arrangements at the periphery. This model helps explain the political union with Wales in the 1530s and with Scotland in 1707. Even after formal union the dual polity continued to operate and to allow a high degree of local autonomy.

Applied to Ireland the model explains the reliance on Protestant settlers and, after the crises of the seventeenth century, on the Protestant Dublin Parliament. Formal union in 1800 followed the first stirrings of (Protestant) Irish nationalism and came during the middle of the severe external crisis with Napoleonic France. The model also explains two crucial aspects of Britain's policy in the twentieth century – lack of commitment to Northern Ireland and inconsistency of policy. In 1921 Lloyd George was ready to sell out the Ulster Unionists in favour of a united Ireland that would remain within the Commonwealth. The High Politics of imperial unity over-rode the local interests of Ulster. More dramatically, in 1940 Churchill offered Irish unity to De Valera in return for his declaration of war on Germany. High Politics again required a sacrifice of an expendable part of the realm. Towards Ireland Britain pursued a policy of subjugation, followed by colonialism, followed by union. For Northern Ireland after 1921, London allowed a free hand – the most extreme variant of the dual polity system. Since 1969 the bipartisan policy of the two major parties at Westminster has aimed at keeping the Irish question so far as is possible out of British politics because Ireland spells trouble for London. The key instrument of that bipartisan policy, the revival of a devolved assembly commanding widespread support, has failed. As a result Britain is now bereft of powerful and acceptable collaborators in Northern Ireland. The Hillsborough Agreement of 1985 (discussed below) appears in this light as an attempt by Britain to bring in Dublin as a collaborator in the governing of Northern Ireland.

The dual polity model carries the implicit conclusion that Britain would abandon Northern Ireland again, as in 1921 and 1940, if this could be done without great costs. Already Northern Ireland enjoys a right to secede from the United Kingdom and the right is regularly tested in referenda. Less dramatically, the model asks what British interests are served by remaining in Northern Ireland. The interests of *capital* seem hardly to be affected at all. The *political parties* have no interest since they do not organise in Northern Ireland. The Labour party has always been emotionally hostile to the 1921 partition and sees a united Ireland as the most desirable theoretical outcome. The Unionist party of Northern Ireland aligned itself at Westminster with the Conservatives until 1974, but since 1974 the fragmented unionist parties have not supported the Conservatives and after 1977 they chose to keep Callaghan's government in power. In both major British parties there is some support for organising in Northern Ireland but the leaderships see the risks and are hostile. Few *bureaucratic interests* are served by remaining in Northern Ireland. For the Treasury Northern Ireland is a major financial liability. For the Ministry of Defence it is a thankless commitment which also exposes a whole range of security problems in Great Britain. For the Foreign and Commonwealth Office Northern Ireland is a major obstacle which complicates Britain's relations with the United States, the European Community and the Republic of Ireland. Indeed

Enoch Powell repeatedly accused the FCO of conspiring to ditch the province and he interpreted the Hillsborough Agreement as part of this FCO strategy. The Northern Ireland Office itself represents no organised interest or community. In contrast to the Scottish or Welsh Office, a necessary claim to ministerial office in Northern Ireland is to have *no* local connection.

Each of these different languages of analysis contributes to our understanding by defining the problem itself quite differently. The Marxist and dual polity models analyse Northern Ireland both from a peripheral (Irish) and a central (British) perspective. The unsuccessful application of liberal solutions offers a warning against easy solutions by the well-intentioned. The nationalist and religious perspectives emphasise the intractability of the conflict while two distinct communities lay claim to the same territory.

Alternative solutions to the Northern Ireland question

There is no solution to the Northern Ireland question that does not carry massive costs. The best starting point for considering alternatives is Richard Rose, *Northern Ireland: a Time of Choice*. In Northern Ireland there is no consensus on the means of politics, let alone the ends, and the state lacks not merely a monopoly of the instruments of violence (a basic defining element of the state) but also lacks a monopoly of what is widely regarded as legitimate violence. In these circumstances, everything becomes difficult. Northern Ireland is not 'state-less' to the same degree as, say, Lebanon, but neither is there a state in Northern Ireland in the normal sense.

(1) *Direct rule and complete integration with the rest of Britain*
Enoch Powell argued for this policy and the increase in parliamentary representation was a necesary (though not sufficient) condition for it. But few Ulstermen favour it because it means rule by non-Ulstermen. For Britain it would make Ireland a permanent and unwelcome ingredient of politics. On the other hand, direct rule may be a tolerable second best for both communities and it has enjoyed the enormous advantage since 1972 of representing the status quo, except to the extent that the Hillsborough Agreement has introduced a new Irish dimension into direct rule.

(2) *An independent Ulster*

Some extremist Unionist politicians would see this outcome as a better long-term solution than the Unionism that they ostensibly support if the alternatives were either union with Ireland or a large degree of power sharing with the Catholic community and an inadequate British security policy. An independent Ulster would probably be born in bloodshed and survive only as a poor and oppressive state. Those in Britain such as Tony Benn who support the more or less immediate withdrawal of British troops and political engagement also support this policy, at least by implication, because an independent Ulster, rather than the united Ireland that they prefer, would follow a British withdrawal.

(3) *Unilateral British withdrawal*

Richard Rose termed this 'Doomsday'. A unilateral withdrawal would probably produce worse consequences that a negotiated withdrawal (though with whom could the British negotiate?) or the planned establishment of an Ulster state. The militants in both communities are heavily armed and would fight for political supremacy. The Republic would almost inevitably be drawn in to defend the Catholic community and its financial and political stability would probably collapse. Quite apart from considerations of political morality, the British government would fear that the fighting would spill over into Great Britain.

(4) *A united Irish state*

Unification is a powerful romantic myth for all Irish nationalists, but as a practical political goal its appeal is probably limited. The SDLP favours unification as a long-term goal but in practice it tolerates British rule and has postponed unification to the very distant future. Only Provisional Sinn Fein/IRA fight and struggle for a united Ireland. Viewed from Dublin, unification is not attractive. The Republic is politically stable (though threatened by the IRA), peaceful (in marked contrast to Northern Ireland) and relatively prosperous. Not only would the tax burdens of unification be enormous but the Republic would probably be unable to cope with a million hostile Protestants in its midst; the successful incorporation of the Protestant minority into the Republic after 1921 is certainly no precedent for the quite different Ulster Protestants. Above all for the Republic's politicians, the only united Ireland imaginable in the short term is one in which the IRA had come to power.

Until recently the Republic made no efforts to meet the objections of the Ulster Protestants to unification. The first significant step in this direction was the publication by Dr Garret Fitzgerald's government in 1984 of the *New Ireland Forum* which, in accepting that unification could come only by consent, effectively ruled it out for the foreseeable future. The *Forum* also discusses confederal and federal forms of government as possible future models which would be less repellent to the Protestants than the classical nationalist concept of a unitary state.

In Britain the Labour Party has traditionally upheld the goal of unity by consent. In the 1983 and 1987 election manifestos consent was interpreted to give the Unionist community a veto on the issue – the position consistently taken by the Thatcher government. However, the Labour party has since modified this policy by emphasising that the goal of unity can be achieved over time by a whole series of political reforms enshrining all-Ireland developments, for instance, cross-border economic co-operation, and the majoritarian veto applies not to these developments but only to the ultimate issue of unification itself. Whether in reality this represents a substantial rather than a rhetorical shift of policy is difficult to assess. Bipartisanship remains the best characterisation of the position of the two major parties.

(5) *Redrawing the Border in a fresh partition*

The 1921 border could be redrawn to transfer to the Republic border areas with a local nationalist majority. However, the border areas are not homogeneously nationalist and there would remain nationalist areas in the north, for instance in West Belfast, whose relative numerical position *vis-à-vis* the majority community would become worse. This solution is attractive to liberal opinion in Britain as a concession to the idea of self-determination but its appeal in Ireland is less. The Unionist political parties are pledged to oppose the concession of a single inch of territory while the IRA, though not perhaps moderate nationalist opinion, demands full unification and an end to the British presence.

One major recent IRA target appears to be the Protestant farmers scattered throughout the border territories. These stand in the way of more cohesive nationalist majorities and their removal would also increase the IRA's tactical freedom in avoiding the British Army.

(6) *Devolution of power to Northern Ireland*

This remains the preferred solution for the British parties. But it is doubtful whether there is a consensus in Northern Ireland for the power-sharing between the two communities which would be a necessary condition of any major restoration of power to Belfast. The Faulknerite rump of the Unionist party favouring power-sharing won only five of the forty-nine Unionist seats in the 1975 convention. After the 1982 assembly elections there was practically no support for power sharing. The SDLP and Sinn Fein, with fourteen and five seats respectively, boycotted the assembly. Ian Paisley's Democratic Unionists with twenty-one seats and the Official Unionists with twenty-six seats both opposed power-sharing, and the Official Unionists boycotted the assembly from 1982 to 1984 in protest against the inadequacy of British security policy.

Devolution without power-sharing is not a realistic option for the British government. In any case, while the army is so heavily deployed to combat the IRA, Britain is so tied into Northern Ireland that devolution could not offer more than a very partial withdrawal.

(7) *Anglo-Irish condominium over Northern Ireland*

This superficially attractive idea involves Britain and the Republic sharing sovereignty and responsibility for Northern Ireland. The two communities there would not only have a choice of citizenships (the Republic already offers passports to residents of Northern Ireland and many Catholics prefer to travel on an Irish passport) but could look either to London or to Dublin as the fount of authority. Although condominium is a form of legal regime governing sovereignty and territory, which are intensely contested in Northern Ireland, the general premises behind this sort of approach is that territorial and sovereignty questions might be approached gradually within a growing web of interdependence between the Republic, Great Britain and Northern Ireland. In practice therefore the condominium concept reflects two developments: firstly, the great and growing links between the Republic and the UK in trade, travel, population movements, etc (a close relationship enhanced by shared membership of the European Community); secondly, the inherent interest of the Republic in Northern Ireland and the vast volume of practical co-operation and relationships that already exist across the border.

The *New Ireland Forum* gives some support to this sort of

approach to the problem. An extreme variant of the condominium approach would be a broader confederation between the Republic and the United Kingdom, recognising that the separation of these two closely related states, which was necessary in 1921, is no longer appropriate within a European Community framework.

The drawback with this approach to the problem, however, is that it adopts a rationalist attitude to questions of territory and sovereignty which retain great political and emotional significance, however anachronistic they may appear to liberal thinking in Britain.

The Hillsborough Agreement of November 1985

Following the failure of the Sunningdale arrangements, direct involvement of the Republic in Britain's Irish policy tended to decline until the election of Mrs Thatcher. Notwithstanding her strong emotional commitment to the Union with Northern Ireland, she has consistently sought to involve the Republic in her policies.

Three factors shaped this striking development. Firstly, the need for co-operation between the security forces of the two states. The border is virtually impossible to police and hence terrorists can easily find refuge in the Republic unless the Irish police are prepared to assist in seeking out terrorists. Secondly, the British government was encouraged by the replacement of Charles Haughey's Fianna Fáil government in Dublin in June 1981 by the less overtly nationalist and much more complaisant Fine Gail-Labour coalition led by Dr Garret Fitzgerald. Mrs Thatcher and Chares Haughey had already met in Dublin in December 1980 to develop closer relations and under Fitzgerald this *rapprochement* accelerated, with the British objective being Irish accession to the European Convention on the Suppression of Terrorism which would allow the extradition of IRA terrorists to Britain for trial. Thirdly, both governments needed to sustain the parliamentary and anti-terrorist SDLP as the vehicle for Northern Irish nationalist aspirations. The hunger strikes damaged the SDLP and benefited Provisional Sinn Fein in the 1982 assembly election. In the 1983 general election the respective shares were 18% and 13% and in the 1985 local council elections the results were 18% and 12%. Throughout the early 1980s the electoral strategy and strength of Provisional Sinn Fein (the 'bullet and the ballot-box') was a powerful factor pushing London and Dublin closer together.

In November 1981 Mrs Thatcher and Dr Fitzgerald held their first summit and agreed to regular political meetings (the 'Anglo-Irish Intergovernmental Council') and to the possible establishment of a parliamentary forum bringing in also the proposed Belfast assembly. Unionist politicians and IRA alike condemned the initiatives but, following a rather difficult period in Anglo-Irish relations when Charles Haughey briefly resumed the premiership, Fitzgerald returned to office and a second summit was held in November 1983. A third followed a year later and, after increasingly intensive bureaucratic exchanges, a fourth summit was held at Hillsborough Castle in November 1985.

At Hillsborough a formal treaty was concluded embodying two principles to govern the policies of the two governments towards Northern Ireland. The first principle was that there could be no change in the status of Northern Ireland as part of the United Kingdom without the consent of the majority of the population. This was the first Irish recognition of a *de jure* Protestant veto on unification and Fitzgerald formally recognised that Protestant consent to unification did not exist. The second principle accepted by the two governments was that the Republic would enjoy a formal status in the government of Northern Ireland. An 'Intergovernmental Conference' established a permanent machinery, located in Northern Ireland, through which the Irish state was to be consulted about Northern Ireland. The Conference was given four specific tasks: economic co-operation across the border; social co-operation across the border; the administration of justice (including extradition); political development in Northern Ireland where Dublin would help to represent the interests of the minority community in the absence of an agreed and widely supported system of devolution. The idea underlying the first two tasks are found in the 1973 Council of Ireland but the second two tasks go much further and give the Republic a role in the constitution of Northern Ireland. The Irish government also agreed to accede to the convention on terrorism allowing the extradition of IRA terrorists from Dublin to London to stand trial for crimes committed within the United Kingdom without their being able to argue successfully in the Dublin courts the claim that the offences were 'political' and non-extraditable.

The treaty claimed not to raise the question of sovereignty in Northern Ireland but in fact it not only represented an unprecedented acceptance by Britain of the legitimate interests of the Republic in Northern Ireland but also gave the Republic a framework within which to defend the interests of the minority community.

The treaty found many staunch enemies and few effective friends. In Dublin it was condemned by Fiannna Fáil as marking a retreat from the claim to unification – a charge echoed in Britain by the left wing of the Labour Party, although the party leadership welcomed the agreement. In Westminster the right wing of the Conservative Party attached the agreement as a retreat from the union with Northern Ireland which would inevitably undermine the confidence of the Unionist parties. In Northern Ireland the agreement was condemned in equally virulent terms, though for exactly opposite reasons, by the Unionist parties and Sinn Fein. It was warmly welcomed by the Alliance and by the SDLP, which had played a major role behind the scenes in the whole process and which now stood as the chief political beneficiary of the agreement. The opponents of the agreement in Northern Ireland carried greater political clout than its supporters. The Unionist parties returned to the assembly in order to demand a referendum on the agreement and, when this was refused, all fifteen Unionist MPs at Westminster resigned over the issue. In by-elections fought in February 1986 fourteen were returned with a clear anti-agreement mandate (the SDLP picking up the other seat). In the face of continuing opposition to the agreement in the assembly in June 1986 the British government decided to dissolve the assembly and to revert again to direct rule. This was the fourth abandonment of Parliament/Assembly since 1972, though direct rule now had the additional element of the Republic's involvement through the Inter-governmental Conference in Belfast. To the continuing war against the IRA was now added a series of violent attacks on the Royal Ulster Constabulary from Protestant paramilitaries.

The Hillsborough Agreement thus had promised a good deal more than it had actually delivered and it remained a focus of opposition to Britain both in the north and in the Republic. During the election campaign in the Republic in 1987 Fianna Fáil continued to denounce the agreement and to threaten withdrawal. However, although the defeat of Dr Fitzgerald was a grave blow to London, the new government of Mr Haughey in fact maintained the agreement and used its procedures to keep up pressure on the British government over such matters as the administration of justice in Northern Ireland. Security co-operation was continued and in some ways extended (for instance, the Republic agreed to the British army's helicopters overflying the Republic) and, after a series of false starts, extraditions from the Republic eventually began. Only the SDLP had real cause to welcome the agreement and in the 1987 general election it consolidated its position *vis-á-vis* Sinn Fein winning 21% to 11.4%, though Sinn Fein retained its seat.

In 1988 the SDLP opened up a formal dialogue with Sinn Fein in an attempt to recreate a unified nationalist position on the Hillsborough basis of working towards Irish unification by consent. Sinn Fein took the more realistic view that agreement by consent ran up directly against the Unionist veto. It also argued that the British position in Northern Ireland was imperialist, against which only a continuing campaign of violence would succeed. In September 1987 the talks were called off and IRA terrorism entered a renewed phase of activity against civilian and military targets in Northern Ireland and Great Britain.

Conclusion

By 1988 the British government had exhausted each of its available paths towards 'normality'. Hillsborough had alienated the Unionists still further without offering any solid advances in terms of the immediate political and military struggle against Sinn Fein/IRA. A consensus in Northern Ireland for devolved rule was further away, than ever. The threat of unilateral withdrawal remained unthinkable. Direct rule and an unending security struggle, plus whatever Hillsborough offered, appeared the only foreseeable future.

Viewed in the longer term however, British policy remains characterised by instability and a desire to minimise the Irish dimension in British politics. The British state has no desire of its own to retain the union which persists only until the Northern Irish people tire of it or the IRA is able to present such massive costs to Britain that withdrawal becomes thinkable. An Irish solution to the Northern Ireland question – whether in the form of Irish unification, a separate Northern Ireland state, or civil war throughout Ireland with a collapse of both political regimes – seems more likely to endure than a solution imposed by Britain.

Reading

D. Birrell, 'Northern Ireland: the obstacles to power sharing', *Political Quarterly*, 1981.

J. G. Bulpitt, *Territory and Power in the United Kingdom*, Manchester University Press, 1983.

A. H. Birch, *Political Integration and Disintegration in the British Isles*, Allen & Unwin, 1978.

W. H. Cox, 'Managing Northern Ireland intergovernmentally: an appraisal of the Anglo-Irish Agreement', *Parliamentary Attanus*, 40, 1987.

W. H. Cox, 'Public opinions and the Anglo-Irish Agreement', *Government and Opposition*, 22, 1987.

B. O'Leary, 'The Anglo-Irish Agreement: folly or state craft?', *West European Politics*, 10, 1987.

R. Rose, *Northern Ireland: a Time of Choice*, Macmillan, 1976.

The Government of Northern Ireland: Proposals for Further Discussion (1980), *Northern Ireland: a Framework for Devolution* (1982) and the *Hillsborough Agreement* (1985) are the three main Conservative Government statements on Northern Ireland in Cmnd 7950, Cmnd 8541 and Cmnd 9657.

New Ireland Forum, Irish Government Publication, Dublin, 1984, was discussed extensively in the British press in May 1984.

Ireland: a chronology of key events

Origins of the conflict

1170 Henry II of England begins conquest of Ireland.

1542 Henry VII proclaimed King of Ireland. Ulster remains Gaelic and unsuppressed.

1603 Ulster now comes under firm English governmental control. Gaelic order vanquished and settlement of Ulster by 175,000 mostly Scots Presbyterians begins.

1641 Catholic revolt involving massacre of Ulster Protestants (Portadown). Cromwellian suppression follows (1649–50).

1688 James II deposed by William & Mary ('Glorious Revolution'), but James still recognised as King by Catholic Ireland.

1689 *Siege of Londonderry* protestants by forces of James II.

1690 *James defeated at the Battle of the Boyne:* Protestant ascendancy now assured.

1782 Irish Parliament set up in Dublin under Henry Gratton, inspired by American Revolution.

1790s *Birth of Irish republicanism by Wolfe Tone,* inspired by French Revolution – attempt at French revolutionary intervention.

1798 Insurrection of Tone's 'United Irishmen' suppressed in particularly savage fashion.

1801 Act of Union Dublin Parliament disappears and Ireland becomes an integral part of the UK.

1820s Daniel O'Connell's Catholic Association succeeds in achieving Catholic emancipation in 1829 but fails in the 1830s and 1840s to force *Repeal* of the Act of Union. O'Connell father of Constitutional – Nationalism.

1845–48 Famine, and Young Ireland Movement: violent rising in 1848 suppressed.

1860s Fenian movement (Irish Republican Brotherhood) gathers momentum and develops a strategy of separatism, republicanism and violence. 1867 insurrection fails.

1870s Irish party in Westminster captured and transformed by Charles Stewart *Parnell* into an organised, disciplined and popularly-based political party.

1886 Gladstone coverted to Parnell's policy of Home Rule for Ireland within the Empire and subject to the Westminster Parliament introduces *First Home Rule Bill*. Defeated in the House of Commons following Liberal defections led by Joseph Chamberlain. One consequence is the destruction of the Liberal Party as a governing party for the next two decades.

1893 Second Home Rule Bill passes House of Commons but defeated in the Lords. Gladstone concludes Home Rule is not possible while the House of Lords powers remain unaltered.

1905 Sinn Fein party founded by Arthur Griffiths and rapidly captured by the IRB (Fenians).

1910 Constitutional crisis following the House of Lords rejection of Lloyd George's 'People's Budget' leads to the return of a Liberal government *dependent* for its Parliamentary majority on Irish Nationalists.

1911 Parliament Act: House of Lords veto replaced by delaying powers.

1912 Liberals introduce Third Home Rule Bill which provokes militant reaction by Ulster and Irish Unionists: *'Home Rule is Rome Rule'*; *'Ulster Will Fight'*.

1912–14 Ireland dividing into armed militias for and against Home Rule.

1914 War with Germany. *Home Rule Bill* placed on The Statute

Book but not to be implemented until the conclusion of war and
then not without further debate.

1916 Dublin Easter Rising   Fifteen leaders executed. Sinn Fein now
overtakes the Nationalist party as the voice of 'Catholic' Ireland.

1918   Sinn Fein wins a majority of seats at The General Election and
in 1919 sets up the First Dáil as an alternative Parliament. IRA
formed in 1919 from IRB.

1919–21   Anglo-Irish War between IRA and 'Black and Tans' –
military auxiliaries.

1920   Government of Ireland Act partitions Ireland.

1921   Anglo-Irish Treaty – confirms Partition and establishes Irish
Free State.

Ulster: emergence of a 'mini – state', 1920–88

*1920–21   The Government of Ireland Act 1920 and Anglo-Irish
Treaty 1921* establish the boundaries of the partitioned island. The
Ulster 'State' consists of six of the nine historic counties which
make up the Province of Ulster. Its Parliament – Stormont – meets
for the first time on 5 June 1921.

1922–72   The Unionist Party dominates the politics of Northern
Ireland. The Roman Catholic minority is represented by the
residual elements of the old Nationalist party but a portion looks to
the remnants of Sinn Fein and the IRA who have not accepted the
1920/21 Anglo-Irish arrangements. Politics seem to be frozen in a
permanent religious/cultural/nationalist time warp. 'Normal' politics based on class/ecocomic/social issues are marginal.

The 'Troubles'

1968   The Civil Rights Movement emerges with new demands
related to jobs, housing and discrimination which starts the process
of destroying the Stomont Parliament and the monolithic Unionist
Party. The IRA re-emerges and the British government reluctantly
gets sucked into the Ulster Crisis.

1969–72 British troops deployed in Belfast and Londonderry as
peacekeepers, ostensibly to protect Catholics from Protestant forces
of 'law and order'. The position quickly changes and British troops
find themselves confronting IRA as well.

1972   Stormont Parliament prorogued and Ulster now directly ruled
from Westminster via a Northern Ireland Secretary of State and
Northern Ireland Office in Belfast.

1973   Sunningdale Conference; New Assembly elections.

1974   Power-sharing Executive established to deal with all internal Northern Ireland affairs. Representatives of the Official Unionist, Social Democratic and Labour and Alliance parties participate in Executive. *Opposed by Ian Paisley's DUP and Ulster Loyalist Workers' Council whose strike brought it down in May 1974.*

1980   Anglo-Irish Council established to break the deadlock by reviewing the 'totality of relations within these islands'. Joint studies on new institutional structures, citizenship rights, economic co-operation, security, etc., commence.

1982   Northern Ireland Assembly reconvened. Unionist parties oppose revival of power-sharing and Nationalist and Republican parties, i.e. SDLP and Sinn Fein, boycott the body. *Hunger strikes – ten republicans die, including Bobby Sands.*

1985   Anglo-Irish Agreement. Both governments accept that the present constitutional status of Northern Ireland can only change with the consent of the majority. Established regular ministerial meetings via a consultative inter-governmental conference. A permanent secretariat of civil servants from both Britain and Ireland is located in Belfast to deal with political, security and legal questions, and to promote cross-border co-operation. Vigorously opposed by Unionists and rejected by Sinn Fein as irrelevant.

(Chronology drawn up by John McHugh, Manchester Polytechnic)

16 *Bill Jones*

Crime and punishment

This chapter examines the perennially topical problem of law and order, seeking to place it within the context of the current political debate. Law and order in relation to political ideas is examined together with the extent of crime, its causes and society's responses to it.

Law and order and political ideas

The attitudes we have towards law and order depend to a substantial degree upon our assessments of what human nature is really like. Some philosophers have taken a pessimistic view. For Thomas Hobbes human nature was such that in a state of nature, life would be, in his famous phrase, 'nasty, solitary, brutish and short'. Machiavelli was more specific: 'it may be said of men in general that they are ungrateful, voluble dissemblers, anxious to avoid danger and covetous of gain'. Others were more sanguine. Rousseau, for example, believed that 'man is naturally good and only by institutions is he made bad'. Similarly Marx, following his precept that 'environment determines consciousness', believed that it was the harshness of the capitalist economic system which was responsible for man's shortcomings.

For pessimists like Hobbes, chaotic anarchy could only be prevented through the agency of an all-powerful state, a 'Leviathan' which could impose order through overwhelming force. For optimists like Marx the problem of lawlessness could only be solved by fundamental changes in society which would refashion human nature and produce laws based upon fairness and justice rather than the interests of the capitalist ruling class.

The debate about law and order still revolves around these familiar and ultimately unresolvable themes. Conservatives tend to support the pessimistic or what they would call 'realistic' analysis. They believe 'respect for the rule of laws is the basis of free and civilised society' (1979 Manifesto) and

(1) See the problem of crime primarily from the viewpoint of its victims rather than its perpetrators.

(2) Support a deterrent strategy, i.e. stiffer penalties.

(3) Believe individuals have free will and should be accountable for their actions. Everyone, rich and poor, has the choice of obeying or breaking the law but if they take the latter course they should be in no doubt as to the penalties they must face.

Labour, the SLD and the SDP tend to take a more optimistic line. They believe that

(1) Crime has social causes, e.g. poverty, poor housing, unemployment, which are remediable through social policy.

(2) Deterrent strategies involving greater police powers and penalties should not be pursued to the point when civil liberties are unacceptably eroded.

(3) The criminal has rights too: penal policy should be humanised and more emphasis placed on rehabilitation rather than punishment.

In the late seventies Mrs Thatcher took up a tough right-wing stance, stating in the run-up to the 1979 election that 'The demand in this country will be for two things: less tax and more law and order' (*Daily Telegraph,* 29 March 1979). The Manifesto reflected this emphasis on law and order, claiming that 'Labour has undermined it'. During the campaign, 87% of Conservative candidates mentioned this subject in election addresses. There is little doubt that all this rhetoric struck a resonant note: an ITN election night survey indicated that 23% of respondents who had switched their support to the Conservatives had done so primarily over this issue. The Conservatives have clearly succeeded in making themselves the party of 'law and order'. A MORI poll for the *Sunday Times* in November 1985 revealed that 45% of those questioned judged the Tories best equipped to deal with increasing crime, compared with 19% for Labour and 9% for the Alliance. The irony here is that, according to their opponents' analyses (see below), it is Conservative economic and social policies which are exacerbating the causes of crime in the first place.

The extent of the problem: is there a crime wave?

'The number of crimes in England and Wales is nearly half as much again as it was in 1973', stated the Conservative 1979 Manifesto. Mrs Thatcher's governments, however, have not stemmed the tide; notifiable offences rose by over 50% from 2.5 million in 1979 to 3.7 in 1988. Table 5 gives the details. The figures for 1988 show a slight decrease in total offences but this is explained largely by a reduction in crimes against property (nearly 95% of the total). Sustained increases in sexual offences and violent crime give grounds for considerable concern. The number of notifiable offences recorded by the police in which firearms were reported to have been used also increased, according to 1985 Home Office figures, from under 3,000 in 1974 to over 9,000 in 1983. The rioting in several inner-city areas in 1981 and 1985 alarmed the British public and led some to question whether law and order itself was breaking down.

Furthermore, the Home Office-sponsored *British Crime Survey* (BCS) of 1981 suggested that large numbers of offences are never reported and hence never recorded, e.g. half of all burglaries, over 90% of vandalism, nearly 90% of robberies and over 70% of sexual offences. The 'dark figure' of unrecorded crime in fact may be four or five times higher than official police figures.

In statistical terms these figures might well be interpreted as the 'crime wave' of which the Conservatives and the popular press make so much. However, a number of important qualifications have to be made which challenge this conclusion.

(1) It is far from clear whether the level of unrecorded crime has increased by the same proportions as recorded crime. One Home Office survey of burglary and theft concluded that the actual rise in these offences was only *1% per year* from 1972–80 compared with the officially recorded figure of *4% per year*. It was the *proportion* of crimes recorded which had sharply increased, in this instance possibly because of more widespread availability of telephones and use of property insurance.

(2) Much crime is relatively trivial, recorded or not. The 1984 BCS showed that 62% of vandalism cases, 60% of motor vehicles thefts, 63% of burglaries and 51% of thefts from the person were not reported to the police because no damage was involved and no

Table 5   Notifiable offences recorded by police by offence group

	1981	1982	1983	1984	Percentage increase 1985	1986	1987	1988	
Violence against the person	+3	+8	+2	+3	+7	+3	+12	158.2	(+12.2)
Sexual offences	−8	+2	+1	−1	+6	+6	+11	26.5	(+5.5)
Burglary	+16	+16	−	−1	+6	+7	−3	817.8	(−9.1)
Robbery	+35	+3	−3	+13	+10	+9	+9	31.4	(−3.7)
Thefts & handling stolen goods	+10	+10	−3	+6	+4	+6	+2	1,931.3	(−5.9)
Fraud & forgery	+1	+15	−1	+7	+16	−1	−	133.9	(+0.7)
Criminal damage	+8	+8	+6	+8	+3	+8	+7	593.9	(+0.8)
Other offences	−	−7	−	+19	+17	−	+16	22.7	(+17.4)
TOTAL	+10	+10	−1	+8	+3	+7	+1	3,715.8	(−4.5)

Source: Home Office Statistical Bulletin, 16 March 1989.

property taken. In 1984 65% of home burglaries committed involved thefts of property worth less than £100.

(3) Britain is less violent now than it used to be. A report by E. G. Dunning and others from Leicester University revealed that whilst reported violent disturbances in the UK (excluding Northern Ireland) had increased since the war years the rate in 1975 was less than a third of that of 1900, *despite* a 46% increase in the population during that period.

(4) In a society of material plenty and the 'hard sell', the opportunities for crime are much greater and the motivation sharper. And the growth of more plentiful laws and regulations – especially at work – means that there are more crimes now to commit.

(5) More efficient police recording procedures also help explain the increase, together with the 10% increase in police manpower since 1979 available for such duties.

(6) When placed in certain perspectives the chances of being the victim of crime is remarkably low. The 1981 BCS (p. 15) showed that

a statistically average person of 16 or over can expect
   * a robbery once every five centuries (not attempts)
   * an assault resulting in injury (even if slight) once every century.
   * the family car to be stolen or taken by joyriders once every sixty years.
   * a burglary in the house once every forty years.

As the BCS observes, 'small upward changes in either reporting or recording can all too readily create a "crime wave" ' (p. 14). Can we conclude, then – as some on the left do – that the crime wave is merely a creation of the press and politicians playing upon popular fears for political gain? Perhaps. Some experts use the above factors to explain the fifteenfold increase in crime in 1981 compared with the early 1930s. Others disagree and assert that sharp real increases have occurred particularly in violent crime, burglary, robbery and theft. Moreover, statistical averages mask the fact that for certain people, i.e. young, working-class males, especially blacks, living in areas like the inner cities, the risks are much higher. For example, survey evidence indicates that you are twice as likely to be burgled if you are an unskilled worker than if you are a professional. Thirty-five per cent of burglaries occur in inner-city areas according to the 1984 BCS: whilst 12% of householders on poor council estates had been burgled in the previous year only 3% suffered similarly in the middle-class suburbs.

Crime wave or not, crime is indeed a major problem as anyone, especially old people, who have suffered the trauma of a burglary know only too well. Certainly statistics can lie, newspapers sensationalise and politicians exaggerate but there is a legitimate cause for concern. Moreover, the principal victims of crime are not, as one might expect, the propertied middle class, but those least able to afford loss: working-class people themselves.

Fear of crime is arguably as much of a problem as crime itself, blighting peoples' lives and causing yet more crime through emptying streets at night and thus removing social constraints upon criminal actions. The BCS revealed that 60% of elderly women living in inner-city areas felt 'very unsafe' when walking alone in their locality after dark. Twenty-five per cent of all women aged 16–24 never go out on their own at any time of the day for fear of attack and 41% of all women aged thirty and under confess to being 'very worried' about the risk of rape.

The irony is that fear of crime seems to be experienced in inverse proportion to actual risk; for example, only 1% of men aged 16–30 felt 'very unsafe' yet they are the group most likely to be victims: women over sixty, on the other hand, are the least likely to be victims of crime. Again, statisticians, the press and politicians can be blamed for whipping up unnecessary and morbid fears but it is also understandable that the old and frail should fear what, for them, might be catastrophic – even if rare – events.

In February 1989 a Home Office Working Party on the fear of crime was established under the chairmanship of Michael Grade.

The causes of crime

What are the causes of crime? Two broad analyses can be identified which typify positions on the right and left; many 'centrist' positions, of course, exist in between them.

The right-wing analysis
This approach sees crime as fundamentally a matter of values.

(1) Human beings have a natural disposition towards acts which give personal pleasure or advantage, even at the expense of others; as Mrs Thatcher asserts, 'man is inherently sinful'. This predilection is kept in check by the ideas and habits of self-discipline which have been inculcated by the church, family life, social institutions, the law

and those entrusted with authority.

(2) The ideas and actions of the left, so the analysis runs, have eroded this self-discipline by rejecting religion, crucially weakening the role of the family and undermining both the law and traditional institutions like schools. This misguided permissiveness, combined with the over-protective institutions of the welfare state, have created an atmosphere in which citizens have abandoned self-restraint and discipline for free licence and reliance upon the state.

(3) Excessive immigration of alien peoples, say the right, has created tensions and further weakened cultural restraints against lawless behaviour.

(4) Trade unions, aided actively by extremist left-wing groups and tacitly by the Labour Party, have increasingly ignored the law and used violence and intimidation – 'the rule of the mob' to quote Mrs Thatcher – to achieve their industrial and political objectives.

The left-wing analysis
This puts the blame for crime principally at the door of the economic system. This approach:

(1) Dismisses right-wing arguments as a mere rationalisation of ruling-class interests; many of the 'values' which workers are enjoined to embrace are those which favour not them but the ruling middle class.

(2) Asserts that capitalism produces great inequalities of wealth and gives vastly inferior life chances to the poor whilst imbuing them with an ideology of material acquisition and career success. Because capitalism denies what it induces people to pursue it causes crime. American radical Angela Davies puts the argument in its purest form: 'The real criminals in this society are not all the people who populate the prisons across the state but those who have stolen the wealth of the world from the people.'

(3) Sees the law as protecting the privileges of the rich through prosecuting and punishing 'working-class crime' such as robbery and vandalism with much greater energy than 'middle-class crime', e.g. fraud and expenses fiddling. For example, in 1981 the state lost £4 million a week through social security frauds and made 576 prosecutions, yet lost £80 million through tax evasion and made only two prosecutions per week. Moreover, since 1979 the Conservative government has taken on 1,000 social security investigators yet has actually reduced the size of the tax inspectorate (Downes, p. 5).

(4) The racial allegation is deliberately used by the right to stir up ill-informed prejudice and divert attention from the real causes of crime.

Mrs Thatcher summed up the right-wing analysis in 1988 when she blamed the rising crime rate on 'the professional progressiveness among broadcasters, social workers and politicians, who have created a fog of excuses in which the mugger and burglar operate' (*Observer*, 20 March 1988).

Roy Hattersley encapsulated the left's riposte in 1989 when he said that 'The callous individualism that has been encouraged by Mrs Thatcher and her ministers over the past 10 years is directly responsible for the increase in violent crime over the past decade' (*Guardian*, 2 January 1989).

Responses to crime

Just as political opinions differ over the causes of crime, so there are sharp disagreements as to the most effective and morally acceptable responses to it.

Changes in values

At the most fundamental level, politicians argue, society must change so that values will alter and crimes be reduced. The extent of this change usually constitutes the ideological aims of the political creed involved. For right-wing Conservatives this would entail the creation of a free market economy and the dismantling of the welfare state; this would help facilitate a return to the law-abiding virtues of the Victorian era with its emphasis upon family life and obligation, self-reliance and personal accountability. For the socialist the necessary changes in values will only occur when the economy is based upon co-operation, not competition, with more equal distribution of wealth and life opportunities. How long will it take to effect these changes? As long as rival political ideologies are locked in insoluble conflict neither side will win; even Mrs Thatcher's huge 1987 majority has not enabled her to move very far towards her stated goals. It does not follow either that any political analysis is correct, that any wholly victorious political ideology will substantially reduce crime. Inevitably, in the meantime much emphasis is placed upon effective police action.

Policing

Conservatives believe a strengthened police force is an essential high-priority response to the increase in crime. Accordingly, between 1979 and 1983 they raised spending on the police by over 20%, increased the number of police in England and Wales by 9,500 to 120,000, raised police pay by some 30%, improved anti-riot equipment and put more policemen back on the beat. Mrs Thatcher and her ministers were emphatic in their praise for the police throughout the extended bitterness of the 1984 miners' strike and were keen that police powers should be increased through the Criminal Evidence Bill. This measure extended powers for the police regarding: stop and search (including body searches); road checks; the search of premises; and, most contentiously, detention of suspects without trial for up to ninety-six hours instead of the previous twenty-four hours, and for the first thirty-six hours incommunicado, without access to legal advice. On the other hand, the Act created, against fierce police criticism, an independent authority to investigate complaints against the police instead of the previous procedure controlled by the police themselves. In 1986 a new Public Order Act gave the police more power and discretion to curb or control demonstrations, marches and picketing.

Criticisms of this pro-police line are offered by left and centrist spokesmen, academic experts and many others.

(a) Labour left-wingers assert that the police pay awards were a deliberate ploy by Mrs Thatcher to buy their support for their role in containing the social disruption which she knew her policies would cause.

(b) Some experts point out that spending on the police is not especially cost-effective in that (i) only a tiny party of their time is spent on crime-fighting – the major part spent on other duties (Downes, p. 12); (ii) increased beat duty – according to a 1984 Home Office Study – offers only a negligible deterrent to crime.

(c) Other critics believe that all is not well in the police force, pointing out that

(i) The 'clear-up' rate of reported crimes has actually dropped from over 40% in the late seventies to 35% in 1988.

(ii) Despite vigorous earlier denials by the police and their supporters, investigations in the seventies revealed extensive corruption, especially in the Metropolitan Police. 'Altogether eighteen men of varying ranks from constable to commander were sentenced to over a hundred years imprisonment, including terms of 12, 10 and 8 years in the worst cases' (Sir Robert Mark, *In the Office of Constable,* 1978, ch. 20).

(iii) A report into the Metropolitan Police by the Policy Studies Institute revealed widespread racist and sexist attitudes together with frequent drunkenness on duty. Yet despite this, and the occasional well-publicised incompetence – e.g. the shooting of the innocent Stephen Waldorf in mistake for the wanted David Martin of 1983 – only 10% of Londoners registered complete lack of confidence in their police. The majority were satisfied with the service provided.

(d) At present the police are allowed to arrest and prosecute. Critics have long called for an independent prosecuting service for England and Wales, rather like the system used in Scotland.

(e) Those concerned with civil liberties identify a worrying erosion since Mrs Thatcher has been in power. The Police and Criminal Evidence Act was seen to give the police a frightening amount of power and the new Public Order Act was criticised as more draconian than any similar legislation in America, France or West Germany.

(f) The received wisdom that the best policing is carried out by forces in close touch with local communities was strengthened by the 1981 riots in Brixton where it was obvious that relations had collapsed. Labour and centrist critics stress the importance of this approach and urge that local police forces be made formally accountable to local communities.

(g) The specially trained Special Patrol Groups for use in public order roles have been condemned by many critics as provocative and aggressive. Moreover, the use of police – again specially trained – in support of disturbances caused by government industrial relations policy – most notably the 1984 miners' strike – has been condemned by left-wing critics as a quasi-political role for what should be a wholly non-political body. Gerald Kaufman, Labour's Shadow Home Secretary, was particularly worried by the formation of the National Reporting Centre, the centralised body which co-ordinated action against the flying pickets. He feared the 'embryonic growth of an uncontrolled national police force . . . a potential national police militia' (*Guardian,* 7 September 1984). A study by Gerry Northam appeared in 1988 to support this view, detecting a 'secret slide towards a paramilitary policing system throughout Britain'.

(h) Concern has also been voiced that the police have been

allowed to use a wide range of surveillance techniques, e.g. phone taps, which constitute severe erosions of civil liberties.

Penal policy

Once offenders have been apprehended by the police and found guilty by the courts, they have to be dealt with in some suitable fashion. What principles should underlie their treatment?

Right-wing Conservatives believe in retribution and deterrence. Wrongdoers must be punished according to the severity of their crimes to the extent that they – and other potential criminals – will be deterred from committing such acts in the future. If crimes continue to increase notwithstanding, then penalties clearly need to be increased even further. Mrs Thatcher told a conference of the American Bar Association in July 1985 of 'the very real anxiety of ordinary people that too many sentences do not fit the crime'. Sentencing policy in the courts has appeared to reflect this feeling. Between 1984 and 1987 sentences handed down to criminals using firearms to resist arrest increased on average from 3.4 to 6.7 years. Sentences for rape increased from 3·8 to 6·2 years and robbery with firearms from 5·7 to 7·0 years.

The Conservative Party Conference, encouraged by Mrs Thatcher, regularly calls for stiffer penalties. This often leads to home secretaries, faced with the complex reality of crime and punishment in society, being trapped by their own vote-winning rhetoric: William Whitelaw was booed by Conference in 1981 and Douglas Hurd has received much criticism for his stand against the return of capital punishment.

(a) Capital punishment   Surveys regularly show that some three-quarters of the electorate favour the return of capital punishment for murder. Since 1979 scores of eager new Tory MPs have crowded into Parliaments at successive elections, having made capital punishment one of their election platforms. When it has come to the vote, however, many have changed their minds as Table 6 shows.

The answer seems to be that even the most enthusiastic 'hangers' think again when they consider the case adduced against their own retributive and deterrent arguments: it would be a retrograde step for civilised society; Britain in any case has a low level of murders – 662 in 1986 compared with over 18,000 in the USA; there is little or no evidence to suggest that murders have increased appreciably since

Table 6 *MPs voting for capital punishment*

	19 July 1979	13 July 1983	7 June 1988
Conservatives elected in:			
1987			42
1983		64	55
1979	57	43	38
before 1979	174	141	71
Other parties	12	15	12
Total	243	263	218

Source: The Economist, 11 June 1988.

the death penalty was abolished; it would put added pressures upon judges and juries; it would remove the possibility of freeing those wrongly convicted; and in the case of political terrorists would merely play into their hands through making them martyrs. During the 8 June 1988 debate Douglas Hurd pointed out that

Fierce honourable argument immediately after the event is one thing. It is quite another to institute slow, cold processes of justice, with months filled with arguments of lawyers and the hearing of appeals, at the end of which the Home Secretary may decide, long after the event, that the offender should cease to exist. An execution in this way can surely give only fleeting satisfaction, if any, to the public or those who knew the victim.

The House agreed: on a free vote they decided by 341 votes to 218 against the reintroduction of the death penalty.

(*b*) *Prisons* The tendency of courts in recent years to commit more people to prison – from 16% of adult males convicted of indictable offences in England and Wales in 1973, to 20% in 1983 – has created a number of problems and occasioned much criticism along the following lines:

(*i*) To deprive people of their liberty is a very severe punishment which should be used rarely, e.g. 'only where there is extreme danger to the community' (Lea & Young, p. 267).

(*ii*) The aim of prison should be to rehabilitate, not merely to punish. The Barlinnie Special Unit in Glasgow revealed that even hardened criminals – Jimmy Boyle is the best known – can be reclaimed for society, given appropriate attitudes and resources.

(*iii*) Les than 10% of those in prison are murderers, rapists and armed robbers whilst about one-half are there for persistent, non-serious offences: alternative sentences could and should be found for the latter.

(iv) A wealth of respectable evidence suggests that prison is not only very expensive – £850 million in 1988 – but ineffective. The Advisory Council on the Penal System reported: 'Neither practical experience nor the results of research in recent years have established the superiority of custodial over non-custodial methods in their effect upon renewed recidivism.' Indeed there is evidence to suggest that the enclosed criminal sub-culture of prison actually encourages recidivism. A NACRO report produced in 1985 revealed that the UK imprisons 274 people per 100,000 of the population compared with 207 in Italy, 199 in West Germany, 140 in France and 78 in Portugal. Only the USA, USSR and South Africa imprison more. The report concludes that our use of prison is 'both excessive and ineffective'. The fact that one-third of our prison population is there for burglary and that 60% of prisoners are re-convicted within two years would appear to support this view.

(v) According to Whitelaw himself, the conditions in our prisons are an 'affront to civilised society'. In 1978 there were 42,220 prisoners: 9.7% more than the prisons had been designed for. By February 1989, despite a much publicised prison-building programme, the figure had risen to 55,729. Conditions are insanitary and desperately overcrowded: 5,300 live three to a cell designed for one, often without toilet or washing facilities, whilst 14,000 are kept two to a cell. To deprive offenders of their liberty is one thing but to lock them up in such conditions for up to twenty-three hours a day with minimal work and educational opportunities is to add an inhuman dimension to an already harsh punishment. Many reformers call for: legislation to protect prisoners' rights regarding conditions – especially cell space; better leisure services inside prisons and better resettlement care for those leaving prison.

(vi) Some research by criminologists and polling organisations suggests that public opinion is less retributive than right-wingers claim. The 1984 British Crime Survey revealed that 67% thought fines were better than prison for non-violent offences. And a 1985 NACRO poll showed that only a third of people burgled believed that the offenders concerned should have been imprisoned.

(c) *Non-custodial alternatives*   Opponents of prison as the answer to crime look to alternatives which will reclaim offenders for the law-abiding majority in society and will also do something to help their victims. In recent years the government has begun to look with increasing favour upon such approaches.

(i) *Victim restitution* schemes have been very successfully experimented with in America: offenders are brought face to face with their victims and required to make amends.

(ii) *Community service orders* whereby offenders work off their debt to society through undertaking worthwhile tasks have been in existence for some time. In 1981 only 5% of indictable offenders were dealt with in this way but many urge its more extensive use.

(iii) *Other alternatives* to prison like fines, probation, supervision orders are also urged as preferable, more effective alternatives to prison. Whitelaw's attempt to introduce a supervised early release scheme for short-term prisoners was nipped in the bid by opposition from the senior echelons of the judiciary and his own right wing. There seems to be less opposition to 'tagging', a system whereby prisoners are released on condition they wear a small electronic transmitter and report regularly to the authorities on their movements. Some critics, such as Downes, also point out that prison is used more for working-class crimes; middle-class crime, which is largely financial and occupational, is 'almost invariably dealt with informally or by negotiation rather than by the police and the courts' (p. 9). Over one-half of Britain's apprehended criminals are under twenty-one and a fifteen-year-old boy is nearly six times more likely to show up in the statistics than the average male.

(d) *Juvenile crime* The response, by both Labour and Conservative government, has been greatly to increase custodial sentences: they actually rose at *four times* the rate of juvenile crime during the seventies. The present Conservative government has reinforced this trend by its establishment of detention centres with tough military regimes to deter young offenders from a life of crime by a 'short, sharp shock'. Critics argue, however, that such treatment is mostly counter-productive: it merely serves to alienate young people and socialise them into the alternative sub-culture of the criminal world. The return to crime rate from detention centres is now close to 80% within two years – little different from ordinary youth custody centres – and the experiment is generally held to have failed. The Home Secretary has encouraged police to use cautions more liberally – they did so 50% more often in 1987 than 1977.

(e) *Crime prevention*   This approach asks whether money spent on preventing crime might not be more cost-effective than policing and punishment of offenders. It lays some responsibility upon individuals and the community to make crime more difficult and therefore less likely. The need to rehabilitate offenders and thus reduce recidivism has already been mentioned but a number of other possibilities exist.

(i) A greater sense of community awareness and responsibility could be inculcated, especially in young people. In Cuba and China, for example, regular street meetings put moral pressure on people to be law-abiding and greater efforts are made to reabsorb offenders into society.

(ii) France has set up a powerful crime prevention council, with branches in all major towns, which has targeted educational and training programmes at young people most likely to drift into crime. Perhaps as a result France has been the only European country to report a substantial fall in its crime rate.

(iii) Property can be made more secure by individuals, companies and public services. In West Germany car thefts plummeted after the introduction of steering-column locks in the sixties; in Sweden cheque-card frauds did likewise when affixed photographs were introduced as a requirement; crime and vandalism on tube trains are reduced when closed-circuit television is installed.

(iv) Neighbourhood Watch schemes, whereby residents undertake to keep a look-out for and report crime in their area, have burgeoned in recent years. Some 40,000 schemes have been created, a large proportion of them in London. One negative result, however, appears to have been a compensating increase in street crime. A variation on this approach was worked out in a valley near Caerphilly where residents marked valuables with their postcode and indicated the fact with window stickers. The result? A 40% decrease in burglaries.

Concluding comments

The apparent halting of the 'crime wave' in 1988 has been claimed by some Conservatives as evidence of successful policies. Quite possibly it merely reflects demographic factors. During the seventies the crime-prone 15–19 age group increased by 16%. Since 1985, however, the age group has been declining and will be 26% less by 1993.

The Conservative government seems to have shifted its emphasis from a narrowly retributive approach – except for serious violent offences – towards a cautious acceptance of non-custodial alternatives and crime prevention measures. Whilst formally denying that crime has social causes (the 1985 riots were 'not a cry for help but a cry for loot', according to Douglas Hurd) certain government campaigns have tacitly accepted the connection.

Such a policy development can only be applauded. Deteriorating socio-economic conditions like poverty and youth unemployment have created what has been described as an 'underclass' and a related sub-culture which accepts crime as a rational everyday response to the problems which life increasingly poses.

Reading

John Benyon & Colin Bourn (eds.), *The Police: Powers, Procedures and Properties,* Pergamon, 1986.

David Downes, *Law and Order: Theft of an Issue,* Fabian Tract 490, Fabian Society, 1983. (An excellent informative essay written from a committed position.)

Home Office Research Unit, *Fear of Crime,* HMSO, 1984.

Home Office Statistical Bulletins, Issue 5/84 (15 March 1984), 16/86 (12 June 1986) and 36/88 (14 December 1988).

Mike Hough & Pat Mayhew, *The British Crime Survey,* A Home Office Research and Planning Unit Report, No. 76, HMSO, 1983.

J. Lea & J. Young, *What is to be done about Law and Order? Crisis in the Eighties,* Penguin, 1984. (A clear and interesting discussion by two sociologists.)

Colin Moore & John Brown, *Community Versus Crime,* Bedford Square Press, 1981.

National Association for the Care and Resettlement of Offenders (NACRO), *The Use of Imprisonment – Some Facts and Figures.* (169 Clapham Road, London SW9 0PV.)

Gerry Northam, *Shooting in the Dark: Riot Police in Britain,* Faber & Faber, 1988.

Lord Windlesham, *Responses to Crime,* OUP, 1988.

I am grateful to Dr Ken Pease for useful comments on this chapter.

17 *Geoffrey Lee*

Nuclear weapons and the peace movement

This chapter examines the emergence of nuclear weapons as a key issue in British politics during the 1980s. Taking place against radical changes in East–West relations, the chapter will look at the effects in Britain in two major phases – the increasing awareness of and protest against nuclear weapons up to 1985 and then the abatement of that protest during and after 1986, together with the political implications.

Awareness and protest

(1) *The context*
Deteriorating East–West relations   The 1977 proposal by the Carter administration to deploy the neutron bomb in Europe was an important one – the concept of a weapon that emitted more radiation to kill people, without as much damage to buildings through blast, seemed immoral to many and focused attention upon shifts in Pentagon strategy which appeared to bring nuclear war nearer. However, the strongly negative European response to the neutron bomb (one million signatures to a Dutch petition) led to its deferment and an important success for the protesters.

The election of Ronald Reagan in 1980 produced further alarm. Committed to increased defence spending and viewing Soviet Communism as 'evil', Reagan had repudiated Carter's SALT II (Strategic Arms Limitation Treaty). In 1981 he spoke of his belief in the possibility of a 'limited' nuclear war in Europe, and Secretary of State Haig mentioned the possibility of dropping a 'demonstration' bomb on the East. The deployment of Cruise and Pershing II missiles, agreed in 1979, seemed to make war a more feasible option and in 1982 the *New York Times* released US Defense Department plans for a protracted nuclear war.

In March 1983 President Reagan issued his 'Star Wars' directive to scientists for the development of laser defence systems – a potentially seriously destabilising measure – and during the year the Soviets broke off three sets of arms limitations talks – on intermediate range nuclear weapons, the Strategic Arms Reduction Talks (START) and on accidental nuclear war. Threatening to 'launch on warning', the USSR increased its stocks of SS20 and SS22 missiles and moved the latter into East Germany and Czechoslovakia – in range of Britain. The Bradford University School of Peace Studies predicted a doubling of arsenals within ten years. In 1980 BBC Radio announced an opinion poll showing that 40% of respondents thought nuclear war likely within ten years.

While distrust of the Soviet Union remained high in the light of its policy towards Poland and invasion of Afghanistan, more people questioned the US relationship. Plans for a new nuclear war bunker (1982) and the possible deployment of Minuteman missiles in Britain (1984) were revealed, and a central issue became the control of Cruise missiles based in Britain. A 1983 poll showed 73% distrusting American guarantees of joint control of Cruise missiles (*Sunday Times*, 30 October 1983), and a 1986/87 pan-European Marplan study showed that 35% approved of American nuclear weapons being based in the UK while 56% disapproved. More preferred a European or independent system to maintaining existing military links with the USA, and there was less belief in the Americans' commitment to multilateral nuclear disarmament than in that of the Soviet Union (57% and 52% 'no' answers respectively) (*Guardian*, 16 February 1987).

(2) *New weapons*

(a) *Accuracy* Not only was the number of weapons increasing in the late 1970s and early 1980s, but they were undergoing a technological change: Pershing II and Cruise missiles were deemed to be highly accurate. Cruise, SS20s and the MX system (an American plan to install 200 intercontinental ballistic missiles under 6,000 square miles of desert) were all mobile systems. Mobility and accuracy against military targets were said by many experts to increase the likelihood of use.

(b) *Accidents* The Americans estimated that thirty-six accidents involving nuclear weapons had occurred since 1945, including the very near explosion of a twenty-four megaton bomb in North Carolina and the contamination of Palormares, Spain, after three ten-megaton bombs were dislodged in 1966. Between 1950 and 1976, sixteen submarine collisions occurred in Soviet waters.

Technological advances have not improved the risks – it was disclosed that the USA Airforce Defense computer, NORAD, produced two false alarms every three days by 1983. In August 1984 the US Navy recalled a third of its Trident missiles because of faulty microchip mechanisms. During one year, 3,647 people with access to nuclear weapons were moved due to alcoholism, drug abuse, mental illness or indiscipline (US Congressional evidence). And in May 1986 the US Navy admitted to 628 incidents and two accidents involving nuclear weapons over twenty years, including submarines running aground near Gibraltar and in the Irish Sea. A Yankee class submarine sank in the Atlantic after one of its missiles exploded. Fears that exercises were turning into real launches had led to desperate switching off of the power supply in Kansas in 1980 and four years later, to the crew of a minuteman missile in Wyoming parking an armoured car on top of a silo.

Nearer home, a nuclear warhead transporter skidded in icy conditions in Wiltshire in 1987 and turned over in a field.

(c) *Cost* Critics have claimed that defence spending in the UK, which exceeds expenditure on the NHS, has a distorting effect on the economy. Besides the 10% of government income, it takes 60% of technological resources – the Ministry of Defence alone employs 25,000 of our best scientists and engineers. Within the defence budget it is claimed that the nuclear deterrence has a distorting effect on conventional defence. In October 1988 the Labour party claimed that the latter had fallen by 8% over five years and would drop a further 10% by 1992 as Trident spending rose.

Trident has been particularly singled out for criticism, as original costings soon doubled to 10–12 billion. CND translate this into £200 for every man, woman and child, or the yearly food bill for seven million families. Alternatively, for the price of two Trident submarines half the Third World could be given primary schools and teacher training facilities. (Kennard and Sissons).

(3) *Opposition to nuclear weapons*
Wider movements
Peace groups in Britain have been assisted by being part of a wider opposition, which did not exist during the 1960s period of CND activity.

(a) *European Nuclear Disarmament (END)* END was formed in 1980 when it was decided that national protest was insufficient. The culmination came in October 1981 with rallies of 250,000 in Bonn, 100,000 in Oslo, 50,000 in Paris, 50,000 in Potsdam (E. Germany), 80,000 in Helsinki, 120,000 in Brussels, 150,000 in London and a similar number in Rome. The demonstration in Amsterdam brought out 500,000 (one-thirtieth of the Dutch population). END's role is one of publication and communication – linking groups as diverse as the Campaign Against Military Bases in Iceland, West German Greens, Dutch Interchurch Peace Council and Italian Eurocommunists.
   In July 1982 END organised its convention to press for a nuclear-free western Europe. Three months later two million protested against Cruise and Pershing II missiles.

(b) *US Freeze Campaign* Gaining publicity and strength at the same time was the American Nuclear Weapons Freeze Campaign. Only months before, American protest was confined to a few groups such as SANE and Pax Christi; by 1982 60% of US voters, the bishops and the House of Representatives supported the 'freeze'. In November 1985 a Freeze Campaign was launched in the UK, with the support of senior politicians from all parties.

(c) *Environmentalists* The rise of Friends of the Earth, Greenpeace and the Ecology Party in the early 1970s coincided with a lull in CND activity. Indeed, the latter had favoured 'atoms for peace' in its early days. Gradually their aims began to coincide as the effects of radiation were explored. *Non-Nuclear Futures* by Amory Lovins, and the Flowers Report of 1976 drew attention to the link between civil and military nuclear processes. The 1977 Windscale inquiry and the 1977 Anti-Nuclear Campaign cemented the alliance. CND and FOE give mutual support at demonstrations, and in 1984 jointly campaigned against the Sizewell nuclear reactor.

British activities

(1) *Information*
Information about preparations for and the effects of nuclear war is the lifeblood of the peace movement. Governments' habit of secrecy often stores up trouble – such as the revelation in 1980 that a secret £1 billion modernisation of Polaris missiles (Chevaline) had been undertaken.

Perhaps the most effective impact came through film. In 1976 CND's membership increased as it staged 'All Against the Bomb' on BBC 2's *Open Door* programme. In the same year they purchased *The War Game,* commissioned by the BBC in 1965 but not shown for fear of 'irrational reaction'; this still powerful film was shown to 20,000 people over the next two years. Dramas have included *The Day After,* seen by 70 million in America and 15 million in Britain, and *Threads,* a two-hour British production showing the devastation of Sheffield and ensuing horrors. On the documentary side were *QED: A Guide to Armageddon* (July 1982), *The Truth Game* (ITV October 1982) and *Panorama*'s screening of the official pre-war film for the public (spring 1982).

The Civil Defence pamplet 'Protect and Survive' was a restricted document but was released for sale by the Home Office. Its practical DIY advice on building a shelter includes the removal of potentially incendiary newspapers and the disposal of dead members of the family. By 1982 E. P. Thompson's riposte *Protest and Survive* had sold over 100,000 copies.

The Home Office also provided predictions of the holocaust through its civil defence exercises – Operation Square Leg envisaged twenty-nine million dead, and Hard Rock was said to have been scaled down to an unrealistic three million to preserve morale. CND sold the maps of devastation. In November 1983 a copy of the computerised training course on post-nuclear Britain 'reached' the *Sunday Times.*

The GLC commissioned a £475,000 study which reported in March 1986 after 2 years that in an attack on London one-third would try to leave amid panic, food-hoarding and desertion of jobs.

The British Medical Association assisted the process by conducting a two-year study into the effect of nuclear war and reported, in

March 1983, that even one bomb would overwhelm the health service and any more would mean chaos. Doctors then demanded non-co-operation with government plans, and a Royal College of Nursing report saw no role for their own service. Plans to store medical supplies, issue a new NHS war plan and the stockpiling of 56 million ration cards showed the Government was pressing on regardless.

The BMA revised upwards by 10 million to 26 million those who would be killed and it was revealed that not merely would the ill be left to die as drugs ran out but that doctors would select who should die – giving preference to groups such as mechanics, nurses and market gardeners. These detailed but unreal images raised awareness. Many physicians thought planning a waste of time – in March 1986 45% of health authorities had not started and 10% did not intend to.

(2) *The tactics and organisation of the peace movement*
(a) *Resources* Their most important asset is expertise. Like the 1960s CND, the 1980s version is predominantly middle class and professional. The main developments seem to have been the greater involvement of women and the perception of disarmament as a moral rather than a political issue.

The rise of the CND was phenomenal – a tenfold increase in membership between 1980–2. By 1983 there were 54,000 national members, joining for £9, with some 250,000 members attached to local groups, plus Youth CND. The turnover of CND's thirteen booklets was £250,000 (half its income), it sold a million badges (at 20p) in two years, and sales of stickers and necklaces increased at 50% per month. Its journal, *Sanity,* with a print order of 60,000 and monthly advertising worth £4,000 improved in quality. Expanding into three buildings and employing twenty-eight full-time staff, CND clearly had the financial resources it required (statistics: *Observer,* 20 June 1982).

The peace movement can call on respected names to give credibility to its politics – citing Lord Mountbatten on the effects of a nuclear war, Lords Carver and Zuckerman on 'limited' nuclear war, and the supreme Allied Commander, General Rogers on conventional containment. Within its own ranks are credible and renowned authorities: Scientists Against Nuclear Arms (SANA), Christian CND and even 2 Generals for Peace. The involvement of personalities such as actresses also attracts publicity.

(b) *Diversification*   As already indicated, there are several strands to the 1980s peace movement. National CND itself expanded its Council in 1981 to include five delegates from each region and there is representation there for specialist sections – Youth, Christian, Trade Union, Student, Labour, Liberal and Green CND. 1,000 organisations including trade unions such as NALGO, NUPE, TGWU and ASTMS, are affiliated. But much of the strength of CND is at local levels where 'Against the Missiles' groups organise and act. This combination meant CND was stronger than the 1960s version, which was overtly dependent on key personalities, and had no central organisation until 1966, envisaging only a short campaign.

Other parallel groups include the Greenham Common peace camp women, who retain their independence from CND, and the local authorities who had declared their areas 'nuclear-free zones'. Seventy-three local councils attended a meeting in Manchester in 1982, and to date 200 zones have been declared.

(c) *Tactics*
– *Arguments:* as in the case of cost, the peace movement has been adept at enabling people to understand the scope of the subject. Hence a Trident submarine is described as being able to reduce 160 cities to the state of Hiroshima, and that the UK's Trident force could produce 7,000 Hiroshimas. Accepting that the electorate was not yet persuaded on nuclear disarmament or leaving NATO, CND concentred on softer targets – Trident and Cruise. In 1982 63% disapproved of Trident (ORC, *The Guardian,* 27 February 1982) and in September 1985 in a Gallup poll this was still 64%. Three-quarters of a December 1985 Gallup poll sample disagreed with a NATO strategy of first nuclear use, and 60% said Britain should leave if there was no change.
– *Marches and demonstrations* – in June 1982, for example, 250,000 people attended a Hyde Park rally and two years later CND filled Trafalgar Square and blocked off the US Embassy in Grosvenor Square in a disciplined first attempt at non-violent direct action. Conscious of the criticism of 1960s CND for 'Trafalgar Squarism', other approaches to publicity have been followed. In 1983 a human chain, over fourteen miles long, of 70,000 people linked three nuclear establishments, and the following year attention was switched to the Barrow warship yards. In October 1985 CND could still organise a march of 100,000 people in Hyde Park and form a

peace symbol from 20,000 people.

– *Non-violent direct action (NVDA)* – often involving civil disobedience, such action has an honourable tradition which includes Gan-
dhi and Luther King. The division between constitutional CND and
the Direct Action Committee (DAC) and then the Committee of 100
in the 1960s (which organised sit-down protests at bases and in
Trafalgar Square) cost the movement dearly. The issue did not pose
the same problem in the 1980's, as CND accepted NVDA in 1981 and
reaffirmed the decision in 1982 and 1984 with a call for a four-year
guerrilla campaign at Molesworth. It is left to members to decide to
take such action and whether to agree to be 'bound over' or go to
gaol. A Legal Advice Pack was produced in 1984 and seminars held.
The Greenham women conducted several operations – climbing
silos, cutting the perimeter fence and camping inside. The arrival of
Cruise in November 1983 led to 141 arrests at Greenham and 300 at
the House of Commons. The Americans conceded two years later
that cruise deployment had been disrupted by protests. One of the
most remarkable examples of direct action was revealed in November 1988 – that two nuclear disarmers had 'sprung' soviet spy George
Blake from prison 22 years earlier and smuggled him to East
Germany.

– *Emotional protest* – The women of the peace camps believe they
have added a new emotional dimension to the campaign, rejecting
the rational, 'male' game of bargaining over numbers and types of
missiles. There can be no doubting the powerful symbolism of toys,
clothes and pictures of children hung on the Greenham wire in 1982.

– *Local campaigns* – An action manual, 'What do we do after we've
shown *The War Game?*', provides CND members with detailed
advice on the mechanics of organising meetings, finding information,
writing to the press and on the psychology of attitude change.

– *The law* – nuclear-free-zone councils have tried to use the law and
its loopholes to stop the transportation of nuclear materials and delay
planning applications, and they achieved a notable success in 1982
when their non-co-operation with operation Hard Rock forced the
cancellation of the civil defence exercise. And just as the Committee
of 100 wanted to 'fill the gaols', there were fears that the Greenham
arrests would clog both courts and gaols. The Court of Appeal
restored their right to vote in Newbury, and in 1988 the Crown Court
ruled as illegal the Ministry of Defence regulations used to secure
over 1,000 convictions because they ignored medieval rights of

residents. It was further revealed that the MOD buildings had been
built on common land without permission and criminal damage cases
were postponed. MOD attempts to extricate itself from legal
entanglements and delay by abolishing the rights simply extended
the process. CND Cymru won a decision of maladministration
against Carmarthen district council from the Ombudsman for late
granting of planning permission and huge overspending on a nuclear
emergency control centre.

CND did not win its case against MI5's telephone tapping of its
vice-president in 1987 but claimed to have established the right to
seek redress and to have removed the government's ability to block
reviews of alleged abuses by citing national security.

(3) *Party politics*
(a) *Labour*   Canon Collins and the early leaders of CND had made
winning the Labour Party to unilateral nuclear disarmament a key
objective and this they achieved at the 1960 conference. The refusal
of Labour's leaders to accept it, the reversal in 1961 with Gaitskill's
opposition and subsequent acceptance in government of Polaris all
precipitated CND's decline. Labour's adherence to unilateralism in
1980, 1981, 1982 and at the 1983 general election was a major fillip
for the peace movement. The party and CND keep a distance from
each other for their mutual advantage, however: CND's appeal has
to be broader to persuade people who would vote on the centre right
and it has to be more radical to keep up the momentum. It suits
Labour that CND goes further in wishing to leave NATO, in wishing
to close all 131 US bases, and in wanting to divert nuclear weapons
expenditure away from defence altogether.

Labour's 1984 'Defence and security for Britain' envisaged the
UK disposing of its own nuclear weapons and of US nuclear bases,
strengthening conventional forces and campaigning for 'no first use'
and then abolition of nuclear weapons in NATO. In May 1985 Mr
Gorbachev offered Neil Kinnock to reduce weapons on a one-by-
one basis and not target Britain if all nuclear weapons were
removed.

By mid-1986 Labour was committed to negotiating the removal of
US nuclear bases within a month of taking office, a position only
strengthened by the use of US bases to bomb Libya. It believed that
by abolishing Trident it could save up to £2 billion a year by 1991 and
by reducing commitments outside NATO (such as the Falklands) it

could restructure around 15% of the defence budget into conventional weapons. In the wake of Chernobyl the main 'nuclear' problem for Labour centred on demands that all such power stations should be phased out.

(b) *The Alliance*   The division within the Liberal Party which existed at the time of the 1983 general election was continued in 1984 and 1986 when the Assembly again voted against the leadership. Both the Liberals and SDP opposed buying Trident. Dr Owen's views on limiting the number of CND-supporting Alliance candidates did not go down with Liberals, suspicious of attempts to impose a freeze policy on them. Most serious was the attempt by senior SDP spokesmen to replace Polaris by sea-launched cruise missiles. First suggested by John Cartwright in November 1984, the issue developed into a major row by June 1986 with Dr Owen at odds with the Liberals and SDP President Shirley Williams, who accused him of selected reading of a policy document. A Gallup poll showed 51% of SDP candidates favouring replacement, while 83% of Liberal candidates were against.

The SDP–Liberal commission on defence reported in June 1986 after eight months: it stressed commitment to Nato, joint European policies, cancelling Trident and keeping Polaris for ten years, a more active UK role in disarmament and for a comprehensive test-ban treaty. Party leaders then had to contend with Dr Owen openly demanding a replacement for Polaris and CND–Liberals questioning the credentials of those producing this 'fudge'. The leadership of the two parties then narrowed the issue to one of timing on Polaris, and David Steel sought to remove divisive references to previous policy at the Liberal assembly. The rank and file there rebuffed this and voted for a non-nuclear defence. It took until the end of the year for the leadership to agree a settlement – to postpone a choice of minimum deterrent until after the election.

(c) *The Conservative party*   The government was committed to the deployment of Trident and cruise, seeking multilateral cuts while continuing tests, and reaffirmed support of NATO and US bases. Opinion polls showed defence to be a big vote-winner for the Conservatives, with a thirteen-point lead over Labour, and only 46% of Alliance voters preferring their own policies to 24% trusting the government more (Marplan, *Guardian*, 12 December 1986).

(d) *Others*   The ecologists and nationalists similarly support unilateralism and indeed the SNP are closest to CND policy in wishing
also to leave NATO. CND itself voted against adopting party status
in 1980 and kept its own members active and interested prior to the
1983 general election by conducting a Peace Canvass. At the election
itself they took legal advice about the Representation of the Peoples
Act 1948 and then, to the anger of Conservatives, they encouraged
voters – especially in marginal constituencies – to vote only for
candidates opposed to nuclear weapons. Such an attempt to bring a
'sanction' to bear is rare for a cause group (in contrast to an interest
group with economic power such as a trade union). CND also tried to
use the 1983 European elections as a referendum on Cruise and
Pershing.

Disarmament and decline

(1) *The context*
Improving East–West relations   Mr Gorbachev began to move the
Soviet's position in January 1986 by accepting the zero reduction on
intermediate-range weapons. His conditions on British and French
nuclear weapons, Star Wars, and linkage to strategic talks were then
dropped and obstacles such as verification and Pershing 1A warheads
were removed. The INF agreement was signed as both peace cam-
paigners and 'show-of-force' deployment advocates claimed the
credit.

Meanwhile the strategic arms (START) talks continued in Geneva
and Mr Gorbachev persistently seized the initiative by proposing the
abolition of short-range weapons and, in 1988, cutting Soviet conventional forces by ½ million. Conditions imposed by NATO and by
the Conservative government in Britain were undermined and the
changes were cautiously welcomed. With a nuclear-free Europe
beckoning there was every chance that the Soviets would require
Trident to be phased out through the START process.

Opinion in Europe had shifted. On the one hand there had been a
move to the right on defence in countries such as Spain, Greece and
Belgium, removing exploitatable divisions. And attitudes to the
superpowers altered as the USSR pressed disarmament to foster
economic reform and as the US became a potential trading adversary
to an integrated Europe – likely to insist on Europeans shouldering
more of their own defence burden.

(2) *Counter-measures*

(a) *Opposition* Having been taken off guard by the anti-nuclear movement, the Conservative government gradually organised opposition. Elements of the public relations campaign included:

(i) *Ministers' speeches* Speeches and their reproduction in the press emphasised the Soviet nuclear capability and programme, that Soviet intentions had to be doubted and that nuclear weapons had preserved peace in Europe for some forty years.

President Reagan's initiative of November 1981 of a 'zero option', whereby deployment of Cruise and Pershing II missiles would be halted if SS missiles were removed, was seized upon as proof of NATO's good intentions. The Falklands war was said to demonstrate a need to deter aggressors. NATO was sufficiently disturbed by 1981 to try to co-ordinate its response to the peace movements.

(ii) *Counter-information* In November 1981 the Conservative party issued a briefing document on the advantages of multilateral disarmament. The Ministry of Defence commissioned a twenty-minute film at a cost of £70,000, called *The Peace Game* which emphasised Soviet expansion. And a pamphlet called 'The balanced view' was prepared by the Central Office of Information for distribution to schools and colleges. It warned against neglecting defences, 'as in the 1930s'. In 1982 the Foreign Office had published a leaflet 'The Nuclear Debate' in response to requests from organisations for an alternative view to nuclear disarmament. By July 1984 the Home Office was issuing more credible documents on nuclear and chemical attacks.

(iii) *Bolstering civil defence* The government sought to re-establish the credibility of civil defence in the aftermath of the abandonment of Hard Rock 82. It was argued that peacetime emergencies as well as conventional attacks warranted civil defence, and a free Home Office pamphlet warned that nuclear fallout from a war elsewhere could spread over Britain. Even in a nuclear war involving the UK, it was asserted that millions could be saved by preparation.

To assuage public opinion the government let it be known in January 1983 that the Home Office was working on radical plans to evacuate twelve million people or more from high-risk areas in the event of war, conceding that the previous 'stay put' policy lacked credibility. At the same time the government sought to exercise its authority and in October 1983 new regulations were issued obliging local authorities to carry out civil defence duties under the 1948 Civil

Defence Act, and providing 100% grants for communications, training and expenses. In November 1984 the Home Office threatened to send in its own experts and bill ratepayers, and in 1986 it began a three-year programme with six-monthly targets to ensure twenty communication centres were built every year – or councils would face the loss of grant.

(iv) *Direct criticism and action* A reason advanced for the appointment of Michael Heseltine as Secretary of State for Defence in 1983 was his ability to mount a vigorous campaign for Trident and Cruise missiles. He established a unit, Defence Secretariat 19, to combat the rise of CND. In one of the first speeches, unilateralists were described as 'woolly people in woolly hats' (*Guardian,* 3 March 1983). CND were soon claiming that a 'smear' campaign was being waged against them. As early as 1981 Conservatives had said that he KGB had spent 100 million dollars on its anti-neutron bomb campaign in the West. It was asserted that Soviet Spetsnaz had infiltrated the Greenham camps (*Jane's Defence Weekly,* 1986). In April 1983 Michael Heseltine wrote to all Conservative MPs and candidates in marginal seats setting out biographical details of CND's national council and naming thirty officials said to be past or present Labour or Communist party members. In the High Court in 1986 it was claimed that MI5 had tapped telephones to provide information which was passed to DS19 and that Mr Heseltine had then leaked it to the *Daily Telegraph.* He had to deny that he had put pressure on Cardinal Home to remove Monsignor Bruce Kent from the general secretaryship of CND and confine him to church duties. Similarly the Lord Chancellor had to deny that there was a direct ban on CND members being magistrates, after a dismissed magistrate was not allowed to take her case to the High Court. Government scientists were told in 1986 that they would not be promoted unless they worked on the Trident missile.

The strong new line could be seen when the Ministry of Defence resorted to a nineteenth-century statute to draft a new by-law making trespass a criminal offence. Learning from Greenham, 1,500 Royal engineers, 600 MOD police and 900 civilian police (supported by Mr Heseltine in a flak jacket) evicted the 150 Rainbow villagers at Molesworth without warning over Easter 1985. Local passes were issued and people stopped twenty miles away, as in the miners' strike. Meanwhile the MOD tried to buy land at Greenham to close the peace camp.

Citizens' Advice Bureaux suffered a cut to their grant partly because of 'inappropriate political activity' (*Sunday Times,* 10 April 1983) and membership of CND was said to be a relevant factor during positive vetting of civil servants for sensitive posts. Besides open criticism, the government continued to use what CND describe as 'repressive tolerance', treating them as a temporary, misguided phenomenon – as an outsider, uninfluential pressure group.

(v) *Secrecy* The authorities continued to withhold information where possible – a booklet on advice to farmers after a nuclear war was not put on sale at the time of the general election of 1983. In 1983 Mr Heseltine persuaded Caspar Weinberger, US Defence Secretary, to withdraw from a televised debate with Thompson because of the impending election and, it was claimed, fear of embarrassment. The full power of the state, through the Official Secrets Act, was used against Sarah Tisdall – a civil servant goaled for six months for leaking Cruise arrival information to the *Guardian* in March 1984. Many described the story as merely politically embarrassing to the government and the sentence as harsh. The revised 'Protect and Survive' was not published in 1986 as previously planned, for fear of ridicule.

(b) *Pressure groups* By definition, the main problem facing pressure groups opposing the policies of the peace movement is not to appear to be pro-war. It is not therefore surprising that countervailing groups have been slow to emerge and flourish, but having done so they were able to go further in their criticisms and language. They included the British Atlantic committee, Council of Arms Control, Committee for Peace with Freedom, Campaign for Defence and Multilateral Disarmament and the Coalition for Peace Through Security. The Coalition was perhaps the most aggressive – it organised a secret briefing of political, military and business figures on lobbying, mailing and opinion-forming techniques. CND claimed that spies had come to CND offices under false pretences, and some had joined CND. CND lost a High Court copyright action against the Coalition for parodying its symbol with a hammer and sickle. Most visible was the group Women for Defence, founded by Lady Olga Maitland in 1983. While some of its activities, such as an attempted Trafalgar Square rally and visit to the 1984 Labour party Conference were not successes, they did attract considerable publicity.

(c) *Local authorities* Far from being nuclear-free zones, some Conservative-controlled councils restricted peace-group activities, such as meetings and exhibitions. Conservative researchers working for Norman Tebbit gave assistance by detailing the cost of nuclear-free zones – £10 million to co-ordinate, £½ million per year in Greater Manchester and £¼ million for Sheffield's 'peace budget'. Newbury District Council persistently tried to evict the Greenham women, who by September 1983 were said to have cost the public £2 million, mainly through police costs.

(d) *Individuals* Prominent critics included papal envoy Archbishop Helm who rebuked Mgr Kent and disarmers as 'useful idiots' for the Russians. There were also acts of violence by individuals and groups against peace groups and offices, and local interest groups, such as Ratepayers Against Greenham Encampments, were formed.

(e) *The press* News coverage, particularly of the Greenham women, has not always been favourable. It has dwelt upon the squalor of the camps, with pictures of punks, stories of a 'starving baby' and a baby born at Greenham, of families abandoned, 'scrounging' social security payments, and 'strident feminists', 'burly lesbians' (*Sun,* 14 December 1982). Conflict among the different groupings was similarly reported in 1987.

(3) *Internal problems in the peace movement*
(a) *Digression* The 1960s CND turned its attention to the Vietnam war and in doing so weakened its message and lost the support of pacifists. There was a similar attempt in 1981 to line the movement up against the government in a 'Jobs Not Bombs' campaign. By 1985 there were divisions in CND between the END supporters who favoured a cross-party coalition for non-nuclear defence, and who also wanted stronger support for Nicaragua, and those who oppose NATO membership – concentrated in the Youth, Green and Labour organisations. Feeling that CND had lost its way – towards education and away from resistance – 500 'activists' met in Manchester in 1985. By this time Rainbow Villagers, Peace Convoy hippies and broader teenage movements were involved, with the Greenham Women producing literature called 'Widening the Web' on Namibia, prison conditions, South Africa, sexism and inner cities. By 1987 the 'yellow gate' group at Greenham, organised from the King's Cross Women's

Centre, were accusing other groups at the camp and CND of being racist. Their leader, Ms Wilmette Brown, was elected on to CND's council – a former member of the Black Panther Party, she claimed her purpose was 'to integrate anti-racism, anti-sexism and anti-poverty into the mainstream of CND' (*Guardian*, 22 November 1987).

Less directly damaging was the overlap with the concern over civil nuclear power and links with environmentalists. The Chernobyl disaster of 1986, the admission during that year that civil plutonium had been used by the military and concern over waste dumps – all focused attention on the wider issue. In 1987 CND's Hyde Park demonstration was a joint one with Friends of the Earth.

(b) *Infiltration* As a successful vehicle, entryists try to take control of its direction. Just as the Anti-Nazi League had to deal with members of the Socialist Workers' Party and Socialist League, so CND in 1981 and 1982 saw attempts to link it to wider struggles, industrial action and more public opposition to NATO. In August 1983, to combat this, all the officers and executive committee of its Youth Section were suspended. During the 1985 Easter weekend, Class War, an anarchist group, infiltrated the demonstrations at Molesworth. The problems at Greenham have been noted above. These lead to:

(c) *Alienation* Non-violent direct action runs the risk of alientating both peace movement members and the general public. CND had had problems in 1984 with a splinter group, Peace Anonymous, which organised a 'die-in' at the Cenotaph and wanted to blockade the Lancaster House Summit of May 1984.

(d) *Public opinion* A fundamental problem is that the majority of British people are not yet ready to abandon nuclear weapons, nor to ensure greater 'safety' by leaving the nuclear alliance, NATO. In 1981 23% wished to abandon nuclear weapons, 56% to maintain them and 18% improve them (*Guardian*/Marplan, 22 April 1981). In October 1983 16% wished to abandon, 63% to maintain, and 14% to improve (*Guardian*/Marplan, 22 October 1983). To try to change this CND launched a campaign in 1986 to convince the public of the futility of nuclear weapons in clear language. But an October 1985 Gallup poll showed a first-ever majority of 52% to 35% for keeping cruise missiles, and in November 1988 almost 50% of Britons were shown to be in favour of the Trident programme, with 39% against (Gallup poll, *Independent,* 19 November 1988).

The pan-European Marplan survey of 1987 referred to earlier showed the Britons most determined to hang on to nuclear weapons, even more than France – 61% and 57% respectively. However, the minority for abolition had risen to 34% from the 21% in 1983 – in Germany and Italy the figures were 57% and 79%.

(e) *Momentum*   In view of government indifference and public implacability there is a danger that members lessen their efforts or accept partial successes. This befell CND in its early phase as fatigue set in and the 1963 Test Ban Treaty was agreed.

By 1985 the superpowers were talking again and attention had switched to other issues, such as famine in Africa. While incidents could still revive interest, e.g., the Chernobyl disaster, US abandonment of SALT 2 in May 1986 or their raids on Libya the month before, the pre-cruise intensity could not be maintained. The Star Wars issue seemed too complex and to worry governments more. Significantly the April 1988 Aldermaston March was not merely against Trident and 'nukes' but 'No Nostalgia'.

The government learned that the best way to deal with the campaign was to ignore it. Through acting against the peace movement in a robust manner the government had had some success but it also raised some sensitive issues. The politically controversial work of the ministry's special unit raised doubts about civil servants' involvement – and the unit was dismantled in September 1983. By impugning the motives and delving into the background of CND leaders, ministers left themselves open to counter-charges of factual errors and unworthy manoeuvres. The central dilemma was inescapable – by responding to and criticising the peace movement, the government gave it what it wanted most – publicity.

On the other hand, when CND had made their point about knowing cruise missile routes and had won planning permission to build an £88 million shelter for the people of Hertford – the gestures and publicity ended there. The objective of becoming an influencer of governments was a long way away – the MOD threatened to withdraw information from parliamentary committees if even Labour MPs with CND sympathies were on them.

(4) *Party politics: The 1987 general election and its aftermath*

(a) The government gave prominence to nuclear deterrence in the defence estimate paper of May 1987, in contrast to the low profile given previously. The first section contained a justification for retention, followed by sections questioning the dependability of the Soviet leadership, a description of Nato's nuclear strategy, the 'essential' role of the US forces in Europe, and the 'minimum' level of Tridents' capability. The nuclear deterrent was costed at £882 million out of a total defence budget of £18,782 million – the fourth highest in Nato.

(b) *Labour* Neil Kinnock launched Labour's non-nuclear defence manifesto, 'Modern Britain in a Modern World', in December 1986 – firm in its resolve to dispose of Britain's weapons and remove American nuclear bases within the lifetime of a Parliament. The policy was announced early to enable persuasion to begin early and avoid the disunity of the 1983 election. Claiming that Trident would lead to a 30% reduction on spending on new defence equipment, Labour promised to restore a fifty-warship navy, re-equipping the army in Germany and commissioning a new European fighter aircraft.

Neil Kinnock embarked on a week-long visit to the USA as the policy was launched – to persuade and to be seen to persuade the Americans of its viability. It came under an immediate attack – by General Rogers, Nato supreme commander, by Nato defence ministers, the US Secretary of State, Norman Tebbit (who staged a visit to New York) and by the Prime Minister, who accused Labour of abandoning the bipartisan policy of their predecessors.

Labour's policy came under fire during the second week of the general election of May 1987. A story in the *Sunday Telegraph* that General Rogers was advising a withdrawal of US troops from Britain if Labour was elected was denied but gave rise to speculation of warning shots and destabilisation. Neil Kinnock's statement on television that a Soviet occupation would be 'untenable' gave rise to Conservative attacks of 'surrender', 'guerillas against occupation, after 900 years', 'refugees in our own land'. The Alliance, setting aside their position of being above this and bringing forward their assault by three days, spoke of a 'Dad's Army' and referred to Soviet atrocities. The Tory – inclined newspapers wrote of 'White flags' (*Express* and *Mail*) and 'Brother Kinnock says nowt because he knows nowt' (*Sun*). There were few analyses either of the problems of Labour's pro-Nato/anti-nuclear policy or the changing defence picture. Only the Oxford Research Group argued that the Americans would not risk opposition, because their intelligence-gathering facilities were more important.

The issue continued seriously to damage Labour after its defeat. Signs in May 1988 that Neil Kinnock was modifying unilateralism in a new situation of not needing to give 'something for nothing' led to opposition from the TGWU and disruption at the party conference, the resignation of defence spokesman Denzil Davies and disillusion on both left and right as belated denials of a policy change were made. Amid doubts about his leadership Neil Kinnock indicated that constituencies could be balloted on the issue and the proposed policy review debate began to detail the other options to scrapping Trident – putting it into the strategic arms negotiations, freeze it at the level of Polaris, look for a reciprocal deal with the USSR for cancellation, keep Polaris and freeze Trident spending, count Trident as American, or develop a minimum deterrent with France. Those pressing for change did not believe Labour was electable unless unilateralism was abjured, while the moral principle of opposition to nuclear weapons supervened for others.

(c) *The Alliance* The government was also able to pick at the 'brittle alliance' between Dr Owen and the Liberals – with a manifesto commitment to scrap Trident, they had no alternative and could not rule it out.

These policy differences featured after the election as the SDP split with the formation of the new Social and Liberal Democrat Party. The latter then began to modify its stance too as Paddy Ashdown indicated acceptance of Trident in September 1988. With its members divided on the issue for the same reasons as the Labour party, it began to review the same options of restricted firepower and European co-operation.

(d) *CND* CND was not active during the election campaign itself, having done its lobbying in fifty marginals beforehand.

Having claimed credit for forcing the pace of disarmament, it turned its attention to modifying its image. Employing an advertising agency, Creative Sales, it was decided to give less prominence to its logo – its connotations of perpetual radical protest were felt to be counter-productive. The times had changed.

Reading

Central Office of Information, *The Nuclear Debate*, 1982.

H. Clark, S. Crown, A. McKee & H. MacPherson, *Preparing for Non-Violent Direct Action, Peace News*/CND 1984.

A. Cook & G. Kirk, *Greenham Women Everywhere*, Pluto, 1984.

P. Kennard & R. Sissons, *No to Nuclear Weapons*, Pluto, 1981.

J. Minnion & P. Bolsover (eds.), *The CND Story*, Allison & Busby, 1983.

Andrée Shepherd, 'The politics of nuclear protest in the fifties: CND and the early New Left', *Teaching Politics*, September 1986, pp. 476–91.

P. Webber, G. Wilkinson & B. Rubin, *Crisis Over Cruise*, Penguin, 1983.

Chronology of development

1945 Only 21% of British disapprove of use of A-bomb against Japan.

1950 British Peace Committee claim one million signatures on Stockholm Peace Appeal.

1952 Sit-down protest at War Office and Aldermaston.

1954 H-Bomb National Campaign founded. Coventry City Council disbands Civil Defence Committee as 'waste of time and public money'.

1957 Protest boat sails to stop H-Bomb test at Christmas Island. Labour Party H-Bomb Campaign Committee rallies 4,000 in Trafalgar Square.
National Committee for Abolition of Nuclear Weapons Tests transfers funds to new body – CND. Members: Bertrand Russell, Sir Julian Huxley, Michael Foot, James Cameron, J. B. Priestley.

1958 Britain agrees to four US Thor missiles bases in E. Anglia. Gallup poll – 80% expect half UK population to die in war. Gerald Holtom invents symbol ☮. Aldermaston march.

1959 Aldermaston march – 20,000 in Trafalgar Square.
Direct Action Committee organises civil disobedience at bases.
Voter's Veto in election campaign.
Support risen from 25% to 30%.

1960 Committee of 100, led by Russell, breaks away from CND.

1961 Sit-downs and arrests – 1,314 in Trafalgar Square.
Arrest at bases, including 100 at Greenham Common.
450 CND groups; *Sanity* – 45,000 circulation.

1962 150,000 in Hyde Park Rally.
Cuban missile crisis.

1963 'Spies for peace' reveal bunkers and HQs.
Partial Test Ban Treaty signed.

1970 Festival of Life in Hackney attracts 20,000.

1973 Weeks of action in Scotland.
Labour Party Conference votes for unilateralism.

1978 Neutron bomb petition.

1980 Chevaline modernisation of Polaris revealed.
Panorama shows 'Protect and Survive'.
Manchester City Council declares nuclear free zone.
80,000 at Trafalgar Square rally.

1981 Women for Life on Earth march from S. Wales to Greenham
Common.
42 nuclear free zones.
CND membership 30,000.
Demonstration in European cities by over one million people.
President Reagan offers zero option.

1982 140 nuclear free zones.
Operation 'Hard Rock' abandoned.
Greenham women ring base. Eleven women gaoled.
Hyde Park demonstration by ¼ million.

1983 Cruise arrives – 700 arrests.
Human chain between bases.
National membership of CND 54,000. Total membership
110,000.
CND non-violent action in Grosvenor Square.

1984 Liberal Assembly again votes to remove cruise missiles.
Labour reaffirms unilateral nuclear disarmament.
Several attempts to evict Greenham women.
Nuclear free zones cover ½ to ⅓ of England, all Wales.

1985 100,000 march to Hyde Park.
20,000 demonstrate at Molesworth, proposed second cruise
missile site.
Greenham Peace Camp numbers fall to 40.
CND Secretary General Bruce Kent and Chairwoman Joan
Ruddock stand down.

1986 CND membership falls to 91,000, 25% not renewing subscriptions. No large Easter rallies.

Alliance dissension over replacement of Polaris. Support slumps in opinion polls.

Amalgamated Engineering Union disaffiliates from CND.

Chernobyl nuclear power station disaster in USSR.

1987 INF agreement signed, removing class of medium-range missiles.

CND membership falls to 75,000, national membership to 230,000.

General election: defence a major issue, with Labour policy attacked as 'defeatist'.

1988 First cruise missiles leave UK for destruction.

President Reagan expresses wish to 'eliminate' nuclear weapons.

President Gorbachev announces to UN a 20% cut in Soviet conventional forces – ½ million troops.

Confusion and dissent in Labour party over nuclear weapons issue – defence spokesman resigns and slump in polls.